The Association 'Cherish'

The Association 'Cherish'

The Story of America's First Folk-Rock Band

Malcolm C. Searles

A Dojotone Publication in association with Troubador Publishing Ltd.

Matador
9 Priory Business Park,
Wistow Road, Kibworth Beauchamp,
. Leicestershire. LE8 0RX
Tel: 0116 279 2299
Email: books@troubador.co.uk
Web: www.troubador.co.uk/matador
Twitter: @matadorbooks

ISBN 978 1789013 610

British Library Cataloguing in Publication Data.
A catalogue record for this book is available from the British Library.

Typeset in 11pt Minion Pro by Troubador Publishing Ltd, Leicester, UK

Matador is an imprint of Troubador Publishing Ltd

Special thanks to my wonderful wife Louise for, once again, allowing and tolerating the time it takes for me to pull together such a project as this. Without you…

xxx

CONTENTS

1. ENTER THE YOUNG   1

2. THE TIME IT IS TODAY   19

3. YOU HEAR ME CALL YOUR NAME   32

4. BETTER TIMES   44

5. AND THEN... ALONG COMES MARY   58

6. CHERISH IS THE WORD   72

7. CHANGES   86

8. SONGS IN THE WIND   97

9. GOTTA TRAVEL ON   117

10. WASN'T IT A BIT LIKE NOW?   132

11. A BIRTHDAY MORNING   150

12. COME ON IN   166

13. TIME FOR LIVIN'   177

14. SIX MAN BAND   192

15. IT'S GOTTA BE REAL   201

16. UNDER BRANCHES   213

17. JUST ABOUT THE SAME   224

18. ONCE UPON A WHEEL   237

19. RIDGE RIDERS   252

20. KICKING THE GONG AROUND   267

21. NAMES, TAGS...   285

22. LIFE IS A CARNIVAL   300

23. TIME TO GET HIGH   323

24. THE BACKSEAT OF HEAVEN   340

25. NEW MEMORIES   356

26. HAPPY TOGETHER   372

27. A LITTLE BIT MORE   386

28. JUST THE RIGHT SOUND   401

29. ONE MORE TIME...   419

SELECTED DISCOGRAPHY   431

CREDITS   439

PREFACE

The auction starts. It was only by chance that I had stumbled across this particular music-related auction site two days previous. Up until that point I was convinced I had completed work on the book you now hold. The final 'i' had been dotted and the final 't' had been crossed I had reassured myself. But then, whilst casually sifting through the various online auction houses, typing in 'The Association' and perusing the many, many often unrelated items on offer, I hit pay dirt. The jackpot. The perfect ending to my research...

At that very moment, as I looked down at the screen in front of me, there was an audible intake of breath, and my eyes widened bug-sized. Shoot! An original Radio Recorders multi-track tape, dated April 7th 1965, the band's first successful recording session at the Hollywood studio was on offer before me, the keeper of said item for over fifty years having recently passed on, and although the estimated selling price made me a little wary, it was way out of my price range, the opening bid required was... just about... within my grasp. Maybe. With a little help. With some financial assistance from a good friend and fellow Association collector, living across the pond, I put in a pre-auction opening bid... and now, here I was, patiently waiting for Lot 158 to start.

Shoot again! There were some serious collectors watching it seemed. A signed guitar by the recently departed Tom Petty went for big $$$, then an

Elvis master reel from the same source made my eyes water with the price it was snapped up for. Eventually, two hours later, Lot 158. I held my breath. It started. Thirty seconds later… still nothing… my opening offer stood firm. Like a giant colossus that refused to be brought to its knees (OK, so I'm over dramatizing this for effect but…). Another thirty seconds. Still no response. Then… BAM! The auction for Lot 158 ended! *WHAT*?!! Short and sweet. Very sweet. With no other bidder. I sat there and looked at the screen as it flashed the word 'winner' before my very eyes. A surreal moment, frozen in time…

Fast forward four weeks. Here I am, sitting nervously in the small Audio Restoration studio operated by a friend of mine. The newly arrived 52 year-old Scotch reel, baked for protection, was delicately placed onto the Tascam tape machine, and the spools started spinning.

The guitars, the drums… and the voices. *Those* voices…

Please note that the concert dates listed throughout this book are just a mere selection of the touring schedule the band undertook throughout the years, and is by no means a definitive reference.

INTRODUCTION

1966

...nd the radio frequencies crackle as the harmonious sounds gush forth out of the tiny transistor speakers, across the airwaves of America. With notes blending in harmony, the amalgamation of tenors, baritones and bass vocals, combining with the driving backbeat of guitars, bass and percussion, hit home amongst the general populous of the listening teenage audience across the vast continent. It was hip. It was groovy. It was a new sound...

Think 'harmony' in American popular music and immediately the images of the Wilson brothers, Brian, Carl and Dennis, decked in candy-striped shirt freedom, singing alongside their cousin and friends, spring to mind. Good vibrations in the sum-sum-summertime. Cruisin' on the crest of a wave. Alternatively, take a step further back in time, to the closing years of the previous decade, when two good looking teenage brothers broke into the recording industry with songs about clowns, dreams and bird dogs, all sung in unison and in perfect harmony. These acts, along with many more from across the decades and the musical divides, will be forever linked with musical perfection. Time capsules for the vocal harmonies they so sweetly delivered, mixed with a little, or a lot of rock 'n' roll, via recorded works and/or live appearances, performed before thousands of adoring and devoted followers.

But there is one other act, one that time has perhaps sadly neglected to keep in the same musical hemisphere as those mentioned. One that, despite their relative anonymity as individual artists, came together as a part of the new and exciting folk-rock boom to create some of the finest examples of harmonious pop, rock and ballads from that glorious era, pre-Nixon, pre-Woodstock, pre-whatever. However, not only did they survive, they outlived that phase, recording and touring long after The Beatles, The Byrds, The Lovin' Spoonful and so many other bands had all fragmented, blowin' in the wind, and the legacy they left, and continue to leave, speaks for itself...

Five *Billboard* Top 10 hits, two U.S. Number One hits, three multi-million selling releases, the second most played song in American radio 20th century history, *Billboard* magazine's Number Two song of 1966 (and I challenge you to name the Number One song off the top of your head!)* – that very same year that saw the release of "Good Vibrations", "I'm A Believer", "Paperback Writer", "Monday Monday" and "Paint It Black"... and a career that still continues to this very day. Constantly on the road, touring across the vast reaches of the United States, they are recognized as being one of the, if not *the* hardest working band of that era.

When I first started writing this story, a labor of love, somewhat naturally for a project such as this I stumbled across a number of hurdles *en route*. Some of the principal players and important associates are no longer with us, others preferred to retain their privacy, whilst others still, I'm delighted to say, were more than happy and willing to contribute or assist in whatever way possible... to a degree. That's the nature of researching such a work I guess, and I'm honored that the assistance of these generous folk made the book what it is today. And I sincerely thank them all (credits and contributions can be found at the rear of the work). However, fifty years of music making, music collecting, or simply fifty years of aging can play havoc with the memory cells and dealing with numerous different people, all with their own... at times *differing* version of the events that unfolded... Well, need I say more?

In addition, such an 'association' is often guarded. Private in what it reveals. What goes on within the inner circles of such a collective often stays there, unknown to those who view in from the outside. And so it became apparent during the research. A lot of what went on between the core members of the band remains exclusively under wraps to only those privileged few... which leaves documenting such a lengthy career open to conjecture and speculation at times. However, I have attempted to overlook such speculative assumptions – although, I confess, even I may have been drawn into it such questionable areas at times – and, instead, present as close to the full story of this collective as we are ever likely to get. To read. To see. It may not be the *definitive* version of events as they unfolded. We would need to get all of the surviving band members together, and the families of those no longer with us, to even attempt such a task... and then throw in the record labels, management figureheads, press agents... and with decades now having passed that scenario seems highly unlikely, but what you have here remains faithful, and detailed, to the many trials and tribulations that befell the chosen few.

The principal band members themselves, for many unforgiving musical historians and collectors, may still remain anonymous. But for anyone who lives, breathes, works and/or collects such wonderful musical artifacts that befell upon us during that heady mid-'60s to early '70s era then the creations that this particular six-man, seven-man or, for a brief moment during the 1972 touring schedule, eight-man band offered up still stand tall, these fifty-plus years later. Be they folk, pop, rock, ballad, jazz, blues... sunshine or otherwise, from the 1965 debut of "Babe I'm Gonna Leave You" through to fading refrain of 1972s "Little Road And A Stone To Roll", and subsequently beyond, or indeed prior to, this was a fascinating era, and not only for the band themselves – all forty-one recognized musicians and singers that have passed through the Association studio or touring ranks at one time or another, however briefly. Researching, writing and reading was an enthralling road of discovery which, I hope, you may well enjoy traveling alongside, for however long you wish to journey... for the time it is today.

Ladies and Gentlemen... Enter The Young

The Author. 2017.

---

* For the record, the Billboard Number One song for 1966 was "Ballad Of The Green Berets" by SSG. Barry Sadler

Colecchio Management promotional artwork

CHAPTER ONE

ENTER THE YOUNG

It was the fall of 1962, and when Jules Gary Alexander, a short, wiry-haired U.S. Naval technician hailing from Tennessee, walked away from the house party on the rainy mountainside slope, not far from the beach at Pearl Harbor in Hawaii where he was currently stationed, he could not have foreseen that the person he had just met, a tall, dark former U.S. National Guard sergeant, with whom he had just spent time talking and playing music, would have such an impact on his future. Indeed, he possibly thought no more of the recent meeting, and quite probably imagined he would never even see the stranger ever again, despite the vague suggestion that if they were ever in the same town… Fortunately, on this occasion, his potential instincts were way off base, and they would indeed meet again, a full year later, having both completed their individual tours of duty, and fate would guide them together to success, in another time, another place.

Jules was born on September 25th 1943 in the city of Chattanooga, a growing metropolis known as the 'Dynamo of Dixie', located in the southern region of Tennessee, and situated on the eastern banks of the Tennessee River. His parents, Jay and Jean, divorced when he was still a young boy and his father moved out of the family home, leaving the youngster with his mother and an extended family, including his grandparents and an uncle, living under the same roof until he was a teenager.

"My full name is Jules Gary Alexander," he was to recount to the author during 2017, "but I grew up in the south, and Jules sounded too much like 'jew', which was very racist, and so my family didn't want to call me Jules. It wasn't a great name to grow up with so they called me Gary, and that's all I knew until I learned that Jules was my first name much later on. But everyone called me Gary, so that's what it was…"

Both his mother and grandmother were artists to a certain degree themselves, with his grandmother, on his mother's side, being a talented piano player, whilst Jean herself specialized in photographic restoration, and Jules maintained the family values and his grandmother's interest in music during his formative years. He first picked up a guitar when a friend of his mother's loaned him a Silvertone archtop acoustic model, and he taught himself the rudimentary chords on that, but when he was sixteen years of age his mother Jean remarried and she and her new husband packed up their belongings and relocated the family out west, to the golden state of California, settling in Pomona, a heavily urbanized area of Los Angeles county approximately 25 miles east of downtown L.A., and it was there that Jules was bought his very first guitar, a gift from his mother, an inexpensive Fender Telecaster, a popular mass-produced solid body model.

Whilst attending the local Pomona High School he began to swiftly develop his guitar technique, influenced by the heavy rhythm 'n' blues sounds he heard on the radio, and it was in school that he formed his first band with a number of his tenth grade classmates, and one in particular; a British student from Liverpool named Terry Watson, a former classmate of James Paul McCartney at Liverpool Institute High School for Boys. With the young band subsequently utilizing the name of Terry & The Twisters, a tag that has now sadly disappeared from the annals of rock 'n' rock history, they even got as far as recording one of their songs, written by Watson, at the nearby Pal Recording Studios, located in Cucamonga, CA, later famed for being the same studio that gave us such surf monsters as "Wipe Out" by The Surfaris and The Chantays "Pipeline".

As Jules recalled to authors Marti Smiley Childs and Jeff March, for their detailed overview of The Association band members in *Where Have All The Pop Stars Gone?* (published in 2011 via EditPros LLC), "We played pure rock and roll. We'd play school functions, and on Saturday nights we'd play for dances at the YMCA, and we played at park events. There were only about two other bands in that entire area at the time I started, so we were working.

I mean, if you had a guitar and you had a band, you were in demand. We weren't bad either; we were really pretty good."[1]

This was also the era of musical diversity as well, with the fresh sounds of rock 'n' roll music rubbing shoulders in the best-selling lists with either finger-snappin' doo-wop, originally from the darker street corners of the eastern shoreline, or the more traditional barbershop harmonies, wafting across the airwaves in suits and candy-striped shirts. Subsequently, Jules' very first record purchases were often varying between artists as diverse as Buddy Holly, with his hiccupping, rhythmic rockin' sound, and the far gentler, sweet synchronizations of The Hi-Lo's

However, change was in the air, and such was his dislike for lessons that in 1960, one year short of his graduation, he quit school. He continued in conversation: "A friend of mine, Arnie Mount said, 'Are you having a good time?' I said, 'No, I hate school.' He said, 'Let's go join the Navy' so I said, 'OK, let's go.' So we did. I was an apprentice at an observatory in Chattanooga when I was a kid, (and) I knew optics and telescope repair and optical instrument repair, having done it for a number of years, so they (the Navy) put me right into optics, and I worked on binoculars and periscopes and other instruments."[1]

Despite the seemingly little thought that had gone into his impulsive career move, Jules remained as a Navy technician for just over three years, during which time he continued on with studies away from the classroom.

"I was incarcerated in Uncle Sam's Canoe Club for three years, four months, twenty-eight days, seventeen hours and twenty-two minutes..." he later joked, "in which time I took several classes in advanced mathematics, calculus, physics and several mid-Eastern philosophies". However, his musical grounding during his brief sojourn with Terry & The Twisters was never far from his mind and many off-duty moments were spent with a guitar in his hand, mixing with fellow Naval musicians, even whilst on board ship. At one point, whilst stationed on board the submarine tender USS Nereus in San Diego, Jules, along with fellow recruit and guitarist Michael Whalen and a Navy dental tech by the name of Sharon Workman, combined together and started playing as a folk trio, initially calling themselves 'Sharon, Michael & Alex'...

"It was around 1963 and I was a dental tech in the Navy, stationed at MCRD, San Diego," recalls Sharon today. "One day, off duty, I was taking a long walk when I heard a voice shout out my name. It was Michael Whalen, calling from a passing car. He and I had sung together on the beach a while back when, one evening, he had joined up with a group I was with, so I knew him slightly. I approached the car and he said, 'I know this guy who's a great guitarist! Maybe we can all get together?' so I told him how to reach me and I soon heard from him. We started meeting at an apartment Alex shared with another guy; I knew Jules as 'Alex' in those days. We clicked immediately and had a great sound. Michael singing lead, Alex harmonizing and me, filling in with a third part and lots of ad lib; both the guys on guitar.

"We all knew the popular folk music, primarily the Peter, Paul & Mary numbers, and sang those, as well as drawing from other sources. We had SO much fun together, joking around and bantering when we weren't singing. Our practices were a blast. They'd often start with Michael declaring, 'Let's wail!' and when the guys thought we were ready to take our show on the road we auditioned to sing at The Land of Oden, a neat coffee house in the area. We made a number of appearances there and I remember that Mason Williams was also performing on one of the nights we did. This was followed by shows at other venues, and it seemed that every time we sang somewhere, we were offered another gig!

"We were doing songs like 'Little Boxes', which was a hit for The Womenfolk, and 'House of the Rising Sun', which I belted out as a solo. Originally we called ourselves Sharon, Michael & Alex, but then we became The Greenstone Singers and finally, our sort of joke name, The Froggy Flats Ramblers. Quite often we did just that; ramble around the city making music...

"I recall that we also sang at a radio station in San Diego. It was a phone-in request show and one of the songs we performed on-air was 'Lemon Tree'. Evidently we must have made a good impression because someone told me a few months later that one of the DJs had been asking 'does anyone know what happened to The Greenstone Singers?'!"

On another occasion, whilst on Navy duty at the Great Lakes Naval Training Center in Illinois, Jules met up with another recruit, Rick Allen, spending the day jamming with the future *Grammy* winner, and blues/B3 specialist.

Jules: "While I was stationed at Pearl Harbor, I didn't have much to do except play music during my off times. So I just played and played, mainly by myself. Just learning. I started playing with a few people – then it was hootenannies, of course, because it was during the very early folk era. And so that's really where I learned a whole lot and found myself performing more, and more, and more, and more."[1]

Sharon Workman (now Sharon Degonia) continues: "With the sound we had, Michael, Alex and myself, I really believe that if we could have stayed together longer, we'd have really taken off. But it wasn't on the cards. The guys got out of the Navy and went on up to Los Angeles and I lost touch with them…"

In 1963, following his departure from the Navy ranks, Jules returned home to the family house in Pomona, Southern California. By then the folk music circuit was in full resurgence, driven by the success of the movement amongst the college students throughout the country, with small clubs springing up in cities all over the States, all full of youngsters wishing to learn and emulate the recent triumphs of the popular acts of the day. With Jules still intent on honing his love of music he began to frequent the clubs, coffeehouses and nightspots around the area, including the popular Ice House venue, over on Mentor Avenue in Pasadena, where he became acquainted with one of the sound and lighting crew who worked there, nineteen-year-old fellow musician Russell Giguere.

Then, on one fateful day later that year, Jules ventured into a club located between Upland and Claremont, The Meeting Place, only to discover a familiar face working amongst the crowded room, a face he had last seen, months earlier, in Pearl Harbor, Hawaii.

Terry Kirkman grew up in a musical environment. Both of his parents were extremely talented musicians, as was his elder brother Richard, and it was only a matter of time before Terry was to become equally as enamored.

His father, Gordon Kirkman, had grown up in Hays, Kansas, the largest city in the northwestern region of the state and he played in local dance bands, both singing and performing on soprano saxophone. His mother, Lois, had spent much of her childhood traveling all around the vast state, the result of growing up as a part of a Methodist minister's family, changing churches every few years. She was a music major and played the organ in her father's congregation, as well as playing piano but, with the family reputation to behold, she was the minister's daughter after all, she couldn't let it be known that many of her evenings were also spent playing the pipe organ and the piano whilst the silent movies played at the local movie theater. She was also a teacher and, according to Terry in later years, whilst stunningly gifted as a musician, she was also renowned for her commanding presence on the local pinball machines. She met Gordon whilst attending Hays High School and they married whilst still young, bringing two boys into the world. Terry, the youngest by five years, was born in Salina, on December 13th 1939.

"Both of my parents had come from very educated, very realized parentage, but both of them were working people. My father never lived up to his dreams of owning a theater or a shoe store, and he ended up being a parts manager for a Ford's auto garage. I never thought of us as being poor, but we sure weren't rich! My dad's father built hospitals and theaters in the Midwest and if you see the movie *Paper Moon*, there's a scene between Tatum and Ryan O'Neil, a pivotal scene set in little coffee shop, and across the street is a Fox Theater that my grandfather built. My maternal grandfather built churches and was head pastor of Kansas Wesleyan University." [1/51]

Then, in 1943, whilst Terry was just 3 years of age, Gordon Kirkman, who was now working for the large Montgomery Ward retail chain, transferred from his Kansas base, journeying the 1300-mile route west to the store in Pomona, California, and resettling his family in nearby Chino, a small farming settlement in the shadows of the Chino Hills, surrounded by the orange groves and citrus trees of a post-war Southern California.

Nevertheless, being embraced by music at such an early age was clearly beneficial for the youngster, and his mother started off his own development by teaching him to play the marimba, encouraging him to learn such tunes as the Christian hymn "Jesus Loves Me", or the patriotic "God Bless America". However, his youth was never easy as he was later to recall in conversation: "I never really felt like I fit in. I wasn't a townie. On a school day I would get on a bus and go out into the country with some other kids, but I was never a part of any social scene..."

By 1954, whilst attending Chino High School, Terry began to follow in his father's footsteps, picking up the saxophone, learning to play by ear as he sat in with the shows at the popular Centro Basco restaurant on Central Avenue in Chino, teaching himself the intricate finger movements.

"My whole family was musical but I never saw my father play professionally or sing, and my first learned instrument was when I started playing tuba in 7th grade. My best friend was a Hungarian kid by the name of Frank Kozma, and his older brother Jim played monster clarinet in the restaurant, and he was a one-man band, and Frank and I just played behind him. Not knowing the songs I would just turn my back to the dancers and, with my tenor saxophone, I would listen to Jim and Frank and get what key it was and how it went, and being a tuba player, who only played the harmonies, I would just pick it up and then turn around on the second verse or chorus and join in! I was born with the ability to play the harmonies or counterpoint. I had no idea really how to play saxophone. I just fingered it like I did the little flutes I played when I was a kid. And that was my first paid gig, I was paid, maybe around $5 for that…"[51]

Graduating from Chino High School in 1957 he started attending Chaffey College in Alto Loma where, tall, with slicked back hair and a youthful beard growing through, he settled into a routine as Rally Chairman and a member of the men's Glee Club and the concert choir. He also continued with his musical development, contributing the tuba to the 120-piece college orchestra.

"They had an incredible music department that could play almost anything that was out in front of them."

In an interview with Steve Stanley, author of the sleeve notes for the Association's Now Sounds CD reissue series, Terry explained what happened next: "One day after class (in college), I walked around the corner, took a look at him and said, 'Who, or what, the hell is that?!'"[2]

With a familiar dark mustache already in growth, 'that' was Frank Vincent Zappa…

Although he had been born in the eastern seaport of Baltimore, Frank Zappa's family had moved west, to the warmer climes of California, for health reasons during 1952, and despite only attending Chaffey for one semester, attending (in his own words) 'for the express purpose of meeting girls', he was a bright, highly intelligent individual.

"My father wanted me to go to college," Frank would later state, "but I said no. I was interested in music; I didn't want to go to college. So I hung out at home for a while, but there was nobody to talk to, everybody else being at college, so I finally decided I should go too. That was very ugly. I stayed for about a year."[3]

For the next twelve months or so, bonding over a mutual love of music, Terry and Frank began performing folk, blues and jazz together at local coffee houses around the region.

"It wasn't like we were ever a formal act," recalled Terry. "A lot of the reason we played together was that I had a car and he never drove. But then we started writing satirical stuff together. Frank is a genius with a strange and valid perspective. I guess you might say he is a rebel with a cause..."[1/13]

"He was really into (British philosopher) Alan Watts, the ethnic folk thing, and blues. We would tease people with bongo drums and make up music on the spot. I was playing clarinet, singing and playing bongos. We didn't really have a repertoire *per se*. Club people would call us up and essentially want us to make noise or read some poetry. They really didn't have any idea what they wanted. And they'd tell us maybe, 'how about blues? How about ethnic folk music?' We created things together... ethnic folk, Afro-Cuban, blues, sparse jazz, adaptations of Bach and other classics, etc.

"There was a famous place nearby called the Claremont Folk Music Center and we'd all go down there and learn what folk music actually was. We'd grab the Alan Lomax book of ethnic-American folk songs, learn a song on the spot, a simple song, so we could perform it that night! And it might be the only time you ever played that music.

"It was just walking around being rent-a-guys for a new kind of entertainment that nobody understood, or what it was they were supposed to be doing. We also had a very short-lived six-piece band for about three months and we got a gig at the Pomona YMCA. The only recollection I have of it was of us playing our theme song and Jackson Pollock's nephew, John playing the piano. I was fascinated by 'The Morning Theme' from Stravinsky's *Rite of Spring*, and so we turned that into a rhythm 'n' blues melody, and so the theme song to the band was Stravinsky!"[3/51]

This youthful band, known as Frank Zappa's Boogie Men, even had business cards printed up, listing 422 W. "E" Street, Ontario, CA. as their address, but it never really took off.

"I wrote lyrics for some of the stuff Frank wrote, but we were just experimenting with being a completely off-the-wall idea. There was no rock 'n' roll as we were to come to know it. There was 1950s rock 'n' roll but essentially Frank's idea of rock was to be doo-wop, which never appealed to me much at all, except to be as a satirical platform. We were actually even once rent-a-beatniks. We were invited to a party to be real live beatniks, down in Laguna Beach for a bunch of doctors and lawyers, who were taking very serious drugs. We were the rental people and then we watched them vomit a lot."[3/51]

As a footnote to this particular part of his life, in the sleeve notes to his original *Mothers of Invention* album, Frank Zappa gives credit to Terry for helping to inspire his music.

Terry joined the National Guard during his senior year in high school, serving for six years in California and Hawaii, and achieving the rank of sergeant. That role came to an end once it became known he was suffering from Osgood-Schlatter's disease, an inflammation of the ligaments just below the knee joint, and one that the U.S. National Guard deemed unsuitable for their ranks, the result being that, in early 1962, Terry received an honorable discharge.

"I really enjoyed most of my service and the guys I got to do the work with... ordnance, communication and jungle engineering in Hawaii."[1]

So much so that shortly afterwards, accompanied by a couple of his former college friends, he flew back to the islands for a short vacation, and ended up one rainy evening at a party near Pearl Harbor, west of Honolulu, on the island of Oahu, held in the home of a city-based pediatrician. Music, conversation, and new friends were made. Then, returning once more to the mainland, he enrolled as a Journalist and English Major at Orange State College, across the Chino Hills in Fullerton where, during the second semester of '62, he became one of the staff writers for the college's then-new in-house paper *The Titan Times*, graduating to associate editor the following year...

"I majored in journalism but I never had any intention of getting a degree" he later commented, before adding in a subsequent interview: "At this time I became very politicized and discovered there was another place for me to be in the world. I was very attracted to folk music and the civil rights movement. And I saw that as a calling. It was a scene, it was a culture, and it was a cause, and I really wanted to be a part of that common and united voice. With folk music, I couldn't believe what was being sung about. I couldn't believe the accessibility of folk songs. They made you want to sing. A major influence on me, personally, was west coast progressive jazz; Stan Kenton, Chet Baker, Maynard Ferguson... but folk music was a new idiom. The content of the songs was a big draw, talking about peace and freedom, the labor union, whilst being performed in profoundly intimate settings. You were viscerally immersed in the music and you would walk out of the club and your consciousness would be raised. I had never heard anything like that! What were those chords? What was that finger picking? It was better than jazz music, and it was better than rock 'n' roll..."[1/2/13/51]

Subsequently, to help with tuition fees, and to aid his increasing political cause, he found part-time employment tending the bar, manning the ticket booth, and eventually managing one of the local coffeehouses and folk clubs near Upland, just a few miles north from the family home, from where he booked local acts and promoted the shows. It was there, one evening, that his brief friendship with the former US Naval technician was to be rekindled...

The following months would see that friendship between Alexander and Kirkman consolidating and building as they played music, talked and bonded. They got an apartment together on the corner of Yucca and Vine, near the Capitol Records tower, and began to frequent the folk clubs around the greater Los Angeles area, learning and discovering more about the scene, and one club in particular, situated five miles to the west of their apartment, on the busy Santa Monica Boulevard in West Hollywood, became a regular haunt for the duo.

Alexander Douglas Weston had been born in Manhattan, New York, on December 13 1926 and little is known of his formative years. But, by the time he reached adulthood, he had grown into a thin, gangling, authoritative figure with a head for business. Following his relocation to the western coast of the United States he had started up his first venture, the 65-seat Troubadour coffeehouse (specializing in 'entertainment and nearly-gourmet style food') on La Cienega Boulevard in 1957. Four years later he relocated the flourishing business a short walk away, to the much larger 9081 Santa Monica Boulevard premises, where he developed it into a popular nightclub, a home from home for the many folk musicians and young comedians who were flooding into the city from as far afield as Michigan, Oklahoma and Texas, all keen to either present themselves before a small, appreciative crowd on the imposing stage, or to simply hang out in the crowded front bar, talking music, art and politics, with fellow like-minded folk, and draw inspiration from their new surroundings.

"I chose the name 'Troubadour' because troubadours were, historically, men who traveled from town to town during the period when the Church completely blackened out all communication during the Middle Ages..." Doug would later comment. "There were no newspapers and there was no way for people of one town to know what was happening in another town. So these men traveled from place to place and did a chant-like song, which was a living newspaper."

As for his own lofty ambitions, he continued: "I want to stay nineteen years old for the rest of my life, and I want to provide as wide a range of entertainment as possible. I picked up the name of 'West Coast Father of Folk Music' because folk singers would tell one another and usually they could depend on a handout or a free cup of coffee, or a place to stay if they showed up at the Troubadour and said they were in need. People were showing up at my door all the time and it became sort of a stray boys' camp for folk singers![13]

"I am in sympathy with the things they are fighting for politically, economically and emotionally. The hope of the future has always been with the young. I consider myself an older, perhaps more stable, spokesman for the position..."

As the new decade developed, and the popularity of the Los Angeles nightclub scene grew, particularly up on the Sunset Strip, a stone's throw to the north of Santa Monica Boulevard where the flamboyant displayed their wares, the Troubadour continued to pull the crowds in, the lengthy queues outside running parallel with the old railroad tracks that ran down the center of the busy main street. And despite the increasing focus on the newly opened Whisky-A-Go-Go, the jazz-influenced Crescendo or the teen-driven Pandora's Box (situated over at the far eastern end of the strip), Weston, the demanding, long blonde-haired entrepreneur, saw the growing potential of the revitalized folk scene, particularly with the building success of acts such as the New Christy Minstrels and the more established Kingston Trio.

The New Christy Minstrels, a multi-membered gathering of singers, songwriters and instrumentalists, had been formed by 27 year-old Randy Sparks, a native of Leavenworth, Kansas, during the opening months of 1961. Sparks had been performing as a solo musician during the final years of the previous decade, combining his love of folk music with the more traditional Broadway sound. In 1960 he formed the Randy Sparks Trio with his wife, Jackie Miller, and Nick Woods, but soon realized he wanted a larger group and, influenced by a number of the choral acts performing during that era, such as Les Baxter's Balladeers (featuring a youthful David Crosby) and the Norman Luboff Choir, he created a vast fourteen-voice ensemble, calling them the New Christy Minstrels after Christy's Minstrels, a blackface group formed by Philadelphia-born showman Edwin Pearce Christy back in 1842.

Combining the Randy Sparks Trio with another similar band of musicians, The Inn Group, featuring John Forsha, Karol Dugan and the

Alabama-born Jerry Yester, along with a young quartet known as The Fairmont Singers (David Ellingson, Terry Tillman, Robbie Mills and Hal Ayotte), and singer/musicians Billy Cudmore, Terry Wadsworth, Dolan Ellis and Art Podell, this newly formed line-up burst onto the folk scene with a striking vision of color-coordination and cheesy smiles. It was a revelation for the times. Smiling, fresh-faced young people with a generally upbeat and rousing approach to their repertoire, the Minstrels used their style of folk music as a means of entertaining audiences rather than raising their respective consciousness. Ironically, the very lack of controversy made them controversial, especially in traditional folk music circles, where they were deeply resented and frequently derided and yet, for all of their alleged transgressions as a folk group, the New Christy Minstrels immediately won over critics and audiences alike.

It is also worth noting that each member of the band got the spotlight at some point in their shows to demonstrate their particular strengths, and the original line-up proved to be engaging musical personalities, performing as a full ensemble on a certain number of songs, but then also including numbers that spotlighted certain duos and trios within their ranks, resulting with audiences feeling as though they were getting the equivalent of several groups' sounds and performances in the course of a concert set.[4]

The following year, after their initial formation and rehearsals, and now residents of Los Angeles, the Minstrels recorded their debut album for Columbia Records, *Presenting The New Christy Minstrels*, featuring a notable cover rendition of Woody Guthrie's "This Land Is Your Land", although following the departure of the four Fairmont Singers (due to a poorly scheduled prior engagement), the line-up was now reduced to a potentially more manageable ten-piece choir. Nevertheless, the album went on to win not only a *Grammy* award for Best Choral Performance, but it also gained a phenomenal two-year stint in the *Billboard* Top 200 listings. Within the space of twelve months the Minstrels went on to consolidate their immediate popularity, albeit with a change of line-up, although Randy Sparks himself also chose to retire from performances with the band the following year, opting to open his own folk nightclub, the popular Ledbetters on Westwood Boulevard, and concentrate on developing the band from behind the scenes.

All of this immediate success failed to go unnoticed by the astute Doug Weston, and he booked the recently diminished Minstrels line-up, still with Sparks at the helm, and now also scheduled to appear as resident performers on NBC-TV's *The Andy Williams Show*, for a series of debut live performances at his ever growing nightclub on Santa Monica Boulevard during the late summer of 1962, where they subsequently recorded their next album, *The New Christy Minstrels In Person*, live on the Troubadour stage during September of that year. Just prior to this, a further series of changes within the band saw founding members Forsha, Dugan and Yester depart, once again due to conflicting bookings, and, amongst the new arrivals, singer/guitarist Barry McGuire and a young Hawaiian-born ukulele playing singer of Filipino descent named Larry Ramos were added to the line-up. McGuire brought in a dynamic, gravel tone to the proceedings whilst Ramos added a boyishly-good looking charm to the set, in addition to an extraordinary talent. The subsequent re-pressings of their successful debut album from here on in reflected the change in personnel with updated photographs, highlighting the new membership, and the inclusion of Forsha, Dugan and Yester brazenly whitewashed from the sleeve notes.

As regaled in a later Jerry Yester article for *Goldmine* magazine, the Minstrels were only intended initially as a studio aggregation but, whilst The Inn Group were on tour themselves, the album had shot up the charts. Randy Sparks had then phoned Yester, telling him to cancel everything they had planned and return back to L.A. Jerry responded, "I told him we couldn't do that. We had commitments. He would have to count us out. So we ceased to be Minstrels and they went on to sell millions. The Inn Group did nothing and broke up after about six months!"

Despite the top-line draw that the New Christy Minstrels could now bring to his club, Weston also began to take a number of other new performers under his wing, namely a traveling folk trio calling themselves (somewhat appropriately) The Travelers 3, along with a duo going by the name of Robb & Tim, comprising of two young Californians, Robb Royer and Timothy Hallinan.

Charlie Oyama, one third of The Travelers 3 (who, having recently arrived in Los Angeles from their native Hawaii, now roomed together on Sunset Boulevard), states that the trio was also a part of the original set-up for the New Christy Minstrels, before they forged their own path. In conversation with the author Charlie recalled: "We were a part of Randy Sparks' original starting line-up for The Minstrels. When Randy approached us it was just his trio and us when we first started rehearsals. However, before any performances were made we secured an extended contract from the Dunes Hotel and Casino in Las Vegas, which we accepted, so we left. The Fairmount Singers were four young men, 1960 high school graduates, from Eugene, Oregon who were in the process of discussing joining Randy as we were leaving. I knew the Fairmounts because I taught and coached at that high school..."

His bandmate, Peter Apo, shared his own recollections in an interview with the *Hawaiian Star Bulletin*: "The Troubadour was the crossroads for folk music there. People like Hoyt Axton, Judy Collins, (future members of) The Byrds and Buffalo Springfield would play and hang out. It was there that we hooked up with our manager, Leonard Grant. With Leonard's help the band graduated from the small touring circuit to play Las Vegas showrooms and big-city supper clubs. I remember playing places like New York's Blue Angel, where we auditioned with people like Peter, Paul & Mary... and an up-and-comer at the time named Barbra Streisand."

Robb Royer meanwhile, later a member of the folk-rock quartet The Pleasure Fair, and then co-founder of the phenomenally successful soft-rock band Bread (Hallinan would go on to become a successful crime writer), also recalled in conversation with the author, "When Troubadour owner Doug Weston was managing 'Robb & Tim', Doug booked a then-upcoming group which was the sum total of at least seven failed folk acts, known as The New Christy Minstrels, for a two week run. I guess they figured all those failures would add up to one big success and they were right. They caused a sensation. Doug was dazzled. He assumed that huge bands were the coming thing, and he herded all of the stoners and wannabes (who were regulars at the club) in the front room, of which I was one, and up onto the stage to be in his new mega-band, The Men. I did, in fact, take the stage with them, but I looked around and noticed there were around thirteen of us onstage – the Christy's were only ten! Having no desire to be in a thirteen-man group, I slipped off the back of the stage, which was so crowded no one noticed. Doug rehearsed them, and then booked them for several runs..."

It would be a few more years of development and soul-searching before Royer would go on to achieve fame as a part of Bread, and also achieve success as the co-writer of several huge hits for other established artists, winning an *Academy* award *en route* for his efforts.

In recalling the Troubadour, and agreeing with Apo, Robb concludes that: "The Troubadour was the capitol of L.A. folk and early rock. Other clubs such as the Ice House (twenty miles to the east) in Pasadena, or the

Ash Grove over on Melrose, were places where legitimate acts came to play. An audience arrived, a show happened and everybody went home. The Troubadour was a place where at least half a dozen future known rockers were hanging about at all times. Location was part of it. Right at the corner of Santa Monica and Doheny, a central gathering place like Haight Ashbury. Although Doug remodeled it at least a dozen times, it always had some kind of lounge being used as a flophouse. It was also several times the size of those other clubs, so something was always going on. I knew Jules Alexander very well. We wrote a couple of songs together and worked on an idea of his called 'Along The Great Divide', but we never finished it.

"The only place that I can compare the vibe of the Troubadour to was the funhouse on Santa Monica pier that burned down when I was a child. Giant, cavernous, flat black paint indifferently splashed on wallboard or plywood. Style and class created by a total indifference to style and class. And Doug Weston? Bill Graham south. Total whacko, but responsible for countless great moments in rock. So stoned my then-partner Tim once quipped 'even his drugs were on drugs'…"

Jules concurs, "Yes, I remember that Robb knew my wife way back before I met her, so we had mutual friends and then we met and worked a little bit together. We wrote 'The Great Divide' and a couple of others, but they never went anywhere…[37]

"The folk music thing was peaking. Terry and I played together a lot, and we started hanging out in L.A. We got an apartment in L.A., and were regulars at the Troubadour. Everybody in the music business in L.A. in the '60s seemed to hang out there. There were actually three clubs: The Troubadour, the Ash Grove, and Randy Sparks' club, Ledbetters. Randy Sparks' club attracted all the white guys, the white jocks. It was a Christy Minstrels kind of a 'Hi! I'm an American short-haired boy. I'm playing folk music.' And then there was the Troubadour, which was a lot funkier. And there was the Ash Grove, which was blues. But we hung at the Troubadour…[1]

"The place seemed to be made for us. In the few months before the forming of The Men, we made tons of new friends. I had gotten a gig as the guitarist behind Jackie and Gayle, Jackie Miller and Gayle Caldwell, the women members of the New Christy Minstrels who had left that line-up in early '64, and Terry was the musical arranger for a young folk group, The Cherry Hill Singers. We continued to jam with our friends and acquaintance musicos all around and in the Troubadour…"[5]

One very successful series of events at the club, known as the 'Monday hoot nights', were incredibly popular with the visiting crowds. The 'hoots', or 'hootenannies' were initially open-mic nights, whereupon aspiring amateurs, or established musicians could line up and take to the stage themselves, performing under the spotlights before their peers in a relaxed atmosphere, gaining a foothold and a reputation, although such was the demand at these nights that, more often than not, there were more players wanting to get in on the act than there were places available, and on any given Monday evening impromptu duos and trios were often the norm. Simply to get a place in the spotlight. Jim McGuinn, Gene Clark, Hoyt Axton, Ted Bluechel, Michael Nesmith, John Deutschendorf, Linda Ronstadt, Brian Cole, David Crosby and, on occasion, even Latin guitar virtuoso Jose Feliciano – all depending on who knew what song…

However, as the popularity of the event began to take hold, and the Troubadour's status grew around the industry as the in-place to perform at, the 'hoot nights' gradually became a hot-bed for agency-fuelled platform appearances, more so than for the traditional free-for-all fun events that many of the original residents craved.

Terry Kirkman: "Though there were at least a dozen other clubs in the area thriving at the same time, the famous Ash Grove and the Ice House among the best, Doug Weston's Troubadour was definitely the place you had to be seen to really be in the scene. It was arguably one of the most powerful music clubs in the country or maybe even the world at that time. [6/7]

"By 1964 it had become a virtual showcase for powerful agents. Everybody fought politically to get their new acts, their new discoveries, whether they were from another state or from Orange County, fifty miles from L.A., whatever the deal was, people were trying to get on that hoot because the hoots were so powerful and so popular that they would be filled with agents and record companies and people trying to find the next best thing.

"The room was full of people anxious to get up and play and to be seen and to put it together, thirty or forty of whom on any given night were going to become relatively droppable names in American music history". [7]

"The hoots at the Troub were all agony or ecstasy and little in between…" continues Jules, "and if one had the whatever-it-took to go play the Troubadour on a Monday night it might indicate that the player was either truly talented and knew that he or she had a chance to come off well or was absolutely delusional about their abilities. Of course there were the occasional madmen and women that would perform at the hoots that gave a certain gritty *Gong Show* flavor.

"One of the madding crowd was Wild Man Fischer. This guy would get on stage and do the weirdest stuff that I'd ever seen yet. He would start some song or comedy bit then get off into some rant scream about the music business or PGE or his ingrown toenails and wouldn't quit until he was physically dragged off stage. He did it almost every Monday. There would always be the completely stoned out players who would get on stage and forget to play. It happened more than once. Then there were the proto-performance artists; nobody knew what to do with them, one of whom was an incredibly beautiful woman who was over 6'2", barefoot, and way before her time. But the audience tended to want acoustical protest and denim dreams not bare breasted women's angst." [5]

"Wild Man Fischer was one of the craziest acts I'd ever seen," confirms Russ Giguere. "He'd get onstage and play his body! They'd put him on the Monday night hoot to clear out the audience and the funny thing was as soon as he went on stage the audience would start pouring out and all the people in the bar, the musicians, would pour in. He was so interesting!" [36]

One particular Monday evening during 1964 saw Terry and Jules watching the unfolding events on the stage before them, with proprietor Doug Weston standing alongside. Also in evidence that night was bluegrass banjo player, Doug Dillard, who was appalled at the political state that the 'hoots' had formulated into, so, according to Terry, "Dillard looked at the stage that night and said 'this is just bullshit! What happened to the hoot night? What happened to the fun and the sing-along? Let's just hit the stage and do that...'

"He went around and he pitched to everybody he could in the room that night, say there were two hundred people in the Troubadour on a Monday night, and Doug would go around saying, 'You want to get up on stage and play some real folk music? Go ahead and do it.'" [7]

The result was that around twenty or so keen folk musicians of varying abilities clambered up onto the large stage that famed evening alongside the regular MC Tony Mafia, a guitarist himself, all keen to have their voices heard as one.

"They said, 'Well, you have to have a name for your act,' and (responding instinctively) Doug said, 'We're called the Inner Tubes,' and so the MC at this hootenanny gets up and says, 'Okay, here's the Inner Tubes...'"

"I immediately liked (the name). It was the very basis of an inner circle: the 'In Crowd', one that I was actually going to be a part of. So many people wanted to be an Inner Tube that night that it took about a third of our allotted time just to get everybody set up, tuned, and settled on which song to sing first. All we did was pick about four or five songs that everybody could play and sing, and then the whole audience sang and made it into a true hootenanny. From then on, every Monday night, it was the Inner Tubes, but the whole room was singing these songs." [6/7]

Songs reportedly performed by this rough aggregation that night included such standards as "Banks Of The Ohio", "Michael Row The Boat Ashore", "Darlin' Corey" and "This Land Your Land" and the featured masses included such notable names as Elaine 'Spanky' McFarlane, David Crosby and... Ted Bluechel, Jules Alexander, Terry Kirkman and Brian Cole.

According to New York-born guitarist and banjo picker Steve Cohen, another who was present on that night and on many subsequent occasions: "There was no planning or anything that led up to that moment. It was just unrehearsed. It just happened. I remember Gene Clark came in and wanted to play but he was voted out, as there was no more room!"

Terry: "It was twenty-plus minutes of the best musical fun anyone had experienced in some time. All in all quite a blur for me, however, because it was the first time I'd ever sung on any such stage, let alone with such talented people. Little would I have dared dream, though, just how important that night and that stage were going to be for me..." [6]

CHAPTER TWO

THE TIME IT IS TODAY

As the popularity of the Inner Tubes grew, week by week, so did the various musicians who drifted in, and out of the vast interchanging line-up. Jules' former Navy partner Mike Whalen, now a fellow regular at the Troubadour club as a member of a small folk band known as The Cherry Hill Singers, signed up alongside another former Naval colleague, Sanford Delano, as did two of Mike's fellow members of The Cherry Hill Singers (who had already recorded an album for the small HiFi/Life Records label), guitarist Nyles Brown and guitar player and percussionist Ted Bluechel. Also in attendance were two musicians who had drifted down from Portland, Oregon, members of a folk trio known as The Gnu Fokes.

Brian Cole and Bob Page, along with Molly Malarkey, had originally made up this Portland-based act but, after widespread acclaim in their home state had eluded them, the trio had ventured south, to Los Angeles, where they continued to perform in the small clubs or, on occasion, link up with a similar folk-comedy troupe bizarrely labeled The Shaggy Gorillas Minus One Buffalo Fish, another trio originating from Portland who had followed the coastal highway down south, seeking potential success. Brian would often supply upright bass behind this particular group, a talented line-up comprising of Greenwich Village-born bass player Ron Long, and guitarists Brian Bressler and Jon Bunce (the latter soon to be replaced by Mike Neun), whose style of music and improvisational on stage comedy would prove very influential to his own development. They had proven to be a popular success on the Oregon circuit and were hoping to achieve similar levels of achievement in L.A., but it wasn't to be. They even ventured in to the recording studios to cut a number of popular, traditional folk songs, including 'Wayfaring Stanger" and "Pastures Of Plenty", although it remains undocumented as to whether Brian was in attendance during these sessions. A later 1965 version of the act, now performing simply as The Buffalo Fish, and led by Ron Long, also included two relatively recent arrivals to the City of Angels; guitarist Stephen Stills and multi-instrumentalist Peter Halston Thorkelson (who later shortened his name to Peter Tork, once success beckoned).

"Ron Long was a fantastic bass player," recalls Jules. "I worked with him when I first came to Hollywood, playing with Jackie and Gayle from the New Christy Minstrels and Ron was playing bass. Sadly, he suffered a stroke when he was young guy, just twenty-one or twenty-two or something like that. He came back and started playing again but then we lost contact..."

And the Inner Tubes? It seems that this new collection was now proving to be such a success amongst The Troubadour crowds that, just maybe, Doug Weston's earlier acknowledgment of The New Christy Minstrels size and pulling power could be emulated once more by this new gathering. Yet, such was this loose agreement amongst all participants over membership and arrangements that Doug Weston, overseeing the unfolding dramas from the Troubadour balcony, felt a more formal approach was needed to take the next step. He saw the possibilities that were spreading out before him. Subsequently, word was sent out amongst the frenzied weekly gathering that anyone interested in stepping forward and combining the sound into an official, organized line-up should show up the following weekend, whereupon he would oversee the forming of a 'serious' musical act...

However, with over fifty years of history now behind us since Weston first acted upon his instincts, the resulting story as to how events unfolded tend to vary, subject to who was in attendance that day. Jules Alexander, writing in 2002 for his brief, yet thoroughly enjoyable article on the formation of The Men, recalls that over one hundred or so hopefuls turned up to audition in front of Doug that weekend, before being whittled down to a chosen thirteen. Terry Kirkman, by comparison, remembers it very differently, commenting that the amount was much smaller, closer in numbers to the final chosen thirteen.

"There may well have been around thirty or more guys who showed up that evening, but only thirteen of us actually signed up and said 'I want to do this…'" he clarifies. "Certainly none of the name acts or Dillards or Crosby. And no women, just thirteen guys. All of us struggling no-names, out of work and looking for any paying gig we could land. So, as bizarre and manipulative a character as Weston was known to be, we cut a deal right there. With him, seeing just who had accepted his invitation, declaring we should now be called The Men. Not just some men, but… The Men." [6/51]

Whilst both stories have their possibilities, and whilst one is perhaps inclined to follow the smaller version of events, after all, a gathering of over one hundred would surely have generated further headlines, the fact that fellow Troubadour resident Robb Royer also recalls being a part of the troupe, but his name does not appear in the final chosen list, implies that there were indeed numbers beyond the suggested final total.

Thirteen members have been officially linked to having been a part of the first draft of The Men, and rare photographic evidence still survives to confirm these very names. Pictured alongside Jules 'Gary' (as he was still being referred to then) Alexander, strumming an old Mexican 12-string guitar, and Terry Kirkman were Ted Bluechel, Brian Cole, Mike Whalen, Steve Cohen, Harvey Gerst, Howard Wilcox, Nyles Brown, Tony Mafia, Steve Stapenhorst, Bob Page and Sanny Delano and, together, as one united vocal chorus, they formed a formidable folk line-up. Albeit one with a difference.

Terry: "Ted started playing drums. We said 'you play drums, you do this.' Well, you don't have drums in a folk group. Well, you do now! And Harvey Gerst played an electric Gretsch guitar, someone else played electric bass, I don't recall which of our bass players it was, and everyone else played acoustic instruments, guitars and banjo. And if you were looking at it from an arranger's standpoint there were thirteen voices and thirteen instruments, so you had twenty-six voices and instruments to play with!

"If we were arranging a song my frame of reference was Henry Mancini, how to start a song and how to build a song, and the harmonies I was hearing, and that Jules was hearing were influenced by Stan Kenton and The Four Freshmen. The Four Freshmen were one of the big secret missing links in musicology. They had a profound influence on American vocal groups. They voiced their harmonies in a different way, they just nailed it. It was like a horn section. They literally taught me the sound of the Stan Kenton trombone section…"

The following months saw this newly formed aggregation develop their united sound as they took to the stage, not only at The Troubadour, but at other clubs such as the Music Box Theater on Hollywood Boulevard, the Cosmos Folk Club down in Seal Beach, where they performed every Friday and Saturday during the final two weeks of October 1964, and the Mecca, over in Buena Park, where they appeared for a winter season of performances, sharing the bill with fellow Troubadour regular John Deutschendorf every Thursday, Friday and Saturday during November of that year. However, as noted, in a ironic twist for a folk group performing a number of traditional folk tunes, they uniquely utilized the drums, the electric guitar and both an electric fender and an upright bass, alongside the obligatory acoustic guitars and deep harmonies within their act. Decked out in jeans, chambray shirts and cowboy boots they were firmly critiqued by poet, cartoonist and singer-songwriter, Shel Sylverstein as being no more than a 'musical jail break', and it was going completely against the grain for the true folk musician, who, up until now, eschewed the use of electronic amplification.

Terry continued: "We got together and we experimented with these incredible vocal arrangements. And almost nobody else had electrified their instruments yet. But we did anything we wanted. Any time somebody wanted to sing a horn line, or a guitar line, he just did, because there was still a solid harmony group going. It was so much fun…"

Billed as either The World's First Folk Music Revue (a Folk-Rock Chorus) or The World's First and Finest Folk-Rock Group (the 'Rockiest, Swingiest, Folkiest Show in History!'), their performances were proving to be an important step in the union of these two significant genres of popular music and some that were initiating the first, tentative moves towards the worldwide success that a number of associated acts would achieve the following year.

Folk-rock, as compounded by The Men, is simply an amalgamation of folk song and rock-and-roll. It grabs any familiar folk song that is handy, slaps a rock-and-roll beat on its broadside, and wallops the daylight out of it. The result is loud and lively, and jubilation abounds as The Men jolt tradition from such tunes as 'John Henry', 'I'm On My Way', 'Linin' Track', 'Goodnight Irene' and 'Banks Of The Ohio'. Arrangements of 'If I Had Wings', 'Amazing Grace' and 'Railroad Bill' are performed to much acclaim by various members of the chorus in solos, duos and trios. But whether singly or combined, it looks as though The Men are presently selling exactly what the public wants.

The Los Angeles Times
August 1964

Certainly, the recent arrival on American shores of The Beatles, four scruffy-haired rock 'n' rollers hailing from the grimy suburbs of an industrial English seaport, had shaken up the American music industry and whilst many of the dedicated folk musicians, the hardcore gathering of short-haired, guitar picking regulars from New York's Greenwich Village or the newly-born clubs of Los Angeles, looked down upon this British Invasion with disdain, the younger disciples viewed these latest arrivals with curiosity and interest. Particularly those on the western shoreline of the U.S., still buzzing in the aftermath of the frenzied media excitement following the quartets performance at the Hollywood Bowl in August of 1964. They looked, they studied, and they copied…

David Crosby, by now a regular performer on the Los Angeles folk circuit: "They (The Beatles) were our heroes. They were absolutely what we thought we wanted to do. We listened to every note they played, and savored it, and rubbed it on our foreheads, and were duly affected by it. I was in Chicago one time, living with a British guy named Clem Floyd on Well Street, right in the middle of it all. I was singing at Old Town North and Mother Blues and Clem walked in one afternoon with that first Beatles album, *Meet The Beatles*. He put it on, and I just didn't know what to think. It absolutely floored me. Those are folk music changes, but it's got rock and roll backbeat. You can't do that, but they did! Holy yikes!" [8]

Fellow musician, Jim McGuinn, originally a New York resident who made his start on the streets of Greenwich Village before finding a home at the Troubadour concurs: "The blending of folk and rock was something that was inspired by The Beatles when I was working for Bobby Darin in New York. I was in the Brill Building in 1963 and I heard The Beatles and it inspired a combination of folk and rock and I went down to Greenwich Village and I started playing traditional songs with a Beatle beat and gradually, when I went out to the west coast, Gene Clark came along, and David Crosby, and we formed The Byrds around that sound…" [9]

One of their formative recordings, issued during late 1964 when they were still finding their Byrd-wings, resulted in an obscure 45rpm release on the Elektra Records label, "Please Let Me Love You", credited to The Beefeaters and written by McGuinn and Harvey Gerst, co-founding guitarist of The Men.

"Jimmy McGuinn had been the first person to tell us about The Beatles," adds Terry Kirkman. "Jules and I were renting this apartment near Capitol Records in Hollywood, and Jimmy came in and said 'have you heard this group from England? They're like a jet plane!'"

Unquestionably, The Men were also at the very forefront of this new movement, blending the two very diverse styles of modern and traditional music and performing a set that fused the very essence of folk club repartee, from the traditional standards of "John Henry", "Willie The Fireman", "Cripple Creek", "If I Had Wings" and "Winkin', Blinkin' and Nod", all arranged by various band members themselves, to renditions of newer compositions such as "Road To Freedom", "Shelters", "If You Hear My Name" and Bob Dylan's "Tomorrow's A Long Time". On top of that, throw in the occasional smattering of bluegrass and blues, including a newly re-arranged Alexander and Kirkman version of the Ma Rainey 12-bar blues classic "CC Rider". Yet, this thirteen-man partially electrified outfit was more often than not restricted to the local Los Angeles scene and the exposure that the small clubs had to offer. Without a recording deal then folk acts such as this were, sadly, all too much in abundance, albeit many of them without as much talent and originality as The Men could offer. However, Doug Weston certainly did see the possibilities as boundless, intending to take his new prodigies onto that next step and into a recording environment. But, before that could take place, a notable line-up change occurred when Mike Whalen chose to leave the band, the result of him being offered the opportunity to link up with The New Christy Minstrels as a replacement for the departing Barry McGuire.

Jules recalls: "Barry McGuire, the lead singer on (the hit 45) 'Green, Green' had just left The New Christy Minstrels. The Christy's management hired Mike Whalen away from The Men in an agent's heartbeat – very fast and silent to the point of non-existence. They offered Mike great money and the lead singer spot in a hit band. It seemed a good decision for him at the time. It was difficult for The Men to lose our lead singer and difficult for Terry and me personally as we had been fairly close friends with Mike for several years before and would miss the closeness of that good friendship, however we were once again the recipient of great fortune..." [5]

To replace Mike, the band drafted in a relatively unknown figure on the circuit but one that Jules had become acquainted with during his regular visits to the Ice House club, over in Pasadena.

Russell Henry Giguere (*pronounced jig-air*) had been born on the east coast of the United States, in Portsmouth, New Hampshire on October 18th 1943, the only child born to Russell Henry Sr. and Marguerite Mary. Sadly, Russell Jr. never had the opportunity to meet with his father, a Chief Pharmacist's Mate in the U.S. Navy, who was killed during action in the Second World War, a victim of the attack on the USS Plymouth, two months prior to the birth.

Overcoming the tragedy, the years passed and as the decade drew to a close Russell and his mother moved west, settling in San Diego, California to be near his mother's sister. There, Marguerite remarried and gave birth to three more children, giving the youngster the opportunity of a larger, stable family upbringing.

Both music and dance were an essential part of the family household and until his teenage years Russ was a keen participant in various dance competitions around the city. "My aunt was an instructor," he would later recall to Jeff March and Marti Smiley Childs, "and I was into rock and roll dancing in junior high. (But) as soon as I was about fourteen or fifteen I stopped going to dances and folk music took over my life. The fact that I was interested in music was looked upon as being really neat, so they encouraged me to listen to everything. Anything I'd show the slightest bit of interest in, I was just barraged with, so it was great." [1]

Attending both Hoover High and, later, the E.R. Snyder Continuation High School in San Diego, schooling was never a prime focus for him, neglecting to dedicate himself to offering up the mental hard work required to study math and suchlike, instead choosing to concentrate on the more manual, creative classes of woodwork, metalwork and art. Eventually he left school altogether, short of graduating, choosing instead to push all of his attentions onto his music, and teaching himself to play guitar whilst getting by with a series of part-time jobs including casual work in local coffee houses and as a merry-go-round operator at the San Diego Zoo

At the tender age of just nineteen he moved up the coast, to the busy and exciting life of a 1960s Los Angeles, where he found further degrees of employment just outside the city limits, much to his delight, as the lighting and sound director at the popular Ice House folk club in Pasadena run by Bob Stane. Stane, a savvy young entrepreneur with a head for both business and publicity, had previously operated a successful coffee house in San Diego that was frequented by Russ and his school friends.

"We first got together when I had a coffee house, the Upper Cellar, in San Diego," remembers Bob, when questioned by the author during 2016, "and Russ was, at that time, around fifteen years old and did odd jobs for me. At the Ice House, a few years later, he developed into a skilled light and soundman and started to learn performing music. He took in all the lessons I was teaching on being an excellent stage act with wit, humor and sparkling personalities. These were the traits of the acts I hired at the club…"

Another regular face at the Upper Cellar was emerging folk musician and writer Mason Williams, who also recalled: "I was in the Navy in San Diego when I became friends with Russ. I played at the Upper Cellar many times as I was stationed at the amphibious base there so I was a sailor by day and a folk singer by night, and I played all of the folk clubs in San Diego, but the Upper Cellar was the big one. There were a lot of coffee houses that were trying to do what Bob was doing, but they would only last a short time. I recall that Russ made all of the drinks at the club. They didn't serve alcohol so it was just tea and coffee. Then when Bob went up to the Ice House, Russ went along with him, where he worked there as the lighting man. He was such an integral part of what Bob had done before. I remember I used to sit in the booth with him, rather than in the audience. He had his own little speakers in there, so it was the best seat in the house!

"I'd go out there every night of the week, and there was a room next to stage, sort of a green room, where you'd just hang out and talk about songs, talk about this and that with everybody, and a lot of my friends hung out there. Steve Martin, I saw him there a lot, and a guy named David Somerville. The Ice House had this group of regional stars and when they would play there the place would sell out for four or five days in a row. I remember going there with The Smothers Brothers as they liked to put their act together in a small club, just to get the rhythms and such together, and I played guitar and five-string banjo behind them. The Ice House was just an incredibly important place, and Bob just knew how to run a club better than anybody…"

One of Russ's early contacts there was Jules Alexander, fresh out of the U.S. Navy himself and a regular in such haunts, and on occasion the two of them would find the opportunity, any opportunity, to jam together.

Russ: "I moved to L.A. and became the light and sound man at the Ice House in Pasadena. I was still playing guitar and learning my stuff. That's where I met all the guys. Ted was in a group called The Cherry Hill Singers;

I worked lights for them. Terry ran a little folk club out in the valley and he would come in, so I knew him from that, and there was a group called The Gnu Fokes; that's where I knew Brian. [10]

"One night when I was working lights the owner says, 'this guy is late, Russ. Can you go out and do a few tunes?' So Jules was there, and I said, 'Jules, you want to play bass?' He said, 'Sure.' So we went out and did three or four songs until the guy got there."

In fact, Russ's very first appearance on vinyl came about as the result of his job at the club, with the *Jack Linkletter Presents A Folk Festival* LP, issued in 1963 (GNP95), featuring the spoken introduction of Russ, at the very start of the recording, albeit at a mere five seconds in length.

Using the opportunities now laying out before him Russ joined up with a fellow visionary, Randy Sterling, a talented guitar player out of Bakersfield CA., in a short lived folk duo, Sterling & Giguere, but the bookings proved scarce outside of the confines of the Ice House, and the musical partnership that each had foreseen proved incompatible and the act dissolved soon after and yet Russ persisted, learning his craft.

"I think I had a gig at the Ice House, where Russ was working lights," recalls Randy Sterling today. "I had been doing some stuff at the Troubadour, and it was a time when everybody was learning from everybody else, and everybody was sharing with everybody else, and I really hadn't hit my stride yet, but I was a solo performer playing this little repertoire of stuff. I'm not exactly sure how Russ and I connected, but we did, and we said 'well, why don't we put something together as a duo? Let's do it!' I just wanted to play, so we kinda taught each other stuff, like… what's it gonna be? Well, it turned out it wasn't really much of anything! We were very disappointed…

"We did one gig at the Ice House together and then we did one somewhere else… all I can remember was that it was held off of a boat dock somewhere, but it was after this second gig that we both just looked at each other and went 'nah! I don't think this is gonna work.' It was a mutual thing…"

"I was still learning to play guitar better and gaining some confidence on stage." Russ was to later comment. "The hardest thing for me was being on stage. It was so scary. So I just did it 'til I got used to it. I did the Troubadour hoot once a month and the Ice House hoot once a month on Sundays. I knew that if I wanted to do this for a living I better get over it and the best way to do that was play…" [1/36]

Clearly, Jules Alexander saw the potential his friend had: "Terry and I had to practically pry Russ Giguere out of his position at the Pasadena Ice House as lighting director. He was, and is, a massive talent and we were bound and determined to get the boy on stage with us. I had played with him in many jams and hoots and felt that he was an incredible talent." [5]

"If you played at the Ice House, you were friends with Russ," concurs Terry. "Russ did your lights and the interesting thing is that he is colorblind!"

Following the invitation to join them Russ, never having seen The Men perform before, went to see the band play and, after a brief audition whereupon he sang a few songs for them, he officially joined the ranks as a replacement for Whalen. The next stage for the band was a visit to the recording studios…

Doug Weston was so convinced that his band was destined for the big-time that many began to question his sanity over his obsessiveness. He began to envisage signs of numerology, astrology and spirituality, all pointing to the direction of success his 'men' were due to travel upon. And then, in the recording studio, he took it one step too far…

Entering an old movie complex located in Van Nuys, previously used for sound tracking and now utilized as a basic recording facility, The Men must have found the scenario laid out before them that day somewhat bemusing. Weston had construed to lay out two precise, concentric circles on the studio floor, in masking tape, with a star positioned in the center. Protruding from the points of the star were a series of further masking taped lines, each extending to the outer reaches of the larger of the two circles. He then boldly instructed the band members to stand at the exact point the lines crossed, around the circles, commenting that this was, as Jules recollects in his article *The Men*; "numerologically correct and astrologically proper…" [5]

The band, doing as they were instructed, was not convinced, and so it became apparent as they attempted to balance the sound.

"Weston had also positioned us by height, shortest in the inner circle and tallest in the outer circle. As it happened the shortest were the tenors, closer to the mic than the baritones and basses. Tenors voices tend to cut through any recordings so it is wiser to position them relatively farther away from the mic than the baritones or basses. This made no difference to Weston as the integrity of the *Pentathingie* was more important to preserve than mere technological requirements. There were also no mics on the instruments so the back row banjos were lost, as well as the double basses, which were in the back row because mics in those positions would again ruin the balance of the *Pentathingie*. There were no drums because they wouldn't fit in the *Pentathingie*. The first tentative takes on the now forgotten song were wildly tenor heavy having no blend whatsoever with the lower voices, the instruments were not recordable, the lead singers couldn't hear the basses, and the tempo was non-existent. It was a disaster, a train wreck." [5]

"I don't actually remember the session at all..." muses guitarist Steve Cohen today, with fifty years now having passed "but that's exactly the sort of behavior I would expect when I say that Doug seemed unsuited and unbalanced, separated from reality. I recall him doing an interview with someone in the record industry and standing on his head while he did it. Irrational. You just wouldn't think of going to promote an act and standing on your head while talking to an agent..."

With Weston suitably chastened by the experience, and the overall failure of the band's debut in the studio clearly evident, tensions within the massed line-up began to build. Firstly, Doug Weston himself was removed of his mentorship of the group, with the band opting for the management skills of Dean Fredericks and Joe Koistra in his place. Fredericks was a friend of Terry Kirkman, having met him at one of the many evenings frequented at the Troubadour. The club was not only popular with the musical fraternity of the city, but a vast gathering of actors and fellow artists were also regulars of the establishment, either socializing in the front bar by the entrance, or within the inner sanctum, in the club itself, and Fredericks, an upcoming actor with a modicum of success to date (predominantly known for his portrayal as a U.S. Air Force pilot in the eponymous TV series *Steve Canyon*), was one such visitor. With his business acumen extending beyond the pages of a well-worn TV or film script he saw the opportunities that entertainment management had to offer and, in partnership with fellow actor Joe Koistra, they agreed to take The Men under their wing, with Dean having the industry contacts and Joe being the artist liaison. The future looked bright once again... or did it? Was it a wise choice?

"I'm not sure that Dean was the right guy..." continues Steve Cohen. "He was an actor that was looking for another gig, and just before we met him he had turned down an acting role that required that he shave his head and he wasn't willing to do it, so he passed up being the TV guy *Mr Clean*. The guy who did it instead went on to make a small fortune!"

One other moment of significance that took place during that period in the band's history came about one evening, late in 1964, also in the Troubadour club. The band continued to play there, despite the parting of ways with Doug Weston's supervisions, and more often than not, the interest in the troupe brought about some notable attendees in the audience, keen to discover this hot, new property causing a storm. On this one particular occasion, following his success with two best-selling album releases that year (*The Times They Are A-Changin'* and *Another Side*) Greenwich Village folk legend Bob Dylan had happened to drop by the club during a stay in Los Angeles. In residence upon the large stage that evening were The Men who, reportedly, put on a particularly fine show, predominantly for the established cast of musical *The Music Man* who were also in attendance. The band however were unknowing as to who else was watching in the darkened room whilst they were performing underneath the bright stage lights, and it was only following the culmination of their act, after they had returned to the dressing room, that Dylan stepped out of Weston's upstairs office, came down the staircase and professed an interest in jamming with that evenings house band.

Jules: "*The Music Man* cast had earlier got sight of Dylan and wanted to meet him but when he started playing, playing some really good rock 'n' roll licks, and Ted started bashing his drums it turned into a dance fest. We played and danced for a good two hours until we had to stop because we were making too much noise for the neighborhood at 2.00am..." [5]

Drummer Ted Bluechel, pounding away to such '50s classics as "La Bamba" from behind his kit, also recalls the scenario: "Dylan came up on stage and we threw him a guitar that was electrified. He was groovin' on that to the point where he wanted to play a number of songs. The next thing I heard from him was 'Bringing It All Back Home'. He had gone electric. He'd gotten out of the 'A Hard Rain's Gonna Fall' bag and into 'Hey, Mr. Tambourine Man.'" [1]

Steve Cohen: "Harvey Gerst, who was my musical compadre (prior to forming the band), put an electric guitar in Bob Dylan's hand and it would seem that he'd never done this before and when the sun came up the next morning he was still sitting there, captivated by the whole experience..."

Finally, Terry adds: "We were the first folk group to use drums and electric guitar and electric bass, while everybody else played acoustic. He (Dylan) came down from Weston's office and sort of jammed with us, to put it in lay terms, and asked how we were pulling the sound of electrified twelve-string and six-string guitars and a bass, and what kind of drum bass were we using for folk music. He was totally fascinated by our electrified instruments." [6/11]

So can members of The Men justifiably claim to have aided the Minnesota-born minstrel on his journey from folkie to rock icon? Potentially so, but such was the shift in the ever changing music industry at that point that it's undeniable that musicians all over the vast continent were now being exposed to the newer sounds of youth breaking down the barriers. It was only a matter of time before electrification permeated the very foundations of the traditional American music industry. Yes, one could so easily argue that electric guitars had always been there, since the initial rock 'n' roll boom of Elvis Presley, Sun Records, Bill Haley and Chuck Berry, the preceding years of New York's Brill Building's phenomenal rise and success, Philadelphia's clean-cut all-*American Bandstand* products, or, since the shift had moved over to the west coast epicenter of Los Angeles, when the driving staccato guitars of early surf music had wafted in from the sun-kissed beaches on the edge of the great city. But there was no doubt that, with the electrified sounds now also emanating from the doorways of the folk clubs, the times were indeed a-changin'. Especially when the leading bard of the current wave of folk music tells us so…

The British Invasion, heralded in by the breakthrough of The Beatles, was swiftly backed up by the tumultuous reception given to the subsequent swell of following Brit hordes. The Rolling Stones, The Animals, The Kinks, Herman's Hermits, The Hollies… so many boarded the daily BOAC flights from London's Heathrow airport, landing at the newly christened John F. Kennedy terminal in Queens, New York, and despite the vast expanse of land that divided the east coast city with its west coast counterpart, news spread like wildfire amongst the music business executives. If it had long hair and spoke with an Anglophile accent, sign it up, we'll worry about the talent later. Subsequently, electrified instruments, especially guitars, driving that rock 'n' roll beat, and influenced by the actions of what was going on 3,500 miles across the ocean, were stepping right to the fore on the stages all around the country, and the gentler acoustic picking that had filled out the folk clubs for the previous five years were getting put back into their cases and snapped shut. Firmly.

CHAPTER THREE

YOU HEAR ME
CALL YOUR NAME

Theodore John Bluechel, Ted, Teddy, was a striking addition to the original line-up of The Men. The all-round Californian young man. Tall, dark, sporty and exceedingly handsome… and talented to boot. Accomplished not only on the drum kit, from where he would pound away the beat with clockwork precision, but also a gifted rhythm guitarist and vocalist, with previous experience in the recording business prior to his joining the multi-facetted formation.

He was born in San Pedro, just east of the shipping port of Long Beach, CA., on December 2nd 1942; one year after the U.S. had entered the Second World War. The youngest of four children, with two elder sisters and one brother, his parents, Theodore John Sr., a general practitioner, and his mother Elizabeth, brought their young children up in a typically American fashion for the times. After a brief sojourn living in the wilds of Montana, the family returned out to the coast and settled in Torrance, CA. where Ted began attending Huntington Beach Elementary School, followed by North Torrance High, where he became first chair in the percussion section of the All-Southern State California Band. Unfortunately, a minor rule infraction, coupled with petty politics stripped him of a state award so instead, disillusioned with classical drumming, he opted for the college route, attending El Camino Junior College (commencing study the same semester as future Beach Boys, Brian Wilson and Al Jardine) although his early interests and intentions for a professional career in zoology soon dissipated once his fascination for the revitalized, burgeoning folk music scene caught up with him.

"I really got the hook in me after falling in love with the feeling of the music of the Kingston Trio when I was babysitting for my sister my first year in college," recalled Bluechel in an interview *for Where Have All The Pop Stars Gone?* "It just reached my very center, listening to the feeling, the ambience of the music. I was just one of those many people who got hooked into it.

"My father said, 'don't be a musician, son. Get a real job.' And I could go for that for a while, until I got the fever in my blood..." [1]

Whilst studying in his fourth year at El Camino, Ted joined his first musical group, a harmony-based quartet known as The Cherry Hill Singers, made up of four singer/guitarists hailing from various parts of the country, with Texan-born Ken Ballard, Nyles Brown, originating from New Jersey, and the virtuoso guitar and banjo-playing Dave Fractman from Colorado completing the line-up alongside Ted.

Dave Fractman recalls: "Ken Ballard and I go back to 1958 in high school. Then, in 1962, I transferred from the University of Denver, where Nyles and I were fraternity brothers, to Long Beach State. Ted somehow heard of me and found out that I played banjo so he sought me out and we would get together and play. He simply wanted to play folk music. The following year I talked Kenny and Nyles into coming out to California to start a folk group..."

Although Ted had been enamored with a passion for drumming and percussion since he had first seen a marching band, practicing up and down the street outside his elementary school, his interest in folk music had seen him pick up and develop his skills on the guitar as well and alongside his three new friends, the quartet came together during September of 1963, practicing during every moment of availability until they had reached a high enough standard to begin performing in the local folk clubs and coffee bars around Los Angeles, including such notable venues as the Meeting Place, the Troubadour and the Ice House, holding down a residency at the latter venue during May of 1964. Another such appearance was held at a small club up in Beverly Hills known as Ye Little Club, owned by an entertainment manager named Marshall Edson and a popular location for established jazz stars such as Nat King Cole and Anita O'Day to frequent, and it was whilst performing there that a number of songs from The Cherry Hill Singers set were captured onto tape, under the guidance of record label owner Richard Vaughn who had seen the band play and, liking what he heard, had signed them to his own HiFi/Life Records label. These live tapes were subsequently incorporated into a record release shortly afterwards, alongside seven studio recordings, issued on HiFi Records (*The Cherry Hill Singers: An Exciting New Folk Group* L-1020) during early 1964. Produced by Vaughan himself, the selected twelve songs (five of which would later be incorporated into the stage performances for The Men) pulled together a gathering of recent compositions, featuring the works of Rod McKuen ("The World I Used To Know" and "Town & Country") and John Stewart ("Come Along Julie"), alongside a couple of more traditional folk songs such as the popular "Railroad Bill" and "Ride Up".

Certainly the four friends blend together well in harmony on the album, and although the release never quite reaches the pinnacle of some of the many similar offerings from that era for these young musicians, caught up in the rejuvenated folk scene of the 1960s, hanging around in the bars and clubs alongside the likes of Peter, Paul & Mary and The Kingston Trio, this was certainly a big thing to be performing and recording alongside the top folk music stars of the day. However, shortly after the record was released, Fractman left the band, opting to join another local line-up instead, The Lively Set, and in his place came guitarist Mike Whalen, fresh from a stint in the U.S. Navy.

Fractman continues: "With the advent of the hootenanny era, things became quite diluted. I left The Cherry Hill Singers because The Lively Set was just starting up and it was a much better group with more singers and more possibilities. As it worked out, folk groups were in such abundance and The Lively Set could go folk, rock and Vegas-style, which included all of it, and (ultimately) that's why The Cherry Hill Singers finally broke up. There were too many folk groups and not enough work..."

However, this scenario was still to come to pass, and it was during this early period in 1964, with Fractman having moved on, that after meeting up with fellow like-minded souls in the many clubs, Ted and his fellow band members became regular visitors to the Troubadour's own Monday evening hootenanny events where they would join in with the action on the stage, in whatever permutation best suited the occasion. This, in turn, led to Ted and Nyles, accompanied by their new colleague Mike Whalen, joining up with The Inner Tubes and, subsequently, The Men...

*

A similar succession of events also befell one of Ted's new collaborators in The Men. Having traveled down the 1000-mile route from Portland, Oregon to the bright city lights of Los Angeles, Brian Cole, accompanied by his friend and musical partner Bob Page, found himself hustling for paying gigs in the many nightclubs around the vast metropolis.

Brian Leslie Cole had been born on September 8th 1942 to Perry and Violet Swan Cole in the urban port city of Tacoma, in the northwest state of Washington. However, with his father working for the Union Pacific Railroad, the family moved to where the work was, and at young age Brian, along with his elder brother Michael and younger sister Cathy, followed his parents south, down to Portland, Oregon, where his father had taken up a new role within the company. A highly educated, well read and intelligent young man, albeit a reluctant student, Brian attended Madison High School in Portland before graduating and moving on up to Portland State College (and attending the faculty during the same era as Jack Ely, founding member of popular hitmakers The Kingsmen of "Louie Louie" fame).

"In all of High School..." Brian would later recall, "I studied just six hours, and that was to write a term paper, (titled) 'IQ and Its Relation to Psychology', which I wrote purposely to blow the teacher's mind. I used to get lousy grades, but I got 99s for three years in a row on the Iowa tests..."

Intent on developing a career in acting, Brian took to drama classes with a passion, performing in a number of Shakespearean college performances during his time there, often spending his free time thinking up one-act plays, whilst also utilizing his natural comedic talents to full capacity. He also met and fell in love at an early age, marrying his young sweetheart, Vicki Cunningham, on June 17th 1961, when he was just eighteen years of age.

"Think of *Happy Days*," said Vicki, "I was in a car with my friends, and he was with a friend. We dated for more than a year before getting married. I was actually two years older than him, but he lied about his age until I was hooked." [1]

Just eight months later, on February 17th 1962, their first son, Jordan, was born. A second child, Chandler, followed the next year.

"Mom and dad met at Tik Tok, a cruisin' hangout in Portland," recounts Jordan Cole today. "Both were quirky people and they just gelled. Dad was thinking of an acting career then. Music would turn out to be just a way to get to Hollywood…"

During this period Brian had undertaken a number of positions of employment, all deemed necessary to support his young family, from advertising to lumberjack to upholstery, but he continually moved on as each new challenge bored him, commenting later "I have so many interests, I go from one to the next, but music I love. I can't play necessarily that well though. Put it this way… it's not what I started out to do and it's not what I'll wind up doing." [13]

Brian first became interested in music whilst he was still attending High School and his first paying gig, in between college plays, was playing standup bass at a local Portland coffee shop, supporting guitarist Molly Malarkey. Shortly afterwards, they were joined onstage by banjo player Bob Page.

"I was totally immersed in the music of The Kingston Trio," recounts Bob Page, recalling those early days. "In college, we had started a little Kingston Trio-style group called The Statesmen. I didn't play guitar at all but I was willing to learn. The others decided that since I had to start learning an instrument from scratch, and any Kingston Trio type band had to have a banjo, that I should go out and buy a banjo instead and start to learn that. So I did. But about four months later, I heard a guy named Gary Palmer playing bluegrass style banjo and I just went head over heels in that direction…

"When I left The Statesmen I wanted to continue to play music as long as I could so that I didn't have to get a real job. The local coffee house featured a woman who played 12-string guitar named Molly Malarkey, and she had a bass player named Brian Cole. I began to sit in with them and play mostly guitar, but also banjo, mandolin, Dobro, dulcimer and autoharp. The group at that time was called The Molly Malarkey Trio and we played at the Us Coffeehouse and the Hootenanny Club."

Despite some local success, popularity on a wider scale escaped them, and once the two venues were forced to close, both during the same period, the trio began to look at the wider picture in order to continue playing their music. Renaming themselves as The Gnu Fokes, they opted to take their act down to warmer climates, intent on seeking fame and fortune amongst the escalating folk clubs and record labels of Los Angeles, whilst Brian's young family remained behind, sharing a house with his in-laws in Portland until they deemed it a suitable enough time, with Brian earning enough income, to join him. Brian also still harbored ambitions within the acting fraternity,

YOU HEAR ME CALL YOUR NAME

and where better to be placed than in Hollywood, the adopted home of the silver screen?

Arriving in southern California during late November of 1963 the trio starting performing folk sets at a number of the smaller clubs around the city, such as the 23 Skidoo Club over in Westwood, the Villain's Lute in Van Nuys and the Blind Alley Coffee House, further down the coastline in San Diego, occasionally joining up with members of The Shaggy Gorillas Minus One Buffalo Fish, improvising their comedy routines on stage. A rare recording of a Gnu Fokes' live performance, taped during early April of 1964 at the small San Diego venue, still exists, highlighting the development of Brian's comedic inclinations, many of which would be later incorporated into his next successful venture. Supported by the talented 20-year old John Deutschendorf the recording features the trio running through a number of skits and songs, including versions of "Skillet (Good and Greasy)", "The Bike Riders Lament", "Daddy Roll 'em" and a wild spoof of "Puff The Magic Dragon".

Deutschendorf himself would soon adopt a shorter, more commercially viable surname and go onto achieve subsequent fame as John Denver, and Bob Page recalls: "Brian and I used to take turns playing bass for John during his sets, although Brian had other interests, so the job fell mainly to me. John and I would travel from my parents house to San Diego in his old tan Plymouth, whilst Molly and Brian, who shared an apartment in Pasadena, would drive down to the gig in Brian's '57 white Pontiac."

At one stage the trio even ventured into the recording studio, cutting a demo tape so that their new management team, Charlie Greene and Brian Stone, could shop them around but such was the increasing popularity of a number of Greene and Stone's other acts that little attention was paid to the struggling trio. Then, as both Brian and Bob began to focus their attentions on the regular gatherings that were taking place at the Troubadour club over on Santa Monica Boulevard, The Gnu Fokes drifted apart.

"There were two reasons we split," says Bob. "First, Doug Weston wanted to promote and manage The Men and Molly clearly couldn't pass the physical! And second, her father had just passed away and he had left his business to her, and she inherited quite a bit of money. She was extremely talented, not only resembling Cass Elliott in stature, but also vocally as well. When we first hit L.A. we were often mistaken for The Big Three (Elliott's east coast-based folk trio) and (after the split) I really missed working with

Molly and Brian. Brian was an incredibly talented person and The Gnu Fokes were about 75% comedy and 25% music. Brian and I used to go everywhere together in his car, and I had a pad and paper and we wrote skits as he drove. I thought we really gelled together as comedy writers.

"Personally, I thought we treated Molly shabbily and said so to Brian, but he responded 'It's our destiny to become rich and famous. She already is rich…'"

As the career of The Men moved progressively forward under the guidance of their new management team, and 1964 slipped away into the history books, so their relationship with their initial guiding light, Doug Weston, faltered. Eventually, it reached the stage where Weston could do no more for the band and with thirteen hungry mouths to feed the community spirit of the Troubadour's kitchen staff had also reached a breaking point. As a result, the entire group moved together, *en masse*, to a small bungalow in West Hollywood, formerly the home of movie starlet Faye Emerson.

"There were some crazy times there!" laughs Bob Page, "It was an amazing location. We had parties that went on for more than a day. One morning, we woke up and there was someone none of us recognized sleeping in the living room. He had been left at the house on purpose by Harvey Gerst's sister who was trying to get rid of him. It was three days before we asked him to leave! Then, at one of the parties, Ted decided to write on the walls, both inside and out. A neighbor had called the police because of all the noise, so Ted's revenge was to go outside and write on the wall above the front door 'Love thy neighbor… except the old bitch next door!' He must have been Biblically inspired that night because above the fireplace he had written, 'And the angel went upon the mountain and said unto the shepherds, get them sheep outta here, this is cattle country', and above the door to the kitchen he had written, 'And into Jerusalem, Joseph led Mary, who was always riding his ass!'

"Plus, we all remember Brian getting his once a month check from 'railroad retirement'. I recall it being in the neighborhood of $270, which supplemented the $50 the rest of us were each getting from our manager. We were all living on Rice-A-Roni, except for Brian who, when he got his check, would buy a huge steak and a can of beer and sit there eating it at the dining room table!"

"Earmarked for destruction in a couple of years to make way for new apartments, our landlord seemed unconcerned about the fact that thirteen-plus of us were soon calling it home." Terry also recalled for an article he wrote for *The Huffington Post*.

"Immediately known as the Folk House, it gave shelter to all sorts of wandering minstrels and their friends, the Smothers Brothers' sister, Sherry, among them. Those first few pioneering months couldn't have been much more exciting. Striving for new sounds we were treated almost daily to one creative surprise or another, like someone electrifying an acoustic 12-string guitar, autoharp, Dobro or banjo. We drew heavily from sounds from big progressive jazz bands, like Stan Kenton's, and vocal groups like The Four Freshmen and, my personal heroes, The Modern Folk Quartet. All with tight, big booming harmonies. Folk plus rock plus jazz times thirteen hungry guys equaled a whole new sound…" [6]

"I remember this one time…" Steve Cohen says, when recalling those intense experimental days, "Terry said 'I want to bring my friend Frank over here, he's a really good arranger. Let him listen and see if he can help us with the music'. So Frank came over, this wild haired guy, and said 'play me one your songs.' He listened and then said, 'play it one more time' and we played it again, and then he continued 'be patient with me, one more time…' So we did it again, three times through, all thirteen players, and then he walked around each of the people and said things like 'what you're doing is good but on the third verse, play something higher', and then he'd walk up to the next person and say 'what you're doing is a little too busy. Cut it down on the first verse but play a little louder'. He walked around to each of the thirteen people and gave them a little bit of correction so they got the picture. We played it and it was instantly obvious that everything he had done in nine or ten moments had transformed it. We then went through this exact same thing with three different songs, and he gave the feedback and made the improvements. It instantly improved it and this was all before Frank Zappa was a very successful guy. He was just Terry's friend…"

There was also a further attempt to record the group during this period. Having experienced the failure of the earlier Doug Weston-led recording session in Van Nuys the band opted to try cutting the tapes themselves, as Bob Page now remembers:

"The session was held in a little house somewhere, where it took us over forty takes to try and get the vocals right on Jules' arrangement of 'Noah's Dove' (a traditional folk tune, also known as either 'Nora's Dove' or 'Dink's Song'). We finally ended up by having Brian sing the low part and Jules and

I overdubbed the remaining four parts. Sadly, the original acetate that I had either broke, or got lost in the intervening years..."

Little more is known of this particular attempt at getting their distinctive sound down onto tape, or the subsequent outcome, and despite the positivity that emanated from the venture, and the many, dedicated rehearsal days, it appears that more often than not, divisions between the various members were beginning to unfold, and the majority vote on group decisions often spiraled out of control as disagreements took a hold of the united household. The band had had already seen two of its members recently depart the ranks, reducing it down to an eleven-piece unit, but that was still a lot of opinions to be tossed back and forth around the crowded bungalow living room, voices raised in dissention. At one stage during this period Terry Kirkman moved out of the Folk House, getting his own apartment on nearby Melrose Place with his fiancé Judy Gelbord, a waitress at the Troubadour, but with the resurgence of folk music as a living, breathing entity now firmly on the wane, in light of the mop-tops invasion – yeah, yeah, yeah – money was becoming increasingly sparse as the bookings became harder to secure.

Nevertheless, managers Dean Fredericks and Joe Koistra had come to the decision that the band needed to further adopt a more professional approach, to polish up their act, appeal to a wider audience.

Steve Cohen: "They put us in matching outfits. They'd be eleven people with the same shirt and we all went out and had expensive haircuts. I just think of it now as how carefully choreographed it all was. The song would be over and it would be for me to wave a count of three, take two steps backward and hold my guitar out to someone who was choreographically waiting to take it from me and hand me my banjo. Every movement was made to be professional. If somebody was singing a solo there would be a crossover and then a bunch of people would be sitting down on their knees, trained not to do anything to distract from what was going on in the spotlight. It was very carefully done..."

Encouraging the entire band to do so, Fredericks booked some rehearsal time at the Larchmont Hall, a few miles east, over on North Larchmont Boulevard.

"Dean and Joe decided it was time to take the next step toward professionalizing The Men, which did seem very logical..." Jules was to remember, "and to that end (they) hired Ruby Raksin to arrange some music for us. Raksin, brother to renowned composer David Raksin, was a well-known arranger and songwriter himself at the time. He was known for movie and documentary productions. I think we met Raksin once, then a week or so later he came to a rehearsal, score in hand, sheets and sheets of music and a gleam in his eye. We were pretty excited for here it was; an official Hollywood arranger was about to do his thing with us. He issued scores to tenors, basses and baritones and began to show us the song and parts on the piano..." [5]

Sadly, the vision that the Hollywood elite had for this gathering of rag-tag former folk musicians was a world apart from what some of them had imagined, leaving the band in somewhat bemused disarray. Whilst some members were content to go along with this sudden vision of grandeur, others were not quite so convinced over the direction this rehearsal was taking, and a band meeting was hastily called. Raksin meanwhile, reportedly furious that his musical expertise be brought into question, abandoned the session, and with scores in hand left the building immediately, whilst Fredericks and Koistra stood back, seemingly unaware as to the rising tensions, letting the divided band members air their somewhat differing opinions. It soon became apparent, between the heated exchange that followed, that some members were preferring to maintain the original direction the band had planned out, continuing along the acoustic folk music route, potentially into financial insignificance with the sudden decline of the genres popularity, whilst others maintained that the electrification of their music, working on new self-composed projects, was the path forward. Accepted, the vision that Raksin had brought into the hall that afternoon, glorified Hollywood arrangements, was a complete non-event for both warring parties, but it had brought the harboring discontent that was bubbling underneath out like a raging torrent to the fore.

"During the intense meeting, tempers flared, words and concepts were machine gunned at each other. The meeting turned into a battle of paradigms..." summarized Jules. "After a wonderfully loud and sincere rant about the nature of music, evolution and the meaning of life Terry and I led the faction to let evolution have its way. To get more electric, to get newer material, to do songs we were beginning to write..." [5]

"I also remember the day..." adds Steve Cohen. "I can recollect someone pulling out a list and airing their grievance over the arrangements or something and how things were forming up. There were some who were really building up against others, who just stood up to read from their list of seven things or so. It was probably a good idea but it was the breaking point..."

The division within the band was now all too clear for all to see, even to the newest member of the line-up.

"I was in The Men for about a month and a half," Russ Giguere remembered. "It was like running a small community. I had only been in the group for a short while, so I didn't say anything. I'm sitting there saying absolutely nothing, and all of a sudden Jules, our lead guitarist, said, 'I'm tired of all this bull. I just want to make music. I'm out of here.' After he walked out, I said, 'I don't even know what you guys are talking about; I got to go with Jules.' So I stood up and walked out..." [10]

Six members of the band walked out of the rehearsal hall that day, some say it was Terry who walked out first, others suggest it was Jules, but regardless of whoever headed for the doorway first the result was that Terry, Jules and Russ, accompanied by Ted, Brian and Bob Page, soon found themselves outside in the warm Californian evening air, the city lights twinkling around them. Immediately, Jules and Terry launched into their vision of starting a new band, with the musical philosophy they had all just so eagerly spouted five minutes earlier. The others, circling around, wide-eyed and windblown, joined in with the enthusiasm. Either Brian or Bob, no-one can recall exactly who, then noted that out of the six of them, two were tenor singers, two were baritone and two were basses… perfect! Shortly afterwards, they were joined outside by Dean Fredericks and Joe Koistra who, upon hearing of the new ideas being planned on that very spot, offered their support, and the new six-man band, united in their new visualization of togetherness, rode off together into the distance. North onto Melrose Place.

However, with fifty years hindsight, Bob Page now recalls events slightly differently to how history recounts the tale, indicating that the final six members were not necessarily the chosen ones in Terry's mind…

Bob: "Terry contacted the rest of us, including Nyles Brown, who turned him down, and said he had a vision for a new band with six people. I also remember him bringing in a guitarist friend of his who auditioned for the group, Frank Zappa, but he wasn't asked to join. Then we also turned down Mason Williams, although I wanted him in the band very much…"

Nevertheless, soon after, ensconced in Terry's apartment, Terry Kirkman, Jules Gary Alexander, Russ Giguere, Ted Bluechel, Brian Cole and Bob Page sat around drinking, smoking and planning, whilst the two-man management team smoothed things over with the remaining five Men, all of whom were presumably left in a state of bewilderment, anger and frustration, having seen their colleagues abandon the hall, breaking up the partnership (note: a number of the remaining band members continued on working together under the name 'Tony Mafia's Men', whilst others simply opted out, taking odd jobs, disappearing into the vast abundance of anonymity). At some point in the evening, between the various wine glasses being chinked together and the joints being passed around, the inevitable question arose: what to call the new act. Russ's friend Mason Williams, although not present at the time, was even called back into the scenario, as he later recounted:

"Russ contacted me and he said, 'we're trying to find a name for the group' and so I gave him these goofy names, although the only one I now remember was The Guadeloupe Buicks! They were scrabbling around trying to find a name and he gave me a list of three or four things they were considering but I think the name they chose was the perfect one for them…"

Someone at one stage, being reminded of a particular and somewhat tasteless, taboo-defying joke that had been circulating around the entertainment industry since the turn of the century and the Vaudeville era, commented that they should name themselves 'The Aristocrats', that label being the particular punch line to this off-color fragment of adult banter. Needless to say, much humor undoubtedly ensued as the gathering discussed the proposal but, wishing to understand the full meaning of the term, they first asked Terry's fiancé Judy to look up the description in a dictionary.

Terry: "While she was looking up the word '*aristocrat*', she found another word, and said, 'Here's a word that would be good for you guys; '*association*', and its definition is '*a group of people gathered together for a common cause.*'" [6]

Six pages lay the difference between one word and the other in the average English dictionary, over one hundred entries, but a fortuitous and small difference for Judy Gelbord that evening as she thumbed through the pages, searching…

From the English Dictionary:
Association (əsəʊʃɪˈeɪʃ(ə)n) *n*. **1**. A group of people having a common interest; a society or club. **2**. The act of associating or the state of being associated. **3**. friendship

CHAPTER FOUR

BETTER TIMES

As the middle brother of the three boys, James Yester, or Jim, a radar operator in the U.S. Armed Forces, had watched from afar as his younger brother, Jerry, had achieved a rising amount of success with two of the musical bands he had been a member of.

A founding member of The New Christy Minstrels Jerome Alan Yester, Jerry as he was known, born on January 9th 1943, had seen the 1962 recording debut of his multi-faced folk chorus line reach the Top 20 of the U.S. best-selling *Billboard* charts and remain in the lists for the next two years. Then, the following year, having left the wandering minstrel family, he had joined up with the popular Modern Folk Quartet as a replacement for the ailing founder member Stan White and had performed alongside fellow-founders Cyrus Faryar, Henry Diltz and Douglas Farthing Hatlelid (aka 'Chip' Douglas) on their first two album releases for Warner Bros. Records (*The Modern Folk Quartet* in 1963, and *Changes* in 1964), remaining with the group until they disbanded during 1966. However, these early successes weren't even the first ensembles that Jerry had been a part of. Prior to joining up with Randy Sparks and his New Christy Minstrels Jerry had played in a small folk trio known as The Inn Group (note: there were at least three groups from this early '60s folk-era performing under this name around the Los Angeles community, all unrelated), recorded albums as a member of both Les Baxter's Balladeers and The Easy Riders, backed Ernie Sheldon and Joyce James on their 1962 Mercury Records release *Sing Of Laughter, Beauty*

And Compassion and, prior to his elder brother joining the armed services, had performed alongside him in a duo, calling themselves either The Yester Brothers or Jim and Jerry. Together they had played the folk circuit and coffee houses around Los Angeles for over a year. That early partnership, alongside Jim, was to prove the training ground for the two phenomenally successful, and lengthy careers that was to follow.

"Jerry is the baby of the family," Jim was to later recount for *Teen Scoop* magazine. "I'm three years older and we have a brother Ted who is the oldest. But because I was in the middle and Jerry the youngest, we were a lot closer. Jerry and I are very much alike. I'm a Sagittarius and he's Capricorn, and those signs have similar traits."

"I was about twenty-one, and Jerry was seventeen," he continued in a later interview when talking about those formative years. "Our folks were going to move to the desert and Jerry and I didn't want to go there so they found us a little one-bedroom house in Burbank, right across the street from the John Burroughs High School, that was like $50 a month. While Jerry and I were cleaning the house, getting ready to move in, he would play guitar and we would sing Kingston Trio songs. He had been taking guitar lessons for about three years. And a kid next door heard us and came over to ask if we would play for a frat party that was two weeks away. We took the job offer and in the two weeks we had to rehearse Jerry taught me how to play guitar for the twelve songs we knew. One thing led to another, and within a few months we were singing in folk clubs in Hollywood, had a manager, 'Mutt' Cohen, who owned one of the folk clubs on the Sunset Strip – The Unicorn – and we would sing at his club, and he would send us out to other clubs around Southern California, such as the Rouge et Noir in Seal Beach or the Satyr in South Gate, where we first met Larry Ramos. We were doing pretty well…" [33]

"You know, Jim gives me credit for teaching him how to play the guitar" Jerry was to add during the article for *Teen Scoop*. "I taught him a few chords but actually it was his own enthusiasm and determination that enabled him to become a good musician within a week. We did commercial folk stuff and really put on a show. We may not have been that great, but we were certainly polished!"

James Yester had been brought into the world on November 24th 1939, born in the industrial city of Birmingham, Alabama. His father, Larry Yester, was a professional musician, a talented accordion and piano player, who longed for fame and the bright lights of Hollywood and so early in 1942, with two young children alongside, and a third on the way, he moved his young family, alongside his wife Martha, to live in Burbank, Southern California, within touching distance of his dream. Although it was one he was never to fulfill, small roles in the top grossing 1948 movies *Fort Apache* (portraying an accordion player in the band) and *April Showers* did provide some justification to the dream…

At a young age Jim became fascinated with the varying styles of music that he heard over the airwaves, with r'n'b and country music being two of the predominant genres crossing his path.

"As a teenager I listened to a couple of L.A. stations that were mostly playing r'n'b, After I graduated from High School I started working in a pharmaceutical lab owned by a millionaire bird photographer. I was also in a falconry club and had been for several years and one of the other guys in the club already worked there. The owner hired us so he could come and take us out of the company for field trips for the purpose of catching birds for him to photograph. We were hired for our ornithological expertise! During the first two years of working there I rode to work with the other guy and we had to get there almost an hour early each day so we could get a parking space on the street. He was a dyed in the wool country freak, so while we waited for work we would listen to country music every morning for an hour and listen to it on the way home as well…"[33]

"In the falconry club there was also this guy in his mid-20s from the south side of Chicago who played boogie-woogie piano… Meade Lux Lewis, Albert Ammons, Freddie Slack. I used to sit there and watch him play for hours and when he'd take a break, I'd sit down and he'd show me stuff. At that time, we didn't have a piano in the house. I was working, so I rented a piano for $10 a month. That just blew my dad's mind. He was so happy."[1]

This mention of falconry, and of bird watching in general, was to become a life-long fascination for Jim, alongside his music, and afforded him the nickname of 'birdman' during later times. "I'm sort of an out-of-doors freak and I dig ornithology, and if I ever have the time I'll probably go back into falconry, training hawks and owls like I used to do. I was in school when I had my first bird and I don't really think that I ever considered it a hobby. It grew in proportion to the point where it became a way of life, because I was eating, living, sleeping and breathing falconry…"[13]

After attending and graduating from the Notre Dame High School in Sherman Oaks, Jim took the job as a pharmaceutical technician, whilst also furthering his education during the evenings, followed by late nights performing alongside his brother in the folk clubs. A career in the laboratory seemed in the offing for him, with promotion knocking on the door, but with the U.S. draft board bearing down, both education and career were ushered to one side, for now. "At work they wanted to promote me to Assistant Production Manager, but I decided not to because I had the draft hanging over my head. I (also) wasn't sure about the music thing, it happened so easy, so I got teed off and decided, 'Well, I'm just going to get the draft out of the way' so I went and joined the Army..."

The following three years would see Jim complete his basic training in Monterey, before stints in Fort Huachuca, Arizona, just north of the Mexican border, and in Germany saw him through his tour of duty. It was whilst he was stationed in the Bavarian region of Europe that his musical aspirations resurfaced, and he formed a popular forces trio named The Yesteryears, performing both comedy and folk music alongside fellow recruits Dennis Turechek and Jim Kirby. The trio proved so popular amongst the entertainment officers that they were even given leave from their posting and spent a period touring around the continent, entertaining their fellow troops. On the odd occasion, Jim also struck out without his comrades, appearing on stage as 'Jim Yester Alone'.

"After being in the Army and getting sent to Germany I began to realize that I really did like the music thing so whilst I was on leave one weekend in Schweinfurt I went into a music store and bought a classical guitar. I played it for my own amusement but, in the course of things, I requested a transfer as they didn't have the equipment I was trained for so I was transferred to a Medium Tank Battalion in Illesheim, where I was assigned to the Communications Department. In that department were two guys who saw me arrive with a guitar, one guy was a jazz guitarist from Greenwich Village and the other had been in a folk group in college that had recorded an album, and they approached me about an idea of putting a group together, which we did. We built a show, mostly composed of old folk songs that we wrote parodies of about Army life, "Hush Little Baby" became "Hush Little Lifer" and "Puff The Magic Dragon" became "Yuch The Honey Wagon". We sent a tape off to the Entertainment Director in Nurnberg and he freaked! He wound up getting us pulled from our outfit and sent all over Germany and France, entertaining the troops at service clubs. We did that for a good part of the year and even did the All Army Entertainment Contest and made it all the way to the All Europe level where we came in second! The winners went to the States for one week whilst we went on a thirty-day tour of Germany with other acts as part of a big revue! [33]

"There was also one occasion where I borrowed a young lieutenant's car and went technically AWOL to go play a gig at a fancy restaurant in Nurnberg. I was able to return to base with no problem because his car had an Officer's sticker on it. I dodged the Officer of the Day and somehow made bed check! Ah, what we do for our art!"

Having gotten through his posting, finishing his Army career in the German-based radio repair unit, Jim was officially discharged from the Army during October 1964.

"I got out of the Army in '64, in Brooklyn, and my brother and his group, The Modern Folk Quartet, were just slowly progressing into becoming a rock band. They were so cool. I stayed with them for about a month in New York, in the Village. And then wound up going back to California…" [12]

This change in circumstances for The Modern Folk Quartet, going from popular acoustic folk performers to a 'rock band' was not going unnoticed in certain circles. Having gained a formidable reputation as one of the leading lights in the early '60s folk revival, they, along with a number of similar bands, The Men included, saw the potential that electrifying their sound could offer them and they were gaining certain levels of notoriety in doing so…

"We really made our mark at the Troubadour on hootenanny nights," recalled founding member Cyrus Faryar. "The Troubadour was in full swing, everybody was there, and it was the most happening place. And it was also happening in the point of view of agents and manager types, who were there looking to harvest talent. So we sang the hootenanny thing, and to our happy joyful surprise, brought the house down."

For much of 1963, through to 1965, they relocated to the east coast, settling in the popular Greenwich Village area of New York, situated on the west side of Lower Manhattan, and home to the many beatniks, writers and fellow musicians that inhabited the region. Dylan, Paul Simon, Joan Baez, John Phillips, John Sebastian, Peter, Paul & Mary… for many it was regarded as the center of the folk movement. Los Angeles had a revitalized folk sound running throughout its many parallel streets and boulevards, but Greenwich Village, with its bohemian feel and towering tenement blocks, maintained the beating heartbeat.

"In 1965, we began exploring a rock sound as a logical outcome of how we think. We would have had to change our whole mental attitude to stay where we were. We had developed a rock set when we played with the Lovin' Spoonful at the Cafe Wha? in the Village…"

The band's first attempt at cutting their new style in a studio, an obscure 45 released on Warner Bros. entitled "Every Minute Of The Day", went largely unnoticed and so, struggling to find their new identity, the band returned west, back to California, and performed once again in the familiar surroundings of the Troubadour.

"People reeled aghast and some fled as I brought out my Rickenbacker and we were all suddenly electric and cranking out electric tunes. The folkies were largely horrified. There were a lot of purists there, into the whole Appalachian thing. So it took a little bit of time, but we gradually won people over." [14]

"When the rock thing hit, the MFQ were in the middle of it," adds Russ Giguere. "They were considered the ballsiest of the folk groups. I've always been a big fan and if I was in town and they were playing at any club I would be there. The Troubadour was hell to play: the audience was not easy. If you weren't doing well you'd hear whistling, but these guys kicked butt. The audience was blown off their seats. It was not only intellectually exciting, it was physically ass-kicking." [36]

Impressed with this new direction his brother's band were taking their music, Jim hung around in New York for a short period, joining in with the band at times, trying out for various groups under the guidance of Herb Cohen, the Modern Folk Quartet's manager (and the brother of the previously mentioned 'Mutt'), whilst enjoying the vibe of the Village, before news came through that their father Larry, now living with Martha in the small Californian town of Joshua Tree, high up in the Mojave Desert, running a restaurant together, had barely survived an automobile accident, leaving him unable to work, and so abandoning the free-spirited city life Jim headed back across the country to help his mother tend the business.

"I worked at the restaurant for about five months cooking, washing dishes, bar tending and singing behind the piano bar whilst weighing up the options of a career in either music or accountancy. When my dad was able to work again, I moved back to the Los Angeles area…"

By this stage, early spring 1965, the newly christened six-man band, The Association, was contemplating the next move. Dean Fredericks, still acting as band manager, had secured them a property on Ardmore Avenue, a few miles southeast of their Hollywood origins, in which to live, work and breathe in, and they labored fastidiously on their new music.

Some of their many musical friends would drop by once in a while, crashing out in one of the three bedrooms in the property, jamming with the ever-increasing musical rhythms that permeated the walls. MGM recording artist Van Dyke Parks, later an influential part of The Beach Boys saga, was a regular visitor, as was a friend of his, a young songwriter born in New York City but now living out on the west coast, Ruthann Friedman. On another occasion, British folk singer Donovan, on one of his earliest visits across the Atlantic to promote himself, happened to drop by the house, as did Stephen Stills, a fellow resident on the Los Angeles folk circuit.

Their first attempt at recording the new group took place shortly afterwards, with the six band members setting foot in a professional studio for the first time. Western Recorders, located at 6000 Sunset Boulevard, was the location for this historic event, but the actual session failed to result in anything of significance.

"All I can recall is that Hal Blaine was on drums," muses Bob Page, "and Jules and I played guitar, whilst everybody else just sang."

However, the new partnership with Bob wasn't really working out and connecting as they had all hoped. Commitment to the cause, paired with his personal life, was proving hard on him, having relocated from Oregon, and his allegiance was brought into question. Randy Sterling, who was still in close contact with various members of the band, remembers Bob as "a really sweet guy, but you put him onstage and he suffered from, what I call, stage paranoia."

"I was generally a pain in the ass to everybody else," admits Bob. "I was living on and off with a girlfriend in Hollywood, and we had an apartment above Brian Cole, near Normandie Street, but in those days living together was frowned upon, so we told everyone that we were married. We were together off and on for a little over two years. We split up when I finally got tired of her trying to convert me to her born again Christian philosophy. I was also living part-time with my parents over those years and they exerted extreme pressure on me to 'stop playing around and get a real job'. Plus, I didn't really care for the direction the music was taking. I just wanted to play stuff like The Byrds were starting to do…"

"Bob Page was actually only in the group for a matter of weeks," states

Terry. "We'd go to pick him up for rehearsal and he would be in the middle of a tantrum with his 'wife'. He had previously been in a folk-comedy group with Brian, The Gnu Fokes, and they were very smart, but if you had a kid like Brian did, or you had just moved away from your hometown you had a profound amount of stress. I mean, we were living on $50 each, a week…"

Somewhere along the line, Jules Alexander recalled a singer and musician that he had seen and heard on occasions performing at the Troubadour and the Ice House and with Page not fully committed a decision had to be made.

"I was doing an audition over at the Ice House in Pasadena," Jim Yester recalled, "and the owner of the Ice House left me a note saying 'I can't use you right now, but some friends of mine are starting a group and they want you to call them.' So, I called them and the next day went over to see them, and they sang for me, and I sang for them, and Jules Alexander pulled me aside and said, 'Come back in about three days and you can move in with us.' By then, the other guy was gone." [11]

Bob Page: "The guys in the band, especially Jules and Terry, were huge fans of the MFQ; Cyrus Faryar, Doug Hatlelid, Henry Diltz and Jerry Yester, and when they got the opportunity to bring Jim Yester into the fold, they jumped at the opportunity."

Page was diplomatically removed from the band, whereupon he briefly formed another six-piece band named The Lydia E. Pinkham Superior Orchestra, who regularly appeared at both the Ash Grove and Ventura's Back Door amongst other venues, before turning his back on live performing altogether, instead taking up a position at Eagle Music, selling instruments, and eventually relocating to San Diego where he opened up a successful guitar outlet he named The Guitar Store (initially based in Pomona). This, in turn, later evolved into Traditional Music and then, in partnership with his younger brother Tim, they developed the acclaimed Buffalo Bros. business. Having steadily built up the company reputation over the ensuing years Bob finally chose to move on during 2013, upping sticks and moving to a peaceful life in the Azores where he resides to this day.

Clearly, for the band, the move was a fortuitous one with Yester, foregoing the choice of accountancy, immediately fitting into the role with precision, his high tenor vocal register blending in perfectly alongside the other five members.

"The first question we asked Jim was, 'Can you sing as high as your brother?"' adds Russ, already familiar with Jerry's contribution to the distinctive sound of the MFQ harmonies. [36]

"We were all harmony-oriented," Jim continued. "Because of people like The Four Freshmen and The Hi-Lo's, as well as The Kingston Trio, The Limelighters. That was all harmony-oriented. And that's where all of us came out of. I grew up in parochial school and by the third or fourth-grade, I'm singing four-part Latin masses. So I've always been harmony-oriented. I had also taken a correspondence course from Berklee School of Music in Boston when I was in the Army. I never finished the whole course, but it gave me enough knowledge to arrange vocals as well..." [12]

Nevertheless, despite the fresh injection of both talent and enthusiasm from the newest contributor to The Association the band, in the eyes of many, remained visually stagnant for the following weeks. There were no immediate ventures into the spotlight, not even on the stages of the many small clubs they had graced during the preceding years. Instead, by choice, they secluded themselves away, funded by the generosity of their manager, working diligently on crafting a sound, and a vision, unique to them.

"We were not performing," recalled Jim, with a touch a humor in his voice. "We didn't perform anywhere for the first few months we were together. We worked six days a week, eight hours a day, rehearsing, writing, arranging, working on stage presence and all that kind of stuff, so when we eventually started working, we were slick as snot. Our manager was giving us what he could, to keep us alive. He provided a house where four of us lived and originally it was $50 a week per guy. By the time I got in, it was $5! [12]

"But the band just knocked me on my butt! I was just blown out by the visceral power of those many voices. The thing that made it different from most other bands was the six guys, singing with the intensity that a lead sings." [40]

Terry: "We had two tenors, Jim and Jules, two baritones, Russ and I, and Ted and Brian would be the bass, if indeed we were going to do that. Sometimes, any one of us could be singing in three different registers. I would often move between bass and baritone and second tenor, singing the same harmony part. We rehearsed every day in that house on Ardmore, with virtually no interruption. Writing, selecting, arranging songs..."

Russ concurred: "When we first started, we rehearsed every day until we got the sound together." [10]

The timeline would now suggest that this period of intense preparation was, in fact, a mere matter of weeks once Russ had joined the collective, given the benefit of hindsight and the succession of events that played out – from Barry McGuire leaving the New Christy Minstrels (following their European tour in late January 1965), Mike Whalen leaving The Men to replace him and Russ coming in, only for The Men to crumble amongst a morass of internal disagreements one month later, taking us into March 1965, just weeks before the next significant moment in the ongoing narrative.

Jubilee Records was a small independent record label, founded in New York City just after the conclusion of the Second World War. By the turn of the following decade it had begun specializing in releasing records by rhythm 'n' blues artists, and names such as The Cadillacs, The Orioles, Jimmy Reed and John Lee Hooker began to grace the label, adorned with the distinctive multi-colored oval-shaped logo. By the arrival of the 1960s, in order to survive the sudden influx of the new independent labels, smaller companies such as this began to expand their roster, incorporating novelty records and releases featuring the new 'beat' boom on their schedules. In as much the same way as the Indiana-based company, Vee-Jay Records, had tried introducing The Beatles to an American audience, before Capitol realized the potential, then Jubilee had faith in another UK act destined for greatness with London's Dave Clark Five releasing one of their early 45s on the small label. Then, in June 1965, sandwiched in between two obscure releases by Susan Rafey ("The Prince" Jubilee 5504) and The Skyliners ("Everything Is Fine" Jubilee 5506) the name of The Association appeared for the very first time on a record release. Coinciding with the issue – Jubilee 5505 – The Association made their very first public appearance, albeit as a low-key formative one, performing a short six-song set, in the comfortable surroundings of the Troubadour club. Terry Kirkman was later to comment that there was so much commotion going on whilst they were playing that he was actually convinced that they were bombing onstage and it was only at the climax of the set that he realized that it was purely down to the excitement they were generating…

"We got off the stage to a profoundly huge response." [2]

Dean Fredericks had helped negotiate the deal with Jubilee Records after a fruitless period of weeks auditioning the band amongst a plethora of similar sized independent labels, all wary of the new amalgamation of genres that played out before them. In fact, the band had started doing the endless rounds of the labels whilst Bob Page was briefly in the line-up, with Bob recalling to the author; "At one stage we auditioned for Berry Gordy Jr. Something about being the first white group to sign with Motown... but we didn't get signed because Gordy wanted 100% of the publishing rights to any songs we would write, and our managers said that was a deal breaker."

And that wasn't the only stumbling block. The plug was going to be pulled on folk music, they were continuously told as they made the rounds. There's no market for folk music anymore.

Terry Kirkman: "What we were doing, unbeknownst to us, in making that separation from being specifically a contemporary folk act, with the addition of drums, starting to write in a pop idiom where you're actually going to write a modern folk love song, it was a complete music departure from what it was before. We didn't realize that. We didn't know that when we were creating our music in that rental house in Ardmore that we were literally creating a new idiom of music that had not existed before. So when we tried to peddle ourselves to the labels we could not get a record deal because marketing had no place to put us. We already had a standing fan club of 20,000 members. We could sell the Ice House; we could sell the Troubadour in a nanosecond. We were one of the hottest tickets in one of the hottest music towns in the world, but marketing has to have something to sell you to and they thought there was no place to sell The Association. They would come down and listen and say 'Damn! This is really exciting! But what do you call your sound?' 'What radio station would *play* your music?' It was really hard to get your head around something that hadn't existed yet..."

Yet, such was the band's diversifying formula, folk *and* rock music, along with their already loyal support from such a fan base, that Frederick's persistence finally paid off and, with the support of a small yet established label, and a contract for a one-off release laid out before them, the band had stepped into Studio B at Radio Recorders, located along Santa Monica Boulevard in Hollywood, on April 7th 1965, to cut a number of tracks, two of which were to feature on the subsequent record.

"Babe I'm Gonna Leave You", with vocal arrangements credited to Terry Kirkman and ousted member Bob Page on the eventual release, was originally composed by an aspiring folk singer named Anne Bredon whilst she was still a student, majoring in art at Berkeley, CA. during the late 1950s. The song had come to the attention of New York-born singer Joan Baez, via another folkie, Janet Smith, another new performer on the folk circuit, and within a matter of weeks Baez had included it as a part of her live repertoire. By the time of its subsequent appearance on the 1962 album *Joan Baez in Concert Part 1* she had consolidated the promising start she made with her career and was on the path to the phenomenal success she would achieve in later years, and that live album, her third record release by that point, was to reach the Top 10 in the U.S. *Billboard* chart listings and take the song (originally listed as 'Traditional/Arranged by Baez' on the early vinyl issues) to a wide audience across the country.

Unlike the flamenco/Spanish feel that ran throughout the Baez rendition of the song, The Association's cut, appearing as the A-side on the 45, offered up a distinctly bluesy, raw approach, with Russ's plaintive lead vocal well to the fore, and a crescendo of vocal support appearing mid-way, overlaying the barren, almost neglected instrumental track. Notably, the mood was set by the use of a bowed upright bass, as opposed to an electric variation, which paired with the simple rhythm guitar pattern placed the emphasis firmly onto the vocal accompaniment. Largely self-produced, 'with a little help from the engineer' (says Jim Yester), this benefited the track in its primitive, early styling and yet The Association weren't the only band to see the potential of what the composition could offer. Late 1964, totally unconnected as to what was going on over on the western coastline of the U.S., a U.K. beat group going by the name of The Plebs, forming in the leafy, suburban surroundings of Weybridge, Surrey, having also heard the Baez rendition, had cut an r'n'b styled version of the song themselves for the Decca label.

By comparison, the flip-side, "Baby, Can't You Hear Me Call Your Name", a newly copywritten composition by the San Diego-based songwriter Ted Staak (with arrangements credited to Gary Alexander and Terry Kirkman), was not as convincingly strong, falling someway short on production values. Nevertheless, this second offering, which featured early examples of the band's impressive and dense vocal arrangements, and the added inclusion of an extended woodwind solo from Terry, highlighted the potential of what the line-up could offer during this early period of their career. Interestingly, a heavily orchestrated and more polished rendition of this same Staak song also appeared during that same period, issued by Capitol Records and produced by Jack Nitzsche (arranger and conductor for many of Phil Spector's sessions). The artists for this second version were an all-girl group calling themselves The What Four, one of whom, Joellen Shattuck, would go on to become Jim Yester's wife shortly afterwards.

Rumors abound as to what other songs were attempted in the small studio that day, with the old 1920s blues standard, "CC Rider", being suggested by some sources as one of the cuts, along with a newly composed work by Gary/Jules and Terry entitled "You Hear Me Call Your Name" (not to be confused with the Ted Staak composition). However, in 2016, when asked by the author, neither Jim Yester nor Jules Alexander could confirm either notion:

"We may have played around with 'CC Rider'" says Jim, "but I seriously doubt we ever recorded that one."

Nevertheless, when the surviving master reel from that original session finally came to light, during late 2017, it did indeed reveal that an early attempt at recording "You Hear Me Call Your Name" was also tried on that day, albeit one that was listed on the tape legend under the abbreviated title of "Call Your Name". A fourth song, the soon-to-be-forgotten Alexander-Kirkman composition "If You Really Need Somebody" (introduced by the engineer at the session as "I'll Be There"), also made an appearance, although history would now imply that this catchy tune, along with the initial attempt at "Call Your Name", was subsequently shelved and destined for the dusty annals of the vaults.

> If you really need somebody to love you
> If you really need somebody to care
> If you really need somebody to love you
> Look around baby and I'll be there
>
> "If You Really Need Somebody"
> Words and Music by Gary Alexander-Terry Kirkman

Interestingly, the reel also reveals that the lead side of the chosen 45, "Babe I'm Gonna Leave You", utilized the very first takes for both the instrumental track and the vocal overdubs.

Following the release of the eventual single the band took to performing anywhere, and everywhere they could, building up their following, honing their sound into an impressive, cohesive 'live' unit. Early July 1965 saw them hold down a short residency at the Ice House club, over on South Brand Boulevard in Glendale, a partnering venue to the more familiar Pasadena establishment where they were by now consolidating their live reputation with regular appearances. The Glendale Ice House, or 'Under The Ice House' as it was officially named, unlike its more established counterpart, was located in a multi-storied building, with the actual performing venue in an upstairs room, accessed by an old elevator. Yet this was just one of the many such venues that the band took to in order the raise their profile. The late August summer sunshine also saw the band appear at the Fantasyland Theater in Disneyland's Anaheim resort over in Orange County, alongside Bobby Soxx & The Blue Jeans, The Edmundson and The Mustangs and yet, despite these many appearances and the rapturous receptions they received during this period, none of it could convert back into record sales for the debut release and despite their following, and the formation of an Association Admiration Aggregation fan group, the single, driven by a lack of small label non-promotion, swiftly disappeared into obscurity.

Nonetheless, undaunted, October that year saw them once again back in the studio. Such was this reputation that they were now building on the live circuit around Los Angeles and the surrounding regions that the label heads over at Valiant Records, another small yet established independent label, impressed by what they saw during an arranged audition at the Troubadour, offered the band a new deal, a better deal, and a far bigger opportunity...

CHAPTER FIVE

AND THEN...
ALONG COMES MARY

A s the summer months of 1965 began to recede into fall, the accompanying backbeat for much of America's youth was that of a vibrant, new sound. The dynamic affects that The Beatles had founded with their invasion of the establishment the previous year, and the following influx of British groups and artists that had followed swiftly behind them had laid the foundations for a music revolution. The traditional folk music of both east coast, and west, had blended together with this new British rock 'n' roll twist, and the amalgamated folk-rock was now one of the many new genres being talked about across the desks and boardrooms of the record companies and labels. It was being treated with serious attention.

From the formative years of The Jet-Set (and, briefly, The Beefeaters), a youthful trio of folk musicians, namely Jim McGuinn, David Crosby and latter-day New Christy Minstrel Gene Clark, who had developed their combined approach under the new moniker of The Byrds, adding in drummer and Beatle-lookalike Michael Clark and talented bluegrass multi-instrumentalist Chris Hillman on bass, these were some of the new kids on the block, and on January 20th 1965 this line-up had entered the Columbia Records studios on Sunset Boulevard to add their vocals to a track that seasoned record producer Terry Melcher, son of actress Doris Day, had cut in advance, utilizing a core of some of the finest L.A. session musicians available. Of the band themselves only McGuinn appeared on the actual instrumental track, adding in some distinctive 12-string guitar licks alongside the work of Larry Knechtel, Hal Blaine, Jerry Cole and Leon Russell, but the blending of the vocal harmonies that the group provided was to become a familiar trademark of their sound, and for much of the ensuing folk-rock era.

In August 1964, the band's manager, Jim Dickson, had managed to acquire an acetate disc of the then-unreleased Bob Dylan composition "Mr. Tambourine Man", which he felt would make an effective cover for The Jet-Set. Although the band were reportedly unimpressed with the song, they began rehearsing it with a new arrangement, changing the time signature from 2/4 to a more rock-orientated 4/4 configuration in the process and, following on from the January '65 session, with a new band name attached, the release hit the charts during April 1965, flying ever upwards to the very pinnacle of the *Billboard* lists. Dylan himself, following his recent witnessing of The Men's performance at the Troubadour, once again added his support to this new electrification of his music, and appeared alongside The Byrds during a famed performance at Ciro's night club, up on the Sunset Strip, in March of 1965.

"They're doing something really new now", he was to say to the media. "It's like a danceable Bach sound. They're cutting across all kinds of barriers, which most people who sing aren't even hip to..."

Yet it wasn't just The Byrds who were to capitalize on this new pulse that was now dominating the Los Angeles Strip and along the streets of the many American cities and suburbs, from coast to coast. Former Los Angeles surf band The Crossfires, originally rising out of Westchester, south of Santa Monica, had rediscovered their sound and had reinvented themselves as The Turtles, also opting to cover Bob Dylan with their Top 10 updated rock version of "It Ain't Me Babe". Then there was former New Christy Minstrel Barry McGuire who, having left behind his happy, smiley Christy image and taken up the gauntlet of the serious folk-rock protester, had cut the anthemic sounding "Eve Of Destruction" during mid-July of 1965, working alongside composer, arranger and musician Phil 'P.F.' Sloan. As well as McGuire, other new token folkies climbing up the *Billboard* charts included former session singer Cherilyn Sarkisian, now prone to calling herself simply Cher, who, alongside her partner and former Spector sideman Sonny Bono, also reached the very peak of the lists that same year with the million-selling "I Got You Babe". Then, four hundred miles farther up the western coastline, in San Francisco, two popular bands going by the names of The Beau Brummels and We Five developed their early roots in the folk-rock movement before both going on to achieve Top 10 status that same year. Meanwhile, far away to the east, over on the opposite shores, down below the skyscraper horizons and the high-rise apartment blocks of New York City, the youthful duo of Paul Simon and Arthur Garfunkel were popularizing their harmonic sound, often appearing alongside the similar folk-sounding reverberations of The Mugwumps, featuring Cass Elliott, Denny Doherty and Zal Yanovsky, and, later, The Lovin' Spoonful (also including Yanovsky in the ranks), all an essential part of the bohemian Greenwich Village scene, full of coffeehouses and smoke filled basement clubs. And then, of course, there was The Modern Folk Quartet, already establishing their credentials in the genre – and now The Men/ The Association were adding their music into the mix. Each new sound influencing the other. A *potpourri* of invention and interaction…

Even the hardcore, traditional folk clubs from the previous years were now beginning to open up their doors, maybe reluctantly at first, to this newer, harder edged sound that the new breed of talented young artists were bringing along to their establishments. Ledbetters, located down on Westwood Boulevard, founded by Randy Sparks and traditionally a club that was built on the very roots of the conventional folk sounds of the New Christy Minstrels, opened up its stage to many of these young new musicians, amongst them a group calling themselves The Survivors, pulled together by Sparks himself during the early summer of 1965, combining of a number of ex-Troubadour regulars such as Nyles Brown (recently of The Men), Texans Owens 'Boomer' Castleman, John London, Michael Martin Murphey and Michael Nesmith, alongside native Californian Bill Chadwick, Arizona's Carol Stromme and the Hawaiian-born Del Ramos, the nineteen year-old younger brother of the New Christy Minstrels banjo player and singer.

Randy Sparks, still clinging on to his traditions as a folk purist, was later to comment on the band's choice of name: "Everyone else in the folk music business has deserted the ship and gone to rock 'n' roll. In view of the fact that these people represent the last of the big folk groups, we've decided on the name The Survivors…"

Nevertheless, the auditions for the band were not as straight forward for some of the members and Del Ramos, a former art student at both Trade

Tech and Cerritos College, who had recently decided against a career as a commercial artist and who had been taught to play the basic chords on the guitar by his talented elder brother, experienced his entry into the band via a simple twist of fate:

"I had got in my car and gone out to Hollywood, and was driving up Westwood Boulevard and I saw a sign on a cardboard box that said 'auditions', with an arrow pointing down an alley. So I parked my car, grabbed my guitar and walked in…" recalled Del, also in conversation with the author. "There were around thirty-five or forty guys in there waiting. I signed my name in at the door and there was a guy sitting at the back of the room, listening, and two and a half hours later in was my turn. He said 'sing me your favorite song', and my favorite was a song recorded by the New Christy Minstrels, a tune called 'Today'. I love the song so I sang that for him and he said 'what made you choose that song?' and I replied 'I love that song, my brother's in the New Christy Minstrels'. And he replied, 'do you know who I am?' and I said 'not really…' to which he replied 'I'm Randy Sparks, I'm the one who wrote that song! You're the talent we're looking for…' and I got hired for The Survivors on that!"

"We played our hearts out in two-bit clubs from California to Colorado," Bill Chadwick was to comment during 1987. "(We played) folk music, along with light comedy and heavy drama, but all the time dreaming of rock and roll. It was a busy time for all of us. The first show began at 9.00pm and, depending on the size of the crowd, there might be a second, third and sometimes even a fourth show scheduled."

As for the chosen set-list, that too was often changing, night by night, performance by performance, with the band members themselves often bringing in their own compositions for consideration.

Del: "We all brought songs in, and when we liked a tune we'd try it out and if it didn't work out we'd pull it. Sometimes it would work, sometimes it wouldn't. A good example of that is a song that Michael (Nesmith) brought in called 'Different Drum'. He sang it more like a hoedown. It was later recorded by Linda Ronstadt, and at the time we all worked the same nightclubs many times, including Linda, and later, after we had all gone our separate ways, I heard she had recorded it and I said 'Oh, that's Michael's song, How cool…'"

Although Nesmith would go on to become a prominent songwriter in his own field, Randy Sparks did all he could to encourage these young musicians to develop their writing talents, setting up a west coast variation of New York's cubicle writing monopoly. Randy Sterling recalls: "Nyles Brown, Bill Chadwick and I wrote for Randy for a while. We would go to his office building and sit around and talk about everything imaginable, then write songs for six or so hours a day. Sparks was trying to start some sort of 'Brill Building – West' but it really didn't work out. Out of the all the songs we wrote there were maybe two or three that were really worthy of going beyond those walls..."

However, notwithstanding the hard graft, and a subsequent succession of interchanging Survivors line-ups, this new amalgamation of varying talents wasn't to last together too long, despite their grand plans for recording sessions, an album (prematurely entitled *Soul Survivors*) and a promotional tour supporting Nino Tempo and April Stevens, especially once the band's unofficial home, Ledbetters, was virtually destroyed by a mysterious fire during the summer of 1965, forcing the bands who played there to find work elsewhere. The Survivors, for their part, took up a month's residency at the Duke Of York club in Manhattan Beach, commencing on August 31st.

Del remembered, "It was constantly changing, and when Randy figured he could make the group work better he would pull one guy out and put another in his spot, but each member stayed there for quite a while. After all, we were doing up to three concerts a night, six nights a week, so there was a lot of work and a lot of learning. And I remember we had just finished doing three concerts one night, and the crowd had been out of the building for at least five minutes, and somebody must've left a cigarette burning in the trash can and the place went up in, like, seven minutes. I watched it burn. I couldn't believe it..."

Despite the setback, shortly afterwards, during extensive rebuilding of the club, employee Barry Friedman walked in one day, during the second week of September, threw down a copy of *Variety* magazine in front of the band and announced 'why don't you get yourself a steady job?'

"Barry kept an attentive eye on the 'trades' – *Variety, Billboard, Cash Box* and *The Hollywood Reporter*" says Chadwick, "and each morning he would post a list of the cattle calls (open auditions). More often than not an appearance at one of these auditions was a total waste of time, but we kept on going to the interviews..."

Guitarist Nesmith picked up the edition and immediately saw an advertisement within the pages, calling for 'MADNESS!! Folk & Roll

Musicians-Singers. Running parts for 4 insane boys...' to audition for an upcoming television plot. Hey Hey!! It appears that most, if not all of the male members of The Survivors – Mike Nesmith, Bill Chadwick, Del Ramos and Nyles Brown amongst them, tried out for this particular audition, with the tall, woolen-hatted Texan coming out successful at the end (of note, Brown, Chadwick and John London all continued to travel alongside Nesmith for much of the following few years as his career, and that of The Monkees, took the word 'success' to new, unfathomable heights). Nevertheless, following the initial unraveling of The Survivors, Mike, Del, Carol Stromme and various other Ledbetters regulars continued working and playing together, appearing at UCLA's Student Union Coop on November 7th (still working under the Survivors name), and then as a part of another of Randy Spark's manufactured troupes, The New Society, debuting at the refurbished Ledbetters club during early December of 1965 and then appearing on the CBS broadcast of *The Hollywood Talent Scouts* TV show, introduced by actress Donna Douglas. An advertisement promoting the Ledbetter's performance subsequently appeared in the UCLA Daily Bruin on December 8th, listing them as 'Randy Sparks Newest and Positively the Last BFG' (Big Folk Group). Also on the bill were two former members of The Survivors, Owens Castleman and Michael Martin Murphey, now performing under the name of Boomer and Travis: The Texas Twosome.

The New Society went on to achieve a considerable amount of success over the subsequent years, with both Del Ramos and Carol Stromme being a constant presence throughout the run, touring across the country, often with acts such as The Stone Poneys, featuring Linda Ronstadt, opening for them, although Nesmith was only there for the early weeks of the band it would appear, following his successful audition and screen test for the TV pilot, in the fall of 1965.

"We played all over the place," continued Del, reminiscing over the success of The New Society. "Disneyland, Knotts Berry Farm, all of the big theme parks, and lots of college concerts and it went on for, I would say, around three years..."

Justifying the popularity of this new venture the band even released an album on RCA Records during 1966 (*The Barock Sounds* LPM-H3676), featuring a number of Randy Sparks, Bill Chadwick and Michael Martin Murphey compositions and arrangements, crossing over their folk roots with a stronger pop-orientated sound, although the front sleeve design, featuring the seven-piece line-up quaintly dressed in Elizabethan-era costume, may well have hindered the crossover potential into a credible rock world...

By 1965, Valiant Records had issued in upwards of sixty 45rpm releases, since its formation at the very start of the decade but had, thus far, only achieved two moderate successes on the charts. Founded by singer-songwriter Barry DeVorzon, an acute east coast businessman who had worked alongside Dorsey Burnette prior to his forming the label on the west coast alongside his manager Billy Sherman, the label had seen limited chart success with solo artist Shelby Flint, who had a Top 30 hit with "Angel On My Shoulder" back in 1960, followed by DeVorzon's own 1963 release "I Wonder What She's Doin' Tonight", credited to Barry & The Tamerlanes.

Having been made aware of the tumultuous reception that The Association we receiving after each of their shows, DeVorzon and Sherman now arranged to see the band perform a brief five or six song show at the Troubadour, towards the late summer of 1965 and, impressed by what they saw, particularly once the band had launched into their driving rendition of Dylan's "One Too Many Mornings", a regular addition to their new set list, they offered the six-man band a deal with the label, confident they would see chart success as a return. Indeed, such was their faith in the band's performance of that one song in particular that when the band entered the halls of the famed Gold Star Studios in Hollywood, previously the home of Spector's 'Wall of Sound' and many of The Beach Boys classic hits, during October of '65, with DeVorzon himself seated in the producer's chair, "One Too Many Mornings" was one of the two songs worked upon that day.

And how did the choice of "One Too Many Mornings" come about? Jim Yester recalled: "I'm not really sure how that happened! We were rehearsing one day at the house where four of us were living, and there was a knock at the door. We opened it and there was Clark Burroughs (a former member of The Hi-Lo's, one of Jules earliest musical influences). He introduced himself and said he heard we were looking for material and he asked if we would mind listening to some ideas he had for us. He had the idea for a Bob Dylan song, 'One Too Many Mornings', and worked with us on it for most of the day. I don't recall if he ever came back to the house after that but we worked on that arrangement and it became a major part of our set, and when we auditioned for Valiant Records that song and arrangement got us our record deal! Obviously that was a great decision!" [33]

Once in the studio, with Russ standing out front as lead vocalist, albeit at times with a delivery that didn't quite turn on the power as much as was needed (particularly on the two falsetto lines), the amassed vocal arrangements on the final product took the composition a million miles away from where Dylan originally launched the song (as on his 1964 *The Times They Are A-Changin'* LP).

"Barry DeVorzon had produced 'Rhythm of the Rain' with the Cascades, and he wanted to produce us." Jim continued "So he took us into the studio and produced 'One Too Many Mornings', which wasn't really great technically. It was a good record, but we were capable of a lot more." [1]

The second song cut that day, a Jules 'Gary' Alexander original, the r'n'b styled "Forty Times", complete with a wailin' Kirkman harmonica intro, showed real signs of the Beatle/Brit influence that almost everyone in the industry had been exposed to during the previous twelve months, whilst also offering up suggestions of the sunshine-pop that would be revisited in the years to come as the band took their influences to new levels of performance...

"I really, really loved that song..." says Terry today.

With an impressive fan following, the aforementioned Association Admiration Aggregation, now reportedly reaching in excess of 20,000 members, the subsequent 45rpm release, appearing in the stores during November, managed to achieve a certain level of success and whilst failing to break nationally it did hit home in a number of the local chart lists, topping out at number 16 in L.A., and it gave the band yet further encouragement.

Valiant Records general manager, Budd Dolinger, later commented in *Cash Box* trade magazine that "'One Too Many Mornings' demonstrated promise for the short-haired, ivy league hopsack-suited group, and sold extremely well in L.A. as habitués of the nitery stormed local record shops for the Dylan composition, but it was lost nationally in the 1965 Christmas shuffle."

Meanwhile, Bob Stane, working from his base at the Ice House club, over in Pasadena, also contributed some notable involvement as to the local success of the release, recalling: "I pushed the single, 'One Too Many Mornings', as a club owner. KFWB, KHJ and KRLA were the big radio station movers in pop music then and they refused to play the record claiming they 'did not have a copy'. A lie. I kept sending them copies. Canterbury Records was a record store near the Ice House in Pasadena and all the radio stations checked in with Canterbury to see what was selling, so I kept telling my customers to buy lots of singles at Canterbury. They sold 'One Too Many Mornings' like crazy. Finally, one DJ said on his program, 'with a gun to my head I am playing 'One Too Many Mornings' by The Association'. So much for good taste at radio stations!"

Then, to publicize and aid promotion further the band made their first television appearance, guesting on the L.A. based variety show *Hollywood A Go-Go* (originally broadcast as *Ninth Street West* and, briefly, *Ninth Street A Go-Go*), hosted by deejay Sam Riddle and appearing alongside Lesley Gore, Simon & Garfunkel, Bobby Freeman, Donna Loren and The Sunrays, recorded on December 18th 1965, broadcasting across the nation on Christmas Day.

For this early performance, promoting both sides of the single, Brian appeared playing an acoustic stand-up bass whilst both Jules and Russ held acoustic guitars, leaving Jim with the electric lead, Ted (naturally) on drums, and Terry providing tambourine on the A-side and, whilst performing "Forty Times", harmonica. Surrounded on set by the show's regular dance troupe, The Gazzari Dancers, and an audience dancing along with the beat, the band certainly showed no signs of a nervous disposition with their first televised appearance, a result of the endless hours toiling in the clubs, and decked out in matching suit and tie the surviving footage, fifty years adrift of the original taping, remains a pleasure to behold.

In the interim, between the recording and the appearance on the syndicated broadcast the band returned to Glendale's Ice House where, between October and December, they made over twenty appearances, performing the new single alongside a number of other recent compositions, such as the jazzy inflections that ran throughout Jules' "Round Again", and the fast-paced beat of Jules' and Terry's "You Hear Me Call Your Name". In addition, they still featured a number of cover versions within their act, with both the ever-popular "CC Rider" (often the show's opening number), and a mixed tempo harmony drenched rendition of The Coasters hit "Poison Ivy", referencing The Four Freshmen, The Beach Boys, The Platters and a host of other musical influences, now becoming established tunes, as was a take on the Chet Powers/Dino Valenti composition, "Get Together", initially recorded by The Kingston Trio and simply referred to as "Dino's Tune" by the band members.

"'Poison Ivy' was fun, because each verse was arranged in a different genre of music. Rock, bossa nova, country..." recalled Jim. "We refused to cover other people's music, unless it was totally different and (we could make it) totally our own."

It was often during the performance of this particular stage favorite that Terry would take up the unfamiliar role of drummer, sitting behind the kit, further adding to his musical dexterity whilst allowing Ted to venture out towards front of stage, often supplying an additional rhythm guitar to the sound mix. And it all went towards keeping their name and popularity in full view of the public spotlight, whilst headlining alongside acts such as Stewart Clay, Roamin II, Mason Williams, John Barbour, Ben Short, Dave Rene and David Troy, the latter being the then-working pseudonym for David Somerville, former lead singer of doo-wop hit makers, The Diamonds. The subsequent succession of reviews that followed also remained highly positive, as *The Los Angeles Times* was to note during the closing month of the year:

> The Associated six in tailored Ivy suits and vests blast out with hard rock and soft soul. They are excellent musicians with good voices and the kind of verve and youthful warmth that make their wholehearted patter qualify as first-rate showmanship.
>
> *The Los Angeles Times*
> December 1965

Nevertheless, times were still hard from a financial point of view, with six band members to feed and clothe, along with their respective partners, and so a number of the group took to finding alternate area of income. "Some of us were doing demo sessions to bring in extra money," stated Jim during 2014, "and Jules played on a session for Tandyn Almer. Tandyn was a friend of ours that also hung out at the Troubadour in Hollywood, and (Jules) brought an acetate home that night and said, 'Listen to this!'" [12]

Tandyn Almer had been born in Minneapolis, Minnesota in 1942 and had been exposed to music from a very early stage, taking piano lessons at the tender age of just six. By his late teens he was a keen exponent of jazz, both Errol Garner and Eric Dolphy being particular favorites, something that was to become evident once his ability as a songwriter came to fruition, and by the time he hitched a ride to the west coast, sometime during 1960, he had a clear direction in his mind as to how his future would pan out.

The following year, after his arrival in Los Angeles, he became a regular at Doug Weston's Troubadour club, befriending a number of the fellow residents who regularly crashed alongside him.

"A lot of times I would live at the Troubadour," he would later comment. "Because I helped Doug out the club around '61 or so, I always had a key to the place. There would often be a rented piano for some act so I'd go there and play all night. I had the place to myself from closing at 2am until the waitresses started lighting candles the next day at about 7pm." [15]

However, after a few years of exposure to the differing styles of music that regularly performed up on the formidable stage of the club his once-prevalent interest in the jazz scene began to fade, and the effects that both The Beatles and Bob Dylan had begun to hold amongst the vast Los Angeles music community also struck a chord with the youthful Tandyn. He signed a deal with a small publishing company, Davon Music, and began to diligently work on his songwriting, whilst also holding down the bass player role in Mason Williams' performing band.

"He was good musician," recalls Mason. "He was my bass player during 1964, and maybe part of '65, I don't remember exactly, and sometimes he would write out tunes for me."

Tandyn: "I got bored with jazz and all this new shit was happening, so pop music became the thing. In December 1964 I first took acid, and it was a great experience because I never wrote lyrics before that. It led to me actually putting words down on paper. I started writing all word-salad type things. Finally, they started making sense, and within a year I wrote 'Along Comes Mary'" [15]

As to the origins of this new composition, a befuddling mixture of marijuana-influenced word play, couplets and shifting rhythms, he continued: "In the spring of 1965 a bunch of people, me and Kim Fowley, Barry McGuire, were interested in getting songs about dope on the air without them knowing. It was like a Trojan horse or something. Van Dyke Parks was in on it also..." [15]

"It's more of a social protest song," suggests Jim Yester. "It's not saying, hey, let's all go out and smoke pot, it's suggesting it's a level playing ground. Pills and alcohol are condoned but not marijuana. It's kinda basically in that direction..."

To cut a demo version of this new composition, he turned to a fellow long-distance traveler, originally from Eau Claire, Wisconsin, but more recently a student of Minneapolis University, now also currently to be found weaving his harmonic magic and sprinkling his own brand of golden fairy dust around the L.A. club and studio scene.

This innovative production protégé, one Curt Boettcher (born January 7th 1944), had started his career early and, as a former member of The GoldeBriars folk group, had cut his teeth in the recording studios during 1964 when the quartet had recorded and released two albums for Epic Records – *GoldeBriars* and *Straight Ahead*. Then, following the band's demise, he had formed a duo named Summer's Children who, as well as releasing two saccharine-pop 45s on APT and Date Records, also performed in various clubs around the city such as Pasadena's Ice House. It was here that he first ran into the newly aggregated Association.

Boettcher: "I come out here gigging, and I played the Pasadena Ice House and a place down in Luna Park [sic] called The Mecca, and The Association's path crossed with mine. At the time they were putting the group together and they asked me if I'd like to be in it. I declined since my group hadn't broken up yet, but we stayed friends. During this time, I was getting my shit together as a producer…" [17]

Whilst Boettcher's claim of becoming a band member is open to much debate (sadly, he passed away in 1987), it is undeniable that his move into studio production was a very astute one as he subsequently brought in around him a regular and close group of friends in whom he knew and trusted could bring to life his musical concepts – vast swathes of shimmering harmonies, including the local Californian-born Lee Mallory amongst others. Mallory had, like so many alongside him, been a regular performer at the Troubadour club during this period and had close association with the members of both The Inner Tubes and The Men. Curt, meanwhile, formed a production company with former Vee Jay Records VP Steve Clark, Our Productions, and had recently become acquainted with Tandyn Almer, hearing the potential in his compositions. Together, they worked up an arrangement for "Along Comes Mary", cutting a demo version of the song during early 1966 with Tandyn himself playing the jazz-influenced piano patterns, Curt supplying the lead vocal in his distinctive delicate tenor, seemingly losing the tempo at times as his voice wavers across the intricate arrangement, accompanied by Jerry Scheff on bass and, following an invitation to participate (and earn some much needed money), occasional associate and fellow Troubadour resident Jules Alexander on guitar.

Unfortunately, despite the obvious potential of the work in question, dissention as to whom should take songwriting credit was to cause ill feeling between Almer, the song's originator, and Boettcher who felt that, as the arranger, he should have shared credit on the final billing. Boettcher's then-wife Claudia later stated that Tandyn had initially composed the song at a much slower speed and that Curt had suggested the faster, up-tempo arrangement and part of the melody that was subsequently demoed, thus justifying his claim, and the feud was to continue in years to come, especially after the subsequent success of the composition. And yet only Almer was to duly benefit as the credited composer. But did he benefit at all? The unreserved media spotlight suddenly befell upon this reluctant individual, forcing him into a public zone he had no experience, or desire to witness.

"My little taste of fame brought me more attention than I wanted" he was to later state. "It cut into my writing hours. On my list of priorities, creativity and freedom are at the top..." [15]

"I actually co-wrote the song..." confirmed Boettcher, in a 1981 conversation with Australian author Stephen J. McParland, "but because of the way it came down, I never did receive any credit for it. It was written while we were all on acid. When I came in to do the session the song was already written out, but as I couldn't read sheet music I just made up my own melody and we cut it that way. It ended up being quite different to how it was originally planned, but that difference, I think, made the song the hit it was..." [16]

Jules Alexander however, in a more recent conversation, counteracts that claim, offering up the version that "Curt did not co-write 'Along Comes Mary'. He, as producer, arranged part of it. He got part of the publishing money due to a deal that was common among many producers at the time, and may still be the case, which was that the producer would get part of the songwriting royalties. Curt may have settled with Tandyn for a flat fee. When the song was written Curt, Tandyn and I were friends. Curt and I co-wrote several songs, hung together, smoked many a joint..."

Regardless of any underlying tensions, or of composing origins, for The Association, "Along Comes Mary" would catapult them into the next phase of their career. Out of the small folk clubs, away from the localized success story, and into the national glare of a watching America...

and then...

along comes

THE ASSOCIATION
singing... along comes mary
& eleven wild new songs
a great valiant effort with
a fantastic new sound

VALIANT RECORDS
MONO 5002 · STEREO 25002

PRODUCED BY C. BOETTCHER FOR OUR PRODUCTIONS   VALIANT RECORDS 6565 SUNSET BLVD. HOLLYWOOD 28 CALIFORNIA

CHAPTER SIX

CHERISH IS THE WORD

"'Along Comes Mary' (is) in the ancient and honorable Dorian mode, the same mode we've heard in Debussy and in the plain-chant. Now who'd have thunk it? The word Dorian obviously comes from the Greek and, in fact, does come originally from the music of ancient Greece. We don't know too much about that old Greek music. What we do know is that the Greek modes eventually made their way to Rome and were taken up by the Roman Catholic Church during the Middle Ages in a somewhat different form. But the church kept the old Greek names for the modes: Dorian, Phrygian, Lydian, Mixolydian, Aeolian, Locrian, and Ionian. Now there's a mouthful for you, I know, but they're much easier to understand than their names are to pronounce. And they are still used today in Catholic churches all over the world, in those beautiful chants called plainsong. To find the Dorian mode on your piano, all you have to do is to start on the note D and play only white notes all the way up to the next and you've got it. Simple.

What is that old Greek mode doing in today's pop music? Well, I'll tell you. The modes have provided a fresh sound, a relief from that old, overused major and minor. For instance, if that swinging opening of 'Along Comes Mary' had been written in the usual, everyday minor mode, it would sound sort of square. Ordinary. But this has a kick in it, and the kick is Dorian..."

Young People's Concert
Leonard Bernstein. 1967

For one as seriously accepted and widely recognized as composer, conductor and lecturer Leonard Bernstein to appreciate the depth to which Almer composed his work in such regard is truly phenomenal and the subsequent public acceptance of the Association's rendition of the song, released on March 8th 1966, with Jim Yester stepping up front to handle the lead vocals – triple tracked to add a warmer, fuller sound to the mix – was equally as positive, driving the song up into the *Billboard* Top 10 and peaking at a lofty #7 position on July 11th during an 11-week run (with The Beatles, Frank Sinatra, The Troggs and Tommy James all holding positions higher up the lists). And yet, were they the first choice to record the composition?

"I believe that (Tandyn) actually wrote it with us in mind," claims Henry Diltz, founding member of the Modern Folk Quartet. "The writer gave us the lead sheet and at the very top it said 'MFQ'. Our group reviewed the song but passed on it. The majority didn't think that it fit as we were still doing more folk stuff. So we turned down 'Along Comes Mary', which immediately went to The Association and they recorded it…" [36]

Another group that had the opportunity of cutting the song was San Francisco's We Five, fronted by Mike Stewart, brother of the Kingston Trio's John Stewart. This came about as the result of the demo disc falling into the hands of Randy Sterling, who was helping the band with their arrangements during that period, having relocated up to the northerly Californian city to further his position within the industry.

Sterling: "By that time I had become a session player. I was now a hot A-list rhythm guitarist ("I Got You Babe", "All I Really Wanna Do") but here I was, now living up in San Francisco, learning about publishing and management and all of that, and I was looking around for songs for We Five, as they've just had this big hit ('You Were On My Mind'), and they're desperately clawing around looking for the next one. I get a package from this guy I had known at the Troubadour, Tandyn Almer, and I'm listening to the demo and I'm going 'Oh my God! This is it! This is a fucking smash hit!' and I take it up to Frank Werber, their producer, and he listens to it and goes 'No! They're talking about marijuana. We ain't doing that!' and I just thought 'fuck!' But I thought this is just perfect for The Association, so I get on the phone and I call, and I think it was Russ who I talked to and said, 'Man, I found this song for you. It's fabulous. It's called 'Along Comes Mary' and he goes 'Oh! Funny you should say that! We just recorded that last week!' I had no idea Jules Alexander was on that demo…"

The Association had initially cut the track just a week or two prior to its release, at the Homewood Studios in Hollywood, a small set-up owned by seasoned record producer Gary Paxton (a former member of the hit duo Skip & Flip and later the producer of the 1962 smash "Monster Mash") and located in his garage, next to his two-story house. When Barry DeVorzon, president of Valiant Records, had agreed to let the band choose their own producer for their single they had opted to utilize Curt Boettcher, a friend of Paxton's, in that role, but it was on the understanding that seasoned session musicians would be brought in to cut the actual tracks. That was fine as the band saw it, knowing that Boettcher had his own crew of professionals to hand.

Curt: "I said, hey guys, I think I can cut it as a producer. I saw their show a million times and knew them inside out. So we went into the studio together with the troops, Ben Benay and all those guys, and that's how it came to pass, with Gary Paxton." [17]

"Our power has always been our singing" Ted Bluechel was to confirm in a 1984 interview with Marty Natchez for *Goldmine* magazine. "I am not a qualified studio drummer and all those (early) tracks were recorded by studio musicians in Gary Paxton's garage that he had converted into a studio. He had four-track equipment set up in an outside trailer."

Also cut in Paxton's ad-hoc studio during the same period were four other songs; a new Yester-Alexander co-composition entitled "Your Own Love", Russ Giguere's enchanting "I'll Be Your Man", the mystical Jules Alexander ballad "Remember" and, finally, the distinctive sunshine pop of Boettcher's own tune, "Better Times", co-written with Lee Mallory (also recorded by The Brothers Cain the following year). Assisting out on the sessions were bass player Jerry Scheff (whose son, Jason, now continues on the family tradition, up until recently holding down the bass role with rock monoliths Chicago), guitarists Ben Benay, Mike Deasy and Mallory himself, keyboard players Michael Henderson and Butch Parker and two drummers and percussionists, James Troxel and Toxey French. Although not acknowledged for any contribution famed Los Angeles session drummer, Hal Blaine, would also later claim credit for playing on "Along Comes Mary" in his autobiography, *The Wrecking Crew*, a fact that, fifty years on, Jules notes may well have rung true:

"Well, what happened was our original drummer in the studio, Jim Troxel, fell ill during one of the actual sessions, which was a blow to us as he was one of the best drummers to work with. He was unbelievable. Other drummers then had to fill in and Hal may have been one of them. I remember knowing Hal for a long, long time and I know he was involved in the beginnings of the band…"

"Some of the songs were recorded in Gary Paxton's living room…" Boettcher went on to say, "and I remember it was a really hot day, and his wife had left a bucket of dirty diapers in the corner so I was in a hurry to finish up the tracks! The rest of them were recorded in a garage, with the recording equipment in a bus in the driveway. Really funky!" [17]

With these initial sessions completed and the five tracks mixed for release the band then took a rather strange option in making the choice as to which songs to release for the third single…

Subud was, and still is an international spiritual movement, founded in Indonesia back in the early part of the twentieth century by the Javan-born Muhammad Subuh Sumohadiwidjojo, a spiritual leader who believed he had established a contact with an energy from a higher power. The basis of the program was an exercise commonly referred to as the *latihan kejiwaan*, which was said to represent guidance from 'the Power of God' or 'the Great Life Force', and Subud members report that over time the *latihan*, which can be approached in the spirit of a scientific experiment, can bring you proof of the spiritual life.

The beliefs of Subuh were respected by a vast amount of fellow advocates, eager to experience this energy he spoke of, and during the 1960s the movement proved incredibly popular amongst the American entertainment industry, the in-crowd, as the culture of the free society, with the desires and wishes to experiment, explore and experience, drew in many activists and supporters, all keenly interested in learning more about the faith, just one of the many Eastern religions and philosophies being discussed freely.

Numerous musicians, poets, and actors took an interest in Subud at its mid-'60s peak, with members of The Byrds, The Beach Boys, The Mamas & The Papas… and The Association being amongst the most notable and media worthy. Roger McGuinn, leader of The Byrds (and formerly known as Jim McGuinn until his involvement in the movement) recalled in a 2006 interview with *Goldmine* magazine:

"I had been flirting with it from the Village. I got interested in it in New York and sorta followed through in L.A. By '67 I was into it whole hog. I switched my middle name. It was Joseph and I switched it to Roger, and (then) started using Roger as a first name.

"There was a Subud house in downtown L.A. on Hope Street, and The Beach Boys used to hang out there. I remember that. Then, Brian (Wilson) formed his own chapter at his house…"

In a later interview with *Rolling Stone* magazine he continued the theme: "It was a small organization out of Indonesia, and frankly, I don't know much about it myself. It was a 'surrender' kind of thing, where you just release yourself to God and it cleans you up. I thought it was cool, a religion without any responsibilities. You didn't have to learn a whole lot or use any props. When Brian Wilson got into it he didn't want to go to the place where they had the meetings. So he sort of developed his own brand of it with his friends. That's when he got really weird. He incorporated acid into it and a few other strange things and drugs were not part of it at all…"

As for The Association, of the band members themselves, Jules Gary Alexander was probably the most vocal in his support for experiencing the Eastern philosophies and uncovering their ways and early publicity material for the band often cited his wishes to travel to India to 'study the mystic religious life there', and yet it was Jim Yester who was to offer his recollections of their involvement in the movement and that of how it played a part in the choosing of the band's third single, with music historian Richie Unterberger for the 2006 reissue of their debut album:

"There were three or four of us that were involved with Subud at that time. Roger McGuinn was also in it, and Cyrus Faryar from the MFQ. We convinced the record company that we were gonna take the five songs we had recorded, and the elders of Subud did this thing called testing, where you would tell them the name of a song, and then they would kind of meditate and tell you yay or nay. We did that, and the two strongest reactions we got were from 'Along Comes Mary' and 'Your Own Love.' Actually, 'Your Own Love' got the strongest reaction from them. That song I wrote after I was in Subud for a while, that's kind of where it was coming from, so for me, that's why that reaction was so positive. Then we went back to the record company and said, 'Okay, these are the two.' And they said, 'Okay.'" [18]

Fifty years after the event this now seems a barely conceivable notion, a PR exercise at best by today's standards, but clearly it was an arrangement that the independently run Valiant Records were prepared to undertake and the forthcoming 45, "Your Own Love" b/w "Along Comes Mary", on the advice of the Subud elders, was prepared for single release almost immediately. Until, that is, deejays issued with advance copies of the release began flipping the record over, entranced by the upbeat syncopated rhythms of the intended B-side, as played by Boettcher's studio team, and the initially chosen leading side, the Jim Yester-Gary Alexander written "Your Own Love", was relegated to the flip in favor of the Tandyn Almer-Curt Boettcher collaborated effort. Smart move…

Almost immediately the single took off, assisted by members of the fanatically strong Association Admiration Aggregation constantly barraging the radio stations for airplay during the first few weeks, with the record hitting the Hot 100 with an initial appearance in the listings at #79, followed by a gradual climb over a seven-week period to its eventual peak. And all of this despite many questioning the suggested lyrical content not-so hidden within the chorus.

One of their many followers at the time was a young 18 year-old named Lois Abrams, hailing from Venice, CA. who was also working as a secretary at the time in the music industry. She was one of the original members of the Association Admiration Aggregation and today, fifty years on, holds true to her memories and recollections of how it all came about:

"They had gotten together at the Troubadour after The Men has disbanded," she recalled during early 2017, "and they had played the Ice House in Pasadena for about a year. There was no overnight sensation here, and they did tons of hard work! After they cut 'Along Comes Mary' and 'Your Own Love' the record was dropped off at a number of the local radio stations and all of us chicks called in and kept requesting to hear it. We all disguised our voices and just flooded the lines! We asked to hear 'Your Own Love' but one of the DJs flipped it over and played 'Mary', but we didn't care which side they played. Away they just went! It was so long ago I can really only remember that it was just us 'ladies with the band' and some close friends and regulars in the AAA. I was dating Ted for around six months during that time and I remember that they all called me Lolo!"

However, it wasn't just the fans that were finding the whole trip exhilarating and one special moment for the band members themselves came when they heard the record being played on the radio for the very first time. According to Jim Yester the band were crammed into Ted's 1959 Chevrolet Impala one hot day, shortly after the release, heading towards

Santa Monica, when the local radio station, KFWB, gave the record the first of many spins…

"We all went bananas…" he remembers. "We were driving over a hill and we heard 'Along Comes Mary' on the radio for the first time, and we were all hanging out the window screaming! It was wonderful!"[11]

Following the initial release of the 45 the band continued with a series of shows in Glendale, performing alongside a variety of locally based acts – including The Greenwood County Singers, Danny Cox and The Texas Twosome – and then, after an April 23rd TV appearance on the popular *Shivaree* TV show (broadcast a full three months later on KABC-7), they once more entered Gary Paxton's home studio arrangement on May 16th, intent on cutting a further series of songs for their potential debut album, having been given the green light to continue recording by Valiant Records. Initial tracks recorded on that day, and also the following day, included one further Almer-Boettcher collaboration, the hypnotic and melancholy "Message Of Our Love", and two other compositions from outside sources, both featuring Russ on lead vocals; a cover of Billy Edd Wheeler's 1963 country/folk crossover, "Blistered", and a new song by two young brothers hailing from Winthrop, Massachusetts, Donald and Richard Addrisi, entitled "Don't Blame It On Me".

'Don' and 'Dick' Addrisi, both musicians and entertainers from their pre-teen years (their parents had been part of a family acrobatic act) had originally ventured out to the west coast during the late 1950s, hoping for parts of the popular variety TV series *The Mickey Mouse Club,* but when that failed to materialize they set their intentions of success as a recording act, signing to (initially) Bob Keane's Del-Fi label, followed by stints at both Imperial and Warner Bros. Sadly, and despite a number of strong releases (including the delightful Everly Brothers influence of "Cherrystone"), success eluded them and by 1966 they had signed on to Valiant Records as staff songwriters.

Jim Yester later recounted, during an interview with WIBM 98 Gold radio: "We used to call them Frik and Frak, and they would show up at the house (on Ardmore) where we lived together. They'd be a knock on the door and we'd open it and there they were, sitting on the front porch, on the floor facing us, using the guitar as an oar, rolling like they were in a canoe into the house, saying 'we have a new song for you!' Then they'd bring an amplifier in, sit on the amplifier, and play us whatever new song they wrote."

Filling out the new sessions were six group originals, all more than competent examples of the band's ever-growing stature as songwriters themselves. Firstly, there was "Changes" and "Round Again", two fairly unorthodox compositions by Jules with intricate melodies weaving in and out of the clever arrangements and production, the latter, featuring a blending of Terry and Russ's shared vocals, having been a staple number of their stage program for a number of months. "Changes" had come about, Jules was later to comment, when Ruthann Friedman was sharing the Ardmore house with the band and she had developed a unique chord progression on a song of hers, "Ringing Bells". Keen to utilize the chord pattern himself Jules had taken it one step further and developed it into a totally new composition, changing the key whilst doing so. There was also one unused song by Jules in the canon, "Flashing Memories", which, he claims, "was one of the first songs I ever wrote". It remained unrecorded.

Then there was Ted's debut as a songwriter, the harmonically delightful "Standing Still", the result courtesy of an inspired evening spent listening to some of The Byrds arrangements. Jules' and Jim's "Come To Me" came next, although this latter recording would remain in the studio vaults for now. Finally, there were the two contributions from Terry, the first of which would eventually open up the debut album, the call-to-arms anthem of "Enter The Young", the inspiration of which reportedly appeared whilst Terry was in his small apartment kitchen, opening a can of cream-styled corn. Needless to say, the can was hastily put to one side as he rushed to write down the melody that was buzzing around in his head, although the initial working title he scribbled on his notepad was "Beware The Young". Vocal tracks for these would be cut a short while afterwards, during an intense four-hour session over in the vast Studio A at the Columbia Studios on Sunset Boulevard.

The final one of these new recordings, and the second of one of Terry Kirkman's contributions, had actually been written a considerable time beforehand and the band had been performing it in its original arrangement for a substantial period during their early stage performances. The initial inspiration for this particular composition, the tempo and the 'feel' of the song, had been loosely based upon The Righteous Brothers 1964 chart-topper "You've Lost That Lovin' Feelin'", with Terry's fascination of his chosen title directing his thought process. Upon release as a 45 "Cherish" would go on to equal the success of that Spector-produced classic, and it would consolidate the band's new standing in both the charts and in the media spotlight although, reportedly, their music publisher fought against the title, believing it was too archaic for a 1966 audience.

"'Cherish' came in one fell swoop. I actually channeled it, or I was channeled. I really don't know what the source was. I've never understood the process nor do I think I will ever understand the process," Terry was to tell journalist Casey Chambers during a 2015 interview. "And there are any number of songwriters out there, poets and writer's writers, and artists of all kinds who will tell you that they've sat down to do something and the next thing you know, it's done. And you don't really know where it came from.

"So between 11:00 pm and 11:37 pm on that particular night, which I know because I got home at exactly 11:00pm and the news had just started, my wife said, 'Do you wanna watch the news?' And I said, 'No, I think I'm gonna try to write this song.' And then when I finished it, I was just barely into Johnny Carson's monologue at 11:37. So in that period of time, that song got written. I mean, we obviously worked on the song for months to make it sound the way it did, but the actual writing of the song just came in one fell swoop..."

Both Terry and Jules continued with the theme in a later (July 1967) edition of the popular *Teen-Set* magazine:

"In the old days..." said Terry "a pop song contained bridge, verse, bridge kind-of-thing. A very confined formula."

"In Cherish" added Jules "there are parts of the song which are neither verse not chorus. Actually, it has two verses, a first type of bridge and a second type of bridge, which all included is not the bridge, but two separate different parts. Then it goes into the verse, which is modulated and the finish is a repeat of the first verse..."

"If you analyze Brian Wilson's writing," Terry concluded, "you'll see that it takes on a more classical form, concerto form, symphony form... like Stravinsky's *Rite Of Spring*, which has many themes. This is the way a lot of popular music composers are turning..."

Fifty years on, and Terry now adds: "When I was around twenty-one, twenty-two years old, in Hawaii, in 1963, I started to hear, not satirical, but fun words to the 'Morning Theme' from *Rite of Spring*. I remember kneeling down and thinking 'Damn! I just wrote a song!' and it wasn't like any of the stuff I was messing around with at the time, with Frank Zappa. I had always written poetry, and written gags, and I was not setting out to be a musician… I just was. I hear music. I didn't know until I was in my twenties that other people didn't hear new music in their head. So I'm like a *savant*. I *receive* music."

Recorded during the May 18th session, and produced by Boettcher with both Gary Paxton and studio engineer Pete Romano assisting, and with session player Doug Rhodes also adding a celesta into the mix, the song initially took shape as a straight forward ballad with, once again, former Hi-Lo's vocalist Clark Burroughs helping with the dense arrangements. The intricate harmonies had also been extensively road-tested before being recorded, albeit without one final addition, one that was to come together in the studio itself.

"We were performing that song long before we recorded it," Russ confirms. "That was one of the few songs I knew was going to be a hit because after the show people would say, 'When are you going to put out 'Cherish' as a single?' (but) it went through quite a bit of an arrangement change. I can remember the day we recorded it and Jim said, 'I have this idea, start 'Cherish'.' We started rehearsing and he started singing, 'Bum, bum, bum-bum.' And we all went, 'Wow! Great!'" [19]

"There never was a demo for 'Cherish'" states Terry. "Jules did the chord charts, and Jim started doing the vocal arrangements…"

For many that distinct vocal introduction, as conceived by Jim Yester, with its continuing presence throughout the song, hit home in the hearts and minds of the listening audience but at the time the song wasn't considered for release as a single record by Valiant and, as a successor to "Along Comes Mary", the choice was initially going to be Terry's "Enter The Young", perhaps a more accessible and youth-orientated release for the American market. An early single mix was even prepared in advance, but, fortunately, a disc jockey in Ohio took it upon himself to promote "Cherish" on his program, causing a regional breakout, and Valiant wisely took note, especially once a Chicago-based distributor convinced the label to press 60,000 copies of "Cherish" as a single, a risky proposition and one that utilized virtually all of the labels free capital at the time, but one that ultimately was to pay dividends.

"Bud Dollinger, Valiant's sole marketing guy, probably more than anyone else, broke us into the major markets. He worked around the clock to push 'Cherish', literally betting the whole farm on this one record," Terry later recalled. "But they really had to question whether they were going to print that many records, with such a limited capital asset, in relation to what the initial sales were. They told us afterwards that they really had to give a lot of consideration that were they really going to sit down and pay for a million records! They did, thankfully..." [40]

On June 24th 1966 the band performed on the variety TV show *Where The Action Is*, broadcast by ABC, promoting the then-current 45 "Along Comes Mary" b/w "Your Own Love" as it climbed towards the peak of its chart career. At the same time, they undertook a short five-day performing residency at the Golden Horseshoe Saloon, located in the Disneyland resort in Anaheim, CA. where they initially faced an unusual reception to performing the current hit single, with the sheriff of Orange County threatening the band with expulsion if they performed the song...

Jim Yester: "We were getting ready to go into Disneyland to play a grad night, and we were meeting some resistance from the security people at Disneyland who didn't want us in there to play 'that there drug song.' And there was this group of nuns from Marymount College walking by and they said, 'Oh, The Association, we love your song about the Virgin Mary!'" [12]

"The song became so popular that all the St. Mary parochial schools in the country taped it for their pep rallies," laughs Ted Bluechel. "I don't think that would have happened if they thought the song was about drugs!" [20]

Needless to say, and despite once again the variables of this particular story differing over the many years that have since passed, subject to whom is recalling the event, with such heavenly support the officials of Orange County and Disneyland backed down and the band played on.

As the popularity of the band increased, and the loyal fan base of the Association Admiration Aggregation grew ever larger, the media awareness and the attention in the press turned towards the young six-man band. Articles began appearing on a regular basis in the music fanzines and magazines, introducing each member of the group to a wider audience, and the teenage focus began to develop a keen interest in this handsome, clean-cut line-up. Both *Teen-Set* and *KRLA Beat*, two popular publications aimed at the teenage music market, published regular articles on the band, whilst the more wise and worldly editions of *The Los Angeles Times* and *Variety* even went as far as to note:

The Association, a sextet of unusual originality and talent, is trying to work its way into the popular folk-rock bag, presently inhabited by Bob Dylan, Sonny & Cher, the Turtles and the Byrds, but their versatility doesn't seem to fit into such a limited genre...

Los Angeles Times

The Association has limitless potential in a strong format that has been so deftly designed, so carefully written, and so handsomely organized it seems a sure hit...

Variety

The Association – Agents of G.R.O.O.V.E.

There's a powerful organization lurking just around the corner, and it isn't undercover anymore. They are out to capture the attention and approval of every single human being in the world, so you'd better watch out. Their name? The Association! But beware – they harbor a distant aversion to tags deep within their souls and about the closest you will come to a definition of their activities is the following statement from Agent 00Terry: "We have a jazz, folk-rock, Dixieland, several other sound-combination, making a unilateral hexagrallagram type of music singing groovy songs."

KRLA Beat

Whilst clearly acknowledging the importance of media presentation, the band members often played up to the lighter-weight publications, offering up a fun-filled, self-deprecating approach, with an underlying cerebral intelligence that few of the teenage readers could have truly appreciated. Spouting words of wisdom to journalists of such candy-filled popcorn publications would scarcely have raised an eyebrow amongst the serious music elite, but such was the rarity of meaningful journals at that time that sharing the pages of the periodicals alongside articles on The Beatles, The Byrds, Paul Revere & The Raiders... and that of a new teenage phenomenon currently breaking out of the Columbia/Screen Gems TV studios in West Hollywood, combining two actors/occasional singers and two serious musicians (including one ex-Troubadour regular), this was pure gold dust for any entertainer setting out along the highway to success.

If anything, the upcoming success story of this televised fabricated foursome, former child actor Micky '*Circus Boy*' Dolenz, east coast folkie Peter Tork, ex-Troubadour stalwart Michael Nesmith and the cherubic British-born song-and-dance man David Jones, was to make the introduction of a clean-cut, fun-filled musical act more acceptable to an American public, wary of the recent British invasion from the dangerous, downright ugly and brooding images of The Rolling Stones, The Kinks and The Animals. This was witty fun, harmless television, reminiscent of the distinctive Marx Brothers brand of humor that many parents had grown up with during the preceding decades, and it turned many a youngster on in such a way that these same parents, now watching over from the doorways of the television room whilst the youngsters sat, glassy-eyed, just a few feet in front of the screen, couldn't help but accept this inoffensive, innocent humor. But did they *really* see it all? Did they catch all of the subtle innuendos that these clever individuals, romping around on the TV screen, were playing out before their kids? Was it really all just good clean fun?

By mid-1966, even The Beatles were beginning to waver away from the nice and polite, witty variation that had landed on the runway at JFK Airport just thirty months before. Whilst in America, the true birthplace of rock 'n' roll music, the candy-striped summer sunshine outlook of The Beach Boys, America's band, was starting to shift gear and move away from the anthemic fun-in-the-sun compositions to a darker, more serious tone, as group leader Brian Wilson crawled away from the sandy beaches of the Californian coastline, retreating into his reclusive psychedelic tent, breathing in the incense and marijuana fumes, high in the Hollywood hills.

Certainly, to a watching and reading audience the appearance that The Association gave out was closer akin to that of The Monkees or Herman's Hermits, another fresh-faced UK import, than to that of the Stones or the equally broody and disruptive Kinks. Suited and booted, with their carefully choreographed stage routines full of witticisms, jokes and comedic interludes, often courtesy of the actor-in-situ Brian Cole, The Association offered up no reason to devalue their creative output or appearance, bar the occasional 'misinterpretation' over the drug-influenced lyrics of their debut hit single. However, unlike The Monkees or the Peter Noone-led Herman's Hermits, The Association members were very much of their own mind from the start. Six head-strong individuals, united in a common desire to reach the peak of their profession, and six highly talented musicians and performers, unstymied by restricting television or managerial contracts, and free to interpret their music as they saw fit. Indeed, such was their desire to reach that pinnacle that, by this stage, mid-1966, they were beginning to question the managerial skills of Dean Fredericks who, despite getting the band regular bookings as their stock level rose, was seeing very little in financial terms in return. Shortly after the release of their debut album, appearing in the stores during July of that year, things were to change…

CHAPTER SEVEN

CHANGES

Jim Yester: "We felt very fortunate to have good record success that early on, because we knew a lot of people who had been together for quite a few years that didn't have that kind of success. So we always considered ourselves very fortunate, but we did have that attitude, that we were going to make it. We knew it was valid. We used to tell a joke; we knew we would make it because scum always rises to the top! But we really were very confident; because we knew what we were doing was different. And it was great fun for us. When we first started out our original manager was an actor, originally a cowboy actor named Freddy Foote. He changed his name to Dean Fredericks and starred in a series called *Steve Canyon*, and he was very wise to all the pitfalls, so we had a lawyer, an accountant, and a P.R. guy, and then Dean and his partner Joe, who also worked at a big Chrysler car sales company, got us a Chrysler New Yorker station wagon, very high line, and a Dodge van with a V-8 stick shift for the equipment. I must say the business side of things was really structured well. Everything was real straight-ahead. Their only drawback was the fact that they were in over their heads when it came to more prestigious bookings. We had a top 10 hit record and were still playing The Golden Bear, a club in Huntington Beach, with no bigger plans on the horizon. They probably would have grown eventually, but time is of the essence and the public has a short memory. You have to be ready to strike while the iron is hot..." [12/33]

Opting to leave the managerial wing of Dean Fredericks and Joe Koistra was clearly the correct move if the band were to take that next step on the ladder of success.

"When you enter the performance scene, you've got to start thinking about more things than just your performance…" Terry was later to comment. "You are the product and if you are not working on a salary basis, but you are your own man, then you have to start checking other people's motivations for wanting to help you progress in your career. Why does your manager want to be your manager? Is he really a good manager? What is he doing for your career?" [22]

"Dean was a wonderful fellow and a good actor but he had no idea about managing a rock and roll band. 'Along Comes Mary' was a hit, and it was making money, but we were only making $500 a week and that was not cool…" summarized Jules Alexander. [1]

Replacing Dean and Joe, the band chose to appoint Pat Colecchio, a Jersey City-born U.S. Navy WWII veteran and a survivor of the Battle of Okinawa who, since leaving the armed forces, had gone on to undertake a variety of careers including managing various sideshow attractions for an array of small carnivals and fairs, working as a bookie whilst also trying out as a boxing reporter, before finally moving into promoting big bands in the vast New York metropolis.

"Pat was my sister-in-law's friend and by that time he was managing a shoe store in Beverly Hills," reveals Terry. "Dean and Joe had tied us into the Associated Booking Corporation, which was [allegedly] a mafia owned company, and we weren't going anywhere. And here was this guy from the east coast who really sounded like he might have something, and we ended up taking on Pat. At the time we had no idea what we were doing, but Pat had the street savvy to get things done."

Jules: "We hired Pat, and the next gig we made a grand for playing thirty minutes. That's probably the biggest punch that the band ever had. He was a hands-on manager, however he respected what we were doing so he stayed out of a lot of things. Musically, he wouldn't say very much unless he really disagreed. If it didn't feel right he would say it…" [37]

"When I started managing the group", Colecchio was to later recall during an interview, "rock and roll had a lot of dead air, especially when someone broke a string. I told the guys, 'You bring the audience way up in your presentation and a string breaks or there's dead air so the audience comes down and you have to bring them up again on the next song. So as soon as something happens, someone get on the microphone and start doing some shtick...

"Some of the biggest names of rock music (later) shared bills with the Association, but many prominent performers learned that it was preferable to play before rather than after the Association because of the band's ability to energize a crowd." [1]

Encouraging the band to entertain their audience, not only with song but also with short skits and comedy slapstick ("I tune by smell and I've got a cold..."), gave the band an all-round Hollywood ethos, encapsulating much of what the golden era of tinsel town had to offer.

"A lot was attitude," believes Jules. "We had a professional attitude. That was a big portion of it. We were doing music that was a strange hybrid between folk music and rock and roll. And nobody quite caught that niche. Nobody quite got it except us. We caught it in that perfect little niche; the right place at the right time." [1]

One of the first roles undertaken by Colecchio was to oversee the promotion for the band's debut album, released during July 1966 under the title *And Then... Along Comes The Association* (Valiant VLM-2002/VLS-25002), and supported by a four-day promotional tour during the opening days of the month, accompanying The Beach Boys and the Tex-Mex sounds of The Sir Douglas Quintet to Las Vegas, Santa Barbara, Fresno and San Diego. With their new album *Pet Sounds* also fresh in the record racks The Beach Boys had to face some harsh criticism during the four-day jaunt, partially due to their outdated appearance in the red candy-striped shirts they still favored, but critics were also quick to point out that they virtually ignored their new Brian Wilson produced album (bar the lone performance of "Sloop John B"), perhaps in recognition to the lukewarm reception it had initially received from the media, choosing instead to concentrate solely on their golden hit era of "Little Deuce Coupe", "I Get Around" and "Surfin' USA". Coming onstage directly after the energy levels generated by The Association could not have been easy, although it wasn't always plain sailing for the six-man line-up, especially when it came to reproducing their big hit on the stage as Jim Yester was to later recall, during 2014:

"It's funny, but after it was a hit we were going on the road on a Friday and on the Thursday I had a motorcycle accident on the Hollywood Freeway, severed a tendon, and (the band) called me in the hospital, from the road, and said, 'Can you dictate the words to Jules for 'Along Comes

Mary'? Nobody in the group knows them!' They had just gotten used to me singing it..." [12]

Dating back to the early live appearances of The Association, and prior to that, to those of The Men, the band members had always placed a premium on quality of sound and performance, both essential keys to the band's success. Russ Giguere was to recall to Chuck Miller for a 2004 edition of *Goldmine*: "Our sound is what we're selling, you know? That was the essence of our being, so we got our own sound system very quickly. When we first toured we had to carry our system, which we traveled with for probably two years. We did that before we even had a record. We'd hit a place and the sound system there was like an assembly for junior college – they'd have three mismatching mics and horrible speakers.

"We were playing, I think, in Santa Barbara with The Beach Boys and the system in the hall sucked blue and green gas, and The Beach Boys came up to us and asked if they could use our sound system. They didn't have their own..."

Although he was no longer a part of The Beach Boys touring circus, choosing to remain back in Los Angeles and concentrate on songwriting and producing, Brian Wilson immediately came out in praise for The Association's new release, claiming it as the "best first album I have ever heard". Packaged within a distinctive cover, dominated by the front image of a green grass overlay, with at least three photographs superimposed on top of each other, all taken by Frederick Poore (a former Art Major from the Los Angeles Art Center) during a photo shoot in L.A.'s Griffith Park, the twelve-track collection peaked at an impressive number 5 in the Top 40 *Billboard* listing, during a fifteen-week run towards the end of the year. And whilst the rear photograph that adorned the sleeve, again taken by Poore (and placed alongside the colorless sleeve notes referencing The Rolling Stones, The Raiders and The Kingsmen, written by Phyllis Burgess, entertainment editor for *Teen* magazine), looked slightly out of sync for the mid-'60s era; the six band members, all in matching suits, posing in front of a vintage automobile, the image of Jim standing underneath an open umbrella (under a presumably blue and cloudless Californian sky) clearly appeared to reference their acknowledgment of The Beatles influence that runs throughout the grooves – The Beatles U.S. release, *The Beatles '65*, had featured all of the fab four sitting underneath umbrellas.

"Yeah, it was very, very Beatlish..." confirmed Jim. "We were all very enamored with The Beatles, we were big fans..." [21]

One other small detail located on the rear of the sleeve offered an address for where fans could mail letters, marked for the attention of the Association Admiration Aggregation, although the location given, 8966 Sunset Boulevard, three miles from Valiant's own official base of operations on Sunset, was no more than a corporate address, used for many artists and celebrities during that era.

As for the material that was selected for the release, Jim was to later comment that "most of those songs we'd been doing in concert for about a year or so anyway. Most of the time everybody had at least one or two songs on an album. We tried to have everybody included. We had a publishing deal where everybody shared in everybody else's publishing. It was very clever. We actually had a publishing deal before we had a record deal. We auditioned for Capitol, and they didn't sign us, but they wouldn't let us out of the building until we gave them a meeting with their head of their publishing because they couldn't believe (we had) a group with six guys, and everybody wrote. And they were all pretty decent songs." [18]

Only Brian Cole was noticeably absent amongst the final list of credited songwriters on the debut album, and he also came away without a lead vocal on the release as well, and yet his presence was all-too clearly felt once the group hit the concert trail once again, to continue promoting the album during the remaining summer dates.

Jim Yester: "Brian's input, mostly, was that he was a front man. He did most of the talking and had a very good sense of comedy timing. He had been involved in Shakespeare in college and he knew a whole bunch of the soliloquies and could rattle them off at any time. He had a really great speaking voice and was real glib, real quick, and his primary function – that and an incredible bass voice that he had. The low parts, a real legit bass singer..." [21/33]

"I never say what I'm thinking..." Brian was to note during a 1967 interview with *KRLA Beat*. "But I talk two-hundred percent as much as the other guys in the group..."

Following the culmination of the brief mini-tour alongside The Beach Boys the band then held down a week's residency at the Glendale Ice House, performing a set list heavily dominated with songs from the album. Both the Ice House, and the City of Glendale itself were quick to acknowledge the success that their resident band had achieved to date and they subsequently designated this particular 'homecoming', July 12th running through to the 17th, as 'Association Week', heavily promoting the shows in the press. The ensuing week the band followed these appearances with two further shows, farther up the coastline, where they headlined a slot at San Francisco's acclaimed 1100-seat Fillmore Auditorium, the founding home of swirling projections and strobe lighting, appearing alongside fellow Los Angelinos The Grass Roots and two of 'Frisco's upcoming young bands; The Quicksilver Messenger Service and Sopwith Camel. The latter of the two shows, held on successive nights, reportedly culminated with two of the city's residents getting married onstage. It remains undocumented as to whether "Cherish" was played at the appropriate time…

With the album now appearing on the streets and in the stores, whilst also achieving significant radio play across the nation, the choice came as how to follow-up the best-selling single "Along Comes Mary" – and despite their initial leaning being towards the equally upbeat "Enter The Young" Valiant Records, encouraged by Pat Colecchio and the demands of a listening radio audience, especially those in the Midwestern states of Ohio and Illinois, opted for a complete about turn and issued the ballad "Cherish" during August of that year. On August 20th 1966 *Billboard* magazine ran the following review:

> Smooth folk-flavored ballad serves a strong follow-up to their initial hit, "Along Comes Mary". Flip: "Don't Blame The Rain"
>
> *Valiant 747*

Despite an initial pressing error on the first run of 45s – the L.A. based Monarch pressing plant erroneously ran the first batch of labels, listing the Addrisi Brothers flip-side composition as "Don't Blame The Rain" (the first line in the lyrics) instead of "Don't Blame It On Me", the correct title – the single took off, becoming an immediate smash. Entering the Hot 100 at number 66 on August 27th, it climbed steadily to the peak position, displacing The Supremes' "You Can't Hurry Love" from the top slot during a 14-week run and stopping The Beatles "Yellow Submarine" ascendance *en route*. Notably, it also became the band's very first international hit, peaking at number 33 on the Australian chart lists (issued via the EMI/Stateside label), despite the fact that "Along Comes Mary" had also seen a worldwide release on a succession of prominent labels. In addition, most of the European versions of the new single also featured the mislabeled B-side on their early pressings. And yet, there was one other little adjustment that appeared on the U.S. 45 label that was seemingly not picked up on in advance. Concerned over the length and running time of the song at over 3 minutes 15 seconds in total, even with a slight edit to the 45 edition, Curt Boettcher, fearing that radio stations would balk at a song that ran for that long, falsified the label detail, listing the track timing at 3 minutes exactly instead. Clearly, no-one picked up on this anomaly although one is now led to smile at the notion of numerous radio shows across the vast nation subsequently running slightly over their allotted time slot... by fifteen seconds, without knowing why! Two months later, The Beach Boys groundbreaking "Good Vibrations" would be released and the three-minute thirty-second time barrier would be broken and accepted.

However, it so nearly wasn't The Association who took the composition up to its lofty heights as, just weeks previously, The New Christy Minstrels, who had been performing the song themselves at recent concerts, had made clear their intentions to record and release the song under the Christy's banner. Terry Kirkman, upon learning of the plans, had other ideas and made his objections known.

The Minstrels had first become aware of "Cherish" when their current lead vocalist, and former member of The Men, Mike Whalen, had somehow gotten a lead sheet of the song from Terry and they had since been receiving rapturous applause at each show they had performed it at. One can only imagine such a sound as a ten-voice choir interpreting the song. Knowing a surefire hit when they heard it they reportedly went and cut a version of it in the studio. Larry Ramos, the young Hawaiian-born vocalist, banjo player and guitarist with The Minstrels, later recalled in discussion with pop writer Sam Tweedle: "We all thought it was a good tune and we learned it so we could record it. We wanted to release it, but we had to get a license from the publisher or the writer. So we were working in L.A. and Terry Kirkman came over, because he was a friend of Mike Whalen, and after the show the manager spoke to Terry and said, "We want the license to release 'Cherish'. Could we record it?" And Terry said, "No, you can't have the license to record it! That's for my group! We're going to release it." [23]

As to whether the New Christy Minstrels ever actually ventured into the studio with the song has been open to debate over the years, but what is widely accepted is the response from the Christy's management team once Terry's refusal to allow the band the release it became apparent.

"You motherfucker! You'll never work another day in show business!!" [2]

Needless to say, Terry and other members of The Association took this idle threat with the necessary pinch of salt it deserved and ultimately released their own version on 45. However, to the New Christy Minstrel's credit, they were without question 100% correct. It was a surefire hit.

"After The Association recorded 'Cherish,'" Terry was to later recount for the 1984 *Goldmine* article, "and it became a big hit, Valiant Records threw a congratulations party for us at their Hollywood office. We were walking out when two principals of Valiant literally took me by the arm, put me in a supply closet, got in my face and offered me $10,000 for the rights to the song! I almost died laughing!"

And so what was the band's next move, with a best-selling Number One hit in their repertoire? They fired the producer…

"Curt was an amazingly talented guy…" said Jim Yester. "And it's a shame that the relationship didn't continue (but) he was starting to not produce us. He was kind of producing himself with us. So that kind of brought that to an end…" [12]

Clearly dissatisfied with the approach that Curt Boettcher was taking in the studio the band dispensed of his services, opting to inform him during a telephone conversation during the summer of 1966. To them it was apparent that Boettcher was intent on developing their sound how *he* saw fit, and not as they saw it. An immensely talented individual, and one who would go on to achieve cult following, if not commercial success, but one whose creative instincts came from his own perspective and, more often than not, he was on opposing paths, walking along his own single-minded route. He was the producer, but they were the band

"The Association are an essential part of the vocal group puzzle, but they always left me feeling deprived." Curt was to recall during a 1974 conversation with *ZigZag* magazine. "Deprived because they never really topped the promise of the first album, never made a classic album…"

Nevertheless, during this mid-1966 period, the band continued developing, both as established performers and songwriters. They began stockpiling material for a proposed second album, with label president Barry DeVorzon offering full support to the project, anticipating a Christmas release schedule. A number of new compositions were already in the locker, some of which would make it onto the eventual release whilst others would remain the vaults for the foreseeable future, or in some cases, would get no further than early rehearsals before being abandoned.

One such tune, written during the final days of Curt Boettcher's involvement with the band, was a joint collaboration between Curt and Jules Alexander entitled "Would You Like To Go". A whimsical composition, full of visionary lyrics of prophets, shiny skies and twinkling eyes, Curt would cut a version himself shortly afterwards as a part of his next venture, an imaginative studio project he entitled *The Ballroom* (as would the pop-psych band The Collage on their eponymous album for the Smash Records label). Sadly, despite the intricate and layered production techniques he used throughout the sessions, fuelled by both his vivid and creative mind and an intense marijuana-influenced recording process, *The Ballroom* album undertaking failed to see a public release until many years later, for an archival 2001 reissue project (although the Boettcher-Alexander tune itself would see a further release during 1968, issued as a part of a later Boettcher endeavor).

Meanwhile, other new compositions registered for copyright during that summer included another collaboration between Jules and Terry; "You May Think", written during a short filming break for a second upcoming appearance on TV's *Where The Action Is*, along with a selection of solo works – Terry's "All Is Mine" and "You Will Never Know", Ted's "Songs In The Wind", Russ's "I'm The One", Jim's "You Can Tell Her", "Memories Of You", "No Fair At All", "The Beginning" and "Listen" (the latter, a collaboration with his wife Joellen) and Jules' "Wordless Song", "Another Time, Another Place", Looking Glass" (again, a collaboration with his then-wife Christie), "Checking Out" and the imaginatively titled "Pandora's Golden Heebie Jeebies". Not all of these would make the final recording sessions for the proposed forthcoming album, but it began to show how prolific the band members were becoming in bringing forth their own compositions into the group environment. Certainly, the recent months, and some may even argue the *recent years*, had seen many established bands taking on the songwriting reins themselves, aware as to the potential monetary values in both royalties and publishing, and the previous reliance on conventional songwriting stables and publishing communities such as New York's Brill Building and Tin Pan Alley, or that of London's Denmark Street region, areas rich in both the talented elite and reputable, and the devious and unscrupulous hustler, diminished somewhat, especially once the emerging commercialism of the in-house Lennon and McCartney team, or that of Jagger and Richards, McGuinn and Crosby, or Wilson and Love became prevalent in the best-selling chart listings around the world. For every small upright piano located in multiple facilitated cubicles, there was a simple guitar, a home-built studio or a sandbox. All it needed was inspiration…

For their part, The Association were unique in their approach to the songwriting aspect of the industry in that (as noted earlier) they had implemented a deal with Capitol Records Publishing at the start of their career, ensuring that for every self-composed song they recorded each member of the band would receive a small percentage of the publishing royalties. Naturally, the songwriter would receive the majority share once all associated fees were dispersed, but every band member, the six equal partners, would benefit from this truly united group approach.

"That was Pat Colecchio's deal," confirms Jules. "We signed with Capitol's publishing, Beachwood Music, and the standard deal then was 50/50, but Pat said 'Wait a minute, we've got six writers here! We don't like that! We want half of your cut!' and we were hot at the time after 'Along Comes Mary', so the publishers got 25% and the band got 75%. If I wrote a song I would get my 50% and then 25% would be split amongst the band. After all, if wasn't for the band then the song wouldn't have made it. It was extremely original…"

Another new song from this era was Jim's "I Was Wrong", and for a short while it appeared that this would see an official release in some form, possibly on the forthcoming album, as the full lyrics and chord charts to this composition appeared in a 1966 slimline publication, *Touch Of Today Volume 3*, a souvenir music book solely devoted to the band. Sadly, this appeared to be rather misleading as the song remained unreleased, and the publication now remains a collectible oddity in the band's memorabilia history.

"I remember that one…" recalled Jim in more recent years when questioned about the song. "It never really got past the demo stage unfortunately. Nice tune though. Kind of a country feel to it…"

I called your name when I was down
But never thought you would hear me
And I looked for you when I was lost
But never thought you'd be near me

"I Was Wrong"
Words and Music by Jim Yester

Immediately, the band began to consider who to replace Boettcher in the
studio, and one name stood out from the very outset. A familiar name to
one and all…

CHAPTER EIGHT

SONGS IN THE WIND

J erry Yester: "They were on the road in Chicago and they rung and said 'we want you to produce our second album', and I said 'you guys are crazy! You've got a number one record and a hot album and you want me to produce your second album? What about Curt?' They said 'Nah. We don't want Curt.' I told them 'You'd better think about this' but they replied 'We thought about it (and) we want you to produce our record.' So I said 'OK, but I think you're crazy but I'll do it...'

So they flew me to Chicago to talk about it and they were just absolutely nuts on the road. I mean, these guys were like kids throwing water balloons. They were into squirt guns and they all fired on me when I arrived..." [21]

Without a significant breakthrough and success eluding them The Modern Folk Quartet had disbanded during July of 1966 and Jerry, looking to find a foothold in the industry, had made his first tentative steps into a solo career, which faltered almost immediately, and record production, working alongside a young singer named Rita Martinson on some demo recordings prior to taking a call from his brother, currently on tour in Chicago.

Jim remembered: "Everybody in the band knew (Jerry) before they knew me, because of the MFQ. The Association had a lot of MFQ input and we were all aware of the group and had watched them work at the Troubadour."[21]

However, changing producers wasn't the only thought on the band's agenda – they wanted to prove their worth as musicians in the studio as well, something that they hadn't had the opportunity to fulfill under the auspices of Curt Boettcher's overseeing eye.

"I woke Barry DeVorzon up early one day and said 'we've got to talk about this album,'" Jerry was to later recount in conversation with Steve Stanley. "I went over, and I explained how the guys were really good and would do the job right…" [2]

DeVorzon, not surprisingly, given that he had two hit singles and a top-selling album on his hands, was keen to continue the formula, utilizing the same session team as before, but Yester was adamant that the band could cut the album themselves, playing every instrument, a move that was going against the grain of a 1966 pattern. Certainly, with a shift in studio management, a number of the top labels and producers were becoming insistent that having the very best studio players cut the tracks in the studio was bringing about much subsequent success. Have the band add the vocals when required, and let them take the songs out on the road themselves, but let the one-take wizards deliver the goods when behind the baffles.

Throughout the mid-'60s, especially within the Los Angeles session industry, a number of highly-paid top-line musicians were being brought in to cut the tracks and, despite the begrudging admiration from the bands themselves, watching over from behind the studio glass, these ace session players were delivering the goods. Time and time again.

A select band of players, many from a background in the jazz clubs, spent endless hours during this period, jumping from studio to studio, toiling away in front of the lead sheets placed before them just moments before, nailing them in one or two takes before packing away their instrument of choice, loading up the car and onto the next session. Western Recorders to Capitol, Columbia to Gold Star. Names that today, fifty years on, appear to grace the sleeves of hundreds of CD and reissue sleeves across the globe, but back then, in the mid-late 1960s, they were the faceless saviors of the industry. Time is money where quality is concerned. Did The Beach Boys play on all of their mid-'60s hit recordings? Did Gary Lewis & The Playboys? The Grass Roots? The Mamas & The Papas? Who cut those early Monkees smash hits? Or was it, at the request of young, knowing producers such as Phil Spector, Brian Wilson, Phil Sloan, Terry Melcher, Gary Usher and Lou Adler, this elite band of players, jumping across the city at the snap of a finger, a free hour in their chaotic schedule and the promise of a top-dollar payout?

Drummer Hal Blaine often headed the troupe, arranging the studio team, putting in the calls, accompanied by a vast array of like-minded performers such as fellow percussionists Jim Gordon and Earl Palmer, guitarists Billy Strange, Glen Campbell, Tommy Tedesco and Barney Kessell, whilst Carol Kaye, Joe Osborn, Max Bennett, Larry Knechtel and Ray Pohlman often held down the bass role, accompanied by keyboard wizards Leon Russell, Don Randi and Knechtel once again. Top that off with the numerous percussion players, brass, reed and woodwind virtuosos and there was a team ready to deliver. However, having seen a similar, albeit smaller crew deliver the tracks on their debut album, The Association were determined to justify their own status as a band this second time around and prove themselves a self-contained unit.

Throughout August and September 1966 the band continued to promote "Cherish", along with the debut album, out on the road, across the nation from as far afield as Poughkeepsie and Newburgh in New York, Terre Haute in Indiana, Sterling, Illinois and Ogden in Utah, before they headed back to their home state where, on September 7th and 8th, they performed at the Carousel Theater in West Covina alongside Sam the Sham & The Pharaohs and Tommy James & The Shondells. The following night the three bands played together again, this time at the Circle Star Theater in San Carlos. Finally, they rounded off this mini-promotional tour with a date at the Civic Auditorium in San Jose, at the end of the month, sharing the billing with The Mamas & The Papas on one of their all-too few concert appearances. In addition, the culmination of this hectic schedule also saw them squeeze in two performances for upcoming TV shows between concert appearances, once again publicizing the current 45. Their appearance on *Boss City*, a Los Angeles daytime TV show, showing on KHJ Channel 9, aired on October 1st, whilst a second appearance on ABC's *Where The Action Is*, performing both "Cherish" and "Along Comes Mary", was broadcast two days later. For this second show the band was filmed being interviewed by host Dick Clark and then lip-syncing to the two songs, surrounded by a casually dressed group of teenagers sitting around a swimming pool whilst they, dressed in smart, dark three-piece suits, looked uncomfortably out of place, especially with Jim balanced precariously on a diving board, playing his guitar as he fronted the band on "Along Come Mary". Nevertheless, the interview segment of the taping provided the viewer with a further insight into their individual persona, with Terry attempting to discuss the band's neo-renaissance awareness, before host Clark cut him off with a more mundane line of questioning, whilst Ted humorously introduced himself as 'The Pig', a reference to his nickname within the line-up, going on to discuss the recent tour and the 'great four-week water war', a description of their recent antics on the road (water balloons and squirt guns), suggesting they got thrown out of every motel they stayed in. This appearance also brought forth the unofficial Association Admiration Aggregation phrase, adorned on thousands of buttons handed out to their fans;

The Association is unnecessary...
like water, sleep, food and love.

The nickname that Ted went by wasn't the only one used within the inner circle. Indeed, such was their close knit bond that a number of others were referenced to in similar humorous fashion – Brank, Bird, Troupe, Freak, Green Kid – all of these were often used in general passing, although Brian also introduced his own personalized names for his bandmates:

"I was Two Kings Nevermore," laughs Jim, "whilst Jules was Diamonds G. Crusader, Russ was Ruse DeGuere, Ted was Punky Coalbubble and Brian referred to himself as Orate Mondo Bituminous!" Indeed, an earlier nicknaming session had even seen former member Bob Page bestowed with the honorable name of Duncan Aircraft Leaflet!

"Brian was this very imaginative person," summarizes Jules. "Highly intellectual to a fault, but he would overthink things a bit!"

Yet their tendency for nicknames and subsequent practical joking wasn't just restricted to soaking each other as a means of breaking the touring monotony of motel rooms.

"Russell, at a party once" related Brian 'Brank' Cole during an interview with *KRLA Beat*, "took a guy who had passed out from an over-indulgence in alcohol, put him in the bathtub, after removing some of his superfluous outer clothing, bought 50 cans of Crisco, warmed them up so they wouldn't hurt him, and let him sit in the Crisco. When he woke up the next morning he was *encased* in Crisco!"

"We don't play practical jokes on each other..." laughed Jules, talking for the same article. "We play *impractical* jokes!"

Still, underneath the mocking humor and tomfoolery played out for the media they still maintained an underlying sincerity, and a professional approach to their chosen path.

Brian: "Pop music is popular because people dig it. If people dig it then whatever they're buying at the time is indicative of the trend that it's going to. And if you want to try to figure out what's going to happen in six months, it will take you six months to figure it out – and by then it will have happened…"

"Pop is in a constant state of Renaissance," continued Russ, reflecting on a more thoughtful outlook. "Pop music is a reflection of everything that's happening…" [13]

Even at this early stage of their collective career, with just two hit singles under their belt, the band, working under the guiding light of a dedicated new manager, was looking towards the future with the possibilities of both a book and a movie script now in the pipeline – the preceding *A Hard Day's Night, Help!, Catch Us If You Can, Ferry Cross The Mersey* and *Hold On!* had all shown the possibilities of what could (or couldn't) be achieved on the silver screen, whilst the September U.S. TV debut of *The Monkees* was also now taking that next decisive step in crossing over the dividing line of music and film, winning an *Emmy* award for its innovative approach along the way. Unfortunately, for The Association, this transition into a secondary medium wasn't to happen and an approved script never came to fruition, depriving the band of a collective move onto celluloid, but with Pat Colecchio at the helm they were clearly keen to search out and uncover the options on offer to them.

Following the culmination of the promotional schedule for the album, and with the single now also firmly ensconced in the upper regions of the best-selling lists, the group reconvened in the recording studio, intent on following up their recent success, and on October 10th 1966, three days after a second show alongside The Mamas & The Papas (held at the Civic Auditorium in San Francisco), they cut the first tracks for "Pandora's Golden Heebie Jeebies" at Western Recorders on Sunset Boulevard, under the production guidance of Jerry Yester

Over the following three weeks, they committed twelve tracks onto tape, writing, performing and singing each and every track themselves, harmonizing together around a single studio microphone whilst Brian, often off on a mic of his own, added the bass tones. However, it was a rushed affair, pulled together without any real time to reflect on the artistic direction that they were either wanting or wishing to take.

"The first albums are always the result of products that you've done up to the time that you get a record contact, and so our first record was tried and proven. We already had a fan following of 20,000 people in Southern California," summarizes Terry, when reviewing the process that resulted in the second release. "But when we came to the second album and we were given just forty days, everybody was scrambling around trying to figure out what we're gonna record. And you haven't played it, and you haven't tried it out on stage. It was a mess! It was like being shoved through a funnel. Had we been given that creative space where the record company would say 'guys, you did so well on your first album why don't we take six months here, and we're going to fund you', which Valiant simply couldn't do… we never had any creative time. There were real arguments, and then you're left trying to evaluate art from a commercial standpoint, not in the context of true artistic quality…" [43]

Jim Yester however, recalls that they did have a few numbers available to them, left over from their early shows, that resulted from the tried and proven method.

"When we got ready to do that second album, we had several things that we'd been performing for a while that hadn't been recorded. So those were probably the first things we took a run at," he states, before explaining, at a later date, how the choice of lead singer also came to pass: "Every song was different. A great deal of them were sung by the writer, but not always. Songs that hadn't been written by one of the group were sometimes assigned to someone by the producer, whilst those written within the group itself were often given to another member by the writer. Jules, who was basically our *de facto* music director when we first started, had me sing 'Along Comes Mary' because the lead singer on the demo was Curt Boettcher, who was a very high voiced tenor, and I was the highest voice in the band."

Amongst those songs chosen for the second album were a number of group highlights, and none more so than Jim's very own "No Fair At All", a gorgeous ballad equally as compelling as the then-current hit single, but overall the album lacked the consistency of its predecessor, with the final mixdown tending to be the moot point of discussion in the ensuing years. Jerry Yester later recalled, "It was just a god-awful production as far as the sound is concerned. I liked it musically but what I learned on that as a first production was leave the engineer alone. Don't get in there saying more highs, more lows, more echo, more drive… I ruined it for that, and Henry

Lewy was a real good engineer and if I had just let him mix it, it would have been 100% better..."

Unfortunately, by the time it came to do the final mix the band were already back out on tour and, to their dissatisfaction, they had little say in how the recordings were finally heard.

"'Renaissance' was mixed whilst we were on the road," commented Ted in later years. "And the pitch was made a little faster. I don't know why. We needed to have top-notch studio guys playing on that. It would have been a lot better, but we wanted to be known for being responsible for our records..." [2]

One certainly cannot fault Ted's admission that seasoned studio players would have added a certain degree of slickness to the proceedings, as would an experienced producer, but the album's charm and longevity is partly down to the raw unpolished approach in which it was tackled and whilst some of the weaker contributions such as "All Is Mine" and "You May Think" may have taken the production level down a notch or three, the highlights that jumped from within the darkened grooves remain amongst the finest from the band's catalog. Jules and Terry's stirring "Angeline" sat comfortably alongside Ted's commercially delightful "Songs In The Wind", and the Subud-influence of "Come To Me" followed on nicely from Jules' thought provoking "Looking Glass". Meanwhile, the up-tempo drive of "You Hear Me Call Your Name", with Ted's impressive drum patterns pushed to the fore, also made a long overdue appearance on vinyl, having first been attempted during the April 1965 debut sessions. However, the central focus of the release fell with the lead-off single from the collection, the striking "Pandora's Golden Heebie Jeebies". Packaged upon release in a full color 7" picture sleeve (the only example of such a U.S. issue in their career), this was a wonderfully creative up-tempo number from Jules' pen, lyrically influenced by a meditational practice, Sant Mat (the path between dark and light), that he had recently taken up. Initially demoed by Jules, in collaboration with Jim and Joellen Yester, the song was something magical, even in its basic form.

"That song was an exercise in meditation," explains Jules. "But we never quite nailed it in the studio. 'Pandora' is about finding the spiritual way. Once you open that box you can't close it!"

Released during the lead-up to the festive season of 1966 the album, titled *Renaissance* (Valiant VLM-5004/VLS-25004), fronted by a striking if somewhat unadventurous Peter Whorf-designed sleeve, featuring an image taken in Russ Giguere's front living room (Whorf was a successful, *Grammy*-nominated art director and photographer, producing many distinctive sleeve layouts during this era, and the son of *Beverly Hillbillies* director Richard Whorf), sadly failed to repeat the success that the debut offering had achieved, despite a number of positive reviews appearing in the press.

The rear of the sleeve was a similarly conservative design, even more so than the debut release, with an 'official' Association Fan Club address now listed as a primary contact – 24 North Mentor, Pasadena, care of Bob Stane, owner of the Ice House. Although, as Bob recalls: "It should have said 'Bob Stane, The Ice House', but the manager of the group didn't want to list the Ice House itself as it wasn't a *prestige* club in Hollywood. Not a good decision. The Ice House was a well-run and reasonably large club with great sound, lighting, atmosphere and comfortable and creative seating. A first class operation that made the others seem crude by comparison. But that is a problem of geography… and delusion."

Unfortunately, the lack of success was followed by a similar story for the 45, a radical departure in style for the band, but one that showed the diversifying talents and approach of each band member.

Said, wrongly, to name-check the Sunset Strip 'Pandora's Box' Club, their most experimental 'A'-side, like the Hollies 'King Midas In Reverse', delves into Greek mythology to find the girl who opens the forbidden chest to unleash evil onto the world, 'freeing locks, Pandora's boxes, devils are expended and I'm finally free'. Echoing future trends by utilizing strange almost out-of-tune harmonies, combined against what was assumed to be a sitar-driven back-drop (actually it's a Japanese stringed instrument called a koto, played by Alexander himself), the ethereal lyrics take a sideways glance at pseudo-profundity, predating the explosion of acid-based imagery by a year. Telling how 'when all the tears are finally cried and I'm finally clean inside, the gentle winds will come and they will dry my mind', until with existential clarity, when he's seen all that life has to offer, 'now all that will be left for me to do is die'. Too downright weird for the kind of mass acceptance that carried their previous hits to the top it remains a totally charming and unique artifact of its time. Oblique and risky, brave or foolish.[25]

Andrew Darlington
Madcap magazine

On the evening of November 4th, after an afternoon recording some radio promotions in the studio, the band performed a show at the Pauley Pavilion in Westwood, L.A., on the campus of UCLA, before regrouping and heading out of LAX airport and across the blue Pacific Ocean, commencing a multi-date tour of cities across the country, starting in Honolulu and culminating one month later with a final show across the border, in Toronto on December 11th.

November 5 1966: Honolulu, HI
November 16 1966: Valparaiso High Gymnasium, Valparaiso, IN
November 18 1966: Ice Chalet, Rockford, IL
November 21 1966: Capitol Theater, Madison, WI
November 23 1966: Aire Crown Theater, Chicago, IL
November 24 1966: Aire Crown Theater, Chicago, IL
November 25 1966: Milwaukee Auditorium, Milwaukee, WI
November 30 1966: Memorial Auditorium, Louisville, KY
December 1 1966: Kiel Opera House, St Louis, MO
December 3 1966: University of Illinois, Champaign, IL
December 4 1966: Clowes Hall, Butler University, Indianapolis, IN
December 8 1966: Civic Arena, Pittsburgh, PA
December 9 1966: Masonic Auditorium, Detroit, MI
December 10 1966: Music Hall, Cleveland, OH
December 11 1966: Toronto, Canada

Accompanying them for much of the tour was the Greenwich Village-formed folk-rock band The Lovin' Spoonful, themselves fresh from a recent run of *Billboard* Top 10 hits, including "Summer In The City", a chart topper during August of that year, whilst England's New Vaudeville Band also joined them for a few of the shows, as did New York's The Left Banke, who appeared at a performance held in Madison, WI. One other band that appeared on stage with The Association during this period was yet another ensemble who had grown out of the Greenwich Village folk scene and who were steadily building a reputation on the live circuit. Led by bass player and vocalist Jesse Colin Young, The Youngbloods finally came to prominence a short while later, hitting big (the second time of asking) with the song "Get Together". However, it was due to the fact that The Association were still utilizing that very song during their live set, as they had been doing since their early shows, and The Youngbloods, liking what they heard whilst on tour with the band, opted to take the song into the studio themselves, initially releasing it in June 1967 (and barely scraping the Top 75) and then again, in June 1969, achieving a Top 5 position in *Billboard*. And yet, contrary to popular myth, it would appear that the New York-based outfit was already highly familiar with the tune, prior to their co-headlining performance, having originally heard it performed at the Cafe A-Go-Go in the Village, sung by fellow resident folkie Buzzy Linhart. The Association, it seems, was merely the catalyst...

Unfortunately, not all of the early winter touring schedule went to plan and unforeseen weather conditions forced the cancellation of a scheduled stop off in Davenport for an appearance, although Russ was still in good spirits as he reported back to *KRLA Beat* midway through the run.

> Well, we are now in an airplane unable to land because of fog, so we can't play Davenport with the Spoonful tonight. Instead we will have to fly to Minneapolis and land there. Oh well, we need an extra night of rest anyway! The tour is going really well and the crowds have been good. This tour is going a little smoother than the others but it is still exhausting...
>
> Russ Giguere
> *KRLA Beat.*
> December 1966

With a set list comprising of a selection from both albums, along with a few choice cover versions, commencing with "Enter The Young" and culminating in an encore of "Pandora's Golden Heebie Jeebies" the six-piece band continued to entertain the crowds with their mixture of rock 'n' roll and slick choreographed humor. Yet, despite the rigors of such a touring schedule, the band still managed to find the time for their inimitable pranks and humor on the road, although it wasn't always at their instigation it seems, as Lovin' Spoonful bass player Steve Boone later recounted. In conversation with a journalist Boone was to later recall that the Spoonful's wild guitarist, Zal Yanovsky, managed to secretly access The Association's dressing room on one occasion during the tour, just prior to a show, and took all of their matching suits and put them on himself. One on top of the other. Come show time, and upon discovering their stage suits were missing, the band was forced to perform in their street clothes and then when the Spoonful came onstage, as the closing act for that particular show, Zal was wearing all of the suits himself, gradually pealing them off, one at a time, to the dismay of the watching Association members!

Surprisingly, despite the continuing efforts of promoting their new releases out on the road, neither the new album nor the single set the charts alight upon issue and those expecting "Cherish" to be replaced at the top of the best-selling lists with the new single were severely disappointed, with a peak position of number 35 during a seven-week run.

Hot on the heels of "Cherish", group has another sure-fire chart topper with this infectious rhythm ballad material. Intriguing arrangement and top vocal work. Valiant 755.

Billboard magazine

"Why that was picked as a single, I'm not really sure, other than the fact that it was probably different from everything else that was going on, which was the case with 'Along Comes Mary'," speculated Jim Yester in conversation with researcher Richie Unterberger. "I think that's why it ('Mary') was successful. It was kind of 180 degrees out of phase from what was going on at the time. But 'Pandora's' was so unusual..." [18]

It didn't help the promotion of the single either when popular KRLA DJ, Sam Riddle, a friend of the band since they first appeared alongside him on the *Hollywood A Go-Go* TV show, actually went on air, panning the release and complaining that the record 'hurt his ears'. Ironically, just as "Pandora..." reached its lowly peak position in the Hot 100 the number one slot was being held down by The New Vaudeville Band, the supporting act on the recent tour, with their novelty success of "Winchester Cathedral".

The album then went on to suffer a similar fate, as December 3rd saw it enter the U.S. charts at a reasonable placing of number thirty, rising to twenty-nine and twenty-six, before taking an abrupt about turn and swiftly falling out after just three more weeks. A significant disappointment. And then more disruption was to follow as the band were then dragged publicly into Los Angeles Supreme Court, following lawsuits filed upon them by their former manager, Dean Fredericks, charging the band with breach of contract, and also by their former publicist, Stan Zipperman, who filed suit for both fraud and breach of contract, asking for $100,000 in punitive damages.

A November edition of *KRLA Beat* reported as such:

The lengthy complaint alleges the following:
- Zipperman's contract for public relations and publicity services was improperly terminated.
- The Association induced Zipperman to execute the contract through fraud.
- It is well known in the industry that Zipperman was substantially responsible for the success of The Association.

Zipperman even went on record as saying, "I am determined to take the case to court where all the true facts will come to light", although the attorney acting on behalf of the band, Lee Colton, denied the contract with Zipperman was binding, adding that there was no time limit specified and that the group had every right to terminate it. Fredericks meanwhile, claimed he had the band tied to a seven-year deal, alleging that the band severed the agreement six years early. The band's Christmas meal that year may have tasted just that little bit bitter.

Although the eventual outcome of the suit was never made public Jim Yester, whilst not recalling the specifics, suggests it may have been settled mutually out of court. "I really don't recall them filing suit," he says today, 'though I'm not surprised. And I really don't remember Stan Zipperman. But as I do recall there was a significant cash settlement in that regard. I'm not sure I ever actually signed a contract with Dean, but it is possible that I did. There was a lot going on in the early days of the band, quite a whirlwind most days, with lots of partying at night!" [33]

Jules Alexander however, recalls the outcome quite clearly. "We lost!" he remembers with a laugh. "He was right. We did breach the contract. However, I don't believe we were smart enough to really battle it..." [37]

And yet, despite the distractions, the demand for their personal appearances was increasing rapidly, and in addition to a number of planned live performances in both Washington state and California during that winter, some of the more established television shows were also now clamoring to add the band to their schedule. One of which was the popular NBC-aired *The Andy Williams Show*, a televised variety outing for the established crooner but one that would bring his self-styled smooth approach to a more modern pop music audience every week. The Association would first appear on the show during December of 1966, performing three songs on the soundstage; "Cherish" and "Changes", as included on the debut album, with the latter featuring Williams himself joining in with a lead vocal (following on from some typical comedic interaction with the band), whilst the final offering was, perhaps surprisingly, not the current single but a smoother *Renaissance* album cut instead, "Looking Glass", one that was perhaps deemed as more appropriate for the audience demographic the show was catering for. Noticeably, and following on from Williams own live vocal take, Russ also stepped forward and performed an admirable live lead on this rendition, as opposed to the standard fare of televised lip-syncing that the band were beginning to get used to. Sadly, the TV ratings did little to increase sales for the second album.

As January 1967 ushered in the New Year, competition in the Hot 100 *Billboard* charts was seriously heating up and one only has to take a look at the best-selling releases of the period to fully appreciate the serious struggle that any new 45 had to compete against to achieve airplay and success. Whilst "I'm A Believer" held down the top spot for the umpteenth week, and "Good Vibrations" made its graceful descent downwards, "Nashville Cats", "Kind Of A Drag", "Ruby Tuesday", "Try A Little Tenderness" and "For What It's Worth" were all gradually making headway, and that was all before the might of the double header: "Penny Lane" b/w "Strawberry Fields Forever" was launched upon a waiting world. And so it was, with a wealth of innovative new compositions being waxed onto vinyl, and with such a variety of heavyweight releases already congesting the radio airwaves, that Valiant Records tentatively chose to release another new Association 45, in the shadow of "Pandora's..." relative failure.

With the success of "Cherish" still fresh in their minds, the executives at the label were keenly aware as to the importance of replicating the phenomenal success of that particular ballad and, clearly, the bold choice of releasing the ambitious "Pandora's Golden Heebie Jeebies" 45 had backfired on them. Subsequently, for the next release, they opted to play it safe once again and go for the big ballad, and immediately pressed up copies of the lilting Jim Yester composition "No Fair At All", coupled with "Looking Glass" as the accompanying B-side. However, the initial mixes of both songs were not deemed quite acceptable for radio airplay and so, encouraged by the label, the band went back into the studios and added an additional layering of overdubs and harmonies.

"The record company thought it would be slicker and more commercial," explained Ted. "We recorded them with single leads at first, but they insisted that the songs needed more voices to get that Association sound. So, on the single, we mixed in more voices." [20]

Interestingly, so *The Beat* magazine was to later explain, the original vocals for the song were cut in an unusual manner – in total darkness. "Cutting in the dark got to be a habit at the studio," Jim clarified. "It all started after seeing Brian Wilson, who is one of our favorite singers, cut in the dark. All the guys said, 'Hey, that's sharp, we'll have to try it'. Solo work is easier when you know everyone in the studio isn't looking at you. You can laugh or cry if you want…

"I was just sitting at the piano going through chord changes when I wrote 'No Fair At All'. It was written to the feel of the song, 'Return To Paradise'. The lyrics were about an actual person and it was just a thing that never did happen…" [24]

Words that, despite coming from a personal viewpoint, once again sadly summed up Valiant's attempt at matching the previous Top 10 successes. A thing that never did happen. Despite the beauty and overall quality of the performance on vinyl, as performed vocally and instrumentally by the band members themselves, the new single once more failed to register with an American record buying public, finishing its climb up the *Billboard* lists at a disappointing number 51 (it should be noted here that the *Billboard* Hot 100 was compiled via a combination of record sales and radio airplay, not just sales alone). Somewhat surprisingly, and despite a similar story following the release of the 45 in Europe and elsewhere (appearing on the London label in the U.K. and on the EMI/Stateside label in Australia), "No Fair At All" proved phenomenally popular out in the distant reaches of the Philippines, reaching the very pinnacle of their somewhat limited chart lists – a fact that went unknown to the band for almost twenty years. Nevertheless, despite the potential popularity that the band could have amassed in such foreign regions, Pat Colecchio, acting on behalf of the band, purposely kept the touring revenue situated solely on home soil for the major part of their collective career, and the possibility of any significant worldwide following was muted somewhat by his actions. Given the potential comparison with the successes that acts such as The Byrds, The Monkees and The Beach Boys were achieving (the latter having just been voted as the Number One Vocal Act in the world in a then-recent UK *New Musical Express* poll) one can only wonder how much The Association missed out on due to Colecchio's restricted view…

However, times were still a-changin', and regardless of the lack of current chart success that the recent releases were bringing, the popularity of their concert performances were still proving top draw. Despite the continuing familiarity of the matching suit and ties, regardless of their peers recent shift to smart but stylish individual dress sense (and the occasional flowing cape), and the inter-song comedy and shtick (they regularly kicked off their performances, and had been doing so for the past twelve months or so, with a recently recorded spoken introduction, conceived by Brian Cole, entitled "The Machine", which theatrically and comically introduced each band member via a fancifully worded piece of improvisation) they were still selling out during their hectic touring schedules.

> Local teeny boppers were out in full force last night to hear mod clad rock'n'rollers – The Association – blast down the walls in Humboldt's State College's men's gymnasium. If more sedate members weren't already piqued by the 60-minute delay (the group's plane was late) they were heading for the exit before the first song was over. For The Association plays only to the young. No one over 25 could have stood the excitement – or the din.
>
> *The Eureka Humboldt Standard*
> January 1967

February would see them, once again, flying across the country, appearing at venues throughout Wisconsin, Nebraska, Ohio and Connecticut but, unfortunately, the pressure was also building on the band members themselves as they flew from city to city, night after night, with shorter and shorter breaks between each tour and recording session and one member in particular was no longer getting the enjoyment of a seemingly constant life on the road. For Jules 'Gary' Alexander a new calling was evident.

"I think that coming out of that (second) album was why he left the group at that time," Terry was later to state. "We suddenly became 'not safe' any longer. We were not able to depend upon the repertoire that we had put together a year and a half before, which we mostly put down on our first album. Suddenly we were confronted with being a successful group who was going to have to go into the studio for a month and record an album. The record company and everybody there wanted you in, and out. Get it down. Nobody there really related to the experience and experiment with recording..." [40]

Jules, in 2000, during a discussion with Jeff March and Marti Smiley Childs, was to add: "I was a terrible, terrible, terrible celebrity, mainly because I didn't like it. I really enjoy my anonymity. It's fun to be high profile, everybody goes 'ooh-ooh' and that kind of stuff, but I'm just not good at it. I think now it's a bit different, but at that time it was just horrid. I got tired of being on the road, and I had to get away. The stress of the group and being on the road for too long with no breaks was too much." [1/2]

"When we went on our first tour we didn't have a dime in our pockets" says Terry today, "and there was an air strike so we were literally driving across the United States of America! Then when 'Cherish' popped it shocked the hell out of everybody and once that happened Pat Colecchio didn't know what to do with us. His only thing was that he needed to keep us on the road as there were so many of us, and everybody needed something to live on, as opposed to pulling us back, honing our creativity, and betting that we could create an act that would make three times the money that we were already making."

As one who had always leaned towards an interest in the far Eastern religions and mysticisms, and had involved himself heavily in both Subud and meditation, Jules' fascination for spiritual satisfaction in such far off locations had been driven for a need to explore them for himself, and regardless that he was now a part of an incredibly successful rock and roll band, his personal values, coupled with an overbearing weariness of the celebrity demands, outweighed the need for devotion and following. Yet, he wasn't about to walk away from his friends and musical partners without consideration, and upon tendering his resignation during the early months of 1967 he made it clear that he would remain with the line-up long enough to allow a suitable replacement to be found and bedded in. After all, there were numerous concert appearances booked in for the immediate future and any subsequent cancellation was surely not a viable option. But who to replace such an integral part of the band?

"Primarily, this was a logistical problem," says Terry, reviewing it over, fifty years after the events. "We were on the road 250 days a year, and the first person that we asked to take his place was Michael Brewer, later of the duo Brewer & Shipley, but that didn't work out."

Michael Brewer, recalling the offer today, explains: "It was a time when many musicians were still hanging out at the Troubadour and other venues and so many paths were crossed. I'm not certain where I met Terry exactly, but we became friends and he would come to my house where many others would gather as well. In fact, Buffalo Springfield formed in the house next to mine and Steve Stills played 'For What It's Worth' for me in my living room, on my guitar, before they even recorded it. They also got their name off a large road construction vehicle parked in front of my house...

"I had a partner, Tom Mastin, and we'd landed a recording contract with Columbia and we had a single coming out. We opened for The Byrds when 'Eight Miles High' was their current release and this was around the same time that Terry and I became friends. To cut a long story short, Mastin & Brewer broke up, and Tom Shipley, whom I'd known from the folk circuit, came to town and lived around the corner from me. We began writing songs for A&M Records, which was a new label then, and the record company suggested we record our own songs. Ruthann Friedman also lived in the neighborhood and would come by and I may have been the first person to hear 'Windy' when she played it in my living room! This was about the time when Terry asked if I'd be interested in joining the group. It was certainly an interesting offer, but Tom and I had our own thing going by then. Also, I figured it was a better idea to have just one partner as opposed to several, and getting to do all our own songs instead of just the occasional song from time to time."

Clearly, for Michael, his developing partnership with fellow acoustic singer-songwriter Tom Shipley held sway, although he wasn't the only early choice for Terry in his quest to replace Jules:

"I would have asked Jerry Yester too if he were not already involved elsewhere," adds Terry. "Jerry would have probably made The Association everything I wanted it to be but he was working in a partnership with his wife..."

It would take a few further weeks of thought provoking enquiries until a third potential addition came into the equation...

As part of Pat Colecchio's overall vision for The Association, it was always a plan that the band be represented in various media aspects throughout the American society, to capitalize on their intellectual nature. Music, movies (the concept of a feature length movie was still in the discussion stage at that time), and print were always high on the agenda and the idea of a related publication, a creative way of expressing the band's artistic leanings in published form, weighed heavily in the schedule during the early months of the year.

"I believe that was Herb Hendler's idea," remembers Jim, when discussing the project. "He was the president of Beachwood Music, the publishing company we were signed to, and he thought we could take advantage of our large fan club and get it happening. We thought it was great fun and had a ball doing it. It was aimed at the same people that bought the teen magazines."

Crank Your Spreaders, also known as *The Association Field Guide & Almanac*, when it finally appeared, hot off the presses during March of 1967, was indeed an artistic and yet rather confusing, and bemusing to many, way for the band to be represented to their youthful audience. It was clearly intended to show the band as a bunch of hip, thoughtful, witty, deep and groovy individuals, influenced by the writings, drawings and poetry of the many authors, poets and musicians who had trodden the well-worn beatnik path before them. And whilst the influence of Beatle John Lennon's published words of witticism in both *In His Own Write* (1964) and *A Spaniard In The Works* (1965) are clear indications as to where the inspirations lay, *Crank Your Spreaders*, whilst an enjoyable piece of light reading, unfortunately fell short of the benchmark those works had set in crossing the divide between author and musician. With Jules still firmly featured within the pages of the collective work it was, unfortunately, also a misplaced timing for the paperback publication, with his imminent departure on the horizon, and the 50-pages held within would surely have left the innocent, teenage audiences who followed the band's every move, autograph books in hand, membership cards to the Association Admiration Aggregation safely stored in their purses and wallets, rather befuddled at the massed self-indulgence laying out before them. And yet, ever aware of the band's overall popularity, the press jumped aboard;

The Greenstone Singers
(c/o Sharon Degonia)

The Gnu Fokes (c/o Jordan Cole)

The Cherry Hill Singers
(by Jay Thompson)

SPC James Yester off duty
(c/o Jim Yester)

The Men at The Cosmos

The Men in concert
(source unknown)

Early publicity shot
(c/o Michael Ochs Archives)

1967 Publicity Photo (source unknown)

Early concert appearance (c/o Michael Ochs Archives)

Larry with Arthur Godfrey
(c/o Tracy Ramos)

Larry and his banjo
(c/o Tracy Ramos)

April 1967 in Lock Haven, PA. One of Larry's first shows whilst Brian recovers
(c/o Rita Michalski)

The Association

Management:
Patrick Colecchio
9000 Sunset Blvd.
Los Angeles 69, Calif.
273-5523

Performing at the Tottenham Court Royal, London, May 1968
(c/o Richard Stirling)

Terry Kirkman
(c/o James Metropole)

Six-Man Band (c/o James Metropole)

Descanso Gardens 1968 (c/o James Metropole)

Rehearsal c.1970 (c/o James Metropole)

AAA logo

Russ and the Beachwood Rangers
(c/o James Metropole)

Brian and Jordan Cole
(c/o Lloyd Phillips)

The Association, Valiant Records group, has written a new book called "Crank Your Spreaders." The content includes prose, poetry, photographs, line drawings and various literary forms, which are difficult to classify.

Publisher is Beachwood Music. Press run of 50,000 copies will be distributed to newsstands.

Billboard
March 1967

The book contains nonsense stories a la John Lennon, doodles both visual and literary, games, words and music to 'Cherish' and 'Pandora's Golden Heebie Jeebies', poetry and biographies of the boys. The poems of Terry Kirkman are particularly nice.

The Florence Alabama Times
March 20 1967

As noted, drawings and doodles, musings and ramblings abound and such advanced knowledge, as befell to writer, musician and pop historian Bob Stanley in his expressive 2013 publication *Yeah, Yeah, Yeah*, would have supremely benefitted and quelled the advancing and confused teenage hoards from writing in to *Teen Set, Tiger Beat, Teen Life* and other such youthful fan fodder.

Stanley notes: "'Crank Your Spreaders', which initially retailed for a dollar at newsstands and was published between the band's second and third albums, is a cheery counter to any perceived conformity or lack of personality. Its odd title is explained on the inside cover. It's the expression used to describe opening or closing a car window prior to launching, or being hit by, a water-bomb, the activity a favored pastime for the band on the road…"

A Poem by Ted Bluechel Jr. for members of the Association Admiration Aggregation (AAA) to use when a commoner parks his car, partially blocking off their driveway.

You are an inconsiderate dumper
Who over my driveway left too much bumper

So it seems so very neat
Next time I'll call the Heat
And you'll quit sending me on a bummer

Crank Your Spreaders
Beachwood Music.
1966/67

CHAPTER NINE

GOTTA TRAVEL ON

Hilario D. Ramos Jr., Larry to family and friends, was born on April 19th 1942 in Waimea, on the island of Kauai in the Hawaiian Islands, just four months after the devastation the islands had suffered at Pearl Harbor. His father, Larry Sr., and his mother Pat ran a dry cleaning business in the islands followed, shortly afterwards, by a series of billiard parlors. Larry Sr. was an artistic individual by nature whilst Pat loved to sing, a trait that her young son clearly inherited as he developed. At just three years of age his father fixed him up an old broken ukulele and encouraged him to play and develop an interest in music.

"I was about three. I had discovered the husk of a ukulele but it didn't have any strings or tuning pegs, and I asked him what it was and he said, 'Do you want to learn how to play?' and I looked at him and said, 'Sure.' So that very day he ran down to the music store and got some catgut strings and tuning pegs, and he fixed it and taught me 'My Bonnie Lies Over the Ocean.'" [23]

Despite that particular tune consisting of just three basic chords, even at such a tender age Larry would spend endless hours practicing and listening to the radio, learning by ear as he picked up the melodies of a number of other popular songs of the day. He even slept with his ukulele by his bedside, so it was there, first thing when he awoke the next morning, ready to play.

A few years later, during the summer of 1949, whilst at the age of seven, he entered a local ukulele talent contest organized by the New York-born television and radio presenter Arthur Godfrey, a fellow ukulele player himself, and despite the presence on the day of many highly regarded players, and being the only child entry, Larry went on to win the day with his performance of "Jealousie". The prize was to be a journey to New York City, and a spot appearing on Godfrey's popular television show, *Arthur Godfrey & His Friends*, airing on prime-time CBS-TV. His response, upon being asked as to whether he would like to make the journey, was simply "I don't know, you'll have to ask my mom…"

Meanwhile, back home, at weekends his mother would take him to work with her, down to the local hotel gift store, where he would sit patiently behind the counter whilst his mother served the customers, strumming his beloved ukulele, practicing those same songs he had just heard wafting over the airwaves.

On one particular day, during the spring of 1950, a female customer had entered the store and was immediately enchanted by the gentle sounds that she heard playing in the background. Enquiring as to where it was coming from the sales assistant informed her that it was, in fact, her son, practicing from behind the counter. Introducing herself as an employee of MGM Pictures, who were currently shooting a movie on location in Kauai at that time (*Pagan Love Song*, released the following winter and starring musical icon Howard Keel), the lady suggested that her producer, the respected Arthur Freed, should hear the youngster play and, shortly afterwards, Freed himself came to the store to hear Larry. Liking what he heard, and deeming it suitable for the South Pacific tone of the current storyline, he offered Larry a small cameo in the film, a short sixty-second appearance singing and accompanying himself on the ukulele to "House Of Singing Bamboo", a song written by the producer himself.

Larry: "They wrote a scene in for me, and I reprised the song that Howard Keel sang at the start of the movie. And it came off great. I saw rushes of it when I came to the mainland from Hawaii when we moved and it didn't make it! It ended up getting left on the cutting room floor because the movie was running over three hours and they had to cut it down. I heard that Howard Keel didn't want that scene in the movie because it showed him up!" [23]

Following the filming for the movie Larry and his mother then journeyed across to the mainland, across to the eastern seaboard, to make his winning appearance on the *Arthur Godfrey & His Friends* broadcast. This show, unlike many of a similar number of variety broadcasts, had begun to veer away from the standard entertainment show, where the stars of the day would churn out their hits and exchange pleasantries whilst they publicized their latest wares. Instead, Godfrey encouraged the promotion of many young and relatively obscure performers, those he named as 'Little Godfreys', and to whom he offered massive national exposure, often on a reoccurring basis. Larry first appeared onscreen during the November 1950 season opening show, which was based around a huge Hawaiian luau theme, featuring fellow Hawaiian entertainers such as dancer, actress and comedienne Hilo Hattie and surf legend Duke Kahanamoku. He later made a further journey to the vast city to appear on the show for a second time the following year, and his appearance was even replicated for a 1951 DC Comics magazine (issue No.48), with a hand drawn image of the youngster prestigiously appearing within the pages alongside Arthur Godfrey and Wonder Woman herself.

Returning to Kauai and playing at a local show on the island, Larry was then discovered by Ann Baker, an up and coming young actress who saw the potential of the talented youngster, believing he would be suited for Hollywood. Subsequently, at Baker's expense, she paid for a further trip to the mainland and then accompanied him around the various studios, auditioning him before a number of prominent movie producers. His first audition was for the role of playing a younger version of Sabu, the popular Indian actor, but his lean frame went against him on this occasion, despite efforts trying to gain some extra weight for the character, and the opportunity went elsewhere. Meanwhile, his family, keen to see his talent develop, and wary of the unrelenting nature of the entertainment industry, followed him to the mainland, setting up home in the southeasterly Los Angeles city of Cudahy during 1952.

Despite never quite breaking through onto Hollywood's silver screen, almost immediately Larry landed a regular spot on the TV show, *Harry Owens & His Royal Hawaiians*, a popular variety broadcast that ran from 1949-1958 and was hosted by the Nebraska-born bandleader who had developed a personal fascination with the music of the islands during the 1930s, following a stint performing at the Royal Hawaiian Hotel in Waikiki. Then, in 1955, following an audition in front of Richard Rodgers and Oscar Hammerstein, Larry took up a role in the touring production of *The King And I*, appearing onstage as one of the King's children every evening, playing directly opposite the then-star of the show, Yul Brynner.

He was also on standby every performance as the understudy for the role of Prince Chulalongkorn, the Crown Prince, and once the show moved on up to the Royal Alexandra Theater in Toronto, for a four week run during July of that year, he had the opportunity to take on the regal position regularly, appearing opposite Leonard Graves, now portraying the lead character.

Larry: "I auditioned for Rodgers and Hammerstein. I actually auditioned to them. I was thirteen and I knew their music, but I didn't know what an honor it was to be auditioning for these guys. They liked what I did, and they hired me and I went on the road as an understudy for the Crown Prince. I got to do the role several times for about a month in Toronto. It was just fun. Anyways, during the time I was the understudy I was also one of the King's kids so I was on stage every night. The Crown Prince was a major part in the play, and I was real happy when I got to play the part because I was able to do something I had never done before, which was acting. It's a lot easier than playing and singing..." [23]

By now Larry was also in attendance at the High School in Bell, California where, gradually, the diversifying musical interests of his peer group began to overshadow his Hawaiian origins. He picked up the guitar, a natural progression, and joined a High School band, a five-piece band named The Defiants, who appeared at various school hops and on local TV stations around the region, even incorporating two of Larry's own recent compositions into their short set-lists; the rockabilly rhythms of "Sippin' Lemonade" and the gentle bluesy-ballad "She's Gone". Nevertheless, despite the musical distractions, he was still keen to further his education and after graduating from High School he went on to attend East L.A. Junior College and Cerritos College in nearby Norwalk, studying political science.

"Most of my family is either into public service, education or law enforcement. I was supposed to have been either a social studies or history teacher, but I found it extremely boring. I enjoyed political science until I figured out that political science is exactly what it says; it's all about politics!" [1]

"(Then) in my first year of college someone said, 'Hey, why don't you come to this frat party we're having?' I'd never been to a fraternity party, I've never been a joiner of any kind, but they said, 'Yeah, come over and have a beer with us,' so I went over there and there were these three guys that had guitars and they were playing a Kingston Trio song. I knew the Kingston Trio from 'Tom Dooley' but I wasn't really a big fan because I thought it was too simple. It was honestly just basic to me." [23]

By this stage, still undecided over any future career, his interest in the local music scene gradually began to take a stronger foothold and during their spare time he and a group of friends started frequenting the local folk clubs. Whilst hanging out at a popular coffeehouse called The Satyr, a nearby club in the South Gate district where the likes of Hoyt Axton, John Hammond, Barry McGuire and fellow folk musicians would come to play, Larry began to take note as to how easy that style of music was to play and, despite his initial reluctance to appreciate the folk genre, his interest took hold.

"I went up to the owner of the club and I said, 'Look, I'm a musician and I'd like to work. How many tunes do I need to know to start playing here?' He said, 'learn a dozen tunes, and come back.'" [1]

Within a week or so, in between his college studies, Larry found himself performing on stage in the club, later moving up to hosting and introducing the acts at the weekly hootenanny nights there and briefly linking up as a member of Frank Miller's Easy Riders, a popular folk trio that had achieved a degree of success the previous decade with the Columbia hit single "Marianne" (and had recently featured Jerry Yester within their ever changing ranks). Shortly afterwards he also guested on Canadian folk singer Cathie Taylor's *In Concert* LP, recorded live at the Mon Ami club in Orange, CA on February 23rd 1962. It was on one such night, whilst appearing at The Satyr during 1962, that Art Podell, guitarist and singer with the New Christy Minstrels came in to watch the talent on show. Impressed with the boyish charm and raw talent of Larry, Art approached the youngster and asked if he would be interested in working with another group of fellow musicians. "What does that entail?" responded the unsure yet inquisitive Larry. Upon being told that it was working within a group of nine others his immediate thought was of how much money they would have to make, to ensure all received equal pay, but once he was informed that this 'big folk band' was booked to appear on the popular *Andy Williams Show*, Larry's interest was piqued enough to find out more…

"I can clearly remember George Greif, our manager, asking as diplomatically as he could what ethnicity Larry was," recalled Art Podell in a recent conversation, "and I mentioned Hawaiian/Filipino. George reflected for a moment and said, 'mmm… that's good! Call him and invite him to come down…'"

"I auditioned for them…" Larry was to say, when recalling the events surrounding him joining up with the New Christy Minstrels, "and they didn't get back to me for several weeks. I thought to myself, 'Was I that bad?' I found out later on that they had to clear me with the producers of the show because I was a non-white!" [1]

Clearly, the racial significance of having a non-white musician performing on the TV screens across the nation could hold major implications for both the TV studios and the group itself, regardless of the talent that Larry could quite clearly bring to the line-up, but it could also work in a positive way for them. After weeks of deliberation, with the network deciding firstly one way and then the other, the official invite to join up with the Minstrels came in mid-1962, offering him the role as vocalist and banjo player, a position that didn't come without further issues. Initially, it was suggested that he take up the post of upright bass player but it was apparent that his smaller stature may cause problems with the largest instrument on the stage and so, even though he didn't regularly play the five-stringed banjo at the time, Jackie Miller quickly showed him the rudimentary requirements for their set list, and because he could pretty much play any stringed instrument he laid his hands on he picked it up quickly. It was a role he would fulfill for the next three-and-a-half years, establishing himself as a key principal within the band, and one who would ensure they remained at the very forefront of their profession, both musically and, due to the very nature of him breaking down the potential non-white racial barrier, within the social aspect of the industry.

Ironically, and despite the New Christy Minstrels tearing down the television walls for a non-white male singer, the exact same scenario befell the band's replacement on *The Andy Williams Show* after the first season. As the Minstrels moved on to greater things a similar ten-piece band, also coming out of the same Hollywood folk clubs, The Good Time Singers, stepped into their shoes. They too had a colored member in their ranks, although for Alexandra Brown, being female also added to the tension. Shortly afterwards, unable to take the pressure and the negativity, she quit the band.

Between 1962 and 1966 Larry appeared on all of the long-playing releases issued by the New Christy Minstrels, from the live *In Person* album (issued in 1963) up until *Chim Chim Cher-ee* (1965), with both Christmas and cowboy albums strewn in between, some of which also featured his own songwriting contributions and co-compositions – "Something Unique In Animal Husbandry" as featured on *In Person* (1963), "Down The Ohio" from *Ramblin'* (1963), "Joe Magarac" from *Land Of Giants* (1964) and "The Rounder" and "Freedom", both from the aforementioned *Chim Chim Cheree* long player (1965) – and they regularly toured across the country, playing up to 300 shows per year to sell-out crowds everywhere, performing a variety of popular and standard folk songs, mixed in with a number of original compositions by the band members or by their founding leader Randy Sparks who, by mid-1963, had retired from the road to oversee their progression from within the walls of his own Ledbetters folk club, over on Westwood. One year later and he would sell up his total interest in the band for $2.5 million. Gravel-voiced vocalist Barry McGuire, another recent addition to the stable, had subsequently taken over as principal director and arranger for their live performances. In addition to their on stage appearances the band remained heavily in demand by the television networks, and alongside their work on the *Andy Williams Show*, they also made guest appearances on *The Dean Martin Show*, *The Red Skelton Show*, *The Bell Telephone Hour*, *The Tonight Show*, *Hootenanny* and *The Julie Andrews Special* amongst the many others, and during the summer of 1964 they actually had their own short-lived NBC series, *Ford Presents The New Christy Minstrels*, sponsored by the Ford Motor Company. They even made prestigious appearances at Carnegie Hall during the winter of 1962, a notable feat for such a new act, and at the White House, on January 14th 1964 where, having originally been booked at the request of John F. Kennedy, they performed on the steps of the grand façade before an audience of President Lyndon B. Johnson and the visiting Italian President, Antonio Segni. Reportedly, according to *Time* magazine the following week, the Minstrels 'flaked the paint from the East Room ceiling with a rousing hootenanny'.

Although he was but one of a large line-up the band clearly saw the potential and, dare one say it, the novelty value that the 'cute brown kid' could add to their shows, and often Larry would step up to front of the stage, wide grin spreading across his face, and play up to that fact. During live performances of the folk favorite "Michael Row The Boat Ashore" he would frequently step forward, banjo in hand, and cheekily take on a faux-Chinese role for a verse or two, slitting his eyes and over accentuating his Asian roots. Other moments of note would see him justifying his increasing status within the group by performing some scintillating banjo-pickin' solos on any number of lively tunes before the nine voices lined up behind him would all chime in, creating a cacophony of choral delights.

Randy Sparks would later comment in an article that was featured in *The Ohio Times Recorder*: "We call Larry our 'precious pineapple' or 'Hawaiian leprechaun'. The kids love him. He gets a great deal of mail and is one of the most popular characters of the group."

It was this intense period of his career that, Larry would later comment, helped him develop his signature style of singing, a vocal blending using the same tone as those surrounding him, whereupon it became virtually impossible to identify a singular voice amongst the overall mix, such was the blend. Members of the band would frequently refer to Larry as 'The Vocal Chameleon', and he regularly worked additional hours in the recording studios, laying down guide vocals to teach the other members how to sing and blend together on new material. And yet, despite his commitment to the band, the schedule they faced was both rigorous and demanding and they spent months on the road and in the studios, and the burden placed upon each individual was so much that, gradually, established band members began to drop out and be replaced. Barry McGuire quit in early 1965, and future Byrds member Gene Clark came and went within the space of two years. The Texan-born Kenny Rogers would join up shortly afterwards…

During 1965 Larry and his wife of twelve months, Helene, whom he had met during 1963 at a party thrown for the band in Reno, Nevada, became the proud parents of twin daughters, Stacy and Tracy, but such were the professional demands upon the Minstrels that Larry had to seek permission to get a day off from performing, to attend the hospital. Barely, twenty-four hours later, and he was back on stage again, in some distant town, banjo in hand. And yet there clearly came a time for Larry when, as had happened with a number of his fellow bandmates, that it became one step too far. One airplane journey too much. One distant stage too many. And in January 1966 he informed the Christy's management team, Sid Garris and George Greif, of his decision to leave. A decision that didn't go down too well.

"You'll never work in show business again if you leave this group," threatened Greif, echoing the very words he had shouted at Terry Kirkman, just a short while earlier, once Kirkman had refused his band permission to release the song "Cherish" as a single.

"I guess I'll have to take that chance," responded Larry, walking away from the band that he had gotten so much from, and had given so much to.

For the New Christy Minstrels that immediately brought about an issue that needed addressing. Not only had they lost a key member of the vocal line-up and their frontline banjo player, but they had also lost their most visual striking point – the distinctive and recognizable ethnic addition. They immediately thought of a solution so as not to lose the impetus and they contacted the one person who could, at best, BE the person they had just lost. A phone call went in to Del Ramos, Larry's younger brother, currently singing and playing guitar and bass in The New Society.

"There were a couple of Jewish gentlemen, really nice guys and they called me in when I was with The New Society" remembers Del Ramos today, "and they said 'we're interested in somebody to replace your brother, Larry. Do you play the banjo?' and I said 'yeah', although I'd never actually touched a banjo before. 'But wait a minute. You want me to BE Larry Ramos?' and they said, essentially, 'yes'. I said 'that's not gonna happen. My brother is a phenomenal talent. I'm in a group but I'm not Larry Ramos. He's one of a kind, there's no way I do it.' So I turned it down.

The New Christy Minstrels wisely opted out of finding a replica of Larry, and added various new members over the coming years, although their moment in the spotlight of American society was, by now, on the wane.

With time now on his hands, and now in his own destiny, Larry signed a solo recording deal with Columbia Records, and issued his debut 45 during October of 1966, under the watchful eye of the former Christy's producer, Allen Stanton, fresh out of the studios himself following production duties on a number of the Byrds recent recordings. Upon release "It'll Take A Little Time" b/w "Gotta Travel On" (Columbia 4-43805), featuring a stellar session crew with Glen Campbell at the helm, sadly disappeared swiftly into obscurity, despite the pleasant nature of both sides and the confidence shown in it by Columbia, opting to release it with a black and white picture sleeve. However, not to be downcast, Larry then ventured out on a promotional jaunt, publicizing the launch of his solo career and performing at a number of small clubs up and down the west coast, in addition to a short residency across the U.S./Mexican border at the La Fiesta theater restaurant in Juarez. He then followed this by then undertaking a brief solo tour of Japan. As fate would then have it, Larry also offered his vocal support at a 1967 studio session for Mike Whalen, another former Minstrel, who was recording a version of a new Jimmy Webb composition, "Where's The Playground Susie" (issued during June of that year as Reprise-0602), under the production guidance of Art Podell (himself a recent departee from the Christy ranks).

Interesting, the flip side of Mike Whalen's single was a song entitled "Universal Love", with the songwriting credits given to both Mike and Judy Whalen, and an unknown third contributor: L. Kirkman. A coincidence or a misspelling?

"I have no knowledge or recollection of that..." muses Terry Kirkman today.

At that time, Terry had been leading the hunt to find a suitable replacement to cover for Jules' upcoming departure from The Association and Art had run into him at the studios whilst they were cutting the track...

"I have a very clear memory of sitting with Terry in the control room..." recalled Art, when questioned by the author during 2016. "My engineer in the studio that day was Jim Messina, who also played bass and guitar on the track, and I remember Terry asking me who I thought might fill a key spot in The Association. Larry had recently left our group and I immediately named Larry as my choice."

"Larry carried a lot of weight," states Terry today, "but if I sat back and looked at it now, it was not the weight that I was looking for. But we had a logistical problem. We had to fill that space with a voice who can sing those parts, and someone who was really competent as a guitarist. It was an interesting move for a lot of reasons. It didn't fit with what The Association already was, and without Jules' input and his strange, unique way of writing, and his probing of different time signatures, all of a sudden there was a more assertive force in the middle of it. In hindsight, and whilst Larry saved our bacon and was a great addition to the group, he also took us into a new area, as he had no tolerance for the artistic stuff that we wanted to do..." [51]

Nevertheless, at that time, the early spring of 1967, Larry's availability was the news that Terry and the group needed and the seeds of an offer were sown. The subsequent plan presented from Pat Colecchio was that Larry would see the band perform in a concert setting, initially at a show held at the Oakland Coliseum near San Francisco on March 25th, where they would be appearing on the same bill as Sly & The Family Stone and Eric Burden's newly reincarnated version of The Animals, and then enter the studio with them, cut some sessions, before venturing out onto the road, acclimatizing to life on the Association trip, watching and learning. And all would go to plan... for a few weeks.

For the remaining dates, held during February and March, Jules remained as an essential member of the touring party. At one point, during early March, they stopped off in New York City to tape an appearance on *Clay Cole's Discotek*, a local east coast TV show airing on WPIX Channel 11, where they appeared alongside Lesley Gore, Tim Rose and The Marvelettes, and it was on this show, broadcast on March 11th, that the U.S. also got to see one of the earliest viewings of a new promotional film from The Beatles, a relatively new concept in music marketing, publicizing their upcoming double A-sided single, pairing "Penny Lane" with 'Strawberry Fields Forever'. Whilst in the city, The Association also took the opportunity to start work on a series of new recordings, intended for the potential third album, and Jerry Yester was flown out from the west coast to oversee production. Two new tracks were worked on, one from Terry's own pen and the other a result of a further submission from the ever persistent Addrisi Brothers, although neither of these New York productions were fully completed, despite some positive values resulting from at least one of the sessions. Instead, the band opted to rework them at a later date, once they were back in Los Angeles.

"I recorded two songs..." Jerry was to say during a 1992 interview with The Lovin' Spoonful biographer Simon Wordsworth. "Ruthann Friedman had come up and played 'Windy' for me, and I went 'naaahhh', to my sorrow. Real nice Ruthann, real nice. I didn't say it to her but... no way. I also heard 'Never My Love' and I thought, 'yeah, it's ok' but I wasn't crazy about it. Then they flew me to New York and we did a version of it, and not a very good one. We also did a version of 'Requiem For The Masses', and I wrote the mass parts, all the 'Kyrie Eleison' parts. I wrote those, and never got any credit for it, but...

"I love the version of 'Requiem...' that we did in New York. I thought it was very soulful, and Joellen, who was Jim's wife at the time, sang on it and it was a real passionate kind of mass singing. Real gooseflesh..."

Not that these were the only new songs on the horizon during the spring of '67 as, whilst staying at the luxurious Warwick Hotel in New York City during the tour, both Russ and Ted were working on new material, Russ with a song entitled "Sometime", whilst Ted, inspired by Brian Wilson, was composing a pretty little number he called "We Love Us".

Unfortunately, upon listening to the results of the New York sessions it appears that Valiant Records didn't view the two new recordings in a particularly positive light and, somewhat hastily some may argue, Jerry Yester was unceremoniously removed from his position as producer for the upcoming album.

"Jerry was family, but we just had to pull the plug on the whole project. It was just not working out..." Terry was to state in *Goldmine* magazine (1984), whilst later adding "We had spent maybe twelve hours in New York City, on the road, exhausted, trying to get vocals down for the (next) album. The day was a complete disaster. People had called, they had the flu, they were exhausted, they were pissed off, 'Why were we playing on the road, why don't you schedule this better?' etc. etc." [7]

Instead, Pat Colecchio, acting on behalf of the group, put forth the option to Valiant of recruiting 'Bones' Howe, an established and highly regarded producer and engineer, stepping into the breach.

"Pat was real excited about The Mamas & The Papas first album *If You Can Believe Your Eyes And Ears*, (and) he contacted Bones, who had engineered that album" says Jim. [1]

The Minneapolis-born Dayton Burr Howe had first made inroads within the recording industry during the mid-1950s, having relocated to Hollywood and taken up a career as an audio engineer for Radio Recorders, where he developed an initial knowledge on recording techniques working alongside legends such as Bing Crosby, Ella Fitzgerald, Ornette Coleman and Mel Torme. By 1961 he had moved on to work at United Recorders who had recently installed vast new banks of technology within their studio mixing desks and where he became an integral part of the development of the multi-tracking and multi-microphone techniques that were to become prevalent during the mid-1960s. Some of the sessions he worked on during his spell at United resulted in the best-selling *Sinatra Swings* album for the Chairman-Of-The-Board himself, however, after just eighteen months he decided that in order to achieve what he personally wanted within the industry he would have to strike out alone.

"I just decided that in order to do what I wanted to do I was going to have to do it independently. My philosophy was that I was twenty-nine years old, and in ten years I'm going to be hitting forty and I'm not going to be able to do that. So if I do it now and I fail, I can always go back to work." [26]

Subsequently, he was also one of the first of his kind to make the move into freelancing, knowledge for hire, whereupon he began engineering for various producers on demand, such as for Lou Adler, working on the recordings of Jan & Dean, Johnny Rivers and The Mamas & The Papas, and for the Snuff Garrett produced sessions for Gary Lewis & The Playboys before, eventually, he moved into production himself, resulting in "It Ain't Me Babe", a Top 10 hit for the Turtles during 1965. On the odd occasion, he even appeared as an instrumentalist himself, adding percussive sounds to the 1964 *Christmas Album* sessions for The Beach Boys and for The Grass Roots 1966 LP *Where Were You When I Needed You?*

"In the halls of Western Recorders, on any afternoon or night, you'd bump in to Brian Wilson, Lou Adler or Snuffy Garrett. Everybody hung around everybody else's sessions. Nobody said, 'You can't come in my session.'" (*Tape Op* magazine 2008)

Following the culmination of their appearances out east, the six members of The Association flew back home to California where, following the show at the Oakland Coliseum, they linked up with the newly appointed Larry Ramos and together they set up camp in small Studio 3 of Western Recorders, accompanied by Bones Howe in the producer's chair, intent on cutting further tracks and vocals for the next album. Jules wasn't in attendance for this new round of sessions, although the idea at this stage was that he would still perform a final few shows with the band, familiarizing Larry with the set, before he stepped away completely.

"I was still around in that period," confirms Jules "But I wasn't involved in the recording of that third album". [37]

By now, news of his imminent departure had reached the media, and articles began appearing in the magazines and newspapers as to his potential plans to travel to India, whilst also introducing Larry as his permanent replacement. The same articles also introduced Russ's new appearance with much fanfare and gusto…

"Gary is leaving the group as far as personal appearances are concerned. Larry Ramos, formerly with The New Christy Minstrels, is replacing him. Right now Larry is on tour with the guys and Gary is along helping to break him in. Gary will continue to write new material for The Association. He left the group merely because continuously being on the road stifled his creatively as far as writing is concerned. Gary has always wanted to go to India, but has made no definite plans."

KRLA Beat

Russ & His Scene:

"Go ahead, ask me why I'm growing a mustache." The explanation for the light brown, five-day growth adorning his upper lip was simple: "I've never had a mustache before." Simplicity isn't the keynote to Russ Giguere, one of six Associates, but directness definitely is. He understands himself as few people ever do. "I have more control over my life than most people have over theirs," he says willingly. "I try to live as spontaneously as possible. I follow my feelings…"

KRLA Beat

THE ASSOCIATION   PRODUCER: BONES HOWE
TRIPLE SESSION-TRACKING SCALE**   (Employer's name) VALIANT RECORDS

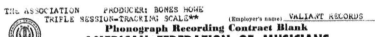

Phonograph Recording Contract Blank
AMERICAN FEDERATION OF MUSICIANS
OF THE UNITED STATES AND CANADA

N⁰ 394840

Local Union No. 47

THIS CONTRACT for the personal services of musicians, made this **28th** day of **March** , 19 **67**

between the undersigned employer (hereinafter called the "employer") and ____ 8 ____ musicians
(hereinafter called the "employees").   (including the leader)

WITNESSETH, That the employer hires the employees as musicians severally on the terms and conditions below, and as further specified on reverse side. The leader represents that the employees already designated have agreed to be bound by said terms and conditions. Each employee yet to be chosen shall be so bound upon agreeing to accept his employment. Each employee may enforce this agreement. The employees severally agree to render collectively to the employer services as musicians in the orchestra under the leadership of

M.R. Pohlman   as follows:

Name and Address of Place of Engagement **Western Recorders, 6000 Sunset Blvd, Hollywood, Calif.**

Date(s) and Hours of Employment **Mar. 28, 67-2 to 6 P.M. & 7:30 to 10:30 P.M. 11: to 2: A.M.**
********************/2-Tracks /1-Track _____ /2-Tracks

Type of Engagement: Recording for phonograph records only.   UNION SCALE   Plus pension contributions as specified on reverse side hereof.

WAGE AGREED UPON $ ____
(Terms and amount)

This wage includes expenses agreed to be reimbursed by the employer in accordance with the attached schedule, or a schedule to be furnished the employer on or before the date of engagement.

To be paid ____   WITHIN 15 DAYS
(Specify when payments are to be made)

Upon request by the American Federation of Musicians of the United States and Canada (herein called the "Federation") or the local in whose jurisdiction the employees shall perform hereunder, the employer either shall make advance payment hereunder or shall post an appropriate bond.

Employer's name and	VALIANT RECORDS	Leader's name	M.R. Pohlman	Local No. 47
authorized signature		Leader's signature		
Street address	6290 Sunset Blvd.	Street address	6171 Rockcliff Dr.	
	Hollywood, Calif. 90028 HO-48144		Hollywood, Calif. 90028	
	City State Phone		City State	

(1) Label Name **VALIANT RECORDS**   Session No. ____

Master No.	No. of Minutes	TITLES OF TUNES	Master No.	No. of Minutes	TITLES OF TUNES
	2:15	REQUIEM		2:14	WINDY
	2:12	ON A QUIET NIGHT		2:20	WANTIN AINT GETTIN, AND
	2:15	HAPPINESS IS			GETTIN AINT GOTTIN.

(2) Employee's Name (As on Social Security Card) Last First Initial	(3) Home Address (Give Street, City and State)	(4) Local Union No.	(5) Social Security Number	(6) Scale Wages	(7) Pension Contribution
(Leader)					
Pohlman, M.R.	L.A. 28, Calif.	47			
Blaine, Hal (contractor)	L.A. 28, Calif.	47			
2 to 6 only-2-Tracks.					
Budimir, Dennis M.	L.A. 27, Calif.	47			
Casey, Alvin W.	L.A. 28, Calif.	47			
7:30 to 2:AM. 3-Tracks.					
Deasy, Michael W.	Van Nuys, Calif.	47			
Howe, Dayton B.	L.A. 27, Calif.	47			
1-Dbl. 3rd Date Only.					
Knechtel, Lawrence W.	Sherman Oaks, Calif.	47			
Osborn, Joe	No. Hollywood, Calif.	47			
(copyist)					
Caton, Roy V.	No. Hollywood, Calif.	47			

ARRANGING BILLS WILL FOLLOW ON LAST CONTRACT ON COMPLETION OF ALBUM............

(8) Total Pension Contributions (Sum of Column (7)) $ **274.52**
Make check payable in this amount to "AFM & EPW Fund."

FOR FUND USE ONLY:

Date pay't rec'd ____ Amt. paid ____ Date posted ____ By ____

Form B-1 Rev 166

CHAPTER TEN

WASN'T IT A BIT LIKE NOW?

B ack in early March of 1967, March 2nd to be exact, whilst the band were still on tour on the eastern coastline, the prestigious annual *Grammy* award ceremony had taken place in Los Angeles, held at the Beverly Hilton Hotel on Wilshire Boulevard. These annual music industry honors, as nominated and chosen by The Recording Academy (an organization of fellow musicians, producers, engineers and other such recording professionals), were set up to recognize the outstanding contributions and performances from the previous year, in this case 1966, and The Association had been nominated in three of the 'Pop' categories, all for their recording of "Cherish". Unfortunately, success didn't come second time around for the song and on the evening itself they lost out in each category (Best Rock & Roll Group Performance went to The Mamas & The Papas with "Monday Monday", Best Rock & Roll Recording went to The New Vaudeville Band with "Winchester Cathedral", and for Best Vocal Group Performance the honor went to The Anita Kerr Quartet with "A Man And A Woman") but, nevertheless, nomination alone was a notable moment of recognition amongst their peer group, and to see the song listed alongside such celebrated works as "Good Vibrations", "Eleanor Rigby", "Guantanamera" and "Last Train To Clarksville" would be both honor and acceptance enough for many.

Back in Los Angeles, with Larry now on board, recording sessions recommenced on March 27th 1967 with a further attempt at the Addrisi Brothers' composition "Never My Love", along with another of their recent offerings, "Autumn Afternoon". However, one of the provisos that Bones Howe brought into the equation was that he insisted on utilizing experienced session musician to cut the actual tracks, a scenario reminiscent of the debut album, and whilst he was more than accommodating as to the input of the various band members, listening to their suggestions – after all, they had to replicate the music on stage – when it came to the tracks themselves he had the final say.

"My deal was twofold." Bones would later recollect with author Ken Sharp, in the expansive history of the '60s studio scene in Sharp's book *Sound Explosion: Inside L.A.'s Studio Factory with The Wrecking Crew*. "We'd choose the material together, and I'd say 'my guys are playing on the records.' The guys in The Association could play fine for the stage but as far as the studio was concerned I didn't want to spend days and days to get one track. I figured I could get more tracks done with the Wrecking Crew and I could get something that was a lot better. The guys were resentful but it was part of the deal…"

"Terry Kirkman was very angry about it," confirms Jim Yester. "He had this big drive for us to do our own stuff…" [27]

"It was the logistics," responds Terry. "We were in one of the music trivia books as the hardest working band in pop music in the world. And that's not a compliment. We were so overworked, so over booked, so undernourished creatively… We would be allotted by Pat Colecchio, the William Morris Booking Agency, and with a Warner Bros. release date already set up, just forty days to do an album. Where nothing had already been done. You may have written a song, or have some ideas, and you're going to start listening to outside material, and you're being asked to record this album in forty days?"

The now-acknowledged name for this seasoned group of studio musicians hadn't come to pass as of that particular era. Indeed, it was only in later years that drummer Hal Blaine coined the phrase 'Wrecking Crew', much to the dissatisfaction of certain members of the circle, and yet Blaine was very much one of Howe's established troupe, called in to perform on The Association's sessions. Working alongside bass players Joe Osborn and Ray Pohlman, keyboard wizard Larry Knechtel, and a revolving circle of guitarists including Mike Deasy and Dennis Budimir, the players set up their instruments under the glaring eyes of the band members and the tapes started rolling.

"Never My Love" hadn't really impressed Jerry Yester when he had first heard the song during the early New York sessions, and Bones Howe pretty much felt the same way once the band had arrived back in Los Angeles and played him the initial recording, despite the enthusiasm for it by label head (who also acted as the Addrisi Brothers music publisher) Barry DeVorzon. However, there was one vital factor missing from the early cut, underplayed by the band themselves on the Yester production, and it was only when Don Addrisi came into the studio, and was randomly playing the composition for Bones, that it all fell together. And all it needed was a simple guitar lick – *dun dun dun dun-dun* – introduced by Don as he fooled about on the guitar.

Once Bones heard that, and ran with the idea of running the lick throughout the entire track, the full potential of the song came into play, and Bones was astute enough to understand that the lick provided the hookline to the recording, and the instrumental bridge, normally filled with a guitar or a saxophone solo, would subsequently work better with a wordless vocal solo. He once again turned to Clark Burroughs for his vocal arranging expertise and between them they developed the wondrous vocal pattern that the group performed before the microphones in the studio, subtly underpinned by the deft keyboard work of Larry Knechtel. In fact, Knechtel's work on the recording is subtle enough that much of his playing lies unnoticed beneath the intricate harmonies, but the piano track caught onto tape, before the vocals were added and it was all edited down for the final mix, features some delicious solo work running on for a further full minute before he winds down, calling out to Howe in the booth "let me hear that back..."

Inspired by the relationship between his brother and his fiancé, Jackie, Dick Addrisi had come up with the title of the song after Don had woken him up at some unearthly hour of the night, excitedly telling him of his marriage proposal, and they had composed the song together at their small Studio City house during the early hours of the morning, before presenting it to DeVorzon. Struck by the delicate beauty of the work, DeVorzon reportedly responded with the throwaway comment 'Gentlemen, you have just written a major song of the 20th century...'

Having unsuccessfully pitched the song to the popular close-harmony trio The Lettermen, Don and Dick were then advised to take it to their friends, The Association. Dick Addrisi remembered: "We tried singing 'Never My Love' (for ourselves) and it sounded like a hula! The people from the record company came and said, 'I know you want to do this song yourself, but if you want to make a lot of money, sing it for The Association'. So we sang it live for The Association in the office…" [28]

Larry Ramos immediately fell in love with the composition, hearing the potential hula and Hawaiian nuances that the song offered, and the tune also caught the ear of Ted Bluechel, who later recalled:

"We had these sessions where we'd all sit down with the record producer, manager and listen to material, and when Dick and Don Addrisi played 'Never My Love' for us I was just knocked over by it, thinking that is a stone-cold hit. But the other guys let it sneak on by. That's why we had each other to lean on and I said 'Let's go back to that song. That's the tune.' After hearing it a second or third time everyone else got behind the wagon, and knew it was a good song." [11]

A number of other sessions followed over the next fortnight as Bones Howe, accompanied by the group members and the session team, worked diligently in preparing the third album. On March 28th, the second full day of recording, the two other songs that Jerry Yester had mulled over were cut in basic form, although both "Windy" and "Requiem For The Masses" would have further time spent on them in the coming weeks, as would "Never My Love".

"Windy" had first been brought to the band's attention by Jim's wife, Joellen, who had initially approached composer and longtime friend, Ruthann Friedman, to see if she had any songs that may be deemed suitable for the sessions. Ruthann, a talented, yet deep and thoughtful folk singer-songwriter, immediately thought of one of her more commercial offerings that she had initially written whilst staying in a small apartment, located below David Crosby's house in Beverly Glen Canyon, out to the west of Hollywood. Pulling it together in a mere twenty-minute writing session, the lyrics had been seen as a way to escape the unwanted attentions of a fellow musician, and to distract her from his annoying habits she had conceived the idea of an imaginary third party… "Windy".

"'Windy' is the *dream* me…" she was later to state.

That recording date, held on March 28th, set up for the initial tracking of five songs according to the surviving AFM session log, and split into three sessions between 6.00pm and 2.00am, comprised of producer Howe, drummer and contractor Hal Blaine, Ray Pohlman and Joe Osborn, both sitting in on bass (although Pohlman left the session early), guitarist Al Casey, who was later joined by Michael Deasy once they started work on one of Deasy's own compositions, and Larry Knechtel once more, who arrived late into the evening work, at 11.00pm. Along with the two aforementioned songs the team also cut the tracks for Phil Sloan's ballad "On A Quiet Night", along with a further Addrisi Brothers tune entitled "Happiness Is" and the quasi-psychedelia of Deasy's "Wantin' Ain't Gettin'", the latter highlighted by the guitarist's own sitar playing. In fact, Deasy had previously cut and produced his own version of this tune (originally titled "Wantin' Ain't Gettin' And Gettin' Ain't Gotten") under the guise of The Flower Pot (Vault Records V-937) but clearly having The Association cut the song afforded him far greater credentials and attention. Not that this established session player and former member of both Richie Valens' and Eddie Cochran's backing bands needed such notoriety.

Once again, justifying his ability for getting the true commercialism out of a song, Bones Howe, along with Ray Pohlman, changed the tempo of "Windy" as it was presented to them, altering it from a waltz to a more upbeat 4/4 time and on the days that the vocal sessions took place, between the 11th and the 13th of the following month, a chorus of singers gathered together in Western Studio 3 to complete the track, the final session reportedly running for almost eleven hours before they achieved a satisfactory result set by their high standards. With Russ and his newly appointed bandmate Larry slated to share the lead vocals, blending as one, standing alongside the band members there was Joellen Yester and Russ's wife Birdie, Ruthann herself and arranger Clark Burroughs with his wife Marilyn, all providing the audible vast refrain during the closing fade.

"The whole group worked very hard on that one," Terry was to comment. "The instrumental track was cut by Bones Howe, and then we started from the bottom with the vocals. We asked our arranger, Clark Burroughs, to help us and we threw all sorts of ideas at him and he was quite critical telling us that certain notes wouldn't make as good a chord as other notes. We didn't leave the studio until around 6.30 the next morning because we had to get a single out. By 8.30am we were on a plane to the next gig… [35]

"We did the song chronologically and the tenors were completely blown by the time we got to the last series of choruses so they came down a register and everyone else went up. Bud Shank also played what would have been my recorder solo, one of my great west coast jazz idols of the '50s."

Nevertheless, with hindsight, in 2017 Terry looked back at the session with a certain amount of distaste in his mouth:

"We chose that song, and on the day of the recording Ray Pohlman took the basic charts into the studio and laid down the basic tracks. Clark Burroughs was then corralled to go in at noon to listen to Ray and to start sketching out a vocal arrangement for what might be. We hadn't touched the song yet. By the time we walked into the studio the process that had begun sounded like Ruthann's song... but it wasn't the spirit of Ruthann's song. We heard the song as a laid back, whimsical thing but we were now looking at... what the fuck?! I walked out into the booth, and Pat Colecchio said 'what do you think?' and I said 'I don't even know that I like it. It's not what we set out to do'. And he replied 'but what do you *think*?' I said, 'OK, if they pop it as a single, in six weeks it'll be Number One!' But when we started laying out that kind of stuff, that decidedly pop stuff, I knew that we were painting ourselves into a corner that we weren't gonna be able to get out of..."

And yet, much of the attention in the coming months, once the sessions were pulled together for eventual release, were focused upon the expansive composition that Terry had brought into the New York studios during the early spring season of 1967 – "Requiem For The Masses". With a variety of inspirational sources combining together this would take the band out of the perceived pigeon-holed 'folk-pop' limitations of the watching media, and into the realms of baroque sophistication, and yet it was a work that Terry had been holding in his mind since his college choral days, performing a version of Mozart's *Requiem In D Minor* alongside his fellow students.

By combining the harmonic influence of the Mozart *Requiem* with the lyrical storytelling abilities of Bob Dylan, notably from his controversial 1963 composition "Who Killed Davey Moore", a tale of tragedy, filled with both question and response, Terry had worked at the concept during his early forays into music but, at that particular time, he didn't have a route to record or release it himself, deeming it to be in need of a massed choir of voices. Instead, he tried offering an early incarnation of the song to the ten-piece New Christy Minstrels, a group vast enough to be able to vocally undertake the challenging work, but the subject matter was deemed too dark for the band by their management, and it was only at a later date, whilst writing a poem about the ongoing U.S. struggles in Vietnam and the last viewpoint of a dying soldier, that he resurrected the idea, developing it into the socially conscious anthem it became. One suitable for the amassed six-part harmonies of The Association. With a military drumbeat, a forlorn and solitary bugle, and a choir reciting the "Kyrie Eleison", the short repeated Greek invocation, it was, and remains a stunning and yet intense composition and production. However, before the album could be finished the band was once again back out on the road, undertaking further concert bookings over in the eastern states of the U.S.

On April 14th 1967, as Terry noted, just hours after the final vocal sessions for "Windy" were completed, and whilst Bones Howe remained in Los Angeles, mixing down the sessions for release, the group were flying into Davidson, North Carolina to commence a series of shows. Both Jules and Larry were now on the tour, albeit with Larry watching and learning from the wings, and yet, on this particular leg, whilst state-hopping between New York and Pennsylvania, they would also discover another familiar face alongside them onstage.

Del Ramos picks up the story: "I was still with The New Society, and we headlined everywhere across the country. We were getting standing ovations, doing three encores a night, and everywhere we went were bringing down the house. And we get to this town in Pennsylvania and I see this big sign on this window, as I was walking around before my sound check, and it says 'The Association', and then somewhere near the bottom, in really small print, it says 'featuring The New Society'. And I was livid! I was so upset! Here we were, headlining everywhere, and who in the heck were The Association? So I went stomping back to my hotel which was adjacent to the venue where we were going to do the concert, and I walked into the elevator and just as I did a guy passes me on the way, and as the elevator shuts and moves up, real slow, I think 'wait a minute, I KNOW that guy that just passed me!' So I get out of the elevator and run down the stairway and coming up the stairs is my brother! I said, 'I thought that was you! Aren't you with The Christy's?' and he says 'no, I'm with a group called The Association!' Well, that tour was the first time that my brother and I shared the same professional stage together, but I was so busy with my career that I didn't even know my brother was with The Association. I didn't even know who they were!

"We opened for them, and after we did our show, with three curtain calls, we were in our dressing room, cooling down, and Terry Kirkman walked into the room and he says, 'Man, that was a fabulous show, but we're gonna extend the intermission for another fifteen minutes. We just want the audience to forget about you for a while!'"

Shortly afterwards came a fateful event that forced a sudden change of hand within the performing entity. Although Jules was now preparing to step away from performing, following one particular show in Philadelphia, possibly even on that same night that Del had first met up with Larry again, Brian Cole had an unfortunate accident, rendering him unable to play bass guitar for the following few dates. Reportedly, as they drove away from the small town they had just played in, Brian was throwing an explosive M80 firecracker out of the car window in a moment of on-tour hi-jinks but, as he let go, the short fuse and the strong wind outside blew the cracker backwards, exploding it in his hand, breaking a number of the bones. The result was that Larry was unexpectedly called onto the stage the following night to play guitar, with Jules switching over to bass, and whilst Brian could still sing his part Larry was still familiarizing himself with the songs.

Terry later remembered the event, sharing his recollections on social media, "He was lighting these huge firecrackers he had just got from Del Ramos and The New Society at a gig we had shared in a small Philadelphia town and as we left he was throwing them out of the rear window, just behind my head. After a few explosions I heard the *pffft* of a very fast fuse followed by (his) scream and a muffled 'pop' all at the same time. We turned the car around immediately and headed back to the town so we could get him to the hospital. Russ was furious that his car and trip to the airport was delayed!"

"I was only supposed to go out and listen to the show," Larry recalled during 2011. "Jules went to bass and he said 'Ramos, you're on tonight,' and I said 'what do you mean I'm on tonight? I don't even know the music!' He says, 'wait a minute, here…' and he gives the albums. 'How much time I got?' I asked him and he says 'show time's at seven,' and I'm like 'it's four o'clock!' But I did it, and in three hours I was onstage.

"I slipped in very easily, and the reason I think I was successful with The Association was because I had done my homework with the New Christy Minstrels. Ensemble singing is a lot different than singing as a soloist. You've got to learn to blend when you're singing with an ensemble. The Association was no different except that there were only six guys instead of ten. So it was much easier…" [23]

With Brian now restricted to a singing role, with his left arm supported in a sling, Larry was swiftly utilized onstage with the little rehearsal time he had available to him but such was his professionalism, earned by the many years and arduous hours as a part of the Christy's package, that the switch was near seamless and the schedule continued unaffected by further calamity.

A week or so later, and two days after they appeared at the Duke University in Durham, North Carolina, once again sharing the bill with The Lovin' Spoonful (during what would be founding member Zal Yanovsky's final tour – he was replaced shortly afterwards by, of all people, Jerry Yester), the first results of their recent recordings sessions, and the first to feature the vocals of the newest recruit, were foisted upon the awaiting world. And with some style. "Windy", paired with Russ Giguere's "Sometime", was released as a single on May 1st 1967 but what was perhaps most immediately significant about the release was the fact that the record label itself no longer bore the distinctive red and black logo of Valiant Records. Instead, in a much publicized buyout, the purchaser was greeted by the orange, circular image, adorned with the familiar Warner Bros. 'WB' imprint. As reported in the press just days beforehand:

Seven year-old Valiant Records has been purchased by Warner Bros. Records for an undisclosed sum in a transaction that places The Association and Shelby Flint, the label's two top-selling acts, on the WB logo. Publishing wing writers Don and Dick Addrisi continue under contract.

Billy Sherman and Barry DeVorzon (the label's founders) had negotiated a release in February 1966. Sherman moves to the Burbank lot to handle the publishing firms. DeVorzon is heading to Europe and will study composition overseas.

Due to the success of The Association (four singles hitting more than 2 million sales, and 2 LPs, 750,000 sales) and Shelby Flint's "Cast Your Fate to the Wind" success last year, Valiant reported 1966 grosses of more than $1 million. As part of the purchase, WB obtained all released and unreleased masters, plus artist contracts. The Association will continue as an independently produced act.

Billboard
April 22 1967

Not that this would have any negative impact of the success of the new 45. If anything, the financial clout and publicity of their newly acquired label would aid the band further and an extensive promotional campaign was duly launched to support the release – *'the most ambitious inaugural singles effort ever mounted*' stated the headline – and paired with the obvious additional commerciality of the recording, one area that was of concern to the ever-creative Terry Kirkman, this ensured maximum awareness in the public eyes... and ears. Still unsure as to how he truly perceived the recording – was it too commercial and too distant from how the songs origins evolved? – and all-too aware as to the depth of its infectious nature, Terry remained reluctant to step into the overly-contagious surroundings of 'sunshine pop', a genre which dangerously crossed the divide between commerciality and pure bubblegum. Fortunately, his concerns proved unfounded as, despite the subsequent success of the release (issued as Warner Bros. 7041), the song maintained a popularity and sophistication that far outlived the synthetic success of many of the era's notable chewy-chewy proclamations.

Entering the *Billboard* charts at number 52 on May 27th, the song took just five weeks to climb to the very top spot, displacing The Rascals and their silky smooth summer anthem, "Groovin'", from the pinnacle following its own two-week run. "Windy", driven by a hugely effective bass riff introduction, would then remain in prime position for four weeks itself before it, in turn, was replaced by The Doors second release, the highly-charged "Light My Fire", a song that ironically featured an uncredited Larry Knechtel playing bass on the session.

To aid further promotion of the release, on May 26th and 28th, having flown back to California after the short tour of the east, with Brian now recovering and Jules (Gary) having stepped away from the band, they filmed two television appearances, the first of which aired that same week on CBS. Titled *The Smothers Brothers Comedy Hour* this was a new, satirical, and somewhat groundbreaking comedy-variety show that, over the course of time, gave airtime to many underground or new musical artists, regardless of political stance or nature. Hosted by two street-wise, musically inclined entertainers and comedians, Tom and Dick Smothers, both popular performers on the folk circuit themselves during the early years of the decade, the show had been launched just three months previously, and within weeks had evolved into a program that, as has often been stated, 'extended the boundaries of what was considered permissible in television satire'.

The show took risks, often paying the network censorship penalty as a result, but it was a commercial success nonetheless, and was considered a 'hip' alternative to the many staid shows that saturated the stations and broadcasting airwaves throughout the industry. This was due, in no doubt, to the roster of credible guests and the talented comedic script writers, including performer/writer Mason Williams, that graced the program each week, as well as the simple fact that, by the mid-1960s, the sale of color televisions began to sky rocket across the country and the creators of *The Smothers Brothers Comedy Hour* were hip to the fact that, by 1967, gaudy colored stage sets were very much in vogue and enhanced the viewing pleasure of the watching audience. Subsequently, notable bands and colorful artists such as Buffalo Springfield, The Doors, The Who, Spanky & Our Gang, Cass Elliott and Janis Ian graced the TV stage, decked in their flowing paisley and pastel finery, alongside the brothers, bringing further acceptance amongst the music community and the show went on to achieve yet further credible status the following year when a surprise cameo appearance by the quiet Beatle, George Harrison, raised the roof of the CBS television studio.

The Association would go on to make a number of appearances on the show and remember the show with affection: Jim Yester: "We did the Smothers Brothers' show and that was neat. The Smothers Brothers were friends from the folk interactions we had had. In fact, two of us, at different times, dated their younger sister, and we were very close with those guys. And, of course, Mason Williams, who was one of their main writers, was a very good friend of ours. We used to share bills with him, do double-bills at the Pasadena Ice House. All of those people were good friends. It was a magical time in the music business..." [12]

For their debut appearance on the show the band, for once stepping out of the matching suits and into more personal formal attire, immediately offered up an example of slick professionalism, paired with the much-lauded comedic shtick they were renowned for. "The Machine", Brian Cole's clockwork introductory piece, often referred by the band as "The Association Machine" due to its performing nature of each member contributing in turn, one by one, was delivered with precision timing, utilizing the now oft-used one liner, 'made in China', when referring to the newly recruited Larry Ramos' Asian roots. Taking the reference with professional humor, and smiling throughout, harkening back to his adventures with his previous band when his ethnicity was played upon to a far greater degree, subsequent concert appearances would see Larry often adding to the wit by commenting that 'they all look alike to me...' when mixing up his fellow members on stage.

Larry: "Terry Kirkman said something to me at the very beginning when he was the leader of the group. He said, 'Larry, you don't have to be that guy anymore.' And I said, 'What do you mean?' He said, 'The guy you were in the Christy's where guys made fun of you and all this other stuff. You don't have to be that guy anymore.' And I said, 'You mean I can be myself now?' And he said, 'Yeah. We want you to be yourself.'" [50]

Clearly, some of racial interaction was still in play.

In more recent years Terry has offered up his own thoughts on his bandmate: "Larry owned himself uniquely. He was well justified in the assurance of his talent and his vocal ability, but he was in search of his own ethnic identity. For a long time he was not comfortable unless he had shtick. On his first tour with us he was wearing suits he had from the Christy's, but by the second tour he had gone to Max Factor in Hollywood and had gotten himself a paste-on mustache. In the first set he would come out as Larry Ramos, the guy you know from the Christy's, but during the second set he would come out and his guitar strap would be made of bandolero bullets and he would have on a Mexican charro outfit, with silver buttons down his pants, and he would be this Mexican guy! He didn't want to be seen as an Asian, he didn't want to be seen as Hawaiian, he wanted to be seen either as a Latin guy or a black, blues singer..." [51]

With introductions made, the band then launched into a rockin' live rendition of "Along Comes Mary", nailing the vocal harmonies with aplomb, before the hosts returned and took time to personally introduce the individual members to the watching audience, although the individual scripts – ranging from Jim's Stan Laurel impersonation, Larry's stereotypical flower lei made of poison ivy and Russ's mustache gag, to Terry, correcting Tom Smothers acknowledgment of his hit composition, "Cherries" – were clearly written for both auto-cue and laugh-a-minute value, more than for improvisation and pure comedy.

Tom: "Terry was the one who wrote the hit song 'Cherries'..."
Dick: "No! 'Cherish'... it was 'Cherish'!"
Tom: "'Cherish'? I thought was 'Cherries'..."
Terry: "No, it was 'Cherish', Tom..."
Tom: "It is? Boy, that sure changes the whole meaning of the song!"

"I usually wrote those intros for them," says Mason Williams today, "because I knew them all so well. They were great! A lot of the rock groups we had on were open to being part of skits, and they were very good about that..."

Ted: "Hi, I am Ted the Pig. I play the drums and hum vocal backgrounds. These are my drums, these are my hums, hmmmmm… I'm a humdrummer"

Terry (upon being asked how they chose the band name): "We didn't pick the name. We were practicing one day and there was a knock on the door. We answered the door and it was us…"

Brian, the true actor in the line-up, with full comedy facial expressions (when asked what future does The Association have): "Well, I think it's too directly bound to its own anguish to be anything other than a cry of total negation carrying within itself the seeds of its own destruction…"

Humorous philosophies aside, the group then returned, now in a more familiar appearance of matching brown suits, to lip-sync along with "Windy". Two days later they appeared on *The Steve Allen Comedy Hour*, a short-lived summer series also filmed for the CBS network, this time performing "Windy" and "Never My Love" from the then-upcoming album, in front of an illuminated backdrop with the band name written in lights, although by the time the taping was aired the album was already on general release.

With recording sessions for the album now in the closing stages, the final dates taking place over the first week of June, the band now looked forward to one particular concert appearance on the calendar, scheduled for June 16th 1967, and located 300 miles up the Californian coastline, in the artistic-focused city of Monterey.

With its picturesque, ocean side vantage point high above the bay, Monterey was already used to an influx of musicians within its small community, having hosted the annual Monterey Jazz Festival since its inception back in 1958. Nevertheless, the decision to host the inaugural International Pop Music Festival, a three-day event to be held within the 7,000 capacity Monterey County Fairground, was seen by many as a way to 'validate rock music as an art form' in much the same way as both the jazz and folk genres were viewed,

Conceived and planned by a number of the industry's 'hip' contingent, including record producer Lou Adler and John Phillips, leader of The Mamas & The Papas, and headed by an elite band of 'directors' (including Phillips, Paul McCartney, Mick Jagger, Donovan, Jim/Roger McGuinn, Terry Melcher, Johnny Rivers and Brian Wilson, amongst others) the general consensus was that this should be a charitable, non-profit event, and the coming together, from start to finish, came to fruition over a brief, yet chaotic two-month period.

Headlining acts, drawn from across the musical divide – rock, pop, blues, folk, east to west, north to south, from the pop sophistication of Los Angeles to the avant-garde and free-formed improvisations of the San Franciscan scene, from New York to London, were booked in to appear over the three days, although the organizers wildly underestimated the pull of such an event. Particularly once the hushed rumors of a long-overdue Beatles re-appearance were whispered amongst the music fraternity, especially with McCartney on the Board of Directors. In truth, this was never a viable or realistic option, not without quadrupling the size of the city boundaries, and the fab four wisely stayed clear of the eventuating masses, estimated anywhere between 20,000 and 90,000 descending on the city and its surrounding areas over the weekend, and instead they chose to send their collective wishes via telegram.

The Beach Boys were one of the early frontrunners for a headlining slot, but wary of their own faltering prominence amongst the musical heavyweights and with Brian Wilson's ailing mental status, despite his position alongside McCartney on the board, coupled with Carl Wilson's ongoing battles with the U.S. draft board, they pulled out at the last minute (although they still supplied their own impressive sound system, which had already been shipped to the festival site), and yet even without such hit-making significance the chosen acts included such notables as The Byrds, Canned Heat, Jefferson Airplane, Buffalo Springfield, Simon & Garfunkel, The Who, Otis Redding, The Grateful Dead, Big Brother & The Holding Company, The Jimi Hendrix Experience and Steve Miller, along with a completely unknown act, listed on the program as The Group With No Name – all topped off with the prestigious Sunday night closing slot for Phillip's own kaftan-clad quartet (supported, musically, by drummer 'Fast' Eddie Hoh, along with the familiar faces of Blaine, Osborn and Knechtel, now often known simply as the 'HGT' – Hollywood's Golden Trio). Sadly, not all could, or would attend, with The Kinks, The Stones and Donovan all absent due to the refusal of entry visas – brought about by recent drug busts or contractual disputes – whilst Bob Dylan was recovering from a recent motorcycle accident, and Frank Zappa downright refused, believing the San Franciscan contingent to be inferior on a musical level and refusing to share the stage with them. Nevertheless, despite their often-viewed un-hip standing amongst such a core band of credible performers, The Association, close friends with Phillips and his bandmates after a series of co-headlining shows together, were invited to open the event, scheduled to appear during the Friday afternoon. When the stage lights finally went on for the first time, and the mics and amps were warmed up, there were flowers, beads and love everywhere… and six guys formally dressed in matching suits, one with the lone concession of a single pink flower placed strategically in his guitar head.

"We were the opening act and we were kind of the sound check and lighting check for the whole festival," Terry was to sardonically comment during a number of interviews in 2015. "It was big. It was an honor. It was historical, and it was really bad. We had just finished the 'Insight Out' album, and we weren't doing those songs yet because we hadn't had rehearsal time to put them together for the stage, so we were not doing 'Never My Love', and we were not doing 'Requiem For The Masses'. We literally went from the studio to home, grabbed some clothes, got on a plane, and flew to Monterey. All we knew was that we were included in this thing that John and Michelle Phillips were doing and that it was in Monterey. We hadn't really thought about it, and I don't think there was anybody else who thought about what it was really going to be like, because nobody had done it yet.

"I think that one of the worst mistakes that we ever did was to do the 'Association Machine', which I had *begged* not to do. 'Don't do that here,' and the next thing I know Brian is starting off with 'Association Machine' and here we go. It knocked us out of the film. John Phillips looked at me one time and said 'sorry about that, but you didn't fit the image'. I thought 'you asked us to be the fucking opening act! How can we not fit the image?' But I honestly believe that had we performed 'Requiem…' we would have been perceived by the public *for ever* in an entirely different context." [7/29/51]

The band had actually kicked off their set with, appropriately, "Enter The Young" but the camera crew were seemingly unprepared as the first notes were struck, and no visual evidence survives of the performance, the result being that, before they launched into the next song, the band were forced to partake in some onstage banter and interaction with the watching audience, giving the crew some additional set-up time. That gave Brian the opportunity to step forward as the cameras started to roll…

Ted Bluechel was later to claim that the subsequent inclusion of "Association Machine" was, literally, a last minute response as, in addition to the camera issues, he also called out to stall the start of the next number whilst he made some final adjustments to his drum kit. Surviving outtake footage from the film would indeed confirm that fact, and Ted can be seen twiddling nuts, bolts and wing-nuts as Brian steps forth...

"For the rest of the three days, we had front row seats and we got to see everybody," summarized Jim Yester. "There was so much camaraderie and all that Summer of Love stuff going on. We stayed at the same little hotel as Big Brother & The Holding Company and got to see Janis interacting with the kids in the group. It was just really cool. So ballsy. I mean, holy shit! I had never seen a performer like that before." [12]

Despite a set-list comprising of "Enter The Young", "Along Comes Mary", "Cherish" and "Windy", the appearance at Monterey did little to enhance their credibility amongst their peer group and, as noted, the band's short performance failed to make the final cut of the subsequent D.A. Pennebaker documentary, *Monterey Pop*, shot on basic 16mm film and created to commemorate the event. An unjust decision with hindsight, especially when one notes the impact that the movie, and the media exposure had on the careers of Joplin, Hendrix *et al.*

Terry: "I later asked John Phillips if he knew what the image for the festival was going in, and he said 'no, we didn't, but after it was all done, and we saw what we had, we created an image... and you didn't fit.'"

In relation to their perceived persona, Jim Yester was later to note: "It was a real strange thing, because the whole premise of The Association when we first started was 'what you see is not what you get'. We wanted to come off as a business image, straight laced, mom and apple pie, and that was the image we projected but everybody in the band was a freak! We were the original flower children before the flower thing ever happened." [40]

Maybe Monterey would have been an appropriate time to start letting the media and the watching audience into the premise...

One noteworthy footnote to the entire Monterey story is the tale surrounding the previously unknown band, The Group With No Name, a folk-rock quintet who appeared on the vast stage mid-way through the Sunday afternoon slot. For almost fifty years their appearance has been shrouded in mystery. No known audio recordings of their set exist, nor does any video footage survive in the Pennebaker archives and yet, research for this book reveals that the five-piece band were made up of founding Modern Folk Quartet member Cyrus Faryar, his wife Renais, a drummer named Terry Crilly (also known as the popular Los Angeles disc jockey Frank Terry), along with the former Travelers 3 bass player Dick Shirley.

And filling out the band was the fifth member, former Association singer and guitarist Jules Alexander.

"John (Phillips) asked us 'Hey, you guys, wanna play?'" states Jules, with a hint of bewilderment in his voice. "So we did! We weren't very good! I think we'd been rehearsing maybe, three or four times and I think that's why we were so surprised! But we said, 'yeah, lets do it!' but it didn't work out…"

Positioned in a revised running order directly after an encore set from the powerhouse that was Janis Joplin, rescheduled so that the cameras could catch her dynamic appearance on film, The Group With No Name played a somewhat muted set themselves, performing just four tunes that they had hastily rehearsed (one rehearsal had taken place the previous week at the preceding Magic Mountain Music Festival, held up in Marin County, CA.), one of which was entitled "Rubber Band" whilst another was a composition from Jules called "Flashing Memories", a song that that harkened back to The Association's debut LP sessions. Following their short set the quintet swiftly disappeared from both the stage and the history books.

"In a way, it was a fearless and heroic thing to attempt," summarized Cyrus Faryar. "We went up there and I think the adrenaline, the novelty and the excitement kind of blew our minds. The song began, and it went in four or five directions at the same time. It didn't flow together in one unit. It became five people. We walked off stage, drenched in sweat, not really knowing what had happened…"[49]

Renais Faryar: "We were like fish in a bowl, you know. We were freaked! The band dissolved as it went offstage…"[49] With Buffalo Springfield following on immediately afterwards, launching their own performance with a rendition of their best-selling hit "For What It's Worth", it's just as well that Cyrus, Jules and friends hadn't taken much time over naming their band…

"I stayed to watch them," comments Jim Yester, before adding with a laugh, "and they were a little rough as I recall, but of course I loved it!"

WINDY CHERISH PANDORA'S GOLDEN HEEBIE JEEBIES NO FAIR AT ALL ALONG COMES MARY THE ASSOCIATION

Management—Patrick Colecchio, 9000 Sunset Blvd., L. A., Calif. 90069
Booking—Associated Booking Corp., New York, Beverly Hills, Chicago, London
Recording—Warner Brothers Records, 4000 Warner Ave., Burbank, Calif.

CHAPTER ELEVEN

A BIRTHDAY MORNING

Just one week separated the cautious applause from a partially stoned, 7,000-strong gathering in Monterey, CA and the cheers of the 2,000 attendees at the Kellogg Auditorium in Battle Creek, Michigan, but that was where The Association found themselves, just seven days after the historic happenings, back out on the road in the distant states of Michigan, Iowa, Hawaii, New York, New Jersey, Pennsylvania, Ohio and Utah, hopping between Holiday Inns and sharing the stage on intermittent dates alongside Buffalo Springfield and The Squires. During the three day stopover in Hawaii, during the second week of July, they appeared as a part of the multi-packaged Donald O'Connor Show, performing alongside the popular folk trio The Wellingtons and Japanese singer/actress Izumi Yukimor. Such was their commitment to touring by this stage that, on this occasion, they even turned down an invitation to perform at the first wedding anniversary party of Frank Sinatra and Mia Farrow, an invitation from Frank himself, opting the spend the day in Waverly, Pennsylvania instead. Their third album, *Insight Out* (W-1696/WS-1696), the title of which was drawn from their ongoing Subud and meditational philosophies, and their first to appear on the Warner Bros. label, had arrived in the stores just days before Monterey and the group was now keen to promote it to their fans and audiences across the nation. Although they had chosen not to perform any of the songs from the release for their Monterey set they gradually began to introduce the new compositions to a listening audience, many of who would have made the purchase the moment the record store doors opened on release day.

Issued with a nicely designed front sleeve, courtesy of Warner Bros. acclaimed art director Ed Thrasher, and containing a series of photographs by the New York-born celebrity snapper Sherman Weisburd, a vast improvement in presentation from the previous two releases, *Insight Out* stands as a perfect example of the power and diversity of The Association, crossing the often blurred lines between rock, pop, psychedelia and folk. From the opening refrains of Terry Kirkman's "Wasn't It A Bit Like Now (Parallel 23)", with its deceptive intro/fade, bookended with another of Terry's compositions, the expansive "Requiem For The Masses", each band member gets the opportunity to vocally shine, often pairing off in the harmonic combination of pop perfection that flows throughout. Ted's delightful "We Love Us" and the Addrisi Brothers "Happiness Is" both offer up a sun-kissed Bluechel/Ramos blend, whilst the opening "Wasn't It..." and "Never My Love' see Terry's voice this time around, smoothly in harmony with Larry, confirming the ability that the newest member of the band had to perfectly sync alongside his partners. Even Brian, more commonly seen supplying harmonies and bass vocals than he was performing solo, standing in front of the microphone alone, offered up his own raucous upbeat version of the Oregon-born folk singer Tim Hardin's "You've Got A Reputation" (abbreviated here to 'Reputation') and then stood alongside Russ, adding his balance to Mike Deasy's Indian raga rhythms on "Wantin' Ain't Gettin'".

"I was one of the ones who pushed for 'Reputation'" notes Jim Yester, "because the Modern Folk Quartet was doing it and their version was so great. When the powers that be agreed to do the song, I was really pumped. Then when I heard what they wanted to do with it, I was horrified. I hear the song more like Timmy did it, and more like the MFQ did it, as a really down blues instead of a frantic freakout. I think Brian pushed it in that direction." [18]

Needless to say, the polished sheen from Bones Howe, and the accomplished performances from the session team, went a long way towards the overall slick sophistication that runs across the vinyl but make no mistake, the six band members themselves contributed a significant depth to the proceedings and the balance between production and performance is flawlessly poised.

With the promotional tour in full flow, and the album now rapidly climbing the *Billboard* charts, eventually peaking at number eight during an impressive 25-week run in the Top 40 list, Warner Bros. set their focus on delivering a follow-up 45 to "Windy" in an effort to maintain the current uplift in momentum the band were experiencing. Despite a healthy choice of options that the album had to offer the selection of "Never My Love" b/w "Requiem For The Masses" was the seemingly obvious one to go with and, following a further overdub and mixing session held at the Western studios on July 27th, the next single was prepared and released on August 9th, as Warner Bros. 7074, ultimately reaching the number two position after seven weeks on the *Billboard* charts during the week of October 7th 1967. It was to remain there for two weeks, sitting patiently behind the Memphis-based band The Box Tops and "The Letter" before its gradual descent downwards. In addition, in what some would often refer to as the secondary U.S. chart lists, as compiled by the *Cash Box* trade magazine, "Never My Love" peaked one place further, reaching the number one slot in that list. However, the longevity that the song has now gone on to endure, almost 50 years after the first release of the work, is simply astounding and a testament to both songwriter and singer. Over the ensuing decades it has now gone on to become a staple within the very framework of American society, registering as the number two most-played song on U.S. radio and television during the entire 20th century. Some feat indeed...

Commenting on its phenomenal success and endurance, composer Dick Addrisi says: "If people tell me they've never heard 'Never My Love', I say, 'That means you've never been in an elevator or a supermarket.' You can't escape the song. It's just there"

It is also worth noting that the 45 release of the song actually fades out earlier than the album cut as, with "Cherish" in mind, an effort was made to keep it under the radio-friendly 3-minute mark.

With the current touring calendar for the band now running into the high summer months there seemed little let-up in their hectic schedule as they continuously flew across the state lines of New York, Michigan, Illinois, Massachusetts, Arkansas, Florida, Colorado and Minnesota during August, squeezing in appearances in their home state just before departure – starting with a run of shows at the impressive outdoor Greek Theater in Los Angeles between July 24th and 30th and then closing out the summer with a slot at the Anaheim Convention Center on the 26th August, sharing the bill with Buffalo Springfield, The Nitty Gritty Dirt Band, The Young Men and The Sunshine Company. For the earlier appearance at the Greek Theater they were billed as 'guest artists' for the week, once again supporting the Hollywood song and dance man, Donald O'Connor, famed for his appearance in the hit movie *Singin' In The Rain*. Sadly, for many, it was a mismatched pairing with reports noting that on some evenings, once dusk had arrived and The Association had appeared onstage following on from O'Connor's late afternoon performance, there was a mass exodus from the older generation, complaining about the 'excess noise' and 'racket'. One can only imagine that the August appearance, with more like-minded bands, would have fared far better.

A few days later they appeared on the bill at the annual Ravinia Festival, held in Highland Park, Illinois over the midweek days of August 2nd and 4th, breaking the attendance record for the event. Whilst at the festival a film crew was also in attendance, capturing a number of the band's songs in full color, including an enthusiastic rendition of "Windy", still residing in the *Billboard* Top 10 at that point, along with a riotous performance of "Reputation" with Brian really driving the band to deliver the goods, squeezing out every note with every sinew of his body, whilst Terry wails away on harmonica and Ted maintains the heavy and steady backbeat.

In between the many live concerts, flights and long haul drives they once again managed to shoehorn in a number of appearances for the television stations, the first of which was for *The Murray the K Special*, a New York-based WPIX broadcast featuring the group, filmed outdoors, lip-syncing to "Windy" and "Requiem For The Masses", and then on the opposite coast, taped on August 25th and airing two weeks later, with a second slot on CBS' *The Smothers Brothers Comedy Hour*, performing both sides of the new 45. For "Never My Love" they were the smiling, affable band, dressed in matching blue suits, offering up the neat, family friendly image, whilst for the accompanying song, introduced by Dick Smothers as "a moving tribute to those who die, without knowing why..." the band conjured up a darker, moodier contrast, outfitted in black on a revolving stage, Ted with a marching snare slung over his shoulder, Terry with a moving, choreographed performance out front. The fact that the band, and indeed the show's producers were brave enough to make such a public statement by performing the song on national TV, "Requiem For The Masses" – a statement questioning the validity of the war in Vietnam, showed the belief they had in this musical *tour de force*. But, sadly, it wasn't one that was shared universally.

"The United States Government stepped on that song," suggested Terry, in separate conversations with journalists Casey Chambers and Robert White, both during 2015. "There was pressure put on the record companies and on disc jockeys not to play the song, (but) Murray the K was playing 'Requiem...', the number one disc jockey in New York. He was asked not to play the record, but he said, 'you know, tell you what? Screw you.' He not only played the record about every hour on the hour, but he put live recordings of wartime horrors in front of it and on the back end of it. It was played every hour on the hour on the moratoriums in New York and Washington D.C. It was the song that later preceded Daniel Ellsberg to the stage in fund-raisers for his Pentagon Papers..." [29/7]

However, it wasn't all such a serious televised tone as, to finish off their Smothers Brothers appearance, they then participated in a short comedy skit alongside fellow guests Greer Garson and Pat Paulson, mocking the fashion sense and trends of the average U.S. male. Decked out in tight fitting pants and wigs of various lengths, nervously glancing across at each whilst they synchronized their routine, this certainly showed how far the band were prepared to travel for acceptability within the industry. And then, as if to acknowledge their acceptance within the elite Hollywood brigade, they subsequently appeared on ABC-TV's weekly variety spectacular *Hollywood Palace*, broadcast on September 5th, appearing alongside hosts Bing Crosby, Milton Berle and Jimmy Durante and a whole bunch of Gleem toothpaste and Raid Mouse Killer sponsored products. After lip-syncing to "Never My Love" during the first half of the hour-long show they later came back on stage where, alongside Crosby, they introduced fellow guest star, the actress, singer and dancer Joey Heatherton, a noticeably attractive addition, a fact that the group clearly played up to with huge smiles and tongues firmly in cheeks. Harmonizing together beautifully, "Joey, Joey-Joey..." they then parted ranks to reveal the diminutive Ms. Heatherton, dressed in a pure white mini skirt and turtleneck sweater combo. It was all very Hollywood glitz; a fact confirmed when they re-appeared during the grand finale, joining in with the ensemble to perform the big show-closing number, "To Be A Performer".

Despite the questionable credibility of such appearances The Association, for a period, appeared to be *the* band on call should such a need, or a vacant guest spot arise.

"We became *the* band for the Smothers Brothers show," Jim Yester confirmed to *Goldmine* in 2004. "A lot of times we were the fill in for *American Bandstand* once they moved their show to L.A. Dick Clark would call our management and say, 'Someone canceled on me. Are the guys in town?' and since we all lived in Hollywood we'd be there in a heartbeat. Doing those shows was so cool. I mean, Durante was such a sweetheart. He was just an angel of a person..." [11/12]

The one particularly notable moment of interest on *Hollywood Palace*, other than their overall professionalism onstage, came when Crosby turned to the six members standing suited and booted alongside him and commented, 'Say, you boys, don't you open at the Cocoanut Grove tonight?" a reference to the upcoming residency the band were scheduled to hold over the following 12-day period at the famed Los Angeles club, located within the prestigious Ambassador Hotel, a location beloved by the Hollywood stars and starlets of the 1920s and 1930s. This indeed was a notable point, seeing that their scheduled series of appearances was to be the very time an 'amplified guitar group' was deemed appropriate enough to work the esteemed room. Needless to say, the press was out in force during the early run of the shows, as were a host of star names:

Russ Giguere: "I remember when the lights came up and I saw Carol Channing and George Burns at the front table, and I about fell over. It was so cool!" [1]

Fortunately, for the staid Ambassador Hotel, The Association's strength is in its vocal chords, with its guitar strumming secondary. Their stage presence is excellent and their utilization of comic bits, including blackouts in one non-singing (portion), based on a 'news-around-the-world' motif, adds a welcome lightness to an otherwise heavy and cerebral potpourri of tunes. Repertoire includes "Never My Love", "Wasn't It A Bit Like Now", "All Is Mine", "Round Again" and "Babe (I'm Gonna Leave You)". A youthful following showed its appreciation, but elders showed their unfamiliarity with this material...

Billboard
September 16 1967

Whilst not a particularly favorable review overall (*The Los Angeles Times* was equally as skeptical), *Billboard* was quick to point out that, in order to play such venues where the audience is clearly a mix of enthusiastic young fan and inquisitive elder, then the act needed more awareness, beyond the depth of just the albums and singles. A fair point to some, and certainly a point worth raising following a similar reception from the earlier Greek Theater audience and it raises the question as to whether the band, under the guidance of Pat Colecchio, and now without the musical diversities that Jules Alexander had often added, were treading too far into the realms of Hollywood acceptability, and away from their roots as a folk/rock band. The Cocoanut Grove was most certainly a prime booking, and one designed to generate publicity, but was it the right publicity? Or is that age-old saying coming true whereupon no publicity is bad publicity, and any publicity is for the good? The recordings that they were generating during this era, either self-composed originals, and/or cover versions, clearly maintained that desire to retain a certain ethos and credibility amongst their peer group, but their willingness to participate and be seen alongside the 'old-vanguard', however sweet or angelic they may be, certainly stood them apart from many of their musical equals. Was the musical portion of their repertoire always geared appropriately towards the attending audience at such venues? Or was the bravado of "Enter The Young", their opening number at the Grove, merely a stand for youth and a brushoff to such outdated venues and aging audiences? When The Beatles appeared on the UK TV variety shows such as *The Morecambe & Wise Show* or *The Ken Dodd Show*, back in 1963, 'pop' music, or even 'beat music', was still in the eyes of many, a novelty. It was simply 'light entertainment'. Now, just four years later, a degree of coolness was casting an ominous shadow over the proceedings and there was a sense of aloofness developing towards what was perceived as 'the establishment'. Would The Byrds have even considered sharing a stage with Durante at all, jazz-hands at full throttle? Would The Lovin' Spoonful or Buffalo Springfield have lowered themselves into a tight pant, wig-wearing spectacle for the sake of promotion? It seems unlikely. But credit where credit is due, and The Association were now getting plenty of work for being such a professional act…

Whilst performing their run at the Cocoanut Grove they also took the opportunity of being in Los Angeles to once again enter the recording studios at Western to lay down some initial tracks for the next series of recordings. As was often the case, whilst in between shows, much of their down-time was spent songwriting, compiling potential songs for the next album, showcasing the compositions for their bandmates at the various band meetings – not that it was always easy presenting the new songs…

"We called material selection meetings. We called them 'hangings'," laughed Jim Yester, remembering these showcases. "You felt like you were bringing your baby to a hanging!" [12]

As was to be expected, with six such-talented musicians, most of who were composing at the same time (with the exception of the seemingly reluctant Brian Cole), the potential input was prolific with almost everyone bringing new songs to the table. Even Larry Ramos, who hadn't been with the band for more than six months by this stage, was contributing a number of new compositions. His true songwriting potential, with the benefit of hindsight, appears to have been somewhat stifled during his lengthy run as a member of The New Christy Minstrels and his artistic creativity, now free of such restraining boundaries, brought forth a healthy burst of songwriting activity. Often working alongside two of his close friends, Tony Ortega (whom he had known for numbers of years) and fellow composer and vocal arranger Bob Alcivar, a former member of the jazz vocal band The Signatures who had first met Larry whilst working with The New Christy Minstrels during 1965, titles such as "Good Feeling Day", "Hear Me Now", "Like Always", "Looking For Evergreens" and "Cryin' Ain't My Sound" were brought into the group selection meets although, in the long run, only one of these particular songs would receive the full Association treatment, a fact that Larry humorously put down to his bandmates 'suffering from bad taste'. For their part the other members of the band were also contributing new songs such as "Birthday Morning", "Everything That Touches You" and "The Time It Is Today".

Encouraged by the success of the writing team, Alcivar placed two of the unused Ramos-Alcivar-Ortega songs, "Hear Me Now" and "Looking For Evergreens", with another local Los Angeles-based harmony band, The Dawnbreakers, comprising of three sisters, Billie Lee, Donnie and Lana Day, along with two talented musicians, Jim Seals and Dash Crofts. The resulting single, issued on Dunhill Records during July of 1967, with vocal arrangements credited to Alcivar, failed to chart but remains a pleasant period piece; sunshine pop at its finest. Sufficiently inspired by the Dawnbreakers sessions the songwriting trio subsequently composed a further new song, titled after one of the Day sisters, "Donnie", and offered it to The Chuck Barris Syndicate, who released it on Dot Records the following year, again featuring the vocal arrangements of Bob Alcivar, and noticeably similar to those of The Association.

September 12th 1967 saw the first tentative round of new Association sessions with a guide track for Jim Yester's "Birthday Morning" attempted. This delightful tune, co-written with an old friend from his falconry club days, Gary Errol 'Skip' Carmel, was one of two new tunes that the duo would bring into the upcoming sessions and with Bones Howe scheduled once again to be behind the studio board, and his stellar session crew out front, augmented at times by members of the band, the new sessions slowly kicked off in a positive vein.

Jim Yester: "Skip and I were both in the falconry club that had been started by Bob Klimes, a childhood mentor of mine and who later did the vocal arrangements for 'Birthday Morning'. Skip had been working on some musical things with Bob and asked if I would work on some things. He also gave me 'Barefoot Gentleman' and asked me to do music for it, so we worked on those two tunes together, but never took it further…"

Following an appearance on the *Joey Bishop Show*, broadcast on September 13th, the remainder of the fall season was, once again, spent out on the road, with a series of seemingly endless one-nighters throughout the latter half of October and into the early winter weeks – the last two weeks of the month saw eleven state crossings alone.

October 11 1967: Eastman Theater, Rochester, NY
October 13 1967: Juniata College, Huntingdon, PA
October 16, 1967: Duquesne University, Pittsburgh, PA
October 17, 1967: Appalachian State University, Boone, NC
October 18, 1967: Dan Cannon Auditorium, St. Leo, FL
October 19, 1967: University of Chattanooga, Chattanooga, TN
October 20, 1967: University of South Florida, Tampa, FL
October 21, 1967: Tennessee Polytechnic Institute, Cookeville, TN
October 26, 1967: Southern Oregon College, Ashland, OR
October 27, 1967: University of Idaho, Moscow, ID
October 28, 1967: Oregon State University, Corvallis, OR
October 30, 1967: Oregon Tech Institute, Klamath Falls, OR

October 31, 1967: Chico State College, Chico, CA
November 1 1967: Humboldt State College, Arcata, CA
November 2 1967: Foothill College, Los Altos Hills, CA
November 7 1967: Idaho State University, Pocatello, ID
November 8 1967: University of Arizona, Tucson, AZ
November 9 1967: Northern Arizona University, Flagstaff, AZ
November 10 1967: El Camino College, Torrance, CA
November 11 1967: California State College, Hayward, CA

During mid-October, whilst briefly back in California, they did manage to book in a session at Western Recorders, cutting a proposed seasonal recording, a version of the ever-popular Bob Wells-Mel Torme composition "The Christmas Song" (as popularized by Nat 'King' Cole amongst many others), but it remained unfinished and unreleased and so it wasn't until November, during a further mid-tour break, that they reconvened once again in the studio, under the guidance of Bones Howe.

A new Terry Kirkman offering, "Everything That Touches You", was one of the first songs attempted during an afternoon demo session held on November 14th with popular session guitarist Randy Sterling, who had known the band since the early days of his duo with Russ at the Ice House, sitting in on bass guitar. Whilst Terry worked out the structures of his new composition, Sterling started tinkering with various lines on his guitar, recalling an old riff he had played years before.

Randy recalls: "For some reason, and to this day I do not know what it was, but Brian Cole had taken a dislike to me and he was always being rude. Not mean, just rude... so, anyway, they came in and said to me 'well, what do you think about starting this off with a bass?' and I remembered this one bass line from around six years before that I had been screwin' around with and I just thought 'I'm gonna use this sucker!' because, by a way of getting back at Brian, I knew it was going to take him at least a week to learn!

"I did it just to piss off Brian, but I remember that a couple of the guys in the group went 'whoa, nice!'"

It worked perfectly and the now-familiar introduction to the song was created. Further sessions for the song would follow shortly, with Joe Osborn sitting in on bass for the final tracking sessions although, even for a player of Osborn's stature, it reportedly still took him at least half an hour to perfect the riff.

Then, as the sessions developed further, various band meets, or 'hangings', were undertaken in order to suggest the eventual song selection and, at one such gathering, held after a particularly lengthy vocal session, songwriter Jimmy Webb was brought in by producer Bones Howe to play the group a new composition he had written especially with the band in mind. Except that it wasn't just *one* song, it was, according to some, an entire 24-minute cantata inspired by the songwriter's love for his girlfriend, a fellow artist named Susan Horton, reportedly crossing over four or five separate songs, but linked by the same theme.

Created during the recording sessions for The 5th Dimension's album *Magic Garden*, a concept work that was co-produced by Bones and Webb and made up almost entirely of Webb compositions, this new idea was certainly an adventurous piece of work by any standards. Bones was to later recall, "During the last four weeks (of The 5th Dimension sessions), Jimmy got this idea to do a cantata. He said... 'I'm gonna write a cantata, and it's gonna be 24 minutes long, and be the whole side of an album, and it'll be broken up into little pieces that could be singles.' He then suggested that The Association would be the perfect group to record the cantata." [30]

Webb, a 21 year-old Oklahoma-born graduate of San Bernardino Valley College of Music, had broken into the songwriting industry courtesy of a 1965 seasonal composition, recorded by The Supremes. The following year, having met singer and producer Johnny Rivers who signed him to a publishing deal, he composed a succession of songs, including future chart smashes "By The Time I Get To Phoenix" and "Where's The Playground Susie?" the latter initially being cut by former New Christy Minstrel Mike Whalen during an extremely fortuitous recording session. In early 1967, with Rivers now working on the debut album for The 5th Dimension, Jimmy contributed five of his songs to the sessions, including the title track, "Up Up and Away" which, when released as a single during May of that year, went on to reach Top 10 status in the *Billboard* charts. During these sessions he also struck up a friendship with production assistant Bones Howe who, shortly afterwards, took over the full production responsibilities for the five-piece harmony group.

Now, over six months on, and Bones was actively promoting the work of Jimmy Webb and, despite the proposed option of inviting all of the band members over to Jimmy's house to hear the new work, manager Pat Colecchio believed it better to have the band listen on neutral ground, suggesting the studio to be a better choice. Subsequently, Webb arrived at Western Recorders that evening and played the new lengthy opus for them, unfortunately splitting his pants in the process, whilst suggesting it be included on their upcoming release – the reputed stipulation being that the entire 24-minute piece came as one package, not a succession of individual songs that could be cherry-picked from the collection. There was also connecting music, interwoven in-between, and Bones thought that they could also expand on that vocally, as The 5th Dimension had recently done so on the conceptual *Magic Garden*.

Bones Howe: "Jimmy was so excited about his song and he sits down at the piano and I say, 'You've got to listen to this all the way through, because it's meant to be one whole side of an LP. It's got several movements, and every one of them could be opened up and we could put it out as a single.' He then played through these pieces and sang them, and went back and played countermelodies, and showed them various things he had in mind for this cantata. It was just a wonderful piece of music. He finishes, and the guys kind of look at each other, and Pat Colecchio goes, 'Maybe Jimmy could go outside for a second and we could talk about this among the guys.' [30/31]

"They closed the door and somebody in the group, I don't remember who, said, 'Any two guys in this group could write a better piece of music than that!' I said, 'You guys are crazy! This is a wonderful concept' to which they replied, 'Yeah, but we'd have to give up the whole side of an album...'" [30]

Ultimately, and unwilling to commit an entire side of their upcoming release to the work, despite an interest in at least two of the integrated sections, including one particularly long and involved piece of shifting tempos that Webb had entitled "MacArthur Park", an extraordinary opus made up of three individual movements – "In The Park", "After The Loves Of My Life" and "Allegro" – they talked it out and stood united. After much discussion they vetoed the offering.

"We were halfway through the album," states Jim Yester, "and we were nearing the end of a 12-hour vocal session and everybody was pretty well fried. We were having problems finishing whatever tune it was we were working on, very complex. And Bones says, 'Take a break. Jimmy's here and he's got something that he's written for you guys.' And he sat down at the piano and played us a cantata with five movements, and the deal was, take the whole 24 minutes or none of it... [12]

"It was great stuff, but there was no way that we could have taken the whole thing. Jimmy was very bitter, and I can't blame him. I'm sure it would have been mind-blowing (but) we were halfway through the album. It's like, okay, whose song is coming off? Had we done that, it would have been trend-setting, and we probably would have reinvented ourselves..." [18]

Unfortunately, it was left to Bones to break the news to Jimmy. "He was really crushed by it," Howe remembers. "I kept saying to their manager, 'There's not one song here that's as good as the cantata that Jimmy brought in. We ought to go back to him.'" [30]

"I was devastated. It's the old cartoon thing; I see the Grammy on wings, flying away. It's like, here's an opportunity to do something really different that nobody else has done. I thought it was a brilliant idea..." [31]

But the decision stood, the band was unprepared to earmark the whole one side of their record to Webb's work. A significant measure of their reasoning, as Jim suggested, was that it would also have resulted in some of their own compositions, already penciled in for inclusion, being dropped – and none of the band was prepared to cross that border. However, the story doesn't end there... as Webb then took the centerpiece of the work, the lengthy "MacArthur Park", and cut the song utilizing British actor Richard Harris, who was recording his own debut album at the time, at the microphone instead. After playing through the work to Harris in London, who enthusiastically responded, "Oh, Jimmy Webb. I love that! I'll make a hit out of that, I will," Webb duly seceded and the reported 24-minute concept was discarded. The decision proved to be a wise one too, seeing the song enter the U.S. charts during early May 1968, before making a gradual ascent upwards, peaking at the number 2 position during the week of June 22nd.

Maybe if the band had pushed him further? Maybe "MacArthur Park" would have benefited from the full six-part harmony. Who knows? And yet maybe the recollections of many of those involved may have also gotten disorientated through the many mists of time. Some versions of the unfolding events have suggested that the band refused the project simply because they were too close to the scheduled ending of the sessions in order to complete the album. They didn't snub the idea, but they simply had no time. However, detailed research would now confirm that Webb actually began recording the backing track for the subsequent hit version of the song over the Christmas period of 1967, and into early 1968, a number of weeks *before* The Association even started polishing up the final tracks for their album. Subsequently, it couldn't have been a matter of not having the time, or having already completed the majority of the sessions. Howe later recalled that Webb played him the proposed piece once all the work on The 5th Dimension's *Magic Garden* album was finished – November 1967 – and that they would 'get together with The Association' once they returned from their current tour, which confirms the mid-November break. Again, this date was far from near the end of the fourth album sessions, which ultimately continued on until February 1968. And as for the remainder of the cantata itself? Jim Yester has commented that the band had approached Webb once again, in more recent years, with the notion of cutting the full concept in its entirety but, sadly, neither Webb nor Howe ever recorded the expansive project onto tape, and Webb never successfully transcribed the music or lyrics onto paper either. Subsequently, Old Father Time eventually took his toll on the memories of all concerned and the melodies and words have faded away. We shall now never hear those now long-forgotten interludes… or could we anyway? The question must be raised that did it ever even exist in such a complex nature, except in the confused 1960s recollections of those who were reportedly there? That theory is brought into being by the simple fact that Jimmy Webb himself, in more recent years (and in his recently published autobiography), has gone on record suggesting that, other than "MacArthur Park", there WERE no other songs of note and there never was an extended cantata. He wrote the one variable piece simply with The Association in mind.

"I played 'MacArthur Park', singing in my tremulous tenor as Bones studiously turned the pages. The band listened courteously to all seven and a half minutes. It felt long to me and I could feel their interest heighten with the up-tempo section, tailored especially for them.

"Various stories have been floated about from time to time about these simple events over the years, (but) The Association were not discourteous and did not mistreat me in any way. Bones was pissed. I just went out and bought new jeans…" [53]

So where did this brazened 24-minute notion come from? Various members of the band, along with Bones Howe, all testify to its existence. Others still refute the fact. Terry Kirkman has gone on record suggesting, "It certainly ran at least eight minutes…" so was the work just "MacArthur Park", and no more, just maybe in an extended format? The mystery remains…

November 18th and 19th 1967 saw the group feature as part of an impressive weekend billing on the west coast, performing in the cavernous 11,000-seat Cow Palace in Daly City, bordering with San Francisco, on the Saturday night, and then at the even larger imposing Hollywood Bowl on the following evening. Performing alongside them on both nights were Sopwith Camel, Eric Burden & The Animals, The Everly Brothers, The Sunshine Company and, still fresh from their momentous slot at The Monterey Festival (and billed as 'Special Guest Stars'), The Who. With at least three chart-topping acts on the bill, and the wild and reckless UK hit makers currently making their own wave of destruction Stateside, it was an impressive line-up and one that came with a certain of publicity surrounding it.

Tickets to the musical extravaganza are free with any purchase of MGM or Warner Brothers stereo album at any Bay Area White Front store, sponsor of the event. TV personality Sam Riddle will produce and emcee the show, which will run for two and one-half hours.

The Oakland Tribune
November 7 1967

In a clever marketing ploy, the more albums you purchased beforehand, the closer to the stage your 'free' seat was, and with The Who scheduled to close the both shows, potentially down to their onstage tendency to wreck both instrument and equipment as a finale, both appearances drew vast crowds (reportedly, Keith Moon sealed their reputation by discarding various parts of his drum kit into the famed Hollywood Bowl moat at the conclusion of their set). Unfortunately, the Hollywood Bowl outdoors show was hit heavily by a torrential rainstorm mid-way through, which threatened to bring proceedings to an early conclusion until, somewhat appropriately, the L.A. pop sounds of The Sunshine Company came onstage and the clouds fortuitously parted…

Four days later and the 3,500-seat Civic Opera House in Chicago hosted The Association for the first time, shadowed over the following weeks by similar sized venues in Texas, Indiana and Michigan, ably supported for part of the tour by a Chicago-based show band named The Mob, fronted by two hit songwriters named Jim Holvay and Gary Biesbier (who achieved greater fame by penning a number of Top 10 hits for The Buckinghams).

Finally, as 1967 drew to a close, and with Lansing, Michigan fading away into the distance, Terry, Jim, Ted, Russ, Brian and Larry found themselves airborne once more, flying back home for the festive season with a short break in their frenetic schedule, spending the last few days of December, and the early part of January 1968 holed up in Western studios, with Bones Howe and his 'crew', cutting further tracks for the upcoming fourth album, including work on a second Yester-Carmel collaboration; the exquisite "Barefoot Gentleman", a pure delight of harmony group vocal texturing, along with a reflective solo work from Russ, "The Time It Is Today", and a brand new Ramos-Alcivar-Ortega jazz-orientated composition entitled "Like Always", featuring some intricate vaudeville piano playing from Larry Knechtel, hidden beneath the vocal backdrop.

"That one was a kind of jazz fusion type thing" Larry would later remark, when recalling the song. "We had a fugue in the middle of it, which went from 3/4 to 4/4 at the fusion. Since we could do that kind of stuff, why not? Why limit yourself to just rock and roll?"

1968 would go on to bring yet further success, albeit with an air of finality around much of the subsequent proceedings. It would see fleeting acceptance in foreign climes, missed opportunities, changes in appearance and then, towards the end of the year a familiar face back within the inner circle – well traveled, but fresh with new ideas and musical directions. It was a time for livin'...

CHAPTER TWELVE

COME ON IN

Since his departure from the band during the early spring of 1967, and his subsequent journey up the coastline to Monterey, Jules Alexander had taken the opportunity to travel. As had been his intention, part of his journey was in visiting areas of secluded, hidden India where he took the opportunity to embrace the traditions, religions and philosophies that surrounded him, 8,000 miles from home. He wasn't the first to travel from Los Angeles to such distant Himalayan hills to reflect on life in such peaceful settings, but such was the fascination and desire to uncover the mystical Indian wisdoms that Jules, along with a number of other associates and friends, studio engineer Henry Lewy included (who had worked on the *Renaissance* LP), became keen advocates on the practices of meditation and subsequently made their own spiritual pilgrimages to experience the methods and lifestyles first hand.

With his former band now riding a huge commercial wave, following the impact that both "Windy" and "Never My Love" were making, Jules (now having decided to formally revert to his given Christian name) and his wife, Christie, and their young daughter Eden, eschewed the celebrity lifestyle and headed east, via Europe and beyond, towards northern India, seeking enlightenment in the shadows of the mountain ranges. Settling in a small village along the banks of the Beas River, a day's journey from the more familiar meditational surroundings of Maharishi Mahesh Yogi's settlement in Rishikesh, the family intended to spend an extended period of time, absorbing the tranquility of the region. Unfortunately, after a few months of reflection, Christie injured her back and with minimal treatment available in such rural settings the family thought it best to return Stateside where she could receive specialist treatment and rest in more comfortable surroundings and so, cutting the experience short, they flew home to Los Angeles. Not that it had all been the idyllic lifestyle that they had envisaged:

"I spent eight or nine months in India" Jules recounted during 1984, "and it gave me an interesting point of view, but for me it didn't work. I discovered I wasn't a recluse who can go off to live in the mountains." [20]

The hardships of rural India, and the luxuries of western civilization are often too diverse a parity to combine, as The Beatles themselves were also to discover when their celebrity party, including wives and friends, along with Donovan, Mia Farrow, The Beach Boys' Mike Love and the world's media descended on the rudimentary settlement in Rishikesh, and settled under the watchful, and some may say roving eye of Maharishi shortly afterwards. Some take to the rigors of basic foods and little comfort with aplomb, others not so, but back home in California, with an influx of new musical ideas in his mind, Jules put the brief sojourn down to experience and, moving forward, he began formulating the idea of putting a new band together, searching for like-minded souls to work alongside. Firstly, he recruited a neighbor of his, a singer and keyboard player named Richard Ellison who also lived up in the Beachwood Canyon district and then, after talking with Brian Cole about the potential idea, he contacted a talented young drummer that Brian was a close friend with, one whom was building up a healthy reputation around the Los Angeles studio scene. Michael Botts, a good-looking Sacramento-born percussionist (and future member of soft-rock band Bread), and an occasional housemate of Brian, had in recent years been working as a member of The Travelers 3, the folk trio (now a quartet) who had originally been a part of the Troubadour stable of artists. With the folk music genre declining in popularity, and the booking schedule for the band slowly drying up, Mike had begun working the studio scene, often bringing along his high school friend and bass playing partner, Joe LaManno, a latter-day Traveler himself, to complete the rhythm section. Once Jules had approached Mike, at his recommendation both LaManno and another friend, Larry Hanson, a former guitarist with the Sacramento-based band Aeriel Landscape, were recruited to the line-up. This new five-piece collection labeled themselves Joshua Fox, and they spent the next few months continuously writing and rehearsing, playing and developing their own unique sound, often accompanied by a young roadie named Darryl Palagi, who would not only work for the new band during their formative performances but who would also go on to find a home with The Association shortly afterwards.

At one stage all five band members actually lived together in a loft on Hollywood Boulevard, affectionately referred to as 'the foxhole', surrounded by equipment supplied by The Association, who even went to the extent of buying groceries and pot for their friends in order to sustain their minimal income. According to Mike Botts' biography, detailed in the book *Bread: A Sweet Surrender* (as written by this author):

> With his experience in the industry to date, plus a certain amount of financial input courtesy of Association royalties, Jules Alexander was thus seen as the undisputed bandleader and it was therefore assumed that they would fall under the wing of The Association's own management arm. Instead, at the suggestion of Mike, Joe and Larry, they opted to go with Charlie Oyama, their former Travelers 3 associate, who was now running a production and management venture. During the initial period of writing, rehearsing and jamming the band gradually began building up a buzz around town and the talk was that they were going to be the next big thing, and so Charlie Oyama set up an audition with Tetragrammaton Records, a label founded by comedian Bill Cosby back at the start of the decade (and most notably famous for 'handling' the infamous Lennon-Ono *Two Virgins* album). The band played a fifteen-minute live set at the loft in Hollywood for label heads Roy Silver and Artie Mogul, and they made an offer on the spot. After all of the negotiations were done, and the contracts were signed, the band began working with one of the label's own producers, but before the actual recording had barely started, the original band broke up, Jules Alexander deciding that it wasn't really working for him. He subsequently left, taking his friend Richard Ellison with him.

> *Bread: A Sweet Surrender*
> Malcolm C. Searles

Charlie Oyama recalls: "It was not a bitter parting, just too 'chemically' influenced. But the company still wanted the remaining members to go ahead with the recording..."

Even without Jules in the band, the remaining band members, along with new recruit Tom Menefee, still delivered a fine album to the label, issued the following year as Tetragrammaton T-125. Comprising of a number of self-composed songs, the highlight of which was the sublime "Billy Goat Capricorn Lover", co-written by Jules and Larry Hansen during the initial formation period of the group and a tune that, once recorded, shared its harmonic influences with the similar styles that the newly united trio of David Crosby, Stephen Stills and Graham Nash were experimenting with at the same time.

It's very funky at times I must say
Seeing your monkey a stone's throw away
Collecting the pennies from people that pray
Marbles and chocolate and things like today
Billy Goat Capricorn Lover, you've got to stay away

"Billy Goat Capricorn Lover"
Words and Music by Jules Alexander-Larry Hansen

Sadly, financial issues at the label resulted in a lack of promotion for the release, and it folded shortly afterwards, depriving not only Joshua Fox of further promotional backing but also that of another release, one that had been issued earlier, during 1968.

Released as T-114, on the same Tetragrammaton label, the lone ten-track album by the band Summerhill would have escaped the watchful eye of many an Association follower during this era. Cut at the famed Wally Heider Studios in Hollywood, and filled with a mixed selection of in-band compositions, crossing heavy rock with folk and blues, country with psychedelia, Cream with The Beatles, the four members who made up this band were lead guitarist Alan Parker, rhythm guitarist Larry Hickman, drummer Doug Burger and, holding down the bass role, and fresh out of The New Society (as were both Parker and Hickman), Del Ramos, Larry's brother.

"When The New Society broke up the girls went their own way and the guys stuck together," confirms Del. "and we went onto Bill Cosby's label. One of the songs I cut for the album, "Bring Me Round", was written in Topanga Canyon. We were living in a band house there, trying to survive, and I just picked up the guitar one night while I was laying around in front of the fireplace and I played this one riff that I thought 'Ah, this is kinda like Cream', so I started writing lyrics to it and at that point we were trying to put the album together, and we needed about three songs, so I said 'I could put some stuff together'. Alan Parker, our lead guitarist, who was a great talent, helped me write some of the lyrics."

Del contributed three songs to the final selection, the above mentioned "Bring Me Round", a heavy riff-laden rocker, the mid-'60s Beatle-ish "It's Gonna Rain", with its fuzz-pop-psychedelia overtones, and the bizarre piano-filled ballad "The Bird", which pairs delicate sensitivity with shotgun sound effects, topped off with an excerpt of Frankie Laine's "Cry Of The Wild Goose". Sad to say, but the virtual non-existence of any financial support that Tetragrammaton was able to offer the release contributed significantly to its lack of success and the album swiftly slid away into obscurity and cult status, as did the band itself a short while later.

Meanwhile, Jules Alexander, still developing his plans for Joshua Fox during this period, was also heavily into a songwriting phase following his return to the United States. With a host of new compositions such as "Sundown Risetime", "Night Amongst The Mirrors", "Everything Is Perfectly What It Is" and "Lovin' Stew" being worked upon during this heady period, all written in partnership with one Jeffrey Comanor, a burgeoning young New York-based hitmaker and a former member of the East Village outfit called The Hi-Five, the immediate future looked immensely satisfying for the former Associate. Indeed, one particular new song was taken into the studios and worked on by none other than Bones Howe, currently dividing his studio time with, not only The Association but a host of other artists, including the immensely popular pop/soul quintet, The 5th Dimension, who had first hit big the previous year with a Johnny Rivers-produced rendition of the Jimmy Webb tune "Up, Up and Away". The 5th Dimension's connection with The Association doesn't stop there however, and for the group's upcoming 1968 album, to be titled *Stoned Soul Picnic*, Howe brought in, not only one of the collaborations between Jules and Comanor, the uptempo "Lovin' Stew", but he also utilized the vocal arranging talents of one Bob Alcivar, first introduced to him as one of Larry Ramos' songwriting partners. Alcivar would go on to become an essential part of the 5th Dimension's vocal arranging team during the peak of their successes to come.

One of the purest slices of sunshine pop the 5th Dimension ever produced, "Lovin' Stew" is a hazily psychedelic layering of strings, horns, and beautiful overdubbed harmonies enlivened by a chorus featuring that all-time sunshine pop mainstay, the "ba-ba-ba" backing vocal. The lyrics feature the sort of metaphor that falls apart if you think about it too long, imagining love as some kind of giant delicatessen…or something like that. "Lovin' Stew" was just an album track, but it's one of the 5th Dimension's most effective blends of pop, psych, and soul.

All Music Review
Stewart Mason

For The Association 1968 commenced with the usual mix of recording dates, still working at Western Recorders, TV appearances and a slew of cross country concerts. The first week of January saw further session work undertaken on both "Everything That Touches You" and "Birthday Morning", with key players Hal Blaine, Joe Osborn and Larry Knechtel all in attendance, Osborn nailing the intricate bass line intro to the first tune, as laid out for him by Randy Sterling two months earlier, whilst the complex vocal arrangements, as constructed by Bob Alcivar for his own first studio session with the band, were performed supremely. Presumably, both songs were completed in one long sitting as that same week saw the band lip-sync to both completed tracks for a recording on *The Smothers Brothers Comedy Hour*, scheduled for broadcast on the 14th of that month. Smartly dressed in unmatching (yes, *unmatching!*) browns, whites and oranges for the first slot they put in, as to be expected, a slick polished performance, with Terry and a freshly-mustachioed Jim providing the sweet blending of the lead vocals, whilst for the slower ballad they appeared in equally daring individual outfits, patterned shirts and vests, with Jim in a high turtle-necked zippered jacket and top. Finally, it seemed, they were a-movin' with the times and were opting to venture away from the staid, matching suits of the previous years, although Terry's on-set placement, center stage, behind a small electric keyboard, unconvincingly following the dexterous fingering of Larry Knechtel's studio work, and Ted's attempt to mimic Hal Blaine's flourishes, were a moot point. Nevertheless, the talented studio musicians who created these intricate patterns were, more often than not, equally willing to help the actual band members themselves in recreating their parts, despite a lack of reciprocation towards their anonymity status…

Jim Yester: "In '68 the (Wrecking Crew) were laying down the music for one of our songs and we were all watching in the booth. Ted was looking at Hal Blaine playing this incredible part, thinking, 'How the hell am I going to play that?' This song had a very difficult, and highly unusual drum part. Hal sat down with Ted and very patiently showed him how to approach it, and play the part, step by step..." [27]

Bass player Joe Osborn remembers: "At one session, the guys in The Association said 'Please don't tell anybody that you guys played on the records.' They wanted their fans to think they played..."

"I wanted to put the names (of the session players) on the back of the album when it was finished. And they wouldn't let me..." summarizes Bones Howe. [27]

January 1968 saw The Association honored with a *Bill Gavin* award for the 'Best Pop-Rock Artist', a privilege bestowed on a select few courtesy of the U.S. Radio Programming Society, with the notable runners-up in that particular category being a former mop-topped quartet from Liverpool, still plowing their own groundbreaking field. Shortly afterwards they were presented with a series of gold disc awards by Joe Smith, the General Manager for Warner Bros. Records, acknowledging the phenomenal sales figures for both the *And Then... Along Comes The Association* and *Insight Out* albums, along with their "Never My Love" 45.

January 1968 was the month The Association received their gold record for the (first) album, signifying sales of one million. "It was recorded before I joined the group," admits Larry Ramos, "but it's still pretty good anyway!"

Their fourth long object d'art is due out any day now. Says Ted of the latest: "Ten of the cuts on it are original compositions and, as any group, we like to grow. We are trying some new things, especially a lot of new vocal concepts on this album."

Patty Johnson
KRLA Beat

With the deadline for delivering their completed fourth album looming the remainder of January and early February was spent toiling in the studio, delivering the best work they possibly could within the restricted time frame permitted. Even then, they were still committed to a number of concerts in between the many stressful vocal sessions, appearing at the Community Concourse in San Diego on January 6th, with Gary Puckett & The Union Gap, and then two weeks later at a U.C.L.A. performance, lining up onstage alongside Miriam Makeba, Oscar Brown Jr., Jean Pace and The Stone Poneys, the latter act featuring their old Troubadour and Ice House friend Linda Ronstadt. A second televised appearance on *The Joey Bishop Show* was also broadcast that same week.

Back in the studio, amongst the many new tunes that they were now working on for the album, in addition to those previously listed, were the inventive shifting patterns of Ted's "Hear In Here" (Ted later commenting that he was late in attending the vocal session, causing a delay to the day's process), Terry's imaginative multi-part "The Bus Song", incorporating Bob Alcivar's vocal arrangement on the live barbershop bridge, along with another opportunity for Jim to deliver one of his beautiful ballads with the smooth, string-laden sounds of "Rose Petals, Incense And A Kitten" which, despite the overtly saccharine labeling, was truly a highlight of Bones' production techniques and that of the album's co-arrangers Ray Pohlman (who wrote most of the charts for the sessions), Bill Holman and Alcivar. Ace session guitarist Tommy Tedesco ('the most recorded guitarist in history' according to *Guitar Player* magazine) provided the gentle acoustic guitar work, sitting amongst a wash of harmonies and a subtle string section, led by violinist Sidney Sharp, the latter so reminiscent of the Al DeLory arrangements utilized on the Jimmy Webb-Glen Campbell hits from that same era.

"We sat in the booth and did rough mixes of those multi-movement songs," reveals Terry, when reminiscing over the *Birthday* sessions, "and people were crying! We never got that in the final mix. The technology could never get that in the mix and press it. It never captured it. I had long conversations with Bill Holman who did the horns on that, and nobody had ever asked him to voice horns like we did before. Two tubas, two French horns and two flugelhorns, and it would replicate the male vocal sound. He'd never had to do that before.

"Now days I also get a chill when I think of the middle verse of 'The Bus Song' – 'the hours come, don't go anywhere, the world shrinks down to the kitchen and den, with fleeting thoughts of what might have been, so little time left to prepare' – I am so very much living that scene day to day right now!"

Rounding out the album were three non-band composed tunes, the first of which had come to the groups attention courtesy of an arrangement by the Modern Folk Quartet, by then performing as a quintet following the addition of drummer Eddie Hoh, whilst also dabbling with a potential name change to either The Fat City Four or Your Friends. Fortunately, they wisely avoided both.

Jim and Jerry Yester had first stumbled across the Chicago-born Jo Mapes when they had attended one of her concerts during the early '60s, and Jerry's band had later adapted her composition, "Come On In", for a 1965 appearance on the popular *Shindig* TV show. Mapes was a upcoming singer and songwriter who had moved across to Los Angeles at an early age and had become a regular performer on the then-burgeoning 1960s folk revival circuit, in addition to often appearing on the ABC broadcast *Hootenanny* TV shows. She had written and recorded her own version of the song during 1964 with the inspiration drawing from the songwriter's personal perspective…

Over and over I told myself
I said Jo, you gotta lose the blues now
Get ready for the day when he comes home
I dusted off your pipe and polished up your shoes
Come on in

"Come On In"
Words and Music by Jo Mapes

The MFQ had subsequently taken and re-arranged the song the following year, adding a driving, upbeat tempo, a feature that The Association subsequently incorporated into their own studio rendition of the song, with Terry and Russ blending over the lead vocals and a pulsating, descending bass riff. Unfortunately, that didn't sit too well with Mapes herself: "Jo wasn't real happy about the way each of us did it, 'cause she envisioned much more of a soft kind of folk delivery, and we both had kind of hard-edged, rock things," Jim later recalled.

Indeed, Jo Mapes original version of the song, as featured on her *And You Were On My Mind* LP (FM Records 317), was a far gentler, acoustically arranged take, although this is not to say that the later upbeat arrangement didn't work, far from it, and it went onto make a wonderful introductory opening to the new Association album when it finally hit the stores. In addition, for a short period afterwards, it also became the opening number to the band's concert appearances, held throughout 1968.

Interestingly, that very same week that The Association were recording the final notes for their take of the song, elsewhere in the very same Western Studios building Peter Tork of The Monkees, accompanied by Stephen Stills and Dewey Martin from Buffalo Springfield and Lance Wakely, a friend from Greenwich Village, were also cutting their version of the same song. Coincidence or competition? Planned for an upcoming Monkees album, although ultimately unreleased until a 1990s rarities retrospective appeared, Tork's rendition featured a notably slower understanding, closer to how Mapes had imagined it, dominated by Still's sublime guitar work and Tork's somewhat limited vocal abilities although that could not take away the simple and delightful melody that accompanied each and every variation of the composition.

Jeff Comanor's "Toymaker" was the second of the outside contributions to the upcoming album, propelled by Larry Knechtel's simple clockwork chord pattern on the piano, whilst the final offering, another one from the pen of the reliable Addrisi Brothers, was the most commercial of the tunes to make the final song selection, and one that didn't sit comfortably with some of the more serious members of the band. Once again, as it had been with "Windy", it was almost that one-step too far, one step too close towards the much-maligned bubblegum tendencies that were still prevalent throughout the industry after the initial 'Summer of Love' boom, courtesy of The Lemon Pipers and their late '67 hit "Green Tambourine", followed by The 1910 Fruitgum Company and "Simon Says". The genre would subsequently peak over the following years with the success of The Ohio Express's two hits, "Yummy Yummy Yummy" and "Chewy Chewy", and the epitome of bubblegum; The Archies "Sugar Sugar". Nevertheless, so closely pop-orientated was the new Addrisi brothers composition, "Time For Livin'", that, for a period, The Association veered ominously close to the borderlines that surrounded these differing genres, occasionally sharing ink space within the same media reviews as the above-noted acts, a miscalculation potentially far more damaging than can have been appreciated at the time.

The first the public heard from these new sessions was when the debut single appeared during the early weeks of the year, pairing the Kirkman-penned pop-precision of "Everything That Touches You" with, in a somewhat surprising marketing move, Ted's "We Love Us", a song lifted from the previous album. Needless to say, focus and publicity was heavily driven towards the leading side, ensuring yet another runaway success in the chart lists, with a peak position of number 10 in *Billboard* during early March (ironically, five places below "Simon Says"), and a number 11 placing in *Cash Box*.

> Long-awaited follow-up to "Never My Love" is another compelling ballad with a driving dance beat in strong support. Chalk up another top 10 winner for the smooth group.
>
> *Billboard*
> January 20 1968

It then came as no surprise, that soon after the vocal sessions were completed, and even whilst Bones Howe was still in the studio sweetening the final mixes of the completed album, the band members themselves were once again winging their way, cross country, to their stronghold Midwestern states of Ohio, Nebraska, Illinois and Michigan for a series of shows that ultimately continued on, running through until the late spring, by which time they had crisscrossed through twelve or more further state lines, accompanied at various stages by fellow headlining acts such as Spanky & Our Gang, the jazz-pop crossover appeal of The Ramsey Lewis Trio, or local bands such as Burlington's Brian, Bill, Betty & Tony. For a working band The Association truly took the phrase to the extreme...

CHAPTER THIRTEEN

TIME FOR LIVIN'

February 17 1968: Allentown, PA

February 18 1968: Music Hall, Cincinnati, OH

February 20 1968: Veterans Memorial Auditorium, Columbus, OH

February 21 1968: Public Hall, Cleveland, OH

February 22 1968: Springfield, PA

February 23 1968: Georgia Coliseum, Athens, GA

February 24 1968: Northwestern University, Evanston, IL

February 25 1968: Memorial Gymnasium, Orono, ME

February 29th 1968, and The Association, much like the previous year, were once again up for various nominations at the annual *Grammy* awards. With the phenomenal successes of both "Windy" and "Never My Love" it came as no surprise to see both songs listed amongst the varying categories, with "Windy" up for Best Arrangement and Best Contemporary Vocal, and "Never My Love" falling into the Best Group Vocal Performance category. In addition, the album they had featured on, *Insight Out*, also made the nominations within the Best Contemporary Album category. Sadly, despite the positive response that each release had received, once again all nominations failed to bear fruit as they lost out during the evening awards – held once more at the Beverly Hilton Hotel – to The Beatles and their *Sgt. Pepper's Lonely Hearts Club Band* masterwork (Best Contemporary Album), Bobby Gentry's "Ode To Billie Joe" (Best Arrangement), and, much to Bones Howe's mixed delight, The 5th Dimension and "Up, Up And Away", which scooped both the Best Contemporary Vocal and Best Group Vocal Performance categories. Exactly *who* was Bones rooting for during the evening celebrations?

The same day that the awards took place The Association appeared on a yet another TV variety show, adding further claim as to the distancing from their true folk/rock roots. Wigs and tight-fitting pants were one thing, but a fully choreographed dance routine was another ball game altogether.

The Carol Channing and 101 Men TV Special, hosted by the popular dancer, actress and comedienne, featured the band miming to "Windy", tailored in Edwardian dress, foolishly frolicking across the set, sliding down stairway handrails, and generally playing up to the frivolity of it all. But if that wasn't enough – the band then broke out into a shortened, re-arranged rendition of "Along Comes Mary", substituting the 'Mary' lyric for 'Carol', whilst the hostess and Larry frugged it out before the applauding audience, with Russ joining in alongside.

"Carol asked, 'How many of you can dance?' and only Russ and I raised our hands," said Larry. They were subsequently taught the choreography, and reportedly needed only one rehearsal to get the moves down right. [50]

"We were always pretty comfortable with doing television," says Jim today. "We did so many small local shows when we were starting out, that by the time we got to the bigger shows we were old hands at it. The ones that were most fun were the ones like Carol's show, where we were involved in more than just the music. Like The Smothers Brothers, we were part of skits and got to wear costumes, and they always had the greatest sets for their shows…"

That same month saw another small entry into the Association curiosity file when, over 5,000 miles away, a relatively successful Swedish band named The Hep Stars recorded a version of "Enter The Young" as the opening track on their new *It's Been A Long Long Time* album (Cupol CLPNS-342). Clearly influenced by the harmonic sound developing on the American west coast, this Scandinavian release also featured a version of the Boettcher and Alexander collaboration "Would You Like To Go" (previously cut during the 1966 *Ballroom* sessions) along with four other Boettcher-connected compositions. Quite possibly, other than in their homeland, this Swedish quintet wouldn't have achieved much acknowledgment for their recorded output, and their Association connection would have been lost forever were it not for the fact that the keyboard player, Benny Andersson, then went on to form ABBA, one of the most successful Swedish exports around the globe... ever. Nevertheless, their rendition of the Terry Kirkman tune remained faithful to the original. However, this wasn't the first time that another artist had covered the work of The Association. Indeed, the previous year had seen a number of cover versions grace the record racks and radio airwaves across the U.S., with at least six recognized performers recording their own version of "Cherish" – The Lettermen, The Four Tops, Petula Clark and the sublime Nina Simone included. That same year The Letterman also cut a version of the Addrisi Brothers' "Don't Blame It On Me" for their June '67 *Warm* LP. Other covers of note during the period included Denmark's The Red Squares and the L.A.-based Leathercoated Minds working on 1967 versions of "Along Comes Mary", the latter as a part of the mind-altering *A Trip Down The Sunset Strip* album – a bizarre collection of chemically-enhanced cover songs featuring, amongst others, J.J. Cale making some early formative steps in the recording industry. Then there was Sandy Nelson's instrumental take on "Pandora's Golden Heebie Jeebies", as featured on the Imperial Records *Cheetah Beat* LP, The Teddy Neeley Five and their version of "Autumn Afternoon" (still unreleased by The Association at that time) and the Pittsburgh-based Racket Squad with their authentic 1968 interpretation of Jim's "No Fair At All" (also covered by Buffalo's Subconscious Mind the following year). Mason Williams later cut a version of Jules' and Jim's "Come To Me" (with The Clinger Sisters) whilst, perhaps unsurprisingly, there was also a succession of "Never My Love" recordings, ranging from The Lennon Sisters, Vikki Carr and The Anita Kerr Singers, through to Booker T & The MGs, George Shearing, The Four Freshmen and the obscure UK-based band Plastic Penny. It could be argued that none of them matched the originality, or quality of the Association's versions, but it is in recognition of their output that such established and, in some cases, relatively obscure artists chose to acknowledge and offer up their own interpretations. And there would be more in the coming years...

Birthday, the fourth album to be released by The Association appeared in the stores on March 7th 1968. Issued by Warners Bros. Records (W-1733/WS-1733), and packaged in would-be-psychedelic splendor, featuring a photograph by celebrity snapper George Rodriguez colorfully adapted by artist Wayne Kimbell (who had also designed sleeves for The 5th Dimension, The Nitty Gritty Dirt Band and Johnny Rivers during that same year), the album was eagerly snapped up by the legions of fans across the country and yet, for reasons unclear, and despite the quality that simply oozed from each darkened groove of the vinyl, it failed to connect with the mass populous in the same way that its predecessor had, despite a series of favorable reviews.

> The Association should soon be seeing chart action with this LP of pop melodies. The album promises to develop into a huge hit.
>
> *Cash Box*
> April 1968

Subsequent sales were slow, resulting in a peak appearance at Number 23 in the *Billboard* charts just three months after release, and whilst the lush sounds and pop orchestration that runs throughout the featured eleven song selection highlighted the sophisticated partnership they had formed with Bones Howe as to why it failed to click amongst the record buying population in the quantities it deserved remains a mystery. Certainly, in a chart topped by Simon & Garfunkel's wondrous *Bookends* album, sitting alongside *The Graduate* soundtrack, the listings for June 1968 were filled by a succession of releases certainly not superior by any definition. The Monkees fifth album (and their first non chart-topper), *The Birds, The Bees & The Monkees*, Bobby Goldsboro's *Honey*, Herb Alpert's *Beat Of The Brass* and Aretha Franklin's *Lady Soul* all sat comfortably high on the charts that week, whilst records by Moby Grape, The Lettermen and Ed Ames kept The Association from breaking into the Top 20 with, what some may argue, was their finest collective offering.

Nevertheless, undaunted, and keen to popularize their music to a wider audience, the band issued a follow-up single in the wake of the album's release and made plans to travel abroad, lining up a promotional tour in Europe, despite Pat Colecchio's concerns over the financial payback from such a venture. In the interim, the spring 1968 tour continued, buoyed by the constant demand for personal appearances and the needs of the American public to briefly escape from political issues and the many other social concerns that were flooding the nation's media day by day, such as the increasing deployment of U.S. troops into South-East Asia, street protests and rioting.

The Association, producers of such top hits as "Cherish" and "Windy" played in Patrick Gymnasium Sunday night and the kids packed the place. Tickets were $3 apiece. How many in the crowd? "About 3,100" said Paul Shambio of the University of Vermont Interfraternity Council.

If the kids care that much to pay that much to hear a group, then those guys have something to say that the rest of us don't. They do.

They've been on the road constantly and get home occasionally. Meanwhile, they're playing the riot circuit. They went from Burlington to Baltimore and on to Washington. That wasn't the way they planned it but that's how it turned out.

Larry Ramos: "We don't expect any problems because we'll be working colleges and college kids have enough sense, they're more aware of their position in the world. They aren't in on this race stuff. I have faith in America."

The Burlington Free Press
April 11 1968

With a vast portion of America reeling in turmoil, Civil Rights activist Martin Luther King falling prey to an assassin's bullet just three days prior to their appearance in Vermont, tension amongst the many highly populated cities of the U.S. was high and many a town was engulfed in the riots on a grand scale, but for one brief evening, city by city, town by town, one after another, much of the college population could forget the ongoing battles in an scarred outside world and get caught up in the excitement of the concert tour. And it wasn't just The Association spending endless weeks on the road, playing in nameless towns and colleges. Sharing the bill with the band during the latter end of this particular tour were artists such as Sly & The Family Stone, The Delfonics, Billy Vera & Judy Clay, The Esquires and The Entertainers, and it wasn't just restricted to a select few performers out on the so-called 'riot circuit' either. Many of the headlining bands and artists of that era were constantly out onstage, playing the same circuit in the cities and in the backwoods, thousands of miles from home, spreading the message of peace, love and unity. Heaven knows they needed it. And even if the band threw in the occasional political statement – a requiem for the masses – it was greeted with rapturous applause, from one free-speaking member of the youth culture to another. And it was good money to boot.

And Pat Colecchio knew it. Hence his reluctance to take The Association away from home soil, where the dollar was good, and dally with the foreign Antipodean market, where they were constantly being barraged for touring, or the potentially lucrative European market where, to date, the band had surprisingly failed to garner any significant success, particularly in the U.K. where much of the world's musical focus had shifted in recent years, sustained by the developing fashions on London's Carnaby Street and Kings Road, and the hip crowds and nightlife of the city's epicenter. However, distribution in Europe was a moot point for the band members, who were only too keen to see their success replicated abroad.

"When Warner Bros. bought Valiant records what they didn't get was the international distribution contract," Terry recalls. "Whoever Valiant had, it wasn't who Warner Bros. had, and that was the mistake in the purchase."

To date, and despite six releases on the successful London Records label, and a more recent issue on Warner Bros. once the distribution rights had been settled, The Association had failed to make any indent on the British chart lists, surprisingly so given the U.K.'s seeming penchant for a strong melody and harmony, but with a new 45 pressed for release, the Addrisi Brothers hook-laden "Time For Livin'" WB-7195 (and paired off with "Birthday Morning"), the band planned their debut appearances across the waters.

Despite the reluctance of certain members of the band to record the tune in the first place the choice of "Time For Livin'" as the next single was perhaps driven by the desire for the perfect summer anthem, a melody that gets in the mind and is not easy to shake off, and one that this particular song had in abundance. It reeked of 1968 pop commercialism. Certainly, Larry Ramos, whom, as Terry Kirkman was now becoming all-too-aware, was veering the direction of the band towards a more commercial vein, saw the potential that the unforgettable, yet simple melody had to offer.

Larry: "There was a contingent in the group that said, 'Oh man, it's so bubblegum,' and I said, 'Hey look, it's a good piece of music. It's fun, its summer, let's put it out! Let's dance!'" [24]

Clearly one of the voices opposing the release, Terry had this to say in later years: "'Time For Livin', in my opinion, was a nail in the coffin for The Association. I thought so before we recorded it and fought with the group over it ever being on the album. Pat Colecchio and I both predicted the problems that would arise with a song that basically mundane if it got singles treatment from Warner Bros. We sat in the office and said to the rest of the group 'do *not* do this song! If you put out that song with that insipid lyric, and with everything else that's going on in this country, we're done!' But Bones Howe wanted us to do the song, Warner Bros. wanted us to do the song..."

One other deciding factor in the choice may well have been the result of a questionnaire, put out by the Association Admiration Aggregation in the regular newsletter, asking for members to offer their own opinions for the next single.

Our new album BIRTHDAY will be at your record stores any day now. For those of you who get the album we would like to have you participate in choosing our next single release. We feel good about all the cuts and therefore your opinions would be greatly appreciated. If I may make one suggestion, before you submit your entry listen to the album enough times to make a valid choice.

Pat Colecchio Enterprises

March 1 1968: Northern Illinois University, DeKalb, IL
March 2 1968: City Auditorium, Omaha, NE
March 3 1968: Mason City Auditorium, Mason City, IA
March 4 1968: Elmhurst College, Elmhurst, IL
March 5 1968: McCormick Hall Gym, Illinois State Uni, Normal, IL
March 7 1968: Whiting Auditorium, Flint, MI
March 9 1968: Washington Avenue Armory, Albany, NY
March 10 1968: Eastman Theater, Rochester, NY
March 12 1968: University of Oklahoma, Norman, OK
March 13 1968: Oklahoma State University, Stillwater, OK
March 14 1968: Trinity University, San Antonio, TX
March 15 1968: Texas A&M University, College Station, TX
March 16 1968: Civic Center, Monroe, LA

Once the band had arrived back in Los Angeles, following the culmination of the spring tour, and just before they boarded the airplane to cross the vast Atlantic Ocean for the first time, the six members squeezed in two more TV appearances, both of which aired during the final week of April '68. Surprisingly, neither appearance featured a performance of the new release, with Noel Harrison's *Where The Girls Are* and *The Red Skelton Hour* both focusing on songs that had previously been issued. For the former, broadcast on April 23rd and hosted by the English actor and singer, the band lip-synced to "Everything That Touches You" which, at the time that the pre-production for the show commenced was the current 45 release in circulation (which may explain the choice), before breaking away mid-performance to sit amongst the audience, eyes fully focused upon the girls in attendance, all clearly uncomfortable in such choreographed surroundings. The second song featured on the show was of far more interest as it combined a series of six short individual movies, spliced together into one three-minute featurette, whilst "Windy" played over as the soundtrack. In what today would be deemed as a forerunner to a promotional video, and maybe with the recollections of The Beatles' "Penny Lane"/"Strawberry Fields" footage still in their minds, the band played along for the camera – with Terry sitting at the piano composing, Larry fooling with a series of Monkees cardboard cut outs, and Russ strumming on his guitar with a potato chip. All very surreal, and yet puzzling as to why "Windy" was chosen as the accompanying song? Familiarity? Even with the eventual taping of this particular show a number of weeks in advance of broadcast, with The Byrds, Barbara McNair and Cher also guesting, the preparations would have already been in place for the next album, with the pressing plant machinery warming up and the master reels *en route*. One week later and *The Red Skelton Hour* was broadcast on CBS-TV, this time with three songs featured; "Birthday Morning", "Windy" and "Wasn't It A Bit Like Now (Parallel 23)".

On May 5th 1968, one day after an appearance at the Cornell University in Ithaca, New York, and The Association boarded their flight to Europe for a proposed five-week visit, accompanied by Pete Stefanos, the road manager, and two of their loyal road crew, lighting engineer Ray Staar (then going by the surname of Howton) and soundman Steve Nelson. The first stop was the ancient city of Rome, in Italy where the band were scheduled to perform at the 'First European International Pop Festival' (not to be confused with the 'Monterey International Pop Festival', one year previous), a four-day music-fest held at the Palazzo dello Sport, an impressive indoor arena constructed for the 1960 Rome Olympics. With an array of headlining acts across the four days, including Captain Beefheart & His Magic Band, Donovan, Traffic, Brian Auger with Julie Driscoll & Trinity, Ten Years After and The Byrds,

The Association were booked for the Saturday slot, performing alongside The Move, The Nice and the recently depleted incarnation of Pink Floyd, following the departure of Syd Barrett. In truth, that appeared as a rather mismatched line-up, with the three other acts more inclined to indulge in either wild onstage antics, be it Keith Emerson flipping over his keyboards or Carl Wayne and his fellow Movesters setting off explosives and smoke bombs before a bemused crowd or, in the case of Pink Floyd, engaging in long drawn out instrumentals and navel watching. For their part The Association, who weren't even on the initial drawn up list of invitees (Buffalo Springfield, The Doors and The Lovin' Spoonful reportedly turned down the invitation), put in a respectable performance but, dressed in smart casual suits and playing their lively two-minute pop anthems, seemed at odds with the leather clad The Nice or the long-haired English Floydian hipsters. As for The Move, wallowing in the European successes of recent hits such as "Flowers In The Rain" and "Fire Brigade", they had their short set cut even shorter once the explosives came out and the law enforcement moved in. And the organization of the event proved unquestionably inappropriate as well, with the resulting media, in the aftermath, referring to the gathering as 'a festival that combined chaos and disaster with high hopes and lofty ambition'.

ROME POP FEST DRAWS A ZERO

An international pop music festival held here May 4-7 proved a financial and organizational flop despite the presence of such artists as Donovan, Buffy St Marie, the Pink Floyd and the Byrds. The four evening shows were poorly attended and the amplification system was inadequate.

Billboard

"Rome was wild!" recalled Russ during a 2005 interview. "It was gigantic! They had acts from all over the world. The band that went on before us could play but definitely couldn't sing. The audience started booing and when they wouldn't leave, they rushed the stage! I mean the whole audience jumped up on the stage and literally threw these guys off! They even stole three microphones. Then we had to go on next. It took them 15-20 minutes to get the stage back to order."

Following the disorganization and disappointment of Italy the band flew on to Bremen in Germany, where they taped an appearance on the popular TV show *Beat Club*, sharing the bill once more with Brian Auger, Julie Driscoll & The Trinity. Introduced by top British DJ, Dave Lee Travis, the band ran through a mimed performance of "Time For Livin'", with a recently bearded Ted Bluechel kicking it off with the introductory drum roll and even Terry wholeheartedly joining in, miming the distinctive brass arrangements on his trumpet.

"I had the unenviable task of putting Ted's drums together for each show," says Ray Staar, clearly happy to offer more than his employment as lighting tech would normally require. "And I had this system in place whereby I scratched little notches in the stands, showing me where the stand should go in order for me to know where he likes it, and I tried my best for two years… But every time I set them up he would just redo it!" he adds with a laugh.

Then, with anticipation, the band flew into swinging London for a press conference and three scheduled live performances in the city, the first being an appearance on the UK's top primetime music TV show *Top Of The Pops*, performing the new single. A proposed meeting with The Beatles was even mooted at one point, suggested by Peter Brown from the fab four's own newly formed Apple Corps, but such a gathering never came to pass. Nevertheless, they participated in a series of promotional photo shoots around the capital, posing in front of such illustrious locations as the Prime Minster's residence in Downing Street, and on the grand façade outside the British Museum in Trafalgar Square. Almost unbelievably, with almost fifty years of hindsight, it is now hard to understand the BBC's latter-day decision to wipe off and/or discard many of their old TV footage from the 1960s vaults, a result of recycling the valuable tapes, and The Association's *Top Of The Pops* performance, broadcast on May 9th, was sadly one of those now confirmed as lost. Nevertheless, for many years afterwards, the band members themselves still held fond memories for what was one of their most notable performances outside of the U.S.

Larry: "My memories of London are *Top of the Pops*. There was a little kid running around backstage who was saying hi to everyone he could meet. His name was Elton John!"

Russ: "*Top of the Pops* was fun. When we were on TV in the States we would lip-sync stuff because that's how they did it in those days. For *Top of the Pops* we had to re-record the instrumentals before the show and sang live to the pre-recorded instrumentals 'cause that's how they did it there." [32]

Clearly making an impression amongst their fellow performers in the BBC studio that night, including Herman's Hermits, PJ Proby and The Love Affair, the band then undertook their sole full live performance in the U.K. the following evening at London's famed Tottenham Court Royal venue, home for much of the 1960s to the locally-based Dave Clark Five. The theater was reportedly only about three quarters full, a public clearly unsure as to who these American interlopers were, but DJ David Symonds proclaimed the event to be 'an historic occasion', with the popular U.K. music publication *Record Mirror* reviewing the evening as "they would lift everyone up on a cloud of beautiful vocal and instrumental sounds with 'Cherish', then lower them gently to the ground and sock them on the jaw with a belting version of Dylan's 'One Too Many Mornings'..." That same article also made reference to 'a very funny version of 'Poison Ivy' with church bell sounds, French horn and belting rock.'

Despite the fact that not all the seats were taken, the *New Musical Express* actually stated that their after show party gathered such a crowd that Bill Fowler, assistant to the legendary U.K. media agent Arthur Howes, was unable to get past the doorman and inside.

The following day the touring party briefly jetted across to the European continent for a scheduled appearance in the Netherlands, guesting on the Dutch NCRV-TV broadcast *Twien*, before they returned to London for their third UK appearance, performing a short set at the *New Musical Express* Poll Winners Concert, held on May 12th at the 12,000-seat capacity Wembley Empire Pool. This was an event that took place each year to honor and award the performances from the previous twelve months, as voted for by the *NME* readers and, appearing during the first half of the show, the band put in another spirited performance that impressed even the most sturdier of musical hacks:

> The astonishing musical and vocal mastery of The Association followed – and what a treat they were. All six of them sing and all except the drummer stood in a long line across the stage, each with his own mic, giving out some wonderful sounds. The poignant 'Cherish' was a delight, 'Windy' was greeted with applause and 'Too Many Mornings'

sounded perfect. Surely, on this form, it cannot be long before the big, strong, yet delicate sound of The Association makes it big over here.

UK Music Press

1968

Also appearing at the prestigious event that year, hosted by the star of the top TV show *The Saint*, Roger Moore, were Status Quo, Cliff Richard, The Love Affair, Amen Corner, The Herd, The Move, Dusty Springfield, Scott Walker and, with a surprise guest appearance performing two songs, The Rolling Stones.

You could feel the Empire Pool shaking to its foundations as the roar went up for their first British concert appearance in nearly two years and on came Mick, Brian, Keith, Bill and Charlie. 'Jumpin' Jack Flash', their new single, was inaudible above the din and 'Satisfaction' was only recognizable because of its familiarity – but no-one cared about that. So who says today's pop lacks excitement ?

UK Music Press

1968

Jim Yester recalled "Jagger came to our dressing room and introduced himself and welcomed us to Britain. Very cool. He was so polite and gentlemanly," a fact concurred by Larry: "As I was leaving Mick Jagger was backstage and he took me back into their dressing room where I got to meet the rest of the Stones. His persona was totally different than you see on stage. He's a really nice guy, humble. So were the rest of the Stones, they were all really cool!" [32]

Terry Kirkman was later to sum up their week in the city:

"London memories: beautiful city, great press turnout, great review in the *New Music Express,* meeting Elton John. I must say the most rewarding experience we had in London was doing *Top Of The Pops.* The way they handled our presentation was beautiful, and they looked after us so well. We recorded 'Time For Livin'' live, which is something we're very wary of doing in America. But we worked with their house band and they were so much fun, and so courteous and enthusiastic – we really enjoyed ourselves. (I remember) running inside a bakery on Kings Road to get out of a sudden downpour and tasting samples of everything in the case, and the Playboy

Club and those bunnies, and playing at the annual *NME* concert. We thought the crowd reaction was exceptional considering we were one of twenty acts and that we hadn't been seen before, it was a fun show to do. The Rolling Stones welcoming us so kindly after our set there, and our dressing 'room' in a horse stall for that concert!" [32]

After leaving London behind, along with Ray Staar and Steve Nelson (who weren't needed for the next promotional leg of the tour), they then flew back across the English Channel to Belgium, guesting on the Brussels-based shows *Vibrato* and *Tienerklanken* before, at short notice, being forced to fly back to the U.S. with the remainder of the visit cancelled.

"The tour was interrupted by a strike in Paris," remembers Terry. "We were in Belgium and were on our way to Paris as part of a Warner Bros. five-week 'get to know The Association' tour, then we were going to go to Scandinavia, but the whole continent shut down because of the 1968 riots in Paris. One night I'm in the company of Michelle de Rothschild, and Miss Belgium of the previous year, we're in with the royalty of continental Europe… and the next day we're in Provo, Utah singing to the Mormons at a gig we picked up at the last minute!"

All in all, and excluding the poor promotion and set-up surrounding the inaugural festival in Rome, and the disappointment of an all-too sudden end to the tour, the promotional visit had been a resounding success and the positive reception that they had received could only be a stepping stone on which to build upon, and the need to revisit the distant shores of the U.K. was all too apparent in order to capitalize on this. There were even some initial plans put together to take the group back later that same year to perform a number of shows, and Terry even spoke to the *New Musical Express* at some length about the proposal: "When we went to England this time we realized that we had nothing in our rehearsed patter that would be appropriate to those people. While we can make jokes about George Wallace or LBJ here, though I know about (Prime Minister) Wilson I have no idea what his personality is, nor do I have any idea of how people feel about him. What we'll probably do is work with a European who has a pretty good knowledge of their type of humor and then build an act for that audience."

Sadly, this never came to pass as the band's manager, Pat Colecchio, working out the financial implications from behind his stateside desk, soon concluded that the option of a full tour was non-beneficial from a business perspective. And sadly, that's what it came down to in his eyes: business and the $$$. The May 1968 promotional visit would prove to be the only public European outing of the band's collective career. A fate that many U.K. followers still commiserate over...

Fifty years later, and with despair in his voice, Terry Kirkman summarizes up: "It's one of the most embarrassing things ever! 'Did you tour abroad?' Yes, we did... once!"

THE ASSOCIATION

IN CONCERT

With Special Guest Star

WES MONTGOMERY

May 28 thru June 2 • 1 Week Only

Tues., Wed., Thurs., Fri. at 8:30 P.M. • Sat. at 6:30 & 9:30 P.M. • Sunday at 8:00 P.M.
$2.50, $3.50, $4.50, $5.50

Sunday Matinee at 3:00 P.M.
$2.50, $3.50, $4.50, $5.50

Make check payable to **MELODYLAND THEATRE**,
Box 3460, Anaheim, Calif. (92803)

NAME_____
Please Print

ADDRESS_____PHONE_____

CITY_____ZIP CODE_____
Please enclose self-addressed stamped envelope for return of your tickets

Phone (714) 776-7220

THE ASSOCIATION

Date	Time	Number of Tickets Desired	Price Per Ticket	Total Amount

Payment in full is enclosed. CHECK ☐ MONEY ORDER ☐

☐ Charge to my
BANKAMERICARD # _____

For Theatre Party information call (714) 772-4210

CHAPTER FOURTEEN

SIX MAN BAND

Despite the overtly commercial aspect that "Time For Livin'" offered the single failed to match the successes of the previous releases, even if it did just touch the lower echelons of the British Top 30, offering the group their first significant U.K. sales (settling at a number 23 peak position). Likewise, in the homegrown *Billboard* charts the release had to settle for the disappointing number 39 spot (and number 22 in the rivaling *Cash Box* list), certainly not achieving the heights that Warner Bros. had set for it. But with the touring schedule resuming on May 17th with a performance at BYU in Provo, Utah, followed shortly afterwards by a visit to New Mexico and then a six-day residency at the Melodyland Theater in Anaheim with jazz guitarist Wes Montgomery on the same bill, it was business as usual for the band, albeit with a slightly muted outlook. Sadly, as a side note, one week after performing at the Melodyland venue, Wes Montgomery, a mainstay on the crossover jazz scene, died of a heart attack aged just 45, after returning home to his Indiana residence.

However, from the Association's inside perspective, they had bounced back before after the relative failure of a 45 release, and so there was no saying they wouldn't bounce back again and, so it was, that within a matter of weeks they were back in the studio, cutting tracks for what would become their fifth single for Warner Bros., and the first for a while that had been cut solely for the purposes of a 45 release.

The Association came back to California this week, bringing its own brand of music and fans into sight again. They packed Melodyland on opening night Tuesday. And Wednesday. And Thursday. And they probably did it again last night, and will tonight and tomorrow for the closing concert.

Few of them will be able to vote Tuesday, but they turned out in record numbers to cast a ballot for one of the more inventive music groups of the decade.

The kids liked it, this reviewer did, and the bar losses will undoubtedly be made up by snack bar sales.

The San Bernardino County Sun
June 1st 1968

With the California primary scheduled for the following week the upcoming peoples vote naturally was strong in the minds of the media, hence the above reference in the press, although the tragic events that befell the nation two days later, June 6th 1968, when Robert F. Kennedy fell victim to an assassin's bullet, just two months after Martin Luther King, focused the minds of many back onto the more serious matters at hand. Music was but a brief escape…

They opened with 'Come On In', a groovy cut from their newest album Birthday. Then, after 'Come On In' and 'Along Comes Mary' Terry steps up to the mic and introduces his fellow Associates. Terry is the emcee for the evening. The introductions vary, depending on what the guys happen to be wearing. I'll explain: Russ was wearing an 'outasite rusty' brown corduroy suit and when Terry introduced him he said Russ was disguised as a rusty nail…

The Battle Creek Enquirer
July 27 1968

The Association has gone mod, and a full house at Convention Hall Saturday night didn't mind at all. The suit and ties, which the group sported when it started in show business, are gone. They've been replaced with floral shirts, beads, turtleneck sweaters, ruffles, velvet pants, silk shirts, and a cowboy outfit. The music, still essentially Association stamped, sports new strains of Bob Dylan, Spanky & Our Gang, and sometimes semi-psychedelic sounds.

There was light banter between songs and the audience was a little slow to pick it up at first, maybe because the predominantly junior and senior high school devotees weren't expecting some subtle and sarcastic social commentary along with the music. But they soon caught on and by mid-show were roaring at the group's 'Association Press' program, modeled after the myriad news commentaries now in vogue.

The witty buffoonery continued during the whole show and the audience even found itself clapping for an Association 'psychedelic show' which consisted on a darkened convention hall suddenly lit up with a momentous pop of fans flash bulb cameras. Most momentous however was the music. Amongst the songs was the group's new release, 'Six Man Band', and the fellows introduced it in their typical offhanded, glib manner.

"We're going to play another new song now," said Jim Yester. "New release and all that, you know. It's the only one the record company has guaranteed for six months, or two years, whichever comes first..."

Asbury Park Press
August 5 1968

Recorded during a two-day stop off at Western Recorders during the third week of July, and released on the final day of the month as Warner Bros. 45 7229 (coupled with Larry's "Like Always"), "Six Man Band", a new Terry Kirkman composition, was a departure in sound to the polished productions of the preceding album – with good reason.

The relationship with Bones Howe, as professional and integral as it was to the success of both *Insight Out* and *Birthday*, was becoming more strained as the sessions for the latter album progressed. The fallout from the group's refusal to record the Jimmy Webb cantata, coupled with Howe's in-demand status amongst the studios and the band's continuing desire to record their own songs themselves, ultimately resulted in a parting of the ways and the new 45 bared the simple label credit 'Arranged & Produced by The Association' as evidence. Certainly the sound had a rougher, more progressive approach and the instrumentation was simpler, a counter reaction to the lush orchestration that had been prevalent on the last few releases, with the dominating guitar riff adding a harder edge to the overall arrangement.

"When I wrote 'Six Man Band' I was an angry young man," said Terry, during the 1984 *Goldmine* interview. "The original bridge was an out and out indictment of the administrative edge of the music business. I can't remember what the (original) lyrics were but even the group refused to sing them! So I had to rewrite them…"

Pigeon-holed within the soft-rock category, due in no doubt to the success stories of the gentle "Cherish", "No Fair At All" and "Never My Love", and the slick, smooth productions of "Everything That Touches You" and "Windy", the band were always going to end up in a fight to resume the rock credibility that, perhaps, many of the band members desired and the subsequent sales of the new release, or lack of, proved such a theory to be of reasonable assumption.

> Here's the easy beat funky rocker to put the group right back in the Top 20 of the Hot 100. Clever material.
>
> *Billboard*
> August 1968

Sadly, despite a measure of local success, a peak of number 47 in the national Hot 100 would dispute such a prediction and the fight was on, despite two prominent televised appearances designed to promote the new release. Coinciding the with the issue the band performed on ABC TV's *Dick Cavett Show*, followed a few weeks later by the airing of a new promotional film on the top-rated *American Bandstand*. This film, put together specifically to drive sales for the single, was a compilation of various ad-hoc sequences, casually filming the band in the streets, at the airport, and onstage…

> 'Cause I'm a traveling man
> Yes, I'm a traveling man
> Well, I'm a comer and a goer
> In a six man band
>
> "Six Man Band"
> Words and Music by Terry Kirkman

Perhaps wary of the band's desire to change their sound and their appearance, most members were now sporting facial hair to one degree or another, Warner Bros., in partnership with an overseeing Pat Colecchio, put into plan the forthcoming release of a new compilation album, aimed at the upcoming seasonal market and comprising of the hits, and near misses, from the past few years. With a provisional working title of *Golden Hits Album*, the proposed track selection would range from "One Too Many Mornings" through to "Six-Man Band" and would benefit from a heavy marketing campaign in the lead-up to the bumper Christmas sales. As one chapter closes…

It was almost as if Phase II of The Association was preparing for launch.

August 2 1968: Virginia Beach, VA
August 3 1968: Convention Hall, Asbury Park, NJ
August 4 1968: Carousel Theater, Framingham, MA
August 9, 1968: Illinois State Fairgrounds, Springfield, IL
August 10 1968: Opera House, Chicago, IL
August 11 1968: Opera House, Chicago, IL
August 12 1968: Opera House, Chicago, IL
August 14 1968: Mid-South Coliseum, Memphis, TN
August 16 1968: Hampton Beach Casino, Hampton, NH
August 17 1968: Yale Bowl, New Haven, CT
August 20 1968: Orpheum Theater, Davenport, IA
August 21 1968: Memorial Auditorium, Des Moines, IA
August 22 1968: Mesker Amphitheater, Evansville, IN
August 23 1968: Kentucky State Fair, Louisville, KY

With the successful touring schedule still taking up much of their time – a performances at the Illinois State Fair on August 9th, performing on the same bill as The Who, drew in the region of 24,000 attendees, yet another attendance record – there was one more 45 planned for release before the year was out, and with the rapid decline in the success of their singles releases during the preceding months; "Everything That Touches You" had achieved a Top 10 placing but the following two releases had only managed significantly lower positions, there was still hope that the next release would revive their position near the top of the charts. In a somewhat interesting move it was decided to recut one of their more popular recordings from the first album, and one that had consistently delivered a fantastic response on the concert circuit, and so, during early September, they once again grouped together at United Recorders, followed shortly afterwards by a session at the Wally Heider Studios, to work on a new version of "Enter The Young". As with "Six Man Band" the group took the production reins themselves and, once more, kept the arrangements on a simpler scale to those on their earlier releases with the guitar solo in particular, undertaken by Larry on this occasion, brought to the fore and (unlike the Curt Boettcher produced version from two years earlier) not so lost in the overall final mix. Yet, this was now late 1968 and one wonders how relevant such lyrics were twenty-four months further on? Was "Enter The Young" really as relevant as the call-to-arms it had been when Terry first conceived the lyrics, whilst opening a can of corn back in his 1966 apartment? Warner Bros. assumed so and the new recording, paired off with Russ's "The Time It Is Today", a far more relevant lyric for a 1968 America, was scheduled for release as Warner Bros. 45-7239.

During that same period the Association Admiration Aggregation issued one of their regular newsletters during which they also made mention of another new song that had recently been recorded, at least in early demo form. A new collaboration between Ted Bluechel and 'Skip' Carmel, the co-writer on "Birthday Morning" and "Barefoot Gentleman", "The Nest" was an intense, yet uplifting composition, developing from a downbeat first half into an almost joyous second section, and reminiscent of The Beach Boys' structured vocals during the closing tag. Utilizing the often under-employed vocal range of Brian Cole for the first part it was an attempt by Ted to give Brian a sense of meaning to his role. He was often under-used in the studio, given his lack of lead vocals, and his desire to participate in the band's songwriting activities was seemingly occasional at best, and whilst he was an integral part of the vocal stack, supplying the lower registers amongst the six-piece harmony, once the backing vocals had been cut Brian's work was often completed, and his attentions were often misplaced. This was, after all, the late 1960s when drug use was becoming the norm within the music industry and, without a true focus with which to hold on to, Brian began to experiment that little too deeply, that little too far. He also began to show an interest in collecting, from an outlandish interest in the occult, through to an impressive collection of timepieces, although such was the constant life on the road for the band, the endless touring schedule continuing throughout the late summer and the fall and into the early winter weeks of 1968, that such private and personal moments were all-too few to fully appreciate.

"Brian was very intense," reflects Ray Staar. "I don't think there was a muscle or a bone in Brian's body that was ever completely relaxed. Even when he was asleep! He was just this very politically and socially aware guy who had a clear vision of where he was going, and where the country was going, and if you tried to talk to him in any other way, or tried to deposit any other set of beliefs or ideas then Brian was all over you. His eyes would get huge and he would jump in your face..."

November 1968 saw the release of the proposed hits package, simply retitled *The Association's Greatest Hits,* comprising of nine choice cuts from across their four albums, along with the two recent self-produced recordings, although the version of "Six Man Band" included on the album was a noticeably different mix to that of the recently released 45 release with, once again, an extended fade out absent from the radio-play 45. The much hoped for inclusion of "One Too Many Mornings", pleaded for by a large proportion of the fan following, keen to see it included on an album for the first time, sadly fell by the wayside, a victim of publishing issues, whilst the retitling of Ted's "We Love Us" (originally featured on the *Insight Out* album and the flip-side of "Everything That Touches You"), now listed simply as "We Love", was instigated by Pat Colecchio, who saw it as a superior marketing idea. The noted absence of "Pandora's Golden Heebie Jeebies", a song that had peaked higher in the U.S. charts than three of the other tracks that *did* make the cut, seemed another strange choice although Jules Alexander has since been led to believe that the exclusion was down to a muted ill-feeling over this departure from the band.

"To quote Errol Flynn..." he says today, with a sense of humor in his voice. "It's not what they say about you. It's what they whisper..."

Nevertheless, packaged within a delightful sleeve design by Warners' Art Director Ed Thrasher, resplendent with a photograph that represented the happy, sunshine sounds within, the album soared towards the top regions of the *Billboard* album listings, supported heavily by the weight of the Warner Bros. marketing department. The front image itself, taken by the official band photographer James Metropole during a shoot at the Descanso Botanical Gardens in La Cañada Flintridge, with the six group members posing amongst an abundance of shrubbery next to their reflections from the calm deep blue waters of the small lake, was allegedly a composite of two photographs, expertly melded as one, a notion purportedly coming from a

1984 interview with Russ Giguere and then reported as such in a subsequent article in *Goldmine*. However, Metropole himself disputes the notion:

"I don't know where the idea came from that the Descanso Gardens image is a composite shot," says Jim today. "I shot that one portrait with a Hasselblad and I don't think that transparency was manipulated at all. I just shot them sitting there. It was really just improvising, taking them out. I would set them up against a wall or wherever, do this, do that, but I didn't consider myself an artist – just a guy having fun."

A keen photographer since his younger years, he had first come into contact with the band during the mid-'60s when, having relocated from New York, he encountered Terry Kirkman on a social level (sharing the same Hollywood apartment block as Terry's sister-in-law). Subsequently, with one friendship leading to another, he pressed for any photographic work that Pat Colecchio may be able to push his way. Colecchio then hooked him up with the band's PR film, Freeman & Sutton, and he started a lengthy partnership with the group, not only handling hundreds of publicity photographs (some would adorn later album sleeves), but also working with their press releases and media biographies, whilst accompanying the band on the road for a number of shows as a part of Pat's own company, Colecchio Enterprises.

"We had an office up on Sunset, 9124 Sunset, and Geffen had an office next to us," continued Jim, recalling his time with the band. "I wasn't a part of their everyday workings, I just did their publicity. Pat would call me when he needed something and I'd just take care of it. New pictures or a press kit... and then I went on tour, and I went to Florida, Chicago, New York, San Francisco with them, and what they were doing those days was they were playing colleges and they were making a lot of money, but Nixon later took care of that! Once he got elected Nixon started denying colleges money for concerts..."

The *Greatest Hits* album's rapid chart climb was highlighted by the fact that after a gradual build of sales over the Christmas period it had leapt up from the number 35 spot to the number 6 position within one week, before it climbed to its peak placing of number 4 on February 8th 1969, commencing an 18-week run in the Top 20, in a chart dominated by The Beatles' *White Album* and *Yellow Submarine* releases, Cream's *Goodbye*, Glen Campbell's *Wichita Lineman* and the soundtrack to *Hair*, the hippie counter-culture musical of the times.

To accompany the release, Warner Bros. Records also issued a promotional E.P. featuring six tracks from the album, designed for jukebox purposes and for ease of radio promotion. Packaged in a mini-version of the album sleeve this extended play (EP-S1767) featured "Enter The Young", "No Fair At All", "Windy", "The Time It Is Today", "Everything That Touches You" and "Along Comes Mary" and is today an oft-sought collector's item. However, with a change of heart, the proposed single release of "Enter The Young", despite it having been issued with a catalog reference, was cancelled. Its proposed release date clashing with another related item on the Warner Bros. schedule. Potentially one of a far greater significance. Change that to a seven-man band.

CHAPTER FIFTEEN

IT'S GOTTA BE REAL

ecember 8th 1968 and whilst in New York during a tour of the east coast The Association stopped off at the newly renamed Ed Sullivan Theater on Broadway to record an appearance on the CBS primetime variety show hosted by Sullivan himself. Introduced by the bumbling former New York columnist, the band promoted the recently issued *Greatest Hits* package by performing live versions (as were the requirements of *The Ed Sullivan Show*) of both "Along Comes Mary" and "Never My Love". Both were performed exquisitely before the live audience, before Ed briefly introduced them, shook a few hands and made a few casual remarks about their home states:

"Who's from Kansas?

Alabama?

Who comes from Hawaii? You do, I figured that one out!"

Shortly afterwards, the band made a similar appearance, albeit without the bumbling host, on *The Jonathan Winters Show*.

From the Association Admiration Aggregation newsletter, issued towards the end of 1968:

The guys are up to some pretty exciting things these days. Get ready for some surprises!

In the recording studio they've been brewing up four songs for the soundtrack of a Paramount film called 'Goodbye Columbus'. Paramount thinks the film will be one of the biggest of the year. If the movie is anything like the music that will be the understatement of the year.

Working on the film track recording with the guys is none other than Jules (Gary) Alexander. They have started calling themselves the 7 dwarfs in and around the rehearsal hall. The name won't stay I'm sure but Jules might remain with the group after the movie score is completed.

Having returned from India, and having experimented with the formation of the Joshua Fox band, Jules had come to the conclusion that all he was doing with the new line-up was simply trying to recreate what he had already achieved with The Association all over again. The new band was a fine collection of singers and extremely talented performers, Mike Botts was one of the finest drummers around the Los Angeles scene at that time, but it couldn't match the overall sound that The Association could offer. Few could. "So I said, 'What the fuck am I doing here?' And I went down to an Association rehearsal and rejoined…" [2]

Larry meanwhile, having seen the former co-founder of the band resume his position within the ranks without question, was subsequently put into a position of uncertainty himself. He fully expected to be asked to leave, seeing that he was, in essence, brought in to fill Jules' shoes whilst he was away, never expecting him to return. However, the remaining band members had other ideas, recognizing what he brought into the group, and that he had been co-lead singer on two of their biggest hits to date. Without any debate of note The Association simply expanded into a seven-piece band, adding an additional harmony and guitar into the mix, and allowing Jim to move over to keyboards when required without losing the balance in the sound.

"Jules is a very strong personality, as is Larry, and at times that caused problems. But on the creative end, it is certainly a plus. You can certainly get a lot further out with seven guys," said Jim, recalling events surrounding Jules' return. [18]

The Paramount movie *Goodbye, Columbus*, based on a late 1950s novel by Phillip Roth, and starring an aspiring actress named Ali McGraw in her first leading role, was released to U.S. cinemas during the spring of 1969, and yet the members of the band had been permitted early previews of the movie, three to four months beforehand, so that they could work on a number of songs for the soundtrack.

"Paramount Pictures approached us to do the soundtrack. They were very aware of our music, and they asked us to meet with them" Jim recalls.[18]

However, having flown into New York City directly from a concert in Chattanooga to view an early screening of the film, without any musical soundtrack dubbed onto it, they were then informed they had but one week to come up with three suitable songs, one each to bookend the movie, and one to accompany the love scene montage featuring Ali McGraw's character, Brenda, and her lover Neil, as portrayed by Richard Benjamin. Jim Yester, excited at the prospect, immediately set about working on a composition and within a matter of hours of the screening, whilst walking from his New York hotel down to Greenwich Village, had the concept of the title song mapped out in head. Likewise, Jules and Terry, working alongside another friend, Rita Martinson (who had also worked with Jerry Yester in the studio back in 1966), also conceived their own version of the title song. Still, better to have too many than not enough. Meanwhile, Larry came up with "It's Gotta Be Real", Russ composed "I Still Love You" and Terry put together "So Kind To Me (Brenda's Theme)" alone.

One week later and the band met up again with the studio executives and played them their songs. Pleased with what they heard, they selected three of the propositions, opting for Jim's title tune over the one Jules and Terry had co-authored, and deciding against Russ's tune, giving the band another deadline by which to have the chosen recordings completed. The pressure was then on...

John Patrick Boylan IV, a New York native and recent arrival on the west coast, first began his rise to musical fame alongside his brother Terence in the band Appletree Theater, releasing the concept album *Playback* during 1967 to critical acclaim (John Lennon was one of its most fervent supporters) but commercial failure. He had first encountered The Association whilst working in Greenwich Village's folk scene and then, following the Appletree Theater's disbandment, John had then joined up as one third of the rock outfit Hamilton Streetcar, alongside songwriter Buzz Clifford, whilst also developing an interest in studio production, an area he had first begun to pursue whilst writing, arranging and co-producing Rick Nelson's 1967 release *Another Side Of Rick*. It was whilst he was working on Hamilton Streetcar's debut album out on the west coast (ultimately released on Dot Records during early 1969) that he first came back into contact with The Association.

"They hired me to produce the soundtrack," Boylan later recalled. "Terry Kirkman really liked the Appletree Theater album, and gave me an opportunity. The Association were great singers; they could really get a blend like the Four Freshman or The Beach Boys. They were also very professional. For a first major project, I could not have asked for a better situation. However, there were lots of problems within the band, fighting among themselves. Jules had quit before the big hits (and) he then came back. Larry Ramos, the guy they had originally hired to replace him, stayed, and he had a more commercial sense and Jules was going to be the beatnik to give the group credibility. In the late 1960s, everybody was talking about the Doors and Dylan. The Association was considered lightweight. Bones Howe, a great producer and engineer had turned them into a machine like The 5th Dimension, and they didn't want to do that anymore." [34]

Pairing up with them at the popular Wally Heider Studios, located at the intersection of Selma Avenue and Cahuenga Boulevard in Hollywood, John took over the production responsibilities for the new *Goodbye, Columbus* tracks, laying down a number of polished yet less complex cuts than those his predecessor had produced, with the band members themselves adding to the instrumentation alongside a number of the key session players.

The title track, "Goodbye, Columbus", as composed by Jim Yester, maintained the upbeat, commercial approach of the band's former years, with Jim well to the fore and Larry 'ghosting' vocal support, all filled out with layers of harmonies and backing vocals, whilst both Larry's laid-back, jazzy approach on "It's Gotta Be Real" (on which he supplied both lead and backing vocals) and Terry's melancholy ballad were more soulful arrangements, the latter highlighting the depth, both lyrically and musically, that Terry's work was now beginning to explore. Reportedly, the discarded Giguere composition, "I Still Love You", was also partially cut at these sessions, before being returned to the Warner Bros. vaults.

On February 5th 1969 "Goodbye, Columbus" was issued as the new Association single (WB 45-7267), paired with "The Time It Is Today", thus consigning the notion of a Warner Bros. coupling of "Enter The Young"/"The

Time It Today" to the scrap heap. Sadly, and despite a heavy publicity launch in the music press, the single went on to become the lowest charting single for the band since "Along Comes Mary" first made its steady climb up the lists, almost three years earlier. With a chart high of number 80 in the Hot 100 this was yet another comparative failure in their seesawing success.

A scheduled second appearance on *The Ed Sullivan Show* was also planned for the following month, with the band keen to promote the single, along with another new song they were working on in the studios with John Boylan, but the CBS executives, along with Sullivan himself, wanted the band to perform more familiar material once again and a stalemate was reached, with neither party willing to give way. The result being that the band pulled out of the schedule.

By this stage the band were comfortable working in the studios alongside Boylan and the successful *Goodbye, Columbus* sessions melded sweetly into the next round of studio productions, intended for the following full length album. However, the tensions to which Boylan inferred were still simmering below the surface. What had been a six-man committee, seven with Pat Colecchio on board, was now one extra. One more opinion and one more voice wanting to be heard. In the early days of the band they were still learning, still discovering the boundaries with which they could contribute within. Testing the waters. But now there were seven experienced individuals, astute to the workings of the music industry, for better and for worse, and they all had opinions and voices to be heard. Something would have to give sooner or later.

"The Association was a good name for them, because they were an association of songwriters who were all vying for attention," John Boylan was to add, during a 2003 online interview with the *National Association of Music Merchants*. "They had three or four lead singers, three or four writers, and they all had their own thing to come to the fore. And that tension was good, because it provided competition and made their work better. I lucked out…"

Other projects in the pipeline, with Pat Colecchio driving hard for deals, were a re-publication of *Crank Your Spreaders*, with new photographs and a new layout, the possibility of a joint U.S. tour alongside The Beach Boys and the newly-christened giants of jazz-rock, Blood, Sweat & Tears (with maybe even a partnership in the recording studios as an add-on), and even the possibility of a TV special dedicated solely to the band. Unfortunately, the latter two proved to be no more than pipe dreams, the touring proposal never getting beyond the early management meetings, and yet it was clear that Colecchio still held firm his faith in what the band could offer, despite a floundering chart career.

During the opening months of 1969, and in between concert dates in Oregon, Washington and British Columbia (February 7-9th respectively), and the usual round of eastern state performances – Pennsylvania, New York, Maryland, Ohio, Michigan and Illinois (all during the month of March), the recordings sessions for the next album continued in earnest. With John Boylan in a comfortable position seated in the producer's chair, albeit with a shared credit with the band on the eventual release, they reconvened at the TTG Studios at 1441 North McCadden Place, just off Sunset Boulevard. This relatively new recording facility, set up just three years earlier, had become a hot house for many of the popular bands of the day, impressed with the state of the art, newly installed 16-track Ampex recorders. It was the first studio in Los Angeles to have two 16-track machines available, doubling the capacity of the standard 8-track recorders, and the added attraction of its high decibel capabilities, albeit just from the one room in the building, gave artists such as Frank Zappa, The Doors, Eric Burden and, more recently, Jimi Hendrix, so much more freedom to experiment and create, and at reasonable rates as well, as opposed to the higher end and more restricting, often staid atmosphere the more established studios offered.

The first song they worked on at TTG was Jules' "Love Affair", with Jim taking lead vocal duties. Initial sessions for this soft ballad had taken place just prior to the festive season, but with a gathering of new compositions also ready to go, the finishing touches to this tune were worked upon first. Kicking off with a delicate piano introduction, as played by a talented arranger and performer by the name of Richard Thompson, the track steadily builds with a wealth of harmonies and intricate vocal arrangements, coupled with some sublime guitar interplay from Jules as the song draws to a close (although listening closely to the fade tends to reveal a few mismatched notes coming through heavily on the bass guitar). Working with arranger Bob Alcivar on the album once more, the depth to which the band went to get a suitable arrangement is astonishing at times, particularly in the knowledge that Bones Howe, famed for his polished productions, was no longer on board for this project. The band could so easily have stepped off the gas and stripped back their sound but with this composition in particular it becomes apparent how the transition from one producer to another had little affected their own vision.

"Bob Alcivar is a very spiritual, polite, kind guy," noted Terry, in reference to the vocal arrangements of their friend. "Really talented."

"He is one of the best arrangers on the planet!' concurs Jules. "I can listen to his arrangements over and over and that, as a musician, is seldom done!"

Following their return from the short series of concerts in the Pacific north-west the next song undertaken was one that they would return to, time and time again over the coming weeks, such was its intense nature and vocal arrangements. Written once again by Jules, this time in collaboration with 'Skip' Carmel, "Under Branches" was a fragile, multi-faceted creature, featuring differing tempos and short integrated sections, inventive percussive effects and subtle horn arrangements, all seemingly unrelated musically but gelled beautifully and harmonically together in a similar mold to the fragmented sessions that Brian Wilson had envisaged during his infamous *SMiLE*-era recordings. With Richard Thompson once more adding a lilting piano accompaniment, the group blended their vocals together in unison over a mythological lyric that the duo deliberately strove to deliver.

Gary 'Skip' Carmel was to add significant contributions to the songwriting during this period of the band's existence. Having been introduced to the group via his friendship with Jim, and having worked alongside him, writing lyrics for the *Birthday* album, he then began collaborating with both Jules and Ted for the subsequent release, although one of the songs that he worked on with Jules, "Moontime Bore (She Said)", eventually found its way onto the Joshua Fox album. This particular song, even in its completed form without Jules participation, is distinctly Association-like in its vocal arrangement and quirky melody although, for reasons unclear, only Carmel was credited on the label, issued as a single by the floundering Tetragrammaton label during May 1969.

Other unreleased songs from the duo, as recorded on the BMI database, include "Greatness Unknown" and "Ride Out Alone (Rodeo I Love You)", whilst with Ted he co-composed "The Nest", which had initially been worked on back in the fall of '68, and an unrecorded song entitled "Nerves Of Steel".

"Man, I loved the stuff we did together but he was really hard to write with," reflects Jules today. "I haven't talked to him in years." [37]

Sadly, following the author's interview with Jules, 'Skip' passed away during February 2017, whilst research for this book was still ongoing.

Whilst the sessions were developing, on March 17th 1969 the *Goodbye, Columbus* soundtrack album appeared in the stores, featuring the three songs The Association had contributed to the film. Packaged simply with an attractive close-up photograph of Ms. McGraw, surrounded by a white border with the title and the band name highlighted prominently along the top, the only photograph of the band itself was positioned on the rear of the sleeve, with an image taken by Henry Diltz, a member of the Modern Folk Quartet but, by now, an established photographer as well, although the image in question, taken in a white-washed converted garage at the rear of a property up on Laurel Canyon (owned by Henry's artistic collaborator, Gary Burden), was somewhat lost amongst a wealth of stills and promotional shots from the film.

The remainder of the long-player was filled up with excerpts from the musical score, compiled and composed in the majority by Charles Fox, a 28 year-old musician who was, at that stage, starting his career within the movie business. In the coming years Fox would go on to compose numerous popular television and movie themes (think *Happy Days*, *Love American Style*, *Laverne & Shirley*, *Wonder Woman*…) and then, during 1972, in partnership with lyricist Norman Gimbel, he would co-compose the *Grammy* award winning hit "Killing Me Softly With His Song" for Roberta Flack.

One of the Fox-arranged recordings also featured on the soundtrack release, an instrumental rendition of Jim Yester's title song, actually featured the group adding some harmony background vocals on top.

Jim Yester: "It's a 'Goodbye, Columbus' thing for a montage. It was kind of neat. It's real nice, it's all orchestrated and flutes and all that kind of thing. But it wasn't us. It wasn't our thing. It wasn't the band. It was us vocally. It was still kind of fun." [18]

The film itself went on general release the following month, taking an estimated $10.5 million at the U.S. box office, making it one of the most popular movies of the year, and achieving critical acclaim from both *Variety* magazine and the often vitriolic *New York Times* film critics. It also went on to achieve the *Writers Guild of America* award for 'Best Comedy Adapted from Another Medium', along with a *Golden Globe* award for 'Most Promising Newcomer (Ali McGraw)'. In addition, it also received a prestigious *Academy* award nomination for 'Best Adapted Screenplay'. However, not to be outdone, both Jim Yester and Charles Fox were also nominated for a *Golden Globe* for the instrumental arrangement of the title song, losing out at the 1970 ceremonies to Rod McKuen's theme tune for *The Prime Of Miss Jean Brodie*.

Keeping faith in their investment, Warner Bros. issued the next 45rpm on March 26th 1969, releasing the first of the new tracks intended for the band's fifth studio album, paired off with one from the previous release. With radio play geared towards the newer song, the delightful but questionably non-commercial "Under Branches" – Ted's "Hear in Here" being the flip-side – their faith was admirable, yet sadly misplaced as the single limped to yet another new low, peaking at a meager number 117 position on the *Billboard* charts. Meanwhile, across the seas in the U.K., where the band had briefly made inroads into achieving a small level of success the previous year, the label had effectively lost faith completely. Having failed to capitalize on the spring 1968 promotional tour by opting out of a following summer visit, publicity for the band in Europe had all but dried up and with the lack of chart sales for "Six Man Band", their follow-up to "Time For Livin'", Warner Bros. hadn't released a new 45 in the U.K. for almost six months and when they finally relented, albeit not until September 1969, a belated issue of "Goodbye, Columbus" saw no chart action whatsoever. There were to be no further releases in the U.K. until the spring of 1970 although both Germany and France maintained their limited support by issuing one single apiece from these new sessions.

As if to drive support for the U.S. release, Warner Bros. also pressed up a limited edition promotional 45, pairing off "Under Branches" with "Goodbye, Columbus" (Warner Bros. PRO-324), and issued it solely amongst the radio stations to drum up support in the wake of the film's launch, an admirable marketing ploy in light of the positive reception to the film's release. A guest appearance on the highly rated CBS-TV show *The Glen Campbell Goodtime Hour* shortly afterwards (broadcast on May 7th), performing both songs, was a further attempt to drive publicity and sales of the single but, again, it was to little avail. Maybe the choice of song was wrong? Whilst the quality of the performance cannot be faulted, or that of the Alexander-Carmel composition itself, but as to whether it had the commercialism to be an effective choice for a single is debatable. Certainly there is no immediate hook line incorporated within the 4:30 minute arrangement with which to draw in the radio listener's attention, and for a single release that's a mighty long time to not have that distinctive peg to latch onto. And if one compares it to other equally adventurous recordings of the same era, from "Time Of The Season" and "Hair" to "The Boxer", one can almost touch the commercialism bubbling underneath the surface on each of these releases. Mix that in with the driving beat of "Get Back" and "Proud Mary", or even the slick sophistication of the Bones Howe-produced "Aquarius/Let The Sunshine In", and you can see just what the new Association single had running up against it.

In fact, at one stage there was even the slight possibility of The Association cutting their own version of "Let The Sunshine In", as Ray Staar, who was still holding down the position as lighting engineer, recalls when reminiscing over his time with the group: "I had first joined up with the band just after the Monterey Pop Festival. I was a twenty-one year old kid and I had actually gone to Monterey as a friend of the band, with Terry's sister-in-law and her young son. I was a struggling actor going by the name of Ray Adams, and I had met Judy Kirkman in an acting class. She introduced me to the group, and the next thing I knew, after Monterey, I was helping to set up for the next show. I was just a general gopher for them as well as working the lights. Anyway, much later on, when I was still working with them, we came off the road for maybe a month or so and a friend of mine rolled in from New York City where he'd just seen the musical *Hair*. This would have been around 1968 and at that time, on the west coast, *Hair* was utterly unknown. He brought me a copy of the RCA record, of the original Broadway cast, and the opening number was 'Let The Sunshine In'. The first thing that went across my mind was 'Oh my God! This is a hit for The Association!' So, as I was this sort of loose cannon kid who just said things off hand, I just took the record to Pat Colecchio, and I went into his office and played it for him, saying 'Pat, this is perfect for the guys. It's a smash!' And he just goes 'it's too short! I replied, 'Well, lengthen it somehow! What do I know? Stick it with another song…' And he says 'no, no… it's too hippie. Besides, The Monkees have an album with *Aquarius* in the title and that's gonna reflect badly on the guys!' and I just thought 'what?!'

"Well, two months later and Bones Howe, who had been the band's producer, came out with a version by The 5th Dimension! I was really pissed off! I don't know what happened but that struck me as very weird…"

Further missed opportunities aside, even if the band members themselves were unaware of some of them, the outlook remained positive towards the new recordings; "The (new) album will certainly be a departure from what we've been doing," Terry was to say in a 1969 magazine article. "The content and the instruments are different. I'd say it's funkier, more down to earth."

As the sessions continued, mixed amongst the pre-scheduled concert dates, predominantly in the north-east and down the eastern seaboard, Pat Colecchio was also busy arranging the re-publication of an updated edition of the *Crank Your Spreaders* fan booklet. An initial launch for the early weeks of the New Year was postponed due to a printing error on the newly designed front cover (featuring a black and white image of the band taken in Belgium, during the recent European tour), and necessary rebinding was also undertaken, but the publication was back in the stores in limited quantities, and with newly designed pages within, by early April. Rather surprisingly, and bearing mind the delay in publication, the updated edition failed to include or even acknowledge the return of Jules Alexander to the line-up, opting to feature the six-piece band from the previous year, and whilst the initial page layouts, and updated photographs, would have been drawn up during the early stages of planning it does appear strange, with hindsight, to issue the new edition without him. Especially as three or four months had passed since he rejoined, along with a sequence of brand new recordings… and the fact that they chose to remove his images and contributions from the first edition.

During March the group was presented with an outstanding achievement award by the Loews Theater Group in recognition for the work they had contributed towards the success of the *Goodbye, Columbus* film. In addition, their 1968 *Greatest Hits* album was also certified *RIAA* gold award status, acknowledging half a million shipments across the nation to date (as opposed to sales figures). But, perhaps of more significance to the more politically aware followers of the band, as opposed to the unknowingly innocent teenagers who pinned images of Ted or Russ to their bedroom walls, and potentially more so to the band members themselves, was one further event that took place on April 15th. On that date The Association were cited in the U.S. House of Representatives by Thomas M. Rees, the Democrat representative for California, for their contribution to the field of popular music and for 'better understanding between generations'. During the first session of the 91st Congress the Honorable Mr. Rees stood up before the House and publically praised the group for countering the parental-children divide. As to how President Richard Nixon, or Mr. Rees' fellow Representatives responded remains undocumented...

It is not unusual for Congress to pay tribute to an organization such as this, but I would like to take a moment here to explain why I believe The Association is an unusual group, earning unusual attention.

Perhaps the most important thing The Association has done is span the generation gap, linking young and old. In the pleasing melodic sound of The Association, parents have found something in pop music they can share with their children. Young people are grateful the Association exists and so, apparently, are their parents. So, Mr. President, I think we should express our gratitude too.

Thomas M. Rees
California

CHAPTER SIXTEEN

UNDER BRANCHES

Early April 1969 saw the band continuing to work on new material such as Jim Yester's "What Were The Words", the Ramos-Ortega co-composition "Are You Ready", a John Boylan tune entitled "Yes I Will" and a new work by Terry, "Boy On The Mountain", arranged in collaboration with Richard Thompson, the pianist who had been working with the band since the initial stages of these current sessions.

"Richard was one of the most talented musicians I've ever met in my life," reflects Terry. "I met him when Carol Harris, whom he would later marry, was an A&R person at Elektra Records and my then-wife Judith had asked her to 'come up and live in the A-frame', which was our house, and was the closest house to the Hollywood sign, high up in the hills. And that's where I met Richard. He could play, fix, teach, sight read and build for thirteen different instruments, and I never really ran across anything that he couldn't do. I had previously seen him play in the United States Army Band, and we probably had twenty friends in common, but we had never actually met! And yet we were made for each other…

"He didn't write songs as such but he was profoundly creative, so when I put a song to him that I had written he could instantly interpret what I was trying to do, with all sorts of different styles and different voicings. We did write one song together, 'St. Germaine', a 1960s French movie theme sound, one of my favorite things that no one has ever really heard. It was never recorded (author's note: the song does still exist in demo form), although

Carmen McRae performed it when he was playing with her. But Richard was a difficult friend, as he didn't have a whole lot of boundaries, but he changed my possibilities… musically."

Jim's "What Were The Words" maintained a distinct country-music flavor running throughout its musical arrangement, a new direction for the band, but with the then-current development of the hot L.A. country-rock scene taking a foothold amongst the musicians around town, it was only natural that The Association would be drawn into the movement. But as to what degree they would integrate themselves was unclear at the time. Certainly, by listening to this track, they were keen to explore the possibilities.

Fellow L.A.-based bands such as The Byrds, with their seminal *Sweetheart Of The Rodeo* LP, The Flying Burrito Brothers (*The Gilded Palace Of Sin*), The Nitty Gritty Dirt Band and The Dillards were all taking the country music sound and integrating it into the rock and pop rhythms that blew freely around the beaches and palm trees of southern California, whilst Mike Nesmith, the former Troubadour regular, Survivor and soon-to-be-ex-Monkee (he was to quit the manufactured band that same month) was becoming a pioneer in pushing the boundaries of where the great divide between the genres stood. Indeed, Jim actually wrote "What Were The Words" with The Dillards in mind, the two founding brothers, Doug and Rodney, having known the band members since the early days of the Troubadour folk music revival. However, Doug had recently quit the band over 'musical differences' with his brother and so it was that Jim presented his new song to Rodney.

"I played it for Rodney and he said, 'Oh well, we can't do that. You have to record that!'" Yester laughs. "He wouldn't take it."

Nevertheless, both Doug and Rodney, along with fellow Dillard, the multi-talent Herb Pederson, both contributed to the sessions, as did Dillard sideman, steel guitarist Buddy Emmons, whilst Larry Ramos took control for the vocal arrangements.

With the basic session work for at least eight songs completed by mid-April the band then closed up shop at the TTG Studios and took a brief leave from recording whilst they headed back out on tour, taking in Jim's home state along the way, appearing at the University of Alabama in Tuscaloosa on April 30th, along with subsequent shows in Mississippi, Texas and Ohio. Sharing the stage with them for many of these dates were the bands Mercy and The Guess Who, both of whom would hit Top 10 status themselves the following month with "Love (Can Make You Happy)" and "These Eyes" respectively – a chart rating that, sadly, The Association no longer had access to.

Shortly afterwards, having returned to Los Angeles, the final round of recordings took place, albeit now in the more familiar surroundings of the United Recorders and Western Studios buildings on Sunset Boulevard. The final song selection took in twelve tracks, eleven of which came from pens of the band members themselves, in one combination or another, whilst the range in styles covered the country flavor of the aforementioned "What Were The Words", Jim's lone composition, and Ted's delightful "The Nest", through to the rather bizarre and militant vegetarian slant of Russ's "Broccoli", featuring a vocal co-arrangement from the Giguere-Alexander camp, and a rare contribution from Brian Cole with the unnerving drive of "I Am Up For Europe". Neither of the latter two can be classed as formula material by any standard, with the excessive drum fills and triplets that dominate Brian's standard 4/4 offering (provided by session player Jim Gordon, who contributed to much of the final release) really throwing the listener a curve ball and, with both songs coming straight after the intense harmonies of "Under Branches" on the final track run down, the album certainly crossed the barriers between marketable and left field diversity. Often mentioned within the same breath as The Beach Boys homegrown composition, "Vega-Tables" (later simply retitled "Vegetables"), there can be few other songs like "Broccoli", that extol the benefits of the green-rooted munchies with such genuine sincerity.

If there was one name that stood out amongst the others in overall contributions to the sessions, then Jules Alexander would be that name. With five songwriting credits on the eventual sleeve notes, and a clearly audible input into many of the quirky arrangements that ran throughout the songs, his dominance may be somewhat surprising to many given his recent return to the line-up, and the increasing development of his bandmates' individual input. Certainly, over the past couple of studio albums, *Insight Out* and *Birthday*, it had been Terry Kirkman, with three significant contributions to this new release, who had been seen as the gradually emerging force amongst the band members, and yet it is Jules who once more shines through as the musical weight here.

The last two songs cut for the new album both featured Jules in prominent form, firstly with the rejected *Goodbye, Columbus* title song, written in collaboration with both Terry and Rita Martinson, now reworked lyrically as "Goodbye Forever", and then with the exquisitely delightful and chirpy "Dubuque Blues".

"My song was rejected (for *Goodbye, Columbus*) because they thought it was too strange and weird." Jules was to say in conversation with *Goldmine*. "Ali McGraw, who starred in the film, played a real phony and I tried to define her character in abstract terms. We thought the song was too good to lose so we just changed the lyrics around a little bit and changed the title. If you'll notice, the lyrics are the story of the movie..." [20]

Issued in August that year, the album, simply titled as *The Association* (Warner Bros. WS-1800), but often referred to as either the 'Stonehenge' album, due to the front cover artwork, or '1800' due to the misleading placement of the catalog number on initial pressings, saw a mixed reaction amongst followers of the band, many of whom were seemingly unprepared to advance forward in the same direction to which the band were now intent on taking. In addition, to many, the band were still suffering from the backlash of the "Time For Livin'" bubblegum-effect. The lush arrangements of the so-called 'hit-era', and the Bones Howe-produced successes of *Insight Out* and *Birthday*, were safe ground for much of the music listening audience and the radio stations, but were perhaps deemed as too safe, too 'pop-orientated' by certain aspects of the band who, with John Boylan currently at the helm, were now intent on taking their music farther afield. Closer to their own perception of whom they really were, both as songwriters and musicians, and what their music was truly about.

June saw the release of "Yes I Will", coupled with "I Am Up For Europe", issued as the band's ninth single under the Warner Bros. banner and that too struggled to make any impact on an American audience, bubbling under the Hot 100 and climbing to a peak position three places lower than the previous single – could it get any worse? Written by producer John Boylan, no stranger to songwriting himself (indeed, his latter-day credits include several songwriting kudos for those yellow-hued dysfunctional artists The Simpsons alone), the song, with Russ providing the lead voice, was certainly a contender for the higher reaches of the chart but the baggage that came with The Association brand, the slick, sophisticated sheen, was perhaps too much to bear for those who now tuned their dials into the radio stations across the nation or who passed the dollar across the record store counter, despite the band's best attempt to shake it off and roughen it up at the edges. As John Phillips had so eloquently said to Terry following their exclusion from the *Monterey Pop* film, the band just "didn't fit the image" for a late 1960s America, dominated by Nixon, Vietnam, Creedence Clearwater Revival and, all too soon, the end of the hippie-dream courtesy of an event that shook the Los Angeles community to the core.

And then there was Woodstock...

The single was promoted with a July appearance on ABC's *Joey Bishop Show*, broadcast on the 7th of that month, with the upcoming album track "Dubuque Blues" also being performed. This latter tune would fast become a popular song at many a subsequent concert performance, with the light-hearted country-folk approach, coupled with Jules' own fragile vocal, striking a chord amongst the heartlands of the U.S. Written during a mid-tour break, this homage to the Iowa city, built on the banks of the Mississippi River, inspired Jules to revisit his own memories of growing up back home in Chattanooga. One can only wonder as to the fate of the real 'Anna-Sue'...

Between July 8th and the 13th the group once again returned to fulfill a weeklong residency at Anaheim's Melodyland Theater, where they shared the bill with The Dillards and a satirical seven-piece San Francisco-based improvisational troupe known as The Committee. *The Long Beach Independent* reported the show as such:

It's rock 'n' roll time this week at Melodyland. Extra chairs were necessary on opening night as the Southland's youth – and not a few balding young-at-heart – jammed the Anaheim theater to enjoy The Association. The seven young men, who admit both they and their audience have changed in the four years of their existence, are more at ease, and so is their music.

"What Were The Words" and "Requiem" alone are worth the price of admission. The rotund theater echoes with heavy, enthusiastic applause to a new song, "Dubuque", but dies away for the disappointing "Along Comes Mary".

Pre-intermission fun, purposely avoided by many Association fans, shouldn't have been missed. The Dillards waste no time in getting the evening under way with their fine music and thigh-slapping antics.

The Long Beach Independent
July 19th 1969

Jim: "I loved doing 'What Were The Words' live, because it was just the three of us, Ted, Larry and myself. Ted comes in with the first harmony, below the lead, and then Larry comes in with the third over. And when we go to the chorus, I go to the third over, and Larry takes the melody..."

Upon release on August 2nd, and despite the lack of success the preceding singles had generated, the new album was generally well-received by the media and it subsequently climbed to a respectable number 32 position, despite the somewhat eclectic gathering of songs. Packaged in a gatefold sleeve, with original artwork by one William Crutchfield, an Indianapolis-born artist whom Russ had become acquainted with after he had moved out to the west coast, and who was coincidentally studying the ancient British monolithic structure of Stonehenge at the time the band came a-calling. Taking the theme of the prehistoric monument, and re-working the band name within a painting of the moon's surface, this was first album sleeve that totally excluded an image of the group itself, barring the enclosed lyrical insert that featured photographs by Henry Diltz, but as to what was the relevance of the cuboid earth, or the view of Stonehenge placed mid-Atlantic on the inner spread, only Crutchfield could possibly know. Alas, following the artists passing in 2015, the inspirational thought process presumably passed with him.

The first week of August 1969 saw the band 2,000 miles away from their home state of California, performing before sold out crowds in Wisconsin, New York, New Jersey and Massachusetts. However, on August 8th, and then on the subsequent evening of the 9th, the eyes of the entire nation, as well as many from the world's media, were drawn to the horrific events that took place at 10050 Cielo Drive, a luxurious home in Benedict Canyon, north of Beverly Hills, California. Five people, including actress Sharon Tate and celebrity hair-stylist Jay Sebring were slaughtered that night by a bunch of hippie rag-tag followers of self-proclaimed disciple and ex-convict Charles Manson and his drug-addled premonitions. The following night they were undertaking a similarly gruesome act when they unceremoniously took the lives of Rosemary and Leno LaBianca, putting the attentions onto the golden state for all of the wrong reasons. Paranoia swept the city, gun sales escalated and security was multiplied tenfold, especially once it came to light that Manson had a number of high-level contacts within the L.A. music community. Anyone who sported long hair, or had any notion of hippie-belief, was viewed with suspicion. They had previously said in song that it was the death of Buddy Holly, ten years previously, in a bleak snow filled Iowa field that that was the day the music had died. For many, August 8th 1969 was the day the vision of peace, love and the idealist concept of the California dream died. Brutally...

One week later, and whilst the search was still on for the perpetrators of the crimes, the two nights of horror still unlinked at that stage, focus for some of the media turned its attention to the other side of the nation. To upstate New York where, at a 600-acre dairy farm in Bethal, Sullivan County, owned by Max Yasgur, the Woodstock Music & Art Fair took place over the weekend of 16-17th August, running one additional day either side. Initially expecting a maximum turnout of 50,000 music fans, the roads, railways and all other forms of transport in the region were clogged for days as an estimated 400,000 hippies, beatniks, poets, musicians and all other types of intellectual descended on the small community. Sullivan County declared a state of emergency.

Thirty-two differing acts were scheduled to appear, ranging from the highest paid performances of Jimi Hendrix (who was paid in the region of $15,000 for each of the two sets he performed), Blood, Sweat & Tears, Joan Baez and Creedence Clearwater Revival, down to the relatively new or lowly paid acts such as Santana (who, at the time, were promoting their debut album), former Lovin' Spoonful frontman John Sebastian, Sweetwater and Joe Cocker. However, not all those invited to participate in the event took up the option offered to them. The Doors, The Byrds, Frank Zappa and Spirit all turned down the opportunity, all unaware as to how big and influential the festival would be. After all, did *anyone* really know? Chicago Transit Authority, The Moody Blues, Jethro Tull and Free are other names that have all been linked to the gathering at one stage or another, but mention of The Association has always been overlooked. Omitted from the annals of Woodstock history. And yet Jim Yester still recalls how Pat Colecchio turned down the offer to attend, much in the same way as many others mentioned above, unsure how a weekend in a muddy field in the middle of nowhere was going to benefit or offer resurgence to their career. You take the gamble, you reap the benefit, certainly a motto that befell in favor for Hendrix, Crosby, Stills & Nash and Janis Joplin, who all came away from the weekend, somehow intact, and saw record sales and touring revenue increase significantly, especially once the resulting film, documenting the subsequent events, was released the following year.

"Pat had his shortsightedness as well…" Jim was to state to the author when discussing the band and the impact of their management across the years. "Case in point, not going back to Europe as well as turning down an invitation to Woodstock, although no one knew how that would turn out. I'm sure it would have boosted our cred in the business but hindsight is 20/20…"

With a capacity of a few thousand hardened souls braving the windswept arena in Atlantic City, it was a far cry from the almost half a million muddy, and ultimately very wet festival goers, but there was still a loyal gathering of fans seated before them when The Association played the venue out on the pier, the same weekend as the saga of Woodstock was taking place. With a set list comprising of the more established hits – "Windy", "Never My Love", "Along Comes Mary" and "Cherish", favored older cuts such as "Enter The Young", "Requiem For The Masses", "The Time It Is Today" and the show opener, "One Too Many Mornings", alongside newer tunes such as "Dubuque Blues", "Yes I Will", "Are You Ready", "Goodbye, Columbus", "Under Branches" and "What Were The Words" the band's concert appearances were still bringing in many positive reviews.

> The Association relies mainly on complex and tastefully arranged vocal harmonies for the thrust of their music. Their incomparable ability in this field often obscures the band's tremendous instrumental talent.
>
> *The Washington Evening Star*
>
> Along with the music there was a very nice rapport going between audience and performers. It was created not with very hard work and exaggerated clowning but with a simple, easy going, leisurely style and knowledge of a common intent – to have fun. Everyone did.
>
> *The Cincinnati Enquirer*

They played "Goodbye Columbus" with enthusiasm; "Cherish" better than the record (and) "Under Branches" was exceptional. It was done with only a guitar and electric organ. Seeing five of the group lined up front singing in harmony was impressive and it sounded good.

The Ohio State Lantern

Whilst many of these songs had now been in the set-list for a number of years, the band still delivered these old favorites with a fresh approach, with Ted telling the inquisitive *Ohio State Lantern* "There's a security in doing the same songs over and over, because we know we can do them just right. I try to play each song technically perfect..."

The remainder of 1969 would see the band still touring heavily, still taking their music, both old and new, to the far reaches of the U.S. Following Atlantic City, they ventured out to Nebraska and Indiana, where they were supported by the famed surf-instro demons The Ventures, and then in September it was Utah to Louisiana. The October schedule included both Texas and Indiana, followed by Michigan and Ohio, and November saw the touring cover New York and Kentucky, with return visits to both Ohio and Indiana once again. It was constant and demanding, and yet the reviews were almost always positive and professional. However, as the size of the venues changed over the years, and they were no longer playing the smaller clubs of past glories, then so did their approach to the set, particularly with regards to the comedic shtick and the audience interaction.

"That was mostly due to the type of venues we began playing as we became more popular," says Jim. "Things designed for an intimate audience didn't translate to huge arenas. We kept what could be carried by voice amplification, but things that relied on facial expressions, or slight asides just didn't translate to larger venues, and we were always serious about our music. There was no 'change of direction' as such but touring so much, we were averaging almost 290 days a year on the road, doesn't allow you the time to develop things the same way we did before the road took us away."

"We've been around long enough to know that communication with the audience is essential to a good performance," added Russ, in conversation with the *Cash Box* trade magazine. "(But) we're cutting out a lot of the skits and special material because it tends to take away from the music. That doesn't mean we're going to come on stage, do a set and not say a word..."

Further television appearances during this period saw the seven-man band performing before the cameras on ABC's *American Bandstand*, promoting "Goodbye, Columbus", along with guest slots on *Della!* and a second appearance on *The Ed Sullivan Show*. For this latter showing, broadcast live once more from the Ed Sullivan Theater on Broadway, the group performed two songs of their own choosing, as opposed to their last scheduled appearance on the show when they canceled, having been informed they must perform two of their older hits. This time around they performed "Seven Man Band", the newly updated rewrite of their 1968 single, singing along live to the original "Six Man Band" backing track, *sans* instruments and with a leather-fringe jacketed Terry Kirkman a-groovin' with the beat (note: it wasn't all televised live as certain visual segments were pre-filmed to fit in with the track). They followed this with "Dubuque Blues", executed with supreme confidence, with Brian supplying the wonderful descending lower harmonies behind Jules whilst playing his customized, hand-carved Fender Precision bass, complete with a peace symbol, a butterfly and the world 'love' carved into the woodwork (Russ also owned a hand-carved Stratocaster guitar, with the Statue of Liberty, the Empire State building, the American flag and an eagle in flight, all eloquently carved into the wooden bodywork). Meanwhile, the remaining members, positioned someway to the rear of the set, offer up their usual support, with Jim seated behind a piano. Surely, by releasing this as a single, with the ongoing positivity surrounding the song after virtually each and every concert performance, they would once again achieve their rightful position in the upper reaches of the charts? After all, the November 1969 schedules were suggesting somewhat minor competition from the likes of Bobby Sherman, Steam, The Cuff Links and a cartoon variation based upon the exploits of some of characters from the *Archie Comics* publishing house. Surely none of these would offer up any threat or notoriety in the *Billboard* Top 10?

Coupled with Larry's riff-laden "Are You Ready", a rock-gospel influenced cut featuring Joshua Fox drummer Mike Botts on drums, "Dubuque Blues" was duly released during November, coinciding with *The Ed Sullivan Show* appearance, and with the full support and publicity from Warner Bros. Unbelievably, it sank without trace. Failing to find a position on the *Billboard* charts at all, and barely scraping into the *Cash Box* Hot 100.

The year, and the decade closed out on a somber note, with a lone December guest appearance on *The Merv Griffin Show* the final appearance for 1969. For The Association the 1960s had been a decade of coming together, of incredible highs and, as the decade progressed, new lows. There had been successes, home and abroad, the fame and adulation and all that goes with it, and there had been disappointments, both personal and professional. But what would the new decade bring? Would the band survive on the fading memories that the previous decade had afforded them? Or could they rediscover themselves and resurrect a faltering career?

CHAPTER SEVENTEEN

JUST ABOUT THE SAME

'Rock', or 'pop' music in 1970 was of a mixed bag. There was no clear definition anymore of where one genre started and the other trailed away. Many of the most successful bands of the previous decade had, for better or for worse, faded away, gone their separate ways in acrimonious circumstances, or were in the process of doing so.

The Beatles, the fab-four, the mop-tops – call them what you will – were in the throes of their last waltz or, in the case of Lennon and Ono, waltzing away on the darkened set of the *Let It Be* sound stage. Within three months McCartney would mark the closing of a chapter when he officially called it a day. The Byrds, now with only McGuinn left from their hit-making years, were struggling to make a commercial impact despite the stability and undeniable quality of their current four-man line-up. Likewise, The Beach Boys, still working with a nucleus of the Wilson brothers, Love, Jardine and Johnston, albeit with big brother Brian watching cautiously from behind the curtains of his Bel Air bedroom, were in the process of releasing their gloriously harmonic *Sunflower* album, a work of wonder and a commercial disaster and their lowest charting album to date.

There were exceptional circumstances of course. The Rolling Stones were never going to fade away, not whilst Keith was strumming the chords, and fellow Brits, The Moody Blues and The Who were both reaching creative peaks, but for many of the U.S. bands who were still following in the wake of these super groups, the 1970s offered little consolation or promise. The

Monkees were now reduced to a twosome (the running joke at the time amongst the Colgems staff was that the next album would be credited to 'The Monkee'), The Buckinghams, Harpers Bizarre, Tommy James & The Shondells, The Rascals, The Turtles…

Yes, The Grass Roots and Paul Revere & The Raiders would both have one final flourish in the upper reaches of the charts and, as the new decade kicked off, who was to say The Association wouldn't? Warner Bros. still saw enough commercial potential in the band to continue offering their support. The publicity launch for *The Association* album had seen a number of full-page advertisements in the music press, and they didn't come cheaply. So, encouraged by the labels ongoing financial support, the band re-entered the studio to cut a brand new song for their next release.

Having finished working with The Association back in mid-1966 Curt Boettcher had been involved in a number of subsequent projects, the first of which had been The Ballroom, a studio based project incorporating a similar session team of like-minded souls, including singer and composer Sandy Salisbury. Together they had recorded an album's worth of material, including the collaboration with Jules Alexander, "Would You Like To Go", Unfortunately, only one unsuccessful single from the band was ever officially released during that period and the line-up quickly dissolved. At the same time Boettcher was also involved with seasoned record producer Gary Usher, a veteran of the surf and hot-rod recording scene (and former collaborator with Brian Wilson) and, more recently, the producer for The Byrds 1966 album *Younger Than Yesterday*. Working as a partnership Usher and Boettcher produced the lavishly psychedelic pop of Sagittarius' *Present Tense* (which also included The Ballroom's original version of "Would You Like To Go") and then, by using Usher's clout in the industry and Boettcher's previous successes with both The Association and Tommy Roe (he had produced two 45's for Roe the same year), they convinced Columbia Records to finance Boettcher's next studio project; The Millennium. With an expanded session team, including Sandy Salisbury, Lee Mallory, drummer Ron Edgar, and guitarist Michael Fennelly, along with contributions from seasoned pros such as pedal steel player Red Rhodes and banjoist Doug Dillard, the studio was full of hi-tech sounds, overdubbed vocals and instrumentation. The Millennium project was also noteworthy for being the most expensive, and expansive, album Columbia Records had backed up to that point. Supposedly, it had it all. Robb Royer, founding member of the band Bread, and a former alumni of the Troubadour/The Men era, recalled those heady days in conversation with the author: "We really thought for three or four months there that the Millennium was going to be the biggest thing. Forget The Beatles. And then (the album) came out and did absolutely nothing!"

Despite a lack of commercial success, this 14-track release, issued during 1968, remains a wonderful 'sunshine-pop' timepiece to this very day, fifty years later. However, still with the buzz of creativity surrounding the sessions, Curt and his team went back into the Columbia Studios during the fall of 1968, located at 6121 Sunset Boulevard, intent of starting work on a follow-up release. These later recordings resulted in just two songs being cut, before the project crumbled – "Blight" and "Just About The Same" – the latter of which bared the songwriting credits of Boettcher and Fennelly, along with fellow band members Joey Stec and Doug Rhodes.

"After the first album we began work on a follow-up amidst a hail of bad shit from Columbia. They really came down on us," Curt was to comment in a conversation with journalist Ray McCarthy for *Zig-Zag* magazine. "They thought we were some kind of cosmic hoax! We had recorded two songs, one of which was called 'Just About The Same'. It actually has parts of 'It's You' (from the debut album) in it, where it goes 'aah aah aah aah aah la la la la'. That's from "It's You'. If you take that song and play it backwards, you'll get what I just sang. So, as a little pun, we called it 'Just About The Same' because it was written by playing the tape backwards. We were down, it was a down song, but it had 1930s scat singing, and Michael (Fennelly) and I did two-part scat singing which I thought was really a gas!

"Jack Gold (head of Columbia A&R) heard the two new things, which were really an added dimension of music for The Millennium, and he said, "That's a piece of shit!" And that's all it took. We just disintegrated..." [16]

The two new recordings were placed back in the studio vaults.

With The Millennium now in tatters around him, Boettcher instead worked on various ideas and creations over the following year or so, until in late 1969 he once again reconnected with The Association with the idea of working on a number of new recordings together. Four or five songs were initially mapped out for the revitalized partnership including one new song entitled "Justine", composed by two relatively unknown Boettcher associates named David Batteau and Tommy Logan, along with some new songs by Bob Wachtel, a New York-born composer and the guitarist in the recently re-located L.A. band Twice Nicely. Wachtel would later go on to adopt the nickname of 'Waddy' and become one of L.A.'s hottest and most popular session players during the following decades. Jules also recalls today that another song under consideration was one with the dubious title of "Unzip My Love". "One that was maybe just a little ahead of its time…" he adds with a laugh.

Finally, Boettcher proposed that the band overdub some harmonies onto one of The Millennium's discarded recordings from fifteen months previous, the infectious "Just About The Same". Sadly, despite the concept of cutting a number of these tracks together, this one song would prove to be the only result from the renewed partnership. With Michael Fennelly, Joey Stec and Lee Mallory having all played guitar on the original track, with Doug Rhodes providing the distinctive bass lines, and drums handled by Ron Edgar, the 1968 recording of "Just About The Same" was, essentially, fully completed before it was abandoned, and there was no need for The Association to add any additional accompaniment, other than their own harmony stacks, to make it their own, building on top of what was already there.

"I think it was our idea to work together again," suggests Jules. "But it really didn't work out. As much as he liked the vocals he was very much into the instrumental stuff, and one of the tunes we did with him was on a 16-track, or maybe it was a 24-track, and when it came time to do the vocals I asked him 'how many tracks do we have left to do the vocals?' and he said 'two!' We decided not to go with him for that very reason…" [37]

A somewhat bitter Boettcher would later go on to comment, "I dubbed The Association's vocals on top of The Millennium track, and they couldn't even cut the vocal! They didn't even do the vocal one tenth as good as The Millennium did!" [16]

A harsh claim from the disgruntled producer, as the addition of the overdubbed vocals, cut at the Village Recorders studios over in West L.A. on January 13th 1970, certainly added to the original tapes. As to why the relationship was rekindled in the first place no-one can truly recall the full scenario and maybe, as Jules suggests, it was simply a group idea to try it again, but with John Boylan now moving on to work with a number of other artists, as the demand for his producing abilities increased, The

Association were always looking out for new opportunity. Certainly, the opportunity to record new material was always high on the agenda and a number of potential 'outside' compositions were regularly screened at the band 'hangings' and listening sessions. Songs that have now gone on to become standards of U.S. radio rotation were often played over first at these Association gatherings, more than likely in rough demo form, with the band often missing the opportunity to cut the songs for one reason or another. "He Ain't Heavy (He's My Brother)" (a huge worldwide hit for The Hollies in 1969) has been reported as getting an early demo airing for The Association, as did later smashes for Three Dog Night ("Joy To The World") and Norman Greenbaum ("Spirit In The Sky"). As to whether any of these would have been of any benefit to the band is irrelevant today, as each artist subsequently took the song and arranged it to their own suitability, but one cannot deny that the potential was there in each case if the opportunity had just been taken.

Not that it was always their own careers at the forefront of their minds either. Such was the music community around Los Angeles during the late 1960s/early 1970s that, at any given time, folk would happily join other artists in the studios to help out where needed, or to simply hang out with fellow musicians. The previous year had seen Jules, during a break in the touring schedule, drop by a studio in Chicago to watch local band The New Colony Six whilst they were cutting their next single, the delightful "Barbara, I Love You" – the result being that his own vocal abilities and arrangements were added to the final mix. Likewise, that same period had seen him associating with another local L.A. band, The Joint Effort, managed by a fellow Sant Mat devotee, Bud Mathis. A later article in *Ugly Things* magazine suggested that Jules may have even shown an interest in working with the band on a permanent basis, but today he suggests that his interest in them may have been misrepresented and that, despite his interest in the band and their vocal abilities, he had no intention of joining up with them.

"At that time in L.A. Bud had the only spiritual book store in town, and both he and I were into Sant Mat and we hung out. Bud told me about this band with lots of vocals, and I thought 'God! I'd love to go see them' because we were the only others who did that in rock 'n' roll, but I don't know how it got around that I wanted to join them! I just wanted to see them!" [37]

Additionally, during 1970, Jim Yester aided a group of acclaimed country-rock pioneers – Buddy Emmons, Jay Dee Maness, Red Rhodes,

Sneaky Pete Kleinow and Rusty Young – with their pedal steel *Suite Steel* album, providing rhythm guitar alongside his wife, Joellen, at a number of the sessions. Sitting alongside the Yesters, providing piano, electric guitar and production duties, was the increasingly in-demand John Boylan.

"We were part of a music community that was more of a brotherhood than a competition. We all hung out at the Troubadour together before we all made it and somewhat afterwards as well…" [33]

February 4th 1970 saw the release of "Just About The Same" as Warner Bros. 45-7372. With Terry's "Look At Me, Look At You", the opening cut of *The Association*, as the flip-side this was by far the most commercial offering the band had released for over a year and was a release clearly in sync with the music dominating the charts at that time, so as to why this once again continued the band's concerning decline in chart glory remains bewildering. Underneath the layers of glorious harmony one could argue that it was not an 'Association' tune *per se*, it had no group involvement other than a vocal contribution over an existing track, but that mattered little to a record buying public who, for reasons that remain unclear, forty years after the event, once more chose to push it aside, resulting in a dismal number 106 *Billboard* position. Of interest, the version of "Look At Me, Look At You" as released on the 45 was a different mix to that which had appeared on the earlier album, with Terry overdubbing an additional harmony vocal himself (unlike the album cut which featured Jules). Not that the band had time to dwell on such disappointments. Despite the waning record sales, the demand for concert appearances was as great as ever and Pat Colecchio was keen to see the band pulling in the crowds as much as possible. The university concert circuit was a staple for many bands of the early 1970s era, and from week to week a variety of headlining acts made the rounds between states, performing before cross-legged groups of students, squatting together in enclosed gymnasiums. Many former fellow chart contenders were now content to rebuild their fortunes in such non-prestigious surroundings, their record selling ability now in a comparative slump, hopping to the larger theaters and venues when demand necessitated. One can only relate to the tale of the legendary Beach Boys, million-selling hit-makers of just a few years previous, reduced to performing to just 300 paying attendees at a show in South Dakota during their own late '60s/early '70s slump in popularity. A humbling experience from which to bounce back from. And how…

The first two weeks of March 1970 saw The Association in a similar mixed bag, performing at the 5,500-capacity Felt Forum, Madison Square Gardens in New York City on the first day of the month, in a show that also featured The Byrds, retro rockers Sha Na Na and the Michigan-based psychedelic band The Frost. Interestingly, The Byrds set was recorded for a proposed live album, part of which appeared on their Columbia-released *Untitled* album, released later that year. This was followed, two weeks later, by a slot of The Alfred State College Gym in western New York state, a popular touring venue for the period. A surviving audience recording from the Felt Forum show reveals a strong performance from the seven-man band, still committed to delivering their very best for each performance. From the opening introduction of "One Too Many Mornings", through to the closing refrains of "Enter The Young" the band runs through polished renditions of "The Time It Is Today", "Yes I Will", "Dubuque Blues", "Everything That Touches You", "Goodbye, Columbus", "Requiem For The Masses", "Just About The Same", "Blistered" and "Are You Ready?", alongside the requisite Top 5 hits and a few of the more accessible comedic one-liners.

March 1 1970: Felt Forum, New York City, NY
March 10 1970: Brown County Veterans Arena, Green Bay, WI
March 14 1970: Alfred State College Gymnasium, Alfred, NY
March 15 1970: Glassboro State College, Glassboro, NJ
April 3 1970: University of Utah, Salt Lake City, UT
April 15 1970: Albee Hall, Oshkosh, WI
April 16 1970: University Arena, Eau Claire, WI
April 17 1970: Eastern Michigan University, Ypsilanti, MI
April 18 1970: Purdue University, West Lafayette, IN

Some call them plastic. Some call them hygienic. They aren't deep in today's heavy scene. But The Association is something else. They proved that Tuesday night in the Brown County Arena, especially in their striking climax by performing four of their best-known and most loved hits, "Cherish", "Requiem For The Masses", "Windy" and, as an encore, "Enter The Young".

Strangely, for a group only five years old, it was basically a night for grooving nostalgia. The LA septet hasn't been recording for the past few years, hasn't made the charts and therefore hasn't been in the foreground much. Still, they can't be forgotten, especially with all that talent roaming the stage.

The Green Bay Gazette
March 11 1970

Clearly, despite the obvious misinformation supplied to the media on occasion, the lack of chart success in certain areas was having a devastating effect on the public's awareness of the band. The recent recording and release of *The Association* album hadn't even touched base in certain markets of the country, despite the heavy promotional push from the record label. In the same 1970 edition of the *Green Bay Gazette* Jim Yester was also interviewed for a separate article on the band's current situation, commenting that 'singles and two albums are on tap. One of which will be of a live concert', before adding that 'the product isn't going to change much in direction. The emphasis will remain on vocals, with a creative instrumental base.'

The article went on to refer that, following work on *Goodbye, Columbus*, the band had more offers to do film scores but would only consider that option if, firstly, the project was one they could identify with and, secondly, was one that would ensure them full control over the music.

"Our structure is democratic. There is no leader. Everything is done by a common vote. Once in a while, we may have two feeling one way and five feeling the other. We end up doing what the five want…"

On April 3rd the band traveled to the University of Utah, located in the state capital of Salt Lake City. Traveling alongside them was resident photographer Jim Metropole, along with a mobile recording facility hired from the Wally Heider Studios, headed by producer Ray Pohlman and engineer Michael Shields. Pohlman, a veteran of the recording scene as both producer and session player (as one of the initial first-call players in the Wrecking Crew, he is credited as being the earliest electric bass player in the L.A. studio scene), was charged with capturing the performance onto tape, with a view to releasing the live recording as the next album, as Jim had previously suggested to the media.

"Ray was a good friend socially as well as musically," says Jim Yester. "He also did a lot of work for Bones Howe, who had produced the third and fourth albums. In fact, Ray did most of the charts for those sessions."

As much like the Felt Forum audience recording from the previous month the eventual *Association Live* album, issued by Warner Bros. during

May 1970 (2WS-1868), only captured part of the performance from that night, although running at 77 minutes in total, spread over two discs, the twenty-one songs featured, along with short comedic inserts ("there is good news, there is bad news... then there is Agnews...") and the anti-war short spoken word story of James Thurber, formed the backbone of the set-list (only "Everything That Touches You", "Yes I Will" and "Under Branches" were noticeable absentees).

The performance captured by Pohlman and Shields offers up one of the most satisfying double-album collections from that entire era, highlighting the band in their performing prime, without the need for seasoned session musicians. The high altitude of the venue had initially raised a few concerns, with the thinner air quality potentially causing issues with sustaining long notes and keeping the instruments in tune, but the band had played in the high cities of Utah on numerous occasions before and were fully aware as to the variable effects on their performance, keeping a plentiful supply of oxygen tanks in the dressing room and just off-stage.

Richie Unterberger's CD reissue sleeve notes, released in 2003, recount Jim Yester's reaction to the album: "By and large, it was very representative of what was going on. One of the things I noticed years later in listening to it is, you can really hear the battle that's going on between the two lead guitars. They're trying to top each other all the time, and I wish one of them would have just comped. But it was what it was, and I think by and large, we were all very pleased with it. I think a lot of people were surprised at that time, that we were as strong as we were instrumentally, just on our own. I went out to Wally Heider's truck out in back of the auditorium afterwards and they threw up a rough mix, just brought up all the faders, and the first time they played anything back I went, 'My God! That's how we sound?' I was blown away." [18]

More recently, Terry has commented on social media how the band would often prepare for such a show beforehand, enjoying the atmosphere of the larger arenas and gymnasiums. "We loved warming up before a show in the team showers of the big arenas. (They had) the best echo chambers ever. Sometimes the harmonies would create notes that hadn't even been sung – overtones – and when the echo was right I could even play harmonies with myself on the horn."

Yet, when it came down to the final mixing and listening of the original tapes, it became evident that some of the performance would need additional recording and overdubbing in the studio, once they returned to Los Angeles, just to ensure the quality was uninterrupted throughout the release. Subsequently, certain tracks, especially near the top of the set when microphone difficulties were evident on the tapes, were overdubbed accordingly, although to the album listener the differences remain minimal and barely noticeable, if at all. Terry's flugelhorn solos on "Requiem For The Masses" were also subject to additional studio work, as the sky-hugging Utah altitude had clearly affected the live performance, which sounded flat at times. If the listener were to pay close attention to the eventual release it almost sounded like a second player was standing alongside on stage…

"To say I was playing flat was an understatement! So I re-recorded a second part," Terry confirmed. [20]

One final addition to the album was the added bonus of an opening track, a short Ted Bluechel composition entitled "Dream Girl". "We recorded that upstairs in my bathroom, weeks after the concert," noted Ted, when asked about it in the *Goldmine* article. "It was just a fun thing, and I thought it would be really funny to weasel this song in so we scrambled to the bathroom and acted like we were in the dressing room and bled that into the dressing room track out to the stage!" Sadly, one track also soon fell by the wayside with Brian Cole's recitation of James Thurber's "The Last Flower", spoken as a prelude to "Get Together", edited out of all subsequent pressings and reissues of the album due to a publishing dispute.

> Forgive me if I'm a bit disconnected today; I was up late last night, at a party to welcome the new Association album, a gathering of friends, and press and food and drink, in the recording studio, to preview 'The Association: Live'. It's a complete concert, with tune-ups, funny remarks, offstage comments, applause, and The Association – sometimes off-key but most often exactly on.
>
> It was a very nice party. I don't know too many groups who have the courage to appear at a large gathering where their album is being heard for the first time.
>
> Judy Sims
> *Disc Magazine*
> June 1970

With additional publicity, care of two limited edition 7" 45rpm vinyl pressings, featuring differing 60-second radio promotion spots (WB Pro-413 and 418) issued to the top radio stations:

"Great concerts happen in cities like New York, Los Angeles, San Francisco. For The Association it happened in Salt Lake City..."

...the album went on to reach a high of number 79 position in the *Billboard* Top 200 charts, a respectable placement for a 2-LP live set with a higher retail price than the norm. Packaged in an eye-catching royal blue gatefold sleeve, designed once more by award-winning Warner's Art Director Ed Thrasher, and adorned with raised silver lettering and imitation brocade, along with a series of wonderful full color photographic images taken by Jim Metropole during the same performance as the recording, the offering had one further special inclusion for the long term fan and collector of the band. After much demand they finally had a rendition of the popular "One Too Many Mornings" to put onto the family turntable – the 1965 single version having long been out of print by then. The inclusion of this, a live rendition of their second 45, along with their cover of "Get Together", was a continuing nod back to the early days of their folk club roots when, along with "Poison Ivy", they would feature these cover versions within their set. Fortunately, whilst "Poison Ivy" was dropped from the shows during 1968, the addition of the popular Dylan and Valenti compositions were an added bonus for buyers of the new album.

One further note of interest, to those who scrutinized every printed word within, there was an additional series of credits represented on the inner gatefold sleeve – in small text there was a thank you to a number of the band's own employees for their contribution to the touring set up and two names in particular stood out – Rick Colecchio, Pat's son, who was now also a regular addition to the backstage team, having taken over Ray Staar's former role as lighting engineer, and Darryl Palagi, who had followed Jules over from the Joshua Fox band to join up as road assistant on The Association tour bus. Sound technician Steve Nelson also merited credit in print, as did touring road manager Pete Stefanos and his predecessor, Lee Leibman, now one of Pat's trustworthy office team

Darryl recalls today: "I was working with Joshua Fox when Jules decided to rejoin The Association. About two weeks later I got a call, I believe it was from Jules, with an offer to work with The Association myself, and I accepted the position. As I recall, Joshua Fox was in development from late 1967 to early 1968, the project was only active for a few months and I then went to work with The Association from 1968 to the end of 1969, early 1970, at which time I went on to work with Bread, reuniting with Mike Botts (from Joshua Fox) once more. I seem to recall there may have even been some overlap between The Association's schedule and Bread's schedule.

"The friendship between Mike and Brian Cole was also a primary link between The Association, Bread, and me. We had a pretty strong and direct communication. We were all around each other a great deal at various times. It was a very creative situation. In some ways Joshua Fox brought many of us together for a period of time. The Association was the first touring band I ever worked with and I was sort of swept away by it all. The whole situation was a great rock 'n' roll adventure. I loved all of it and I loved the band. It truly was fun. There was diversity among us all, yet it felt like a brotherhood. The band members and the crew always had access to each other and from my perspective everyone was having a good time. It was hard work, but I was thrilled to be involved. My primary concern was band set-up. Steve Nelson handled the audio, and lights were in the hands of Rick Colecchio, Pat's son. We didn't carry any lighting. As I recall, lighting was pretty much about calling follow spots and cueing whatever we might have had for house lights. A great many of our venues were college gyms. At that time, the college circuit was large and lucrative so we played a number of those venues. It was my first tour, and it was the real deal."

"When I started I knew nothing about stages, let alone lighting," adds Rick Colecchio. "It was all trial and error. Thank God, there weren't big light shows back then, although The Association could have performed with just a flashlight. My theory was to just set the mood in the beginning of the song, and close it down at the end. All the guys needed were their voices and their instruments. The Association was, and still is a finely tuned music machine. We played with some of the top artists over the years, and in my opinion, the original Association was one of, if not *the* best performing bands of the day.

"I started with the band in '68. At that time, Steve Nelson and Pete Stefanos were on the road, with Pete having replaced Lee Leibman as road manager. My dad had wanted Lee to stay at the office and so he had made Pete the road manager. However, I think what happened was, dad said 'until Rick gets the hang of this, Lee you go back out, help Pete and show Rick what to do. He doesn't know crap about any of this. He had a boutique on Madison Avenue last week!'

"Lee took care of the monies, the promoters, and he really knew a lot about lighting. (For) my first gig, he brought me up to the lighting booth and said, 'just keep the lights on!'.

"It was like that until the guys had a bigger soundboard made, which needed more hands in transportation. Enter Darryl. Darryl stayed through the *Live* album and then when he left Merv Matloff came in…

"Naturally a few more European tours could not have hurt, but back then bands weren't getting the dollars they are today. We were playing three or four nights a week in the U.S., so I guess dad felt that the cost of travel and lodging for ten guys, just to play a weekend overseas outweighed our steady flow of income in the states. That is just my thoughts, I never was in the office on decisions.

"The one and only time I disagreed with my dad over his decisions was when he chose not to film the live concert while we were recording the album in Salt Lake City…"

There are two types of groups making rock music today. There are first and foremost the groups that make music for the sake of music. These include The Band and Jefferson Airplane. On the other hand, there are groups whose existence is based on stage performance. Among them are The Who, Crosby, Stills, Nash & Young, and The Association. On their latest album, The Association proves its worth in the world of theatrics. Beginning with a few Top 40 hits, namely 'Along Comes Mary' and 'Goodbye Columbus', the group includes in this two-record set amusing stories, poems and requiems, and on-stage antics which, surprisingly, come out very well on record.

The Association's vocal virtuosity, the variable that sets this group apart from others, is contained here and the instruments, thankfully, are for once considered secondary.

Bill Mackay
Asbury Park Press
August 1970

CHAPTER EIGHTEEN

ONCE UPON A WHEEL

May 1 1970: DePauw University, Greencastle, IN
May 2 1970: Capitol University, Columbus, OH
May 5 1970: MacArthur High School Gymnasium, Decatur, IL
May 6 1970: Mankato State College, Mankato, MN
May 8 1970: Auditorium Theater, Chicago, IL
May 9 1970: Auditorium Theater, Chicago, IL
May 12 1970: Milliken University, Decatur, IL

Following a series of concert performances during early May the band took a short break from touring, returning to Los Angeles to take some personal time before regrouping in the recording studio to start work on their next venture together. However, the constant battles that the seven-strong composite were now regularly facing, often resorting to yelling and screaming as each individual part of the unit demanded their views and opinions heard at their meetings, was slowly bringing down certain members of the band, with the June 1970 edition of the Association Admiration Aggregation newsletter ultimately reporting that 'one of the Associates has decided to extend his vacation, and relax a little while longer than the other Associates. Russ is taking a leave of absence, for how long he doesn't know. During the time that Russ is gone, an old friend of the Association will take his place...'

"Everything was just too contentious. I think it had gotten real big and everything took on such importance'" recalled Russ, when reminiscing over his departure. "Everything was a big fat discussion, which is sort of the way The Men broke up. I really didn't think about going solo. I was just taking a break…"[1/18]

Clearly unhappy with the current position the band was in, both internally and externally, and frustrated by his personal lack of headlining moments, Russ tendered his notice during June 1970, opting to take time out for himself, to take stock, before the pull of the music was once again to bring him back.

Without Russ Giguere in the line-up, it was a new phase for The Association. Although, on a purely instrumental platform, excepting rhythm guitar and percussion, Russ was never a major player in their live or studio performances, but when it came to the actual structure of the group – the concept, creativity and vocal abilities – Russ Giguere was deemed an integral part of the unit, and his departure was viewed by many as creating a significant void. Indeed, many of the earlier comedy routines that the band had amalgamated into their live shows were created from the innovative perception of Russ's thinking. Although they could so easily have reverted back to a six-piece line-up the remaining members opted to replace Russ, maintaining the fuller sound, both instrumentally and vocally, of the seven-man unit, bringing in the multi-talented, classically trained Richard Thompson as the new official associate. Much in the same mold as Terry, and comfortable on numerous instruments – keyboards, woodwinds and horns – Richard had a wealth of experience to hand, having worked on a number of studio projects in the preceding years, predominantly with a jazz base.

"Richard was a godsend," suggest Jim, when asked for his recollections about their then-new recruit. "He was a for real pianist, and I had been holding down that slot as well as rhythm guitar, so he was a most welcome addition as far as I was concerned. He came in to replace Russ as a full member of the band, not just a sideman, and he was immensely talented, and never wore it on his sleeve, and was very supportive of the other guys' talents."

"It was a completely different band," adds Jules. "The whole dynamic changed. Russ was a rhythm guitarist, but he couldn't really add to the musical discussion very much but Richard very much a part of it, and a participant in it. He was one of the finest piano players and probably one of the smartest men I've ever met. To me, he was in the Bill Evans class of piano playing. However, he was not a great singer at all! He could sing background, if he sang on pitch and he came in at the right time! But his contribution was mainly instrumental…"

His musical contributions to John Klemmer's Chicago-based recording of *Blowin' Gold* (1969) and the subsequent *All The Children Cried* (1970) album (working alongside future Association sidemen Wolfgang Melz, Maurice Miller and Art Johnson during the late 1969 sessions), or the jazz-fusion overtones of The Advancement's eponymous album for the Phillips label, along with the Hungarian-born guitarist Gábor Szabó's *Magical Connection* (1970), were all noteworthy examples of his initial growing stature in the industry, and both Richard and bassist Wolfgang Melz had formed a formidable partnership as a part of Szabó's supporting sextet during that period.

Born in San Diego, and having grown up in and around Los Angeles with a Mensa level IQ, he had initially come to the attention of The Association via his friendship with Terry and, secondly, whilst performing as a member of The Cosmic Brotherhood, another jazz-focused L.A. gathering who used to perform regular gigs at the outdoor Pilgrimage Theater in Cahuenga Pass, located near the famous Hollywood Cross, the famed 32-foot monument soaring high in the hills above the Hollywood Freeway.

"I went to see them on a Sunday afternoon," recalls Terry, "and it was very hot out, and I thought 'the last thing I want to do is see a bunch of stoned jazz musicians at this theater in 90 degrees heat', and yet within minutes I had tears rolling out my eyes. The sound just blew my mind! It was the most exciting thing ever…"

After being introduced to the band Richard became a regular addition to the studio sessions that were, ultimately, to develop into 1969s *The Association* album so, by the time he was asked to join the line-up on a permanent basis, he was already fully aware as to how he would slot into the newly reconstructed band demographics, adding both keyboards and horn parts at his Atlantic City debut with the performing band on July 4th and 5th 1970.

Musings
Unattached

Uncombined

Civil wars, symphonies a balloon (Helium or not) weigh grams or pounds

No more than careless terrors (or less) than marriages with grass between barefoot toes

But come the longing onlooker

Blinking the sun of vague and fleeing shadows

Not covered thoughts

But old and unfamiliar miles

New but similar plodding afternoons

A covered wagon baring no explanation

But its creaking wheels

Poetry by Richard Thompson

Late June had seen the band take the first tentative steps back in the studio, the first sessions without Russ, cutting tracks for an all-too rare composition from Brian Cole. Struggling with his mounting dependence on various substances Brian's contributions were, by now, becoming somewhat erratic and the band rallied around their comrade as best they could, but it was fast becoming apparent that it was not going to be an easy ride back for Brian.

"Brian was an extremely intelligent guy," noted Ted. "But he built psychological walls around him to protect himself, (and) he began using drugs to shield himself." [20]

Not that the other band members were wholly innocent themselves. After all, the late 1960s and early 1970s recording studios, backstage lounges and celebrity parties were awash with dope peddlers, dealers and suppliers, offering whatever narcotic you wished to get your hands on and your nostrils around, and the various substances on offer around them were clearly plentiful. A number of the band members had also freely experimented with psychedelics before they were mainstream amongst the music fraternity.

Jim: "It was very early on, when it was still legal as I recall. There was Van Dyke Parks, about five girls and myself. We had one dose, which Van Dyke had put in a pot of tea, which everyone shared, and then he sat on the floor with everyone and read from *The Tibetan Book of the Dead*. How hip!"

Terry Kirkman, who would fall into deep dependence himself during the ensuing years, later recounted in poetry such an inglorious evening spent alongside a group of fellow musicians, sampling the delights of various materials one late 1968 evening in the Tin Angel Café, a popular night spot located in Greenwich Village's Bleecker Street district.

> There were seven or eight of us as I recall
> All high on acclaim and fame
> All topping the charts and breaking girls' hearts
> A covey of dropable names
> Phil Ochs, Timmy Hardin, Brian Cole, Joe Butler
> Zal Yanovsky, Paul Butterfield, and me
> And a couple of other not so droppable names
> Just as [messed] up as we could be.
> All strutting our stories, talkin' women and riches,
> One uppin' each other like mad
> And I remember thinkin' it was the absolute hippest
> Best time that I'd ever had
>
> *Scratch The Surface Of A Poet*
> Terry Kirkman

Ted would later comment to Steve Stanley, for the Now Sounds CD re-issues, that this particular round of sessions for Brian's song, entitled "Traveler's Guide (Spanish Flyer)", was but a fleeting glimpse of his friend contributing to a current recording date with enthusiasm. Sadly, this would appear to be a rare occurrence, as the following months were to see him spiral yet further into dependency.

Shortly afterwards the band began cutting further tracks for a number of other new songs, although not all of these were intended for the next Association project as such, as some were specifically composed with a new documentary film in mind. And despite Jim's earlier comments that, following on from *Goodbye, Columbus*, they hoped to have full autonomy on any soundtrack work they were involved in, for this new work they would once again share the billing alongside other performers.

Sponsored by the giant Coca-Cola corporation ABC-TV were currently to be found working in liaison with the British-born film producer and director David Winters and top-grossing movie star Paul Newman, to produce an hour-long film documenting the history of auto racing. Newman, a huge enthusiast of the sport, was set to narrate the spectacle, working alongside other notable auto fanatics such as Kirk Douglas, Dean Martin, Dick Smothers and Cesar Romero, but an accompanying music soundtrack was also required to add to the background, or whilst the narration gave way to action. The Association or, more directly, Terry Kirkman was asked to provide a number of songs for the project, to be titled *Once Upon A Wheel*, with a proposed soundtrack album set to accompany the release of the film the following year, theatrically in some countries (whilst in the U.S. it was scheduled for broadcast on TV).

Terry himself, who composed three new songs with the concept in mind (a fourth addition offered up for use, "Time For Livin'", was simply the two-year old album cut from the *Birthday* album), later recalled: "It was going to be Coca-Cola's No.1 promotional campaign of the decade! (But) it was a disaster! Coca-Cola had ads printed up, the albums were pressed, and, in the end, they ended up eating the whole thing."

In addition to the promotional ads, Paul Newman aided the campaign, appearing in various magazines talking about the film (whilst wearing a Coca-Cola emblazoned racing jacket), and viewers of the show, upon its eventual release, could also mail order the collectible promotional 8-track cartridges or cassette tapes featuring the accompanying music. However, for reasons that still remain unclear, no official soundtrack album was ever launched to the retailers, and the limited supply of promotional cartridges and cassettes were the only formats produced containing the new recordings, a strange outcome seeing the glowing reviews the documentary went on to achieve.

Spectacular! Paul Newman and celebs performed for director David Winters with *joie de la cause*, abetted by extraordinary editing. A poetic study of man and machines. Incredible effect. Most exciting.

Hollywood Reporter

Warner Bros./Reprise music which is used in a television special about auto racing, will be sold via mail order in special 8-track and cassette packages. The tapes will be sold by Coca-Cola, which sponsors the TV special, 'Once Upon A Wheel', April 18 on ABC-TV. The show's title tune was written by Terry Kirkman and Richard Thompson and performed by The Association.

Billboard

This 13-track promotional release, featuring an image of Newman behind the wheel on the front cover, was distributed exclusively by Coca-Cola in partnership with Warner Bros. Records (catalog reference PRO-444) and featured a variety of artists, all connected, or signed directly to the Warner's label. Some of the recordings appeared solely on this collection, making them much desired rarities amongst collectors, whilst others later appeared on the artists' own releases.

Kenny Rogers & The First Edition "Camptown Ladies"
Arlo Guthrie "Oh, In The Morning" / "Wheel Of Fortune"
Cher "Gentle Foe"
James Taylor "Fire And Rain"
Wilson Pickett "Engine Number 9"
Charles Wright & The Watts 103rd Street Rhythm Band "Your Love"
Fresh Air "Moving Wheels" / "Buddy Can You Spare The Time"
The Association "Once Upon A Wheel" / "First Sound" / "I'm Going To Be A Racin' Star"

For their part The Association, under the production auspices of Terry, and with Richard Thompson undertaking most of the arrangements, cut the three new Kirkman compositions; the title track and "First Sound", both co-written in partnership with Richard, with the latter highlighting Terry's rich baritone range to capacity, along with "I'm Going To Be A Racin' Star", a solid country-influenced tune that featured Brian Cole part singing, part narrating, accompanied by fiddles, pickin' gee-tars and Richard's honky-tonk piano riffs. Working alongside studio arranger Don Randi, himself an experienced Wrecking Crew sessioneer, the tracks were efficiently cut in double quick time – after all, time is money – so much so that Randi reportedly taped the actual track for "Racin' Star" in, literally, double time – i.e. twice the speed Terry had originally envisaged!

"When I found out I called up Ray Pohlman and we were at Laramie Sound the next morning, grabbing guys. Brian sang it in one take and it was mixed and mastered in one hour and 15 minutes… [20]

"The most important song I had written for the film was 'First Sound', and the producers had asked me to go back in and make it thirty seconds longer, which we did, and then it wasn't in the finished product because it was too long! That song just blew my mind…"

As for the title track itself, the soon-to-be-forgotten "Once Upon A Wheel", this kicked off effectively with a rhythmic guitar riff and congas, over a simple string arrangement, before the multi-textured vocals commenced, with Terry to the fore:

Once upon a wheel
Once you've got the feel
Of movin', movin' faster
Make that wheel know you're the master
You've gotta know you might never come down

"Once Upon A Wheel"
Words and Music by Terry Kirkman-Richard Thompson

"I remember those sessions quite well," adds Jim Yester. "That's when Terry was trying to get his producer chops happening. It was his project and we were just extras on the scene. He and Richard did all the arranging and we sang the charts. I don't think anybody made any money on it, as the production costs were pretty outrageous from what I heard later. It was a nice project though and the movie was pretty cool. Most of us were into the racing scene, so we enjoyed that aspect of it…" [33]

With sessions ongoing, some of which would end up on the next studio album, the group resumed its touring schedule, still performing in a mixture of small town auditoriums, universities and, whenever Nixon's budget cutting would allow, smaller college halls.

"Those college concerts were so much fun" recalls Jim today. "The college audiences were so hip, and they got *everything*. We did more comedy then, the patter and inside jokes, and boy, the college audiences just ate that up…"

Another popular performing arena was the larger annual State Fairs, prevalent during the warmer summer months, and between August and September 1971 they graced the stages at both the Nebraska and Wisconsin yearly gatherings.

There were radio ads all that summer stating that The Association would be appearing at the Nebraska State Fair, so I conned my mother into taking me. I recall that, on the ticket booth, *The Association Live* LP had been opened up and stapled to the wall as a sort of advertisement so that the photo-spread served as a teaser to entice people to buy tickets.

Once we were seated I saw Ted showing Jules some drum tricks up on stage and (although) I cannot remember every song they played, I do recall, once they all came up on stage, having trouble finding Russ. I had no inkling at the time that Richard Thompson, who later did a terrible job of introducing "Cherish", had replaced him. I remember Terry doing the 'checking our tuning and readjusting our sound' monologue from the *Live* album and I'm pretty sure Brian performed both "Dubuque Blues" and "Travelers Guide". Larry also performed an absolutely lovely self-composition entitled "Gypsy Boy", whilst Jim sang one of Richard's compositions, "Faith" [sic]. Their last number was "Under Branches" and they did a beautiful job of it, way superior to the album or single. But this was an outdoor concert and the wind had kicked up – and I mean really bad – stuff was just about literally blowing off stage – so the rest of the show was canceled and we drove back to Omaha in quite a nasty storm. Tornado season in Nebraska, don't you know.

Joseph W. Marek
Nebraska State Fair Review

A review of the show also appeared in the following weeks *Lincoln Evening Journal*, confirming the ferocity of the violent storm, whilst remarking how the group, somewhat ironically, didn't get to perform the encore of "Windy" for the 11,000 attendees that evening as, at around the sixty-minute mark, the overhead tarp was ripped to shreds by the wind and rain and the speakers and stage backdrops swayed and toppled…

The mention in the above review of Larry's unrecorded composition, "Gypsy Boy", reminds one of how many works still actually remained in the vaults during the band's successful years of recording or, in some cases, remained solely represented in the performing arena, never even venturing into the confines of a studio environment. From the very early live performances of "CC Rider", "Poison Ivy" and "Get Together", and the debut sessions for "If You Really Need Somebody", through to Curt Boettcher and Lee Mallory's "Better Times", the Addrisi brothers compositions "Autumn Afternoon" and "Decorated For Love", the incomplete "The Christmas Song" and Russ's "I Still Love You", right up to the early 1970s performances of the afore-mentioned

"Gypsy Boy" and "Faith", these were prime examples of how deep the catalog actually ran, and along with a further live excursion for Terry with yet another unreleased song, "Movin'", and studio outtakes from both Jules with "Caney Creek" and Brian with "Conflict", they were but a drop in the ocean of what reportedly remained either under guard in the Warner catacombs or on the ragged set-list sheets that were gaffer–taped nightly to the front of the stages throughout the years. Indeed, it would take almost forty years before a successful run of reissues, specifically designed for compact disc, would see some of these studio rarities finally released to an awaiting fan base. The live performances were not so fortunate… and some were seemingly lost forever once the stage lights dimmed on them for one final time.

"Movin'" was actually quite a radical song," recounts Terry. "It was a call to activism. Get off your ass and do something… that was essentially the theme. But it was hard rock 'n' roll, and it was never recorded."

Yet another new composition would also make its debut concert appearance during the summer of 1970, albeit a brief one, but that too would soon disappear back into the forgotten set-lists of time, a mere footnote in the lengthy performing career of the band members.

Just four years and 15 million record sales ago, 'Along Came Mary', in the guise of The Association's first smash single, and with her the group's first date at the Greek Theater. They were back there Friday and Saturday in a beautifully mounted program, with a sound system so good you could painlessly absorb all the volume and even catch most of the lyrics.

Of the 16 songs performed, 13 were originals born within the septet. All the big ones were there. Even the occasional forays into social commentary are non-controversial: at the Greek they fearlessly took positions against Nazi Germany and smog.

Pianist Richard Thompson, the newest member, offered a legato accompaniment to (Jim) Yester in "Along The Way". Next, a heavy rock beat underpinned Jules Alexander's "Dubuque Blues", throatily sung by Brian Cole. Larry Ramos set a more relaxed vocal groove in "Goodbye Forever", after which Alexander, singing his own folksy "Maybe Iowa Ames", was supported simply by his own acoustic guitar.

"M-a-y-b-a…" corrects Jules today, when talking about his composition. "'Mayba Iowa Ames' was actually about a dream my wife had. She was walking by a thrift store in the dream and there was a mannequin wearing old-fashioned clothes and a heart locket, and as she was looking the locket opened and there was a picture in there. She told me about it and I thought 'Oh, shit! That's song material!'"

"That was a great song," comments Jim today, thinking back on that rarely heard composition by Jules. "We should have recorded it, but we never did. And, yes, I recall that we did perform 'Faith' live as well, but I don't believe that one was ever in the studio with us either…"

When pressed by the author for further thoughts on this catalog of near misses, Jim adds: "'Decorated For Love'? We had the demo of it, and we may have even done a track for it but it never got close to a finished project, whilst 'Better Times', from 1966, was something that Curt was pushing on us. We didn't really want to do it, and we succeeded in keeping it off of the first album.

"'Autumn Afternoon' was never really finished, at least to my recollection. It certainly wasn't going to be on the album (*Insight Out*) anyway. It was for a future project. Likewise, 'Caney Creek' was never done for any album project either. Jules may even have recorded it on his own as the group as a whole never cut it, although it is still one of my all-time favorite songs…" [33]

"I was on the road with the band when I wrote that song," confirms Jules. "But the band didn't find it was what they wanted to do, but that's OK…" [37]

Thankfully, longtime friends and bluegrass specialists The Dillards also saw the potential in the song and cut a version for their seventh album, *Tribute To The American Duck*, released on Poppy Records during 1973. Nevertheless, the notion that the band were prepared to try out new songs in the concert arena, to gauge audience response, sometimes before they had even cut a version in the studio, was indication as to how committed they still were to exploring new avenues and new songs. Not content to sit on their laurels and endlessly rehash the hits of days gone by (the 'rich, warm, brown stuff' as the band referred to them), recounting the halcyon summer of '66, as so many other bands who had achieved similar successes five or six years before were prone to do. "Along The Way", written by Jim, as performed at the Greek Theater in Los Angeles that August, was a prime example. It would be a further two weeks before they took the song into the Sound Recorders Studio, situated on the corner of Yucca and Argyle in Hollywood, followed by a second session at the nearby United Recording one week later, and despite Jim's early arrangement of the song taking it along a country music bearing the feel for it totally changed direction once Richard heard it, and came up with an alternate piano-based rendition, slowing down the tempo, and emphasizing the delicate structures within the ballad. Richard then took it to a producer and arranger by the name of John Andrews Tartaglia, who had previously worked with Paul Anka, Roger Nichols, Al Martino and John Stewart, and he subsequently came up with the elaborate orchestral accompaniment that dominated the second half of the song on the final mix, offering the composition a completely new life.

With a piano accompaniment on the final recording courtesy of their longtime friend and session player Larry Knechtel, perhaps a surprising move with a classically trained pianist now a fully-fledged band member, and with production credits shared between Tartaglia and another longtime acquaintance, Randy Sterling, the beauty of the recording was undeniable from the moment it was issued as the next 45 and the pre-awareness campaign began for the next album. Knechtel's delicate delivery during the opening verses, whilst not quite as captivating as his recent work on Simon & Garfunkel's monumental "Bridge Over Troubled Water", sets the enchanting mood from the opening few bars, accompanied on the 45 mix by a choral of vocal harmony, with Jim's delicate vibrato raising the roof as the sweet string arrangements, courtesy of the full orchestra, build up behind him. It was a good way to start work on the new album, although the sessions that were to follow highlighted the fragmented approach that the band were now working with in the current clime. More often than not, it was just selected band members turning up to specific recording dates, subject to vocal requirements. There was an edge to the sessions, and they were no longer that united front that had built up the vocal stacks during their prolific years and, with each member focusing on their own compositions and recordings, and with session players still in use, studio time became intermittent and disjointed.

"I almost always played guitar," says Jules, when recalling the actual participation of the band members during these sessions. "And Jim and Terry did sometimes, but Brian was not a studio player at all. I had studio chops but Larry Knechtel was a much better studio cat than Richard, whose studio chops were not as good. He was a wonderful live player but not a great studio musician. Knechtel was fantastic…" [37]

Randy Sterling also recalls the strained atmosphere that was prevalent during these sessions: "They were not *The Association* as such. There was something stirring. The comfort level was not there anymore. They just weren't happy and you could almost palpably feel them pulling away from each other. They had asked me to produce with John Tartaglia, and I worked a couple of sessions but Tartaglia had this ego this size of fuckin' Texas! He just thought I was a dumb-ass guitar player. He listened to none of my ideas and wanted to be absolutely in charge of the vocals and I was sitting there, just going 'what the hell am I doing here?'

"And then I noticed that the piano player, Richard Thompson, didn't really give a shit either! I had a couple of little conversations with him, and I just came away feeling that this guy was just clearly in it for the money. That's it. He just didn't give a shit. And then Ted's focus was clearly elsewhere too…"

Other songs cut during the fall/winter sessions of 1970 would include another new composition from Terry called "Silver Morning" (with production credits again shared by the strained Tartaglia and Sterling partnership), a slow, funkier reworking of Larry's "It's Gotta Be Real" (also covered that same year by Roslyn Kind, Barbra Streisand's sister, on her *This Is Roslyn Kind* LP), and a wonderful contribution from Ted entitled "Bring Yourself Home". Whilst not as prolific a songwriter as some of his musical partners the quality that shone through many of Bluechel's offerings has certainly deserved far greater appraisal over the years than what they have seemingly been afforded. "Bring Yourself Home", with its deep resonating and powerful lead vocal from Terry, stands head and shoulders high in the band's catalog and went on to receive a Special Merit Spotlight in *Billboard* when it appeared on a 45 release the following year.

"I decided I wasn't going to sing the lead, but Terry would," said Ted, as noted in the CD reissue sleeve notes. "Nobody asked Terry to sing lead on their songs because Terry had so many of his own songs. Isolationism wasn't working with me. Terry did a good job. It came out nice." [2]

The accompanying "Silver Morning" had been written by Terry at his home, located high in the Hollywood hills off Mulholland, within virtual touching distance of the Hollywood sign. Initially, demoed under the working title of "City Of The Angels Falling", he had been sitting on the front balcony early one morning, watching as the sun rose up over the city below, with Santa Monica in the distant haze, and the lyrics effortlessly flowed;

Silver morning, smog hanging over the city
Hot sun is a–pouring, down through the crowds into the city
California hilltop morning…

"Silver Morning"
Words and Music by Terry Kirkman

With further promotion on the horizon, a televised appearance on NBC's *The Don Knotts Show*, broadcast on October 6th (performing "Silver Morning" and "Traveler's Guide"), the band was back on the treadmill once more, with Richard firmly establishing himself within the set-up, and they saw the remainder of the year out with a succession of live performances across the country, all accompanied by the unfortunate but now-familiar sound of the record returns hitting the bargain bins. Released on October 7th 1970, "Along The Way", coupled with "Traveler's Guide (Spanish Flyer)" (Warner Bros. 45-7429) followed the pattern previously set by "Dubuque Blues" and it failed to register at all on the U.S. charts, despite it receiving rotation on a number of easy-listening stations across the country and achieving success of some of the Top 40 stations across Iowa and Philadelphia.

Fresh approach for the group is this poignant ballad material penned by Jim Yester and performed effectively. Could easily break through and go all the way.

Billboard
1971

With the patience of their record label now wearing decidedly thin as a lack of confidence in their charges began to set in, it would be a further two years before The Association barely dented the Hot 100 once again… and when that was to happen it would be on a new record label.

Greek Theatre

THE

ASSOCIATION

and a very special guest

B.B. KING

★ ★ ★ ★ ★ ★ ★

TWO NIGHTS ONLY

AUGUST 28-29

CHAPTER NINETEEEN

RIDGE RIDERS

Whilst the band were busy mixing work and play, both at home and on the road, their erstwhile partner, having taken time out to himself, was now also hard at work in the recording studio, cutting a series of songs that would ultimately become the first solo album issued by a member of The Association.

With John Boylan sharing the console alongside him, and with the full approval and financial support of Warner Bros. senior executive Joe Smith, along with Pat Colecchio, Russ Giguere made himself comfortable in the Wally Heider Studios in Hollywood during late 1970/early 1971, occasionally shifting over to Western Recorders, committing ten or eleven tracks to tape, ably assisted by a succession of ever-reliable studio musicians and friends. With such notable names as pianist Larry Knechtel, guitarists Ben Benay and Bobby Womack, bassist Lyle Ritz, and drummers Jim Keltner and Russ Kunkel, all working alongside close friends such as former Flying Burrito Brothers' Bernie Leadon and Chris Ethridge, Dillard sidemen Herb Pederson and Buddy Emmons, and Judee Sill, Jerry Yester, Judy Henske and, when not on the road, Jules Alexander, the sessions resulted in an eclectic mix of styles and influences. Some for the good, and some maybe not so...

At times, and upon release, Russ appeared lost over which direction he was trying to place himself and the resulting record. Was he the thinking acoustic troubadour? Or was he a wannabe rocker? Were his r'n'b roots maybe trying to bubble to the surface? Unable to pigeonhole the subsequent release into a specific genre may well have alienated many of the potential listeners and buyers who, in a previous life, may well have jumped at the opportunity to hear more from a member of the harmonically uplifting Association. Yes, the band themselves may have moved on since the heady-harmony days of "Windy" and "Never My Love", but even they would have struggled to acclimatize to the single lead vocal dominating the rootsy sound of John Boylan's "Brother Speed" (previously featured with a much fuller arrangement on the Appletree Theater LP *Playback*) or the funky Motown groove on Smokey Robinson's "Shop Around", featuring the soulful backing vocals of Clydie King, Merry Clayton and former Ikette, Vanetta Fields, along with the legendary guitarist Bobby Womack. Then again, maybe this was Russ being true to himself. Offering up a selection of styles that he was comfortable with. Maybe he had no desire to find a pigeonhole with which to settle into.

Russ himself contributed two songs to the sessions, the first of which, "Now We Begin", featuring the delicate guitar work of future founding-Eagle Bernie Leadon, had been written during his latter-day Association tenure, and this was followed shortly afterwards by the blues influenced pattern of "In New Germany", whilst a new friendship with a singer-songwriter named Bill Martin resulted in two of Martin's compositions also added to the mix. The first of which, "My Plan", a heavenly arrangement of church choirs and organs, relied heavily on the grand scale of Jerry Yester's vocal assemblage, the vocal abilities of Yester, along with his wife, folk singer Judy Henske, and Craig Doerge, paired off with Larry Knechtel's 'Keyboard of The Grand Coulee Dam', a vast theater organ located at the Whitney Recording Studios in Glendale. It was deep, it was vast, and it was immense…

"'My Plan' only had two verses and (Bill) had to write a third one because I had arranged the song for three," Russ informed *Goldmine* back in 1980. "That has to be one of the strangest songs ever written! He also wrote 'Rainmaker' (for Harry Nilsson) which I also considered for the album." [20]

Martin's second offering, the delightful "Rosarita Beach Café" (often mistakenly credited to Warren Zevon, another associate of this band of brothers who also cut his own version during this period) subsequently resulted in one of the session highlights, a wistful tale of loneliness and resignation:

I've got a million dollar bill
And they can't change it
They won't let me leave until my tab is paid
So I might as well settle down here
And buy the house another round
I'm the permanent guest of the Rosarita Beach Café

"Rosarita Beach Café"
Words and Music by Bill Martin

One song that didn't make the final mix was a composition by a young twenty-one-year-old singer-songwriter from Alabama named Jimmie Spheeris. Having traveled to New York City, following a stint out on the west coast, his debut album, *Isle of View*, was in the process of being recorded when Russ and his former bandmates first collectively came across his work. Two tracks that eventually found their way onto *Isle of View* were also cut during the Giguere sessions, the first of which, "Seven Virgins", remained unfinished, although The Association ultimately completed a version themselves which was to appear on their own next studio album. The second Spheeris song, which found a home on side two of the disc, was the gorgeous acoustic ballad "Let It Flow" and it remains a true aural delight from start to end, with some sweet steel guitar from Buddy Emmons lifting it up to a dreamy, lofty height from which it never falls. Even Spheeris' own rendition couldn't top that...

With the album rounded out by re-arranged covers of Randy Newman's "Lovers Prayer" and Judee Sill's decidedly pleasant western-themed "Ridge Rider", the latter featuring the songwriter herself on acoustic guitar (Judee's own version would appear on her debut album, issued five months later), the sessions drew to a close.

"I tried a couple of different guitarists, and they couldn't play the chart," recalled Russ, when recounting the "Ridge Rider" session. "So I called Judee and she put it in a different key than her key, I couldn't sing it in her key. I think she capo'd it way up, and played it a little higher, where I sang below it. (We) recorded it in about a take or two, perfectly of course, as is Judee's way..."[18]

The grand finale to the set was Jules Alexander's Wagnerian, heavily worded (and ultimately far too short) "Pegasus", filled out with a powerful arrangement put together by Russ and studio arranger Al Capps, with Russ himself supplying the fretless zither and a number of the accompanying sound effects, whilst Jules added bass and guitar to the track.

Russ: "That's me playing the wind chimes and bells on the beginning. The thunder was this big printer's sheet..." [20]

"'Pegasus' comes from the mythology of Sant Mat..." tells Jules when discussing the composition in detail, "Pegasus is the means by which one travels from one reality to a finer reality. That's what the whole song is all about."

Recalling this particular era, Jules also makes mention of another unreleased composition he wrote, this one with Judee Sill in mind. "I knew Judee quite well," he says. "We hung out for a long time together and I wrote a song called 'The Last Macaroon' for her! She really liked macaroons and she was over at the house one day and I was determined to be a nice guy and I only had a few macaroons left but the last one was for her. She appreciated that!" he adds with laughter. [37]

Hexagram 16, the debut solo offering from Russ Giguere, appeared in the stores during April of 1971 bearing the distinctive Warner Bros. logo (WS-1910). Labeled after a passage in the *I Ching*, the book of ancient Chinese wisdom, the title referred to a divination called cleromancy by which it chooses a selection of seemingly random numbers. Four numbers, 6 through to 9, can then be turned into a hexagram, which can be referenced within the pages of the much-lauded publication. Hexagram 16 is but one of the 64 hexagrams listed, with this chosen one representing 'providing for', 'excess' and 'enthusiasm'. Certainly, the diversity of the chosen songs highlighted Russ's personal enthusiasm for exploring his musical meanderings, and a total of 52 differing musicians are credited on the rear of the sleeve, along with six studio engineers plus the photographer and sleeve designer, underlining the depth of friendships and the faith that Warner Bros. held in the project – and were still committed to budgeting, despite the concerning lack of sales that were haunting Russ's former band.

With acclaimed art photographer Malcolm Lubliner supplying the images, including a series of symbolic hand gestures, the album also quoted directly from the *I Ching* on the outer sleeve alongside a photograph of the tie-dye adorned musician in thoughtful pose. Sadly, and despite such enthusiasm and excess burned within the grooves, the actual record sales continued the downward trend and the dollar was passed in limited quantities over the counter and made nary a dent in the best-selling lists of the year. Publicity was muted in its praise for the release as well, with a 1971 edition of the *San Bernardino Sun* referencing the release as 'lacking in excitement and a really outstanding selection' despite the fact that the article went on the claim that 'he probably has one of the clearest, most lyrical voices around'. Nevertheless, fervor and passion for this piece has multiplied in the ensuing years and it has subsequently gone on to become a much-cherished artifact within the Association community, warranting a long-overdue reappraisal on compact disc during 2013. Not that the disappointment of the initial sales figures were to play on Russ's mind too much. Keen to take his new musical ventures into unexplored areas, he began his return to the performing arena, and the Beachwood Rangers stepped out into the public eye.

"Russ thought he wanted to lead his own band," comments Jim Yester. "When he first joined The Men he was brought in as *the* lead singer, and in his mind that is where he was at..." – a simple observation that suggests that perhaps Russ missed the comradeship of a close-knit band of brothers, working and playing together, but that he needed the feel, and the white glare of the spotlight shining down on himself. A fact that became apparent a short while later when, alongside a loose aggregation of fellow musicians including Bill Martin, guitarist Scott Shelly, bluegrass banjo and mandolin player Don Beck, steel guitarist Herb Steiner, bassist Gary Sherwood and drummers Dennis Conway and Michael Ney, and a young up and coming songwriter from Illinois named Warren Zevon, all members at varying stages of the new band's evolution, Russ put together The Beachwood Rangers, maintaining the management supervision of Pat Colecchio for guiding their career. A series of official press photographs were even shot by Jim Metropole for distribution and publicity purposes. It would appear that his close friendship with Bill Martin was the guiding force behind the venture, and the fact that Bill was also housemates with various members of Linda Ronstadt's close knit circle of musicians, Herb Steiner included, some of whom were also known to perform as The Beachwood Rangers (and appearing as such on her March 1970 album *Silk Purse*) was evidence that Bill simply carried over the band name into his and Russ's new musical venture, a fact confirmed by Bill's then-wife, former Association Admiration Aggregation member Lois Abrams. She recalls today:

"Bill met Russ through me. I had dated Ted and had stayed friends with them all. Linda Ronstadt and J.D. Souther lived upstairs from Bill and I, and Warren Zevon lived next door and one day we went to round to visit Warren and smoke a doobie, and he said, 'hey, listen to this new song I've just written', and he played us 'Werewolves of London'! We all hung out and we all called ourselves The Beachwood Rangers so Bill and Russ just used the name. They did cut some tracks together but not much became of it. Tons of bands got together and fell apart in those days, and they were all writing and singing at places like the Troubadour and the Ice House. They didn't all 'click'. I do remember them in the studio but as I said not all the bands 'made it'. But Bill was one of a kind – a gentle soul, witty and funny at every turn."

In addition to the Rangers, during that same period, Russ also worked as part of another six-piece band he named Hollywood, an extension of the previous line-up featuring, amongst others, drummer Michael Ney, guitarist Steve Edwards, Scott Shelly, Gary Sherwood and longtime friend singer/ guitarist Lee Mallory but, as with the previous collective, neither act went anywhere of notable significance and, other than a series of brief rehearsals and the occasional live supporting performance, interspersed with endless hours of jamming and fun, both bands swiftly faded away.

> The Beachwood Rangers, a crack troupe of handpicked musician singers, invade and occupy the Ice House in Pasadena today through Sunday. Russ Giguere, formerly one of the mainstays of The Association, is the best known of the group.
>
> Other troops include Don Beck, renowned for his playing of banjo, mandolin and pedal steel guitar. Don also sings tenor. Scott Shelly is a triple treat on guitar, piano and organ. Bill Martin plays all of the above and sings baritone. Gary Sherwood is Bass Man and plays guitar and songs baritone. Dennis Conway drums up a storm. All members write and will be introducing many of their own songs.
>
> *The Pasadena Independent*
> June 30th 1971

Drummer Michael Ney, who shared the interchanging drum stool with Conway in the line-up, recalls: "Basically, we all lived up the path from each other in the Canyon, and we all had a mutual appreciation for a beautiful female fan base. We started playing every day and night, and Russ got us a super rehearsal hangout for twenty-four hour fun, fun fun! We would play anywhere, anytime… Delaney & Bonnie, Albert Collins, early Steely Dan and Boz Scaggs…"

"I was also a Beachwood Ranger," adds Scott Shelly from his home down in Australia, where he now resides, "along with Russ, Bill Martin, Gary Sherwood, Michael Ney, and guitarist Steve Edwards. Russ was putting a band together to do some gigs and somehow I got a call. I had just turned seventeen back in '71, so I was just another kid from the Valley. We rehearsed in one of the Warner Bros. Burbank Studios sound stages, sharing it with Little Feat. Warren sat in for a couple of the rehearsals, and I remember Bill's friend Harry Nilsson dropping in a few times as well. Russ also had a rehearsal place out in Van Nuys decorated with velvet drapes, parachutes and anything else they could find to take the edge off the volume. We're talking ceiling, walls, floor, everything… so it looked like a Bedouin's hangout! Lee Mallory from the original cast of *Hair* also played guitar when The Beachwood Rangers became Hollywood, and I remember gigs at the Ice House in Pasadena and The Whisky in Hollywood where did a combination of covers and originals. I recall we did 'Shop Around', from Russ's album, an original that Gary and I wrote called 'Band Of Angels' and 'Scheherazade', one of Bill Martin's many originals…"

Late June of 1971, going into the early weeks of the following month, saw The Beachwood Rangers perform a number of shows at the Ice House, sharing the weekly bill alongside artists such as The Dillards and Belland & Somerville. However, Russ had actually been considering the concept of the band for a number of months, whilst he was still cutting tracks for his solo album and an advertisement in the *Minneapolis Star Tribune*, placed on March 21st 1971, had already announced the debut solo appearance of:

RUSS GIGUERE

WITH THE BEACHWOOD RANGERS

FORMER LEAD SINGER OF THE ASSOCIATION

SATURDAY MARCH 27TH 8.00PM

MELBY HALL, AUGSBURG COLLEGE, MINNEAPOLIS

TICKETS PRICED AT $3.50 AND $2.50

ALL RESERVED SECTIONS

"I had a band called Hollywood, and another band called The Beachwood Rangers, which was sort of an arty rock and roll group," Russ later confirmed to Jeff March and Marti Smiley Childs for their 2011 publication. "The bands usually had five to six members, and I always had good singers and good writers in my bands..." [1]

A solo performer in his own right, Bill Martin (born in 1945) was an immensely talented musician, composer, screenwriter and humorist, who had already seen significant success as a songwriter for The Monkees (1967s "The Door Into Summer"), The Turtles (1968s "Earth Anthem") and Harry Nilsson ("Rainmaker", also from 1968), and his 1970 spoken word/comedy release for Warner Bros., *Concert For Headphones And Contra-Buffoon In Asia Minor* (WS-1856), had since gone on to achieve cult status, if not commercial success since its initial release, due in no small part to Harry Nilsson's co-production contributions. In addition, his later comedy work with Monkee Mike (1981s *Elephant Parts*) would maintain the ethos for mixing both music and visual comedy that ran throughout his life. Sadly, he passed away in early 2016, aged 70. Nevertheless, following the Beachwood Rangers and Hollywood ventures, both Russ and Bill would go on to explore new territories together, both in and out of the musical field.

The first week of February 1971, and squeezed in between two scheduled performances, one week apart, at the Baylor University in Waco, Texas, the seven-man Association reconvened for a two-day stint in the Gold Star Studios in Los Angeles, the same recording facility that had seen them start on their road to success, five and a half years previous. On this occasion they were to be found cutting the track for their version of a new Jimmy Webb tune, composed during one of Webb's visits to London the previous year, and a tribute (of sorts) to his friend and fellow songwriter, Philip 'P.F.' Sloan.

Last time I saw P.F. Sloan
He was summer burned and winter blown
He turned the corner all alone
But he continued singing

"P.F. Sloan"
Words and Music by Jimmy Webb

The songwriter later explained to *Uncut* magazine how the words came about: "One night, he (Sloan) and I went to see Randy Newman at the Troubadour. We all agreed to come back to my house and play some pool. We were in separate cars, and about halfway there, I realized that P.F.'s car had gone. He'd missed the turn I guess. So I went to my house and everybody said, 'What happened to P.F.?' so I started thinking. The song seemed like a funny idea at first, and then it became a serious piece about a line of communication between writers and the public.

"When Johnny Rivers, Lou Adler and John and Michelle Phillips went into Phillips' house to plan the Monterey Pop Festival, they asked me and P.F. Sloan to stay out on the porch because we were songwriters. And I always wondered about that. I always wondered why was it that songwriters were not as important as anybody else…"

The 'no, no, no, don't sing this song' refrain was written in reference to the way that Webb was viewing the industry from the songwriter's perception, how it was back in 1970. Why is it that it costs two dollars to buy a record and yet the songwriter only gets two cents? If you sing the song then the dollar goes to many, but only a minor share gets back to the songwriter himself. So… don't sing the song. Yet that one particular phrase was also the major disappointing factor for at least one member of the band who, along with his colleagues, felt that overall this was a good shot to get the group back on the charts. It was certainly commercial enough. However, maybe the lyric (perhaps missing the point) should accentuate the positive as opposed to the negative? Get the listener singing…

Jim Yester: "I was hoping we would say "come sing this song" as it's such a fun song to do"[2]

For their own take on "P.F. Sloan" The Association also chose to omit one verse from Webb's original composition…

The London bridge was finally found
They moved it to another town
People gathered around to watch the bridge fall down
But I don't think it will no more

"P.F. Sloan"
Words and Music by Jimmy Webb

bringing the focus on the harmonies of the refrain to the fore and adding a more upbeat pattern to the original arrangement, with Jim's tenor vocals leading the way. For whatever reason, the band also opted to add in Brian's comedic 'country' vocal approach to the session, as previously utilized on

"I'm Going To Be A Racin' Star'" from the *Once Upon A Wheel* sessions; maybe a questionable inclusion, and perhaps taking away some of those more commercial opportunities for the release, but despite this move the vocal harmonies that ran throughout only went to highlight the band's continuing ability to deliver such exquisite planning with perfection. Confident in the new recording they subsequently issued the track as the next 45 single offering (Warner Bros. 7471), strangely paired off with Brian's "Traveler's Guide (Spanish Flyer)", for the second release in succession. They also appeared on the *Andy Williams Show*, their first appearance on the popular variety special for five years, broadcast on February 27th, performing a live rendition of the song to promote the release (in addition to a newly arranged medley of "Everything That Touches You" and "Windy", in collaboration with the host) – but, sadly, it was all to little avail from a sales perspective and it became yet another no-show on the charts. Interestingly, Jimmy Webb's own fine version of the song had also been released as a single, two months previously, on Warner's sister label, Reprise Records, but that too somehow failed to ignite.

Sloan himself was to later recount how he first heard the song:

"The first time I ever heard the song on the air was a divine moment for me," he commented to *SongTalk* journalist Paul Zollo. "I had had all of my royalties suspended, I had absolutely no money and I had no place to live. I was at this hot dog stand on Vine Street, and trying to scrape up 50 cents for a hot dog, and out of the speakers from the hot dog place was that song. The Association was singing it and I was thinking, 'Is this a divine play or what?'

"I thought it was interesting… a difficult song. What was Jimmy Webb trying to deal with? I think it was political, even though I didn't quite understand it. I was kind of flattered."

Music historian Brian Gari, a good friend of P.F., later recalled during a 1985 article in *Goldmine*: "There were political overtones to the song. He (Webb) wrote it sort of paraphrasing who he thought P.F. Sloan was – and in another way he was writing in the genre that Phil was writing in."

"It was an interesting role to play the tragic figure," summarized Sloan. "I was forced to play the tragic role rather than the comedic role that I felt it more to my nature. Many people, even artists who (later) recorded that song, didn't know it was about a real person." [38]

With work continuing a number of other new compositions the new album by The Association, initially scheduled for a release during the opening months of the year, was finally prepared for the early summer of 1971. Housed in a sleeve adorned by a photograph of the band sitting astride an iron stairway, this image came from a series of shots taken by Jim Metropole during a random photo shoot. Breaking out of a rehearsal session held up in the commercial district of Van Nuys, over in the San Fernando Valley, the band posed for the pictures around an empty gas station, part of a small industrial complex across the street from the rehearsal room. Utilizing a series of props that lay around the garage unit; a plank of wood, a builder's construction helmet, even a random basketball, the photographs show the band sitting and standing in front of a series of metallic garage signs – *The World's Best Safety Device: A Careful Man, No Smoking Please* and *Stop Your Motor*. Neither the band, nor Metropole, thought any more of the shoot and it was only when the proofs were being viewed that the one shot, with the seven-man line-up on the staircase with the *Stop Your Motor* sign positioned just above their heads that the first notion of naming the new release accordingly came to light.

"We just decided that that was a good title for the album…" summarizes Jules.

One noticing factor on each of the images taken that day, when studying each shot, is the weary, serious nature that adorns the face of Brian Cole. Unsmiling in the majority of the photographs, including the rear image of the sleeve, perched atop the roof of a battered Morris Minor Traveler automobile (a vehicle that was actually owned by Jules, who in turn had recently purchased it from Ted's wife, Judy), with a recently acquired handlebar mustache hovering above the straightened lip-line, his pattern-hemmed pants holding on to an earlier nostalgic era of flower power, seemingly and sadly at odds with his denim and casually clad partners. Even in the one, unused, solitary smiling image of him taken that day, sharing a basketball prop alongside Larry (available to view in Metropole's portfolio), his darkened eyes appear to tell a tough story.

> Brian is a bit ill. It seems the poor boy works too hard and is now forced to relax, and for those of you who have met Brian, you know what a trial this will be for him.

> *Association Admiration Aggregation* Newsletter
> November 1970

Not that Brian was the only one at odds with the need for future publicity that day. Terry Kirkman also recalls that session as being a relatively unpleasant experience, with his own demeanor being less than enthusiastic towards the camera lens; "Although the session had a tad more grit than most of our PR album fare, I was not happy that particular day. My eyes hurt so very much from the horrible L.A. smog and sun glare and we were in the middle of a rehearsal I wasn't very pleased with…"

It was in July of 1971 that *Stop Your Motor* (Warner Bros. WS 1927) eventually appeared in the stores, a good six months later than initially anticipated. Filled with songs compiled from the recent sessions, co-produced by Ray Pohlman and the band members themselves, along with newly remixed versions of "First Sound" and "I'm Going To Be A Racin' Star" from the ill-fated *Once Upon A Wheel* soundtrack (retitled *"The* First Sound" and "That's Racin'") the album received a mixed response from the media. With vocal arrangements credited to Don Randi a number of these newer, self-composed tunes were definite highlights from the band's recent catalog, with the jazzy instrumentation on Jules' superb "Makes Me Cry (Funny Kind Of Song)", featuring Richard on the piano, sitting alongside Ted's impressive "Bring Yourself Home" as an extremely strong opening pairing. Elsewhere, Jim's stripped back "Along The Way", void of some of the overdubbed harmonies prevalent on the earlier 45 release, still maintained an unparalleled beauty in its' intricate voicing, whilst Terry's visionary lyrics of "Silver Morning" drove home the competitive nature of the band, still resisting the temptation to sit on the laurels of past glories.

The final number of the ten-song collection, the group's rendition of Jimmie Spheeris's countrified "Seven Virgins", featuring Larry's lead, was rearranged with a harder edge than the composers own recording of the song, and it brought the album to a funky, satisfying closure. Albeit one that failed to reignite the record buying public's former passion for the group, barely limping to a lowly number 158 in the album charts, their lowest chart album release to date. It was becoming a familiar story by now, despite a mixed reception in the media.

The Association is alive and kicking and for that the music world should be very thankful. True, the group has not had a smash like 'Cherish' or 'Windy' in recent years, but that doesn't mean they've gone sour. In fact, the group has progressed to the point where I believe they're several years ahead of pop music. With the emergence of soft rock, The Association should rise once again, and 'Stop Your Motor' could just be the vehicle to do it.

Somehow The Association today is only remembered as makers of yesterday's hits. Somehow with 'Stop Your Motor', I think that image will change. Buy it – and do yourself a favor.

The Pennsylvania Daily Notes
July 1971

'Stop Your Motor' is the group's latest release, full of the same fine sounds that produced 'Cherish', 'Along Comes Mary', 'Windy'. The music is the same – soft, wistful harmonies and flawless instrumental techniques but it is lacking any really exciting material. 'Bring Yourself Home', 'Silver Morning', 'It's Gotta Be Real' and 'Travelers Guide' are the best cuts. Tight and well done, long hair and all.

The San Bernardino County Sun
July 1971

Whilst the record sales continued to dwindle with seemingly each new release, their concert draw remained a hugely viable and sustainable option and the 1971 touring schedule saw them continuing to play and perform in a number of notable venues, and none more so than with their return to the Hollywood Bowl on May 1st 1971, headlining the May Day celebrations alongside Joan Baez, The Everly Brothers, Country Joe & The Fish, Redeye and a new funk and soul band hailing from Chicago calling themselves Earth Wind & Fire. However, despite their continuing leanings towards performing their newer material at each show, and the positive reception received for each offering, it was always the old hits, the moments that "Cherish" and "Windy" came across from the vast soundstage speakers, that registered the most with the attending concert goers. And even then, in some of the more hardened locales, that wasn't always enough.

The Association, a seven-man band, visited Des Moines Saturday night (July 31st) and tried hard to please a crowd of about 3,000 who came to Veterans Memorial Auditorium. Their efforts barely succeeded.

Not that they didn't try. They started out with 'Along Comes Mary' and the crowd applauded politely and the group moved on to more of their hits, none of which really got off the ground.

One of the best tunes of the night, 'Bring Yourself Home' is from The Association's newest album, 'Don't Start Your Motor, But Keep On Trucking'. Another plus point was 'Dubuque Blues', a song that apparently went over the heads of the majority of the audience.

At the end, the crowds applauded thoughtfully and left. For the price of a ticket you could buy an 'Association's Greatest Hits' album, stay at home and listen to it.

The Des Moines Register
August 1st 1971

Don't Start Your Motor, But Keep On Trucking? Was the band in playful mood that night?

However, all said, occasions such as this were rare and when the band had visited Larry's home state of Hawaii earlier that summer, appearing at the Polynesian Palace in Waikiki for a week-long residency during early June, they had gone down a storm particularly when, during the encore, with flower leis draped around their necks, they were joined on stage for the very first time by their manager Pat Colecchio, who joyfully joined in on "Enter The Young" to rapturous applause. By the time they commenced the summer touring schedule of 1971, there was also another familiar face joining them amongst the backstage crew. One who would remain loyal to the band's core for many years to come, and who remains an essential part of the story to this very day.

Del Ramos: "As Summerhill was finishing, around 1971, The Association came to me and said 'we want you to work with us', and I said 'but Brian Cole's with you guys.' 'No' they said, 'not playing bass. We want you to do sound for us,' and I said 'I have *no idea* how to do sound! I've never even touched a mixing board!'

But, with an offer to train him in the necessary sound technology requirements, whilst also offering to double his current income with Summerhill as an added bonus, Del was left with little choice but to accept the proposal. How could he not? It would require him stepping off of the stage, putting down his bass guitar and standing behind the scenes but a steady income, job security and family bonds all pull together and by bringing Del on board the band they felt that they had recruited someone they could trust. Someone who understood the music.

"It turns out, he was really good!" says Jules.

"Summerhill were struggling getting concert dates and stuff and I needed the money so I tossed my career into the fire!" Del adds with a smile. "It was a long learning curve for me and I learned a lot about each member. Never did we try to be like anybody else. The music of this band was their own music and their own thinking. I never heard them say anything like 'let's make this sound like a Beach Boys sound, like *Pet Sounds* or something'. They always said 'let's do it this way' or 'the vocals are coming in too early, let's hold it back until the next verse' or something. That's how it worked. I saw it happen. The music of the band was progressing because of Jimmy, Jules, my brother..."

CHAPTER TWENTY

KICKING THE GONG AROUND

Gossip News:

The Association did an interview on a local radio station recently. That is, Jim and Ted did. It was a pleasure to hear their bizarre sense of humor coming over the air. Now that Ted is a father he seems crazier, but in a different way.

It must be moving season; both Jules and Jim are changing houses. Ted moved just recently and Richard took over his home in the canyon. So all seems well at the present time.

The guys are all beautifully tanned from their week in Hawaii. Jim has been spending his time off racing motorcycles. Terry was at a local club the other night to see a new group, 'Rosebud' (Jim's brother Jerry is in it). Well, anyway, the guys are all busy keeping things moving in their own separate lives, as well as in the group.

Association Admiration Aggregation Newsletter

Rosebud was a new venture for Jerry Yester, and one that was also being managed by Pat Colecchio (who was notably increasing his stable of artists during that period, adding both Eric Anderson and Smokestack Lightning to his roster, in addition to The Beachwood Rangers). Having seen The Lovin' Spoonful disband back in 1968 Jerry had then released the album *Farewell Aldebaran* the following year in partnership with his wife, Judy Henske. A diverse gathering of songs, focusing on the vocal talents of

Henske and the strengths of Jerry's arrangements and instrumentation, and issued on Frank Zappa's Straight record label (STS-1052), the album failed to sell in any significant quantity despite acclaim amongst their peer group. Subsequently, the duo followed this up by forming a more conventional, if somewhat experimental rock band, recruiting noted session keyboard player and vocalist Craig Doerge, along with ex-Spanky & Our Gang/ Turtles drummer John Seiter and a respected young bass player named David Vaught, and naming the new collaboration Rosebud. Born in Austin, Texas, Vaught had been playing bass since he was thirteen years of age, joining his brother's popular Los Angeles-based surf band, Bob Vaught & The Renegaids, during 1962 and contributing to their *Surf Crazy* album, released on GNP/Crescendo label that same year.

As a step down from the eclecticism of *Farewell Aldebaran* this new line-up adapted a more direct and democratic approach with Jerry, Judy and Craig all contributing to the songwriting and the vocal sessions, whilst drummer John Seiter also added his voice into the mix. Yet, for all the thoughtful process that went into forming the band, with so much potential, after just one album – 1971s rather uncommercial sounding *Rosebud* – and three live performances, including a show at the Troubadour club attended by Terry Kirkman, the quintet disbanded, the result of Jerry and Judy's marriage dissolving.

Not that Terry had too much time for watching exciting new bands playing in his old haunt, on the very same stage where he had learned his own craft. The band's diary for late September and early October 1971 still had a number of concert performances scheduled, far away from home...

September 18 1971: Pershing Auditorium, Lincoln, NE
September 23 1971: Civic Auditorium, Portland, OR
September 25 1971: Ricks College, Rexburg, ID
September 26 1971: Opera House, Seattle, WA
October 9 1971: West 3rd St Gym, Williamsport, PA
October 10 1971: The Auditorium, Sioux City, IA
October 11 1971: Winona State College, Winona, MN
October 12 1971: Orlando, FL

As nearly 5,000 people left the Memorial Hall Monday evening one could still hear the 'oohs' and 'aahs'. The group had received constant cheers and applause as they performed such favorites as 'Requiem for the Masses', 'Cherish', 'Along Comes Mary' and 'Never My Love'.

At a press conference prior to the show, members of The Association told about the trials and tribulations of stardom. "It's a job," said one member, "just like any other job. We get sick of the long hours, especially when we're on the road like this."

Traveling with the group of seven is a road manager and a work crew of three who are responsible for setting up and packing equipment. Throughout the year, Terry Kirkman, who plays brass, reeds, percussion, recorder and harmonica, said the group makes an average of 100 such public performances. With all the popularity one might ask what kind of money the group makes in a year.

"It's really hard to say," said Kirkman. "We're not sure ourselves." But for the group's public appearances, such as the one Monday night, he estimated that they make more than $1 million a year.

The Winona Daily News
October 12 1971

Living in nice homes in the Hollywood hills and canyons may well have been the benefits of a life on the road, but with the amount of time they spent on tour it also took its toll on their personal lives.

"We were the hardest working band of the '60s," states Terry. "We were traveling at least 250 days a year, (but) it was devastating to our personal lives. We were never home. Ultimately, you sit back and say 'we're doing exactly the same crap *every single day*. What am I doing? The same airport, the same rental car, the same food, the same Holiday Inn, *exactly* the same songs, and you start to get so habituated that it starts to get ingrained. You start to become a caricature of yourself. But we never quite made that millionaire cut, (and) you got a lot of mouths to feed..." [43]

A number of the band members went through a succession of marriage break-ups during these difficult years, Jules and Christie had parted, Brian and Vicki, Jim and Joellen... and even when they were back in their home city, focus was still on the band... most of the time. The article in *The Winona Daily News* continued:

The group admits that three weeks on the road at one time is enough. When they get home they generally relax with their families. Motorcycles are a big hit with many of them. One designs them for a company, another races them, another sells them. Their latest 'thing' is a car they've designed known as 'the box'. At the present time they're looking for the right kind of engine and will hopefully sell the rights to a manufacturer.

Jim recalls: "That all began with Larry Ramos, who was a car nut, seeing an ad in a magazine about a company that had designed a car and were looking for financial backing in trade for stock in the company. After much enthusiastic pleading by Larry, all of us went down to see what it all was. The idea was very progressive and involved a lot of hi-tech engineering and eventually we decided to invest heavily in the company. I'm sure it was against the advice of our financial advisor! The two guys who designed it were great designers, but terrible businessmen! Unfortunately, the car never got past the prototype stage. One of the designers decided to enter it into a race and crashed the car. I don't think it ever recovered from that. After that there were always excuses, but during the time before the crash, Brian Cole had talked me into buying him out, so I took a double loss when it all fell apart! Lesson learned... stick to music!"

With income coming in from the touring schedule, the early winter of 1971 also brought additional residue from record sales and publishing, even if, on this occasion, the sales weren't for their own releases. In between the constant boarding and disembarking numerous flights around the country Terry Kirkman had found the time to assist songwriter and founding member of Blood, Sweat & Tears, Richard Halligan, in composing a song for that band's upcoming album, *Blood, Sweat & Tears 4*. The moody, heavily brass-laden "Cowboys and Indians", featuring the distinctive voice of David Clayton-Thomas, would go on to be one of the highlights of the release and contribute towards another Top 10 album hit for the jazz-rock combo, although Terry had also demoed the song for himself at one early stage. Other demo's that he put onto tape during this period include the unfinished "Time And Time Again", "Wizard" and two with the bizarre working titles of "Mangle When You Mingle" and "Willoughby Wallaby".

"I wrote some... kind of novelty tunes" Terry explains, "but they also had some fairly significant messages tucked in them. So 'Mangle When You Mingle' was...

"You can mangle when you mingle
When you're used to being single
When you're thinking of yourself all alone
You can do and say deceiving things
And blow a good thing happening
And never even know that it was blown…"

whilst "Willoughby Wallaby" (initially conceived a number of years previous), with its joyful refrain of doing 'wallaby things as he hops along, verily, merrily singing the wallaby hopping song' was, quite simply, "one of those things that you write, and you put down, and they're fun."

In response to Terry's humorous ode to the antipodean marsupial, Jules later composed one of his own novelties, bearing the title of "Arno Armadillo".

"Oh, yes! That one was just a little folksie legend about an Italian armadillo", Jules laughs. "That must have been around 1972…"

Their eventual fate remains undocumented…

In addition, during October of 1971, one of the hottest 'pop' stars of the day, one of the biggest teen-idols of the entire industry *ever*, saw fit to cover a version of Terry's "Cherish" for his debut solo album, even going as far as naming the LP after the song, and going on to sell millions of copies as a result. And with a reputation as no more than candy-fluff amongst the serious music elite, it should be noted that David Cassidy's rendition of the song was a fine polished piece of work, although the inclusion of such studio stalwarts as Hal Blaine, Tommy Tedesco and Larry Carlton providing the music certainly aided the sweet, slick sound. Selected from the album as the debut single release the star of the primetime ABC-TV sitcom *The Partridge Family* then took the 45 release into the U.S. *Billboard* Top 10, five years after The Association had taken it to the very peak of the charts. In Australia it went even better, matching the success of the original and reaching the toppermost of the poppermost, whilst in the U.K., the country seemingly most reluctant to accept the original band, the song (paired with "Could It Be Forever") also went Top 10. Recalling the publishing deal that The Association had agreed back in the early days of their collective career, when each and every band member would benefit from record royalties, regardless of who composed the song, must have made such success very sweet for all concerned. Interestingly, Cassidy returned to the Association catalog when cutting his second solo album, *Rock Me Baby*, although his rendition of "Along Comes Mary" never made the final selection.

That same winter season the popular soul and harmony group, The 5th Dimension, achieved a further Top 20 placing in *Billboard* with their own soulful version of "Never My Love", taken from their 2-LP *Live* album. Needless to say, with Larry Knechtel behind the organ and Hal Blaine sitting in on drums (as they had on the original studio cut), and with Bob Alcivar conducting the full orchestra and Bones Howe overseeing and engineering the live concert recording, it was a familiar crew who went to onto achieve satisfaction at the success of the single. Howe would also receive another *Grammy* nomination for his work on the *5th Dimension Live* recording. It is also worth noting that yet another delightful version of the song appeared shortly afterwards, issued as the closing track on The Addrisi Brothers own LP for Columbia Records, *We've Got To Get It On Again*, appearing during 1972.

With the failure of the *Stop Your Motor* album to generate any sales of significance, and one final 45 release on the Warner Bros. label – "That's Racin'" b/w "Makes Me Cry (Funny Kind Of Song)" – their relationship with the record label finally reached a point of no return. After five years of, initially, a fruitful partnership, starting off with some phenomenal highs and some plentiful return, the decline in sales over the past two years had reached the stage where, despite publicity and promotion for each release, the yield for the label was proving minimal at best. And even the parting choice of the final single remained a contentious issue, with far more commercial offerings available to be lifted off the album, although the subsequent result was this was destined to be the fourth occasion that a song had been lifted from the *Stop Your Motor* album, without one of them achieving a notable chart placing. A sad fact considering the quality of the combined work. For the first time as well, the credits on the 45 label also highlighted the individually featured band member on the two songs, with "That's Racin'" listed as *featuring* Brian Cole, and the same for Jules' offering. Clearly, neither the label nor the band no longer knew quite how to market their material…

In a music world where much of the emphasis was now moving towards a heavier, louder approach, with the multi-stacked speaker bands such as Iron Butterfly, Chicago Transit Authority, Creedence Clearwater Revival,

Santana and Led Zeppelin now drawing in the college crowds and, gradually, filling the auditoriums and arenas, and the charts were slowly being clogged up by the likes of pre-pubescent favorites The Jackson 5, The Osmond Brothers and The Partridge Family, the gentler, easy-listening audience that "Cherish" and "Never My Love" had so appealed to were now switching on their AM radios when the likes The Carpenters, Bread, Helen Reddy and Lobo drifted lazily across the airwaves. And then there was the late '60s and early '70s acoustic, singer-songwriter crowd, those who had taken ahold of the Troubadour and its surrounding L.A. clubland, and so effortlessly appealed to the denim-clad, bearded and bedraggled brigade that shared the wooden floorboards of both Topanga and Laurel Canyon, Wonderland Avenue and Lookout Mountain. Crosby, Stills, Nash & Young, James Taylor, Carole King, Jackson Browne, J.D. Souther…

Perhaps there was no longer a place for a harmonically electrified band, with an amalgamation of rock, country, pop, folk, with a smattering of jazz at their roots. Or just maybe, the world was waiting for Don Henley, Glenn Frey and friends to take on the country-rock mantle later that year. And with some style. The baton was being passed…

"We never categorized ourselves," says former member Russ Giguere, "and we didn't like to be categorized by other people. But they did and they always will. Some actually called us a bubblegum band! We never did any bubblegum tunes, we did real music. But the upbeat optimism of The Association was considered too light, too airy, too feel-good." [10]

Around this period rumors also began to circulate as to Terry Kirkman's long-term future within the band, with an Association Admiration Aggregation newsletter appearing to pour water on the hot subject. Reportedly, a dynamic bi-coastal entrepreneur named David Geffen, who had previously acted as the band's agent, was instigating plans to add Terry to his newly founded roster of artists which, to date included singer-songwriters Laura Nyro and Jackson Browne, along with an influential quartet comprising of an ex-Byrd, David Crosby, former Buffalo Springfield guitarists Stephen Stills and Neil Young, and the British-born Hollie, Graham Nash. Both Geffen and his business partner, Elliott Roberts, could see the potential that Terry could add to their burgeoning stable, and Terry had once stayed at Geffen's luxurious New York house when he was out on the east coast. Fortunately, for The Association, such a liaison never came to pass.

Terry recalls, "Around 1971, unbeknownst to the group, or Pat Colecchio, David and I had lunch together. We were socially quite close and he liked hanging out with my wife, and we had a very brief conversation, on the corner of Sunset and Holloway, where he very carefully approached me to ask if I would consider leaving the group to join him and Elliott Roberts, both of whom I liked a lot, in forming a new group with 'others like me'. I didn't think about it too much, and I just said 'I don't think so...' I was really obsessed with maybe turning a corner and making The Association what I had dreamed it would, could, should be, and so David dropped the subject there and it was never brought up again..."

In the aftermath of the incendiary breakup of Crosby, Stills, Nash & Young, following the culmination of their 1970 summer tour, David Geffen was clearly keen to recreate much of the magic his managerial prowess had experienced with 'supergroups'. It was a tantalizing prospect...

With the division between Warner Bros. and The Association clearly irreparable the band was at a turning point and they officially parted company with the might of the Warner's corporation during late 1971. Thankfully, it would seem that salvation was in the wings for a short while later, after a business meeting in New York, they signed a recording deal with Columbia Records, presided over by Clive Davis who, since ascending to the Presidential role of the CBS-owned company in 1967, had doubled its market share due to the astute signings of artists such as Santana, Blood, Sweat & Tears, Chicago, Janis Joplin and Laura Nyro. It was also Davis who insisted that the country music artist, Lynn Anderson, release the country/pop crossover appeal of "(I Never Promised You A) Rose Garden" as her 1970 single, the result of which was a 45 that reached the very pinnacle of the charts in sixteen countries around the world, and was the title track for the biggest selling album by a female country artist for almost three decades. Clive Davis certainly knew talent and potential when he saw it. But could he rejuvenate the fortunes for The Association with such a deal? Was it really possible to implement the fabled fading rock group revival?

By early 1972 recording sessions were underway for what would ultimately be their debut release under the new Columbia contract, and the seventh full studio album for the band, notwithstanding their two soundtrack contributions and the 2-LP live set. The touring schedule was also well underway for the new year, with Peoria and Charleston in Illinois,

Potsdam and Rochester in New York and South Bend, Indiana all hosting the touring party during the opening few weeks of the year, as well as a homecoming show in Salina, Kansas, the birthplace of Terry Kirkman, on May 10th. In addition, a potential and long overdue revisit to the U.K. was back on the cards, also scheduled for May, as reported in an article for *Sounds*, one of the U.K.'s leading music journals.

"I just hope it all works out," commented a keen Terry Kirkman to journalist Jerry Gilbert, before going on to talk about plans for the upcoming album on their new label. "We have had distribution problems in the past but what we intend to do now is put out singles after the album as opposed to before, although the new album is still concentrated on single material. We've not really had anything as big as those early singles although we've gotten some very good airplay."

Jules would also add, during the same article: "I went to India at the same time the group came to England last, but I want to get over very badly. I went away but it just seemed right to come back when I did…"

The album that was to appear on the new label later that spring was clearly an attempt by the band to update their sound with a modern, contemporary vibe. Whilst the previous two studio releases had highlighted an inclination to step away from their more 'pop' orientated roots there had always been underlying current of the '60s sound running throughout the grooves. After all, it was in the DNA of the band. But with another new producer sitting behind the console for the sessions, and a new musical arranger assisting throughout, both of whom harbored an underpinning of jazz music on their résumés, the feel that the new music brought into the studio was far more aligned to a 1970s listening audience than that which they had recorded before.

Jules Alexander commented to *Sounds*: "Some of the stuff we've done before has been pretty good and it's a pity things like 'Stop Your Motor' didn't get out there. That was the last album in the old direction and hopefully we haven't assumed an entirely new direction but we've got closer to what we wanted and what we're really about. We've just selected the best material there is…"

Columbia Records in-house producer Lewis Merenstein was not an obvious choice for the band but he had a good track record, and he came recommended somewhere along the line, and the band accepted his position as they settled into the studios once more.

Merenstein had initially moved to New York during the late 1950s, where he had spent five years as a recording engineer at the Nola Penthouse studio, working with jazz musicians and with producers such as Tom Wilson, who would later go on to work with Bob Dylan. During the following decade he began to undertake the producer's role in his own right, collaborating with artists such as Gladys Knight, Miriam Makeba, The Spencer Davis Group, Cass Elliott and, perhaps most famously, Van Morrison with whom he would conjure up such magical moments as *Astral Weeks* and *Moondance.* Musical arranger Benny Golson on the other hand was a renowned tenor saxophonist, specializing in serious bebop and hardcore jazz during the late 1950s, before venturing away from his chosen area of expertise and entering a composing and arranging career within the studio and orchestral field the following decade. His musical accomplishments during the 1960s would see composing credits on a number of notable television shows such as *Ironside*, *Mannix* and *Mission Impossible,* whilst his arranging work would see acknowledgment on the album sleeves of artists as diverse as Quincy Jones, Peggy Lee, Eric Burden and Cass Elliott. In addition, he also had history with the band, going back to their earliest recording sessions…

"Benny had actually worked with us on one of the first tunes we did," states Jules. "On 'Babe I'm Gonna Leave You', he was right there at the very beginning, and we were real happy to work with him again because he was incredible."

These were some seriously heavyweight studio cats and the continuing presence of veteran vocal arranger Clark Burroughs still on hand only added to the positive vibe that was initially prevalent throughout the early sessions, no doubt aided further still once the seasoned band of session players, predominately with jazz backgrounds themselves, came in to add their input onto the tapes. Guitarists Dennis Budimir, Larry Carlton, Artie Wayne and Dean Parks, saxophonist and bass player Wilton Felder, drummers John Guerin and Milt Holland, and keyboard players Mike Melvoin, Lincoln Mayorga and Don Randi all made significant contributions to the ten recordings that eventually wound up on the album, adding a groove that had been notably absent on the previous releases. One only has to listen to the opening bars of Jules' "Kicking The Gong Around", one of four songs he composed for the album, three of which were written in partnership with Steve Carey, to feel the changes that these new musicians and influences were bringing in.

"Steven Carey and his wife Essie were living in our house with us at the time. It was a *big* house…" laughs Jules, "and we just started writing together.

276

He was quite a good poet, with a really interesting style, very stream of consciousness. That song was pretty much my arrangement. It started out with that bass line, and it just built from there, on and on, It's actually a real simple arrangement if you listen to it, with that bass line and a lot of fill, and it just sorta came about during the playing of it. I think it was Wilton Felder who played the bass and the sax was played by a studio player, I don't know who it was, but he just played it from the top to the end! We were cracking up! We said 'no, just play here, and here', and he played it again and did the same! But he was so good so we just edited out what we didn't want to use! It was hilarious…"

The lyrics that Carey added to Jules' music were perhaps more understandable once one considers his history within contemporary poetry, and an online article overseeing his talents (sadly, he passed away in 1989 following a heart attack, aged just 61) offered a further insight into, what was termed by one journalist, 'the loveliest poetry voice I've ever encountered'.

> His grandfather was Harry Carey, a silent film actor who became a big part of early Hollywood western features associated with John Ford, and his father was Harry Carey, Jr., a popular character actor who was featured in dozens of Westerns, both in film and on TV. Steve subsequently remarked that he had grown up "sitting on the laps of starlets," and it is perhaps for this reason that Carey's poetry has such an obvious spoken component. Surrounded by family and friends who often rehearsed their lines in his presence, he developed an ear for dialogue and the colloquial, and it was no secret that his nuanced and unerring ear often lifted lines from TV or movies and incorporated them into the text of his work. [39]

> Three steps forward and two steps back
> Then count how far you come
> Is this what they mean when they say just to keep on
> Truckin' along

"Kicking The Gong Around"
Words and Music by Jules Alexander and Steven Carey

Continuing the pattern set by the previous releases, whereupon the band members themselves contributed the majority of the compositions, it was again Jules who stepped to the fore once more. With neither Jim, Ted, Richard nor Brian offering up any new songs, and Terry and Larry only contributing one composition apiece, the often-varying styles of Jules' work is subsequently highlighted to a greater degree. Certainly "Gong" has by far and away the funkiest drive of the new tunes, emphasizing the jazz playing of the additional musicians now working alongside them, whilst the calypso rhythms that introduce "Please Don't Go (Round The Bend)" offer up a completely new tangent to the Association catalog.

"It wasn't quite calypso, it wasn't really quite anything!" laughs Jules once more. "That funny mish-mash of timings, especially with the break with a 6/4 over a 4/4. Technically there's some really strange things in it, but that was just a fun song."

"Rainbows Bent" however, another collaboration with Carey, perhaps maintains the most familiarity to the harmonies of former days with the gentle sway of the band vocals supporting the distinctly laid back Alexander lead, ably supported by Larry Ramos on the bridge. And yet, the three overwhelmingly successful offerings on the entire collection come from the pens of Terry Kirkman, with the truly delightful "Come The Fall", Larry Ramos (in collaboration with his brother Del and former New Society/Summerhill guitarist, Larry Hickman) with the acoustic singer-songwriter styled "Indian Wells Woman" and, finally, a cover of John Sebastian's Lovin' Spoonful composition "Darling Be Home Soon", as originally featured on the Spoonful's '67 soundtrack to the previous years *You're A Big Boy Now* movie. It was this particular cut, featuring a sensitive Jim Yester vocal interpretation, with which the band chose to first introduce their new music (disregarding Terry's previous statement that the album would appear first), releasing it as the debut single for the new label (Columbia-45602) on April 18th 1972, backed with the Ramos-Hickman-Ramos song. And for a brief moment it appeared that the resulting move to a new label may have paid off as the release briefly bubbled under the hot 100 before giving up its claim and settling for a Billboard peak of 104. The full album was to follow shortly afterwards, appearing that same month under the title of *Waterbeds In Trinidad!* (Columbia KC-31348).

And how did that title come about?

Jules: "Russ and I had an apartment and we had some friends who lived right next door to us that were cops. And they were really fun guys, real nice, and one of them happened to be from Trinidad. Ted came over one day and they became real tight too. Then this guy had to go back to Trinidad for some reason and he invited Ted to go down with him. Ted just fell in love with it. And, at that time, waterbeds became this 'thing', they were everywhere, and yet there were none in Trinidad! So Ted goes 'let's import waterbeds!' and so they were importing waterbeds in Trinidad! That was the reality of the whole thing."

"That was a silly title!" added Ted, by way of a further explanation, elucidating just that little bit further. "I thought I had invested in a waterbed store in Trinidad and found out it was a front for a drug smuggling operation! I wanted no part of that so I got out…" [20]

"It was so absurd we couldn't ignore it…" summarizes Terry.

Packaged in a sleeve featuring a tinted black and white photograph of the band, taken by one Norris McNamara, surrounded by the snowy wastelands of upstate Illinois, the frozen waters of Lake Michigan to be exact, with the silhouette of a frozen windy city in the hazy background (along with a subtle addition added by the band themselves, a small pile of snow on top of the familiar Columbia logo), the release initially generated some strong supporting promotion from their new label, although that seemingly tailed away fairly swiftly, and yet the band were keen to heap praise upon those who had aided the process of seeing it through to fruition. The inner four-page lyric sheet (featuring a tasteful band photograph courtesy of Jim Metropole), name checked fifty-plus associates who deserved a sincere 'thank you' with, once again, their loyal road crew, family and friends included.

Opening with another cover version, this time a Larry Ramos vocal take on the Ron Davies' composition "Silent Song Through The Land" (previously issued as the title track from the Oklahoma-born composers own album, released during 1970 on A&M Records) and also featuring a polished performance from both Jim and Larry on the Carole King-Gerry Goffin tune "Snow Queen" (first released with a similar vocal arrangement by the Roger Nichols Trio, again on A&M Records, back in December 1966), the album somewhat surprisingly went on to become the band's lowest charting album in their career to date, a major disappointment, reaching a desultory number 194 chart position. However, harsh press reception in some quarters certainly didn't aid the cause;

WATERBEDS IN TRINIDAD! (COLUMBIA KC-31348).

RATING 2.5 STARS.

Haven't progressed at all in the last four years. This is just a rehash of the same old thing. They could be a lot better if they had some better material and arrangements, plus a little motivation.

The Wisconsin Post-Crescent
July 1972

Nevertheless, as the sessions had reached their conclusion, it had become apparent to the band members themselves that the decision to utilize Merenstein in the producer's chair was not perhaps the wisest of choices, especially in light of the ever-widening gulf of opinions that now ran through the ranks;

Jim Yester: "Unfortunately, a great deal of this got shot down by the producer. There was a bit of strife going on within the group and the producer, Lou Merenstein, was a guy who just loved to antagonize people. He would set people up against others and create…" he tails off. "I have no idea why. He just enjoyed doing that, and he got Terry and Larry into a fight. Oh, it was just some horrid things going on. I'm surprised we got the album finished. There was some wonderful stuff on the tape but by the time it was mixed it all just kind of sounded the same. There was a big, wide range to it, and we had some great players. I mean, Larry Carlton… There were a lot of incredible people in there, but he just kind of handcuffed all of them. Real straight, y'know, don't do anything creative. Thanks Lou…"[21]

The album closed out with, what is perhaps with hindsight, a somewhat prophetic inclusion to the proceedings with Brian Cole, his continuing ability to effectively contribute to the band now being brought into question, supplying a heartfelt vocal to the John Stewart composition "Little Road And A Stone To Roll". Whilst Stewart's own acoustic version of the song, from the previous years *Lonesome Picker Rides Again* album, touched the heartstrings, the overly sentimentality of the string arrangement took away some of the personal feel of the song, whereas Brian's electrified rendition, with a delightful supporting chorus of harmonies from his bandmates, in more ways than one offered up the full glory of the tune and nowhere more so than during the extended fading refrain where Brian truly opens up his lungs and delivers, what ultimately became, his epitaph.

Little road and a stone to roll
Little road and a stone to roll

Little road and a stone to roll
Everybody needs a stone to roll

"Little Road And A Stone To Roll"
Words and Music by John Stewart

"Brian was an unhappy individual," says Jim. "At that time we had started going in a different direction and he started doing less. When we first began we did skits and banter, it was more musical theater than it was just a band. I mean, it *was* a band but we also did long involved skits and everything, but the more we started to get away from that the unhappier Brian was. He was not a real great bass player and so his musical forte was this musical theater kind of thing. We tried to help him and we thought we had him off of it…"[21]

With his marriage having collapsed due to his excessive involvement in the rock lifestyle, the drugs and the groupies sadly dividing up the family harmony, Brian continued to spiral ever downwards into the heavy world of substance abuse.

"Smack and cocaine brought him down," summarized Ted. "He started shooting and, by that time, it was too far gone. We worked real hard to break that up (but) everybody has to take responsibility for their own lives…"[20]

The band went out on tour to promote the album, pushing the new songs hard to their ever-loyal following, but Brian was proving increasingly erratic in his performances, to the extent that the band had little choice but to introduce a substitute bass player for their performances, bringing in the German-born Wolfgang Melz, a former partner of Richard Thompson in Gábor Szabó's acclaimed, jazz-flavored backing band. A much-in-demand player due to the dramatic style he utilized whilst playing his Fender, he had worked with John Klemmer, Anita O'Day, Art Pepper, Jimmy Witherspoon and The Doors prior to joining The Association's touring circus and he brought in a solid foundation as accompaniment for Ted in the rhythm section.

With Larry out front on lead guitar, Jim and Jules flitting between frontline guitar and keyboards, Terry on his ever reliable barrage of instrumental prowess whilst Ted provided the beat, and with Richard, usually stage left, on piano and occasional saxophone and horns, that left Brian, reduced to vocal harmonies, standing behind a set of congas and playing along on the tambourine occasionally, looking like a little boy lost to many of the attending audiences. At times those watching on would even suggest that he had little awareness as to whom or to where he was playing…

"We got him to a psychologist," adds Jules "and he was doing a little better. Then he got hold of some really pure stuff..."

On June 20th the expanded eight-piece band had returned for a residency at their spiritual home, the Troubadour club in Hollywood, with Judee Sill supporting them with a thirty-minute set of her own. However, despite the positivity the band felt towards the newer material, and its acceptance from their hardcore following, the media remained unsure as to how far they had truly traveled from their patented formula sound.

At its Troubadour opening Tuesday night The Association could do no wrong. Although it hasn't had a hit record in roughly three years it still commands an adoring public and every song was accorded enthusiastic and sustained applause. The fact remains however, that the eight-man ensemble is caught in something of a musical time warp. It is somewhat distressing to watch talented musicians tread water, especially when one suspects that, given the vocal and instrumental abilities with which The Association are beautifully endowed, they might well be able to strike out in new directions.

The Los Angeles Times
June 22nd 1972

There then followed a journey out east to perform at the annual Schaefer Music Festival, held at the Wollman Rink in New York's Central Park on July 8th, performing alongside Curtis Mayfield and Jackie DeShannon, before continuing with a further series of shows in Michigan and the surrounding states.

Returning to Los Angeles at the end of the month the band took a few days out of the schedule to wind down at home before they were due back out on the road. The second single from the *Waterbeds...* album had seen a release on July 14th (Columbia-45654) but, much like its predecessor, "Come The Fall" b/w "Kicking The Gong Around", had failed to make any dent whatsoever in the Hot 100 and the band were keen to get out onto the stage once again to promote the release.

On August 1st 1972 Brian Cole had made a purchase of heroin to feed his habit, but this batch, unlike previous buys, hadn't been cut in any form other than its purest nature. He saw his former band mate Russ Giguere later that evening and had asked him if he wanted to come over to his house to

Richard Thompson joins in the studio (c/o James Metropole)

Jules Alexander
(c/o James Metropole)

Brian and Larry at the Felt Forum 1970
(c/o Sherry Rayn Barnett)

Stop Your Motor photo session (c/o James Metropole)

With Mike Berkowitz and Wolfgang Melz
(c/o David Nakamura)

David Vaught and Mo Miller join the band
(c/o James Metropole)

1974 publicity image with David Vaught,
Jerry Yester, Mo Miller and Richard
Thompson
(unknown)

Jim Yester
(c/o James Metropole)

Larry Brown and Andy Chapin (left) join c.1975
(c/o Larry Brown)

Homegrown with Del, Larry and Miles Unite (c/o Tracy Ramos)

David Vaught, Russ Levine, Ted, Ric Ulsky, John Tuttle and Jack Harris c. 1978
(c/o Russ Levine)

Jules onstage 1984
(c/o Mike Dennis)

Terry and Larry 1984
(c/o Mike Dennis)

1980s reunion with (l-r) Larry, Ric, Jim, Terry, Jules, Ted and Russ
(c/o Michael Ochs Archives)

Larry and Russ
(c/o Diane Tartaglia)

Larry in 2014
(c/o Tracy Ramos)

Jim Yester (c/o Candy Kayne)

Jules and Bruce Pictor
(c/o Candy Kayne)

2014 with Bruce, Jim, Jules, Del, Jordan and Paul (c/o Pat Smith)

party but, wisely, Russ declined his friend's invitation. Jim Metropole, who was still working for the band in his PR role at the time, just happened to be in their office the next morning with Pat Colecchio, when the telephone rang:

"Brian happened to be buying heroin from a bartender at the Troubadour and he went and bought a hot dose the previous day. He'd previously been shooting cut stuff that was weak and his girlfriend at the time, her name was Linda, called up Patrick in the office that morning, and I was there, and she was screaming down the phone 'Patrick, I can't wake Brian!' Pat dashed out and he drove straight up to Brian's house in the valley, he had a nice little house up there, and that was it. They couldn't wake him..."

"It was very sad," Russ was to later comment to *Goldmine* magazine. "I was already out of the group, but I saw Brian the day before he died."

"We all tried to save him," added Terry, during the same article. "People in the music business would go over to Brian's house and kick his door open, and then you would just pray to God he wasn't hallucinating and shoot you. All sorts of people in the music community tried to save Brian Cole."

Everybody needs a fire inside
Everybody needs a dream to ride
Everybody with a growing soul
Everybody needs a stone to roll

"Little Road And A Stone To Roll"
Words and Music by John Stewart

"Brian was wonderful. He was crazy. He was one of the funniest and brightest people I ever met in my life."

CHAPTER TWENTY-ONE

NAMES, TAGS...

At just 29 years of age Brian Cole had lived, and paid the price of being a rock star in a successful recording and touring band. Unlike many of his fellow sufferers who had trodden the same path of destruction before him – Al Wilson, Jimi Hendrix, Jim Morrison, Janis Joplin – and those who would follow shortly afterwards – Lowell George, Gram Parsons, Danny Whitten – Brian had never publically embodied the dark side of the '60s/'70s era. The music that he had helped create was timeless and to many, the epitome of artistically creative sunshine pop. And, to a degree, they may well be right, but the music that the band recorded during their initial opening salvo, that successful two to three year period, was always that little bit more than just 'pop'. It was experimental. It was vocally challenging. It was an artistic mixture of varying genres and styles that had outlived much of their contemporaries' output. And Brian was there. In the thick of it all. His compositional input may have been to a lesser degree than his multi-faceted partners, and his lead vocal input of a similar stature, but his mere presence was an integral part of the set-up. The only significant difference between Brian Cole and the above list of immense talents was that he had no posthumous luster bestowed upon his reputation following his tragic passing. Nevertheless, his contribution should not be forgotten…

A memorial service was held for Brian two weeks after his passing and his ashes were then returned to his home state of Oregon where they were interred at the Lincoln Mausoleum in Portland. Not that the surviving members and his fellow bandmates had time to sit around and commiserate with each other, and there was no suggestion that the band may split in the aftermath of Brian's death. There were headlining concerts scheduled later that same month and the band simply held strong, regrouped, and on August 16th, a mere fortnight after tragedy had struck, they arrived at the mid-summer Ravinia Festival in Illinois, five years since they had last headlined the same event, appearing two days after homegrown superstars Chicago had ripped through a two-an-a half-hour set for their adoring fans.

"It was rough, but the show has to go on," says Jules today, clearly with sadness still in his voice. "We came from that 1960s business ethic, that show business ethic, and we just stuck to it. We just had to continue, so that's what we did. But it was difficult, very difficult. Death, y'know?"

"Brian Cole, the Association's bass player who died earlier this month, will be replaced by Wolf Gangmelz [sic] when the septet plays Ravinia on Wednesday" ran the misinformed article in *The Chicago Tribune* the previous day, placed alongside a three column review of Chicago's set.

However, with the passing of Brian, and even with Wolfgang now sitting in the touring band on bass guitar, limiting any notable musical absence of their former comrade, the stronger elements of the band still saw fit to restructure the lineup for the new fall touring schedule from that moment onwards. Clearly the set list would have to be re-planned, with any lead vocals that Brian had previously handled either redistributed or dropped entirely, "Reputation" was out and "Dubuque Blues" reverted back to Jules, and although Brian's forte had always been the frontline communication with the audience, along with much of the comedic interplay, particularly during the earlier years, his vocals had still played an integral part of the live performance, albeit from either a lead or a bass harmony. And as Jim noted earlier, much of the onstage banter may have gradually reduced over the more recent months as the band now attempted to portray a serious, contemporary approach to their image, but Brian's former role, despite his debilitating backstage preferences, still brought about a total restructure of their set.

The most decisive move was the introduction of drummer Mike Berkowitz into the rhythm section, pushing fellow founding member Ted Bluechel off his familiar perch and into the now vacant front-of-house conga position, harmonies and tambourine to hand. The addition of Berkowitz, a young yet seasoned professional with touring experience for middle-of-the-road superstars such as Johnny Mathis, Andy Williams and Henry Mancini, may have seemed to many as a harsh snub to the longtime Association drummer and whilst his studio chops may not have always been sufficient enough to play on the band's albums he had become a solid, popular live performer, adding his vocal harmonies and occasional leads to the mix whilst pounding away a driving beat from behind the kit. Nevertheless, his rudimentary abilities still left a lot to be desired for some band members.

"That decision bothered him very much," sighs Jules. "But he had some playing difficulties that he could never get past, or even recognize, so unfortunately he had to be replaced. He was a part of the band, and his voice was a part of it, and he was a great road partner, but that's what happened..." he trails away. "That was when the band started polarizing more or less. Terry and I really wanted to get more specific and we felt that the band as a democracy wasn't always a good idea. We were trying, I think, to maybe take over the band again, which was the way it had started, and we were trying to get that happening again but it just became impossible."

"That was my thing, and Ted was very upset," admits Terry, "as had been Brian before. That was done to free us up in a last ditch attempt to save the group. If we had an actual rhythm section then, maybe, we could be the vocal group that we had dreamed of being. But it was too late. It was so disappointing."

In conversation with the author during 2016, Mike Berkowitz confirmed the disenchantment and harsh treatment that Ted subsequently felt he had handed down to him.

"Ted never wanted to stop playing drums and to this day holds it against Terry for bringing me into the band. Ted and I kind of got along and I always thought he sounded great with the band but the music was progressing and I think that not only Terry, but also Richard and Wolfie wanted another guy. Ideally this allowed Ted to stand up front, sing and play percussion, but he hated it...

"I had met the band in Bloomington, Indiana in May of 1971. I was playing percussion in the house band for the Little 500 show and they were appearing. Terry Kirkman came over to me and struck up a conversation. He liked what I was doing on percussion, which he also played, and I told him my plan to move to L.A. in June of that year. He said to be sure to look him up when I arrived and thought that would be it. I moved to L.A. as planned and began working with Helen Reddy who was very hot at that time. As I was now part of the scene a little, I would either hang out or be performing at the Troubadour, which was *the* place to be in those days for musicians. One night I was there and I see Terry upstairs. I went up and reintroduced myself and we began a friendship. The group had a small studio and storage facility/rehearsal space in Van Nuys and I hung out with Terry a lot in those days. Brian was not around much. With the addition of Wolfie, Terry thought they should have a drummer who was up to the level of both Richard and Wolfgang. They were both virtuoso players, completely at home in jazz, rock and pop, and beyond. Apart from Richard and Wolfie, the three guitarists were first class as well and Terry was able to play his battery of instruments, from flugelhorn to recorders. They weren't studio guys, but they knew and played their music extremely well.

"I always tried to play what Hal or Jim Gordon had played on the original tracks as much as possible. Ted gave me pointers and some things were very helpful. The biggest difference with me on drums was it had more energy. Our rhythm section was phenomenal."

The *Waterbeds In Trinidad!* tour of 1972 ran onto the early winter months of the following year, with venues ranging from Concordia College, located in River Forest, north-east Illinois, down through Jacksonville in Alabama and across to the Santa Fe College in New Mexico. Sadly, the proposed visit across the Atlantic, previously referred to by both Terry and Jules in the U.K. press, fell by the shoreline once more with Pat Colecchio once again putting the financial implications of such a tour before the musical benefits.

"He just felt the market was too small to even mess with…" summarizes Jules regretfully, leaving the small but loyal U.K. contingent of followers once again deprived of seeing and hearing the touring band performing live.

Berkowitz: "We played the Steel Pier in Atlantic City, where Duke Ellington opened for us (Duke had previously supported The Cowsills in the same establishment), and at other venues like Ravinia where we played for 10,000 people. I also recall some State Fairs and smaller venues but the band was still a viable touring act in 1972. We did all the hits plus a lot of the 'Waterbeds…' tunes, which I enjoyed very much. You have to do the hits. This experience was more as being a member of a band for me, which was great."

On September 15th they arrived at the Wisconsin International Fall Festival, held in Kaukuana, appearing during the opening night of the weekend gathering, and on the same bill as The Siegel-Schwall Band, The

New Colony Six, Black Society, The Hound Dog Band and, for one of their final appearances together, the heavy sounds of Michigan's MC5.

FALL FEST
16 Name Bands – 3 Big Days
Adult Admittance Only
ID Cards A Must
Absolutely No Camping
Advance Tickets $4.00 / Gate Admission $5.00

"There were many divisions within the band when I joined and much tension," adds Mike. "I felt it was Terry vs. the band at that point. Jules was more on Terry's wavelength and is a great guy. The political scene of the time entered into the dynamic as well. Larry Ramos led the other faction. He and I weren't close and with Ted on his side, he was a source of much tension. Jim Yester was surfing both sides of the street.

"Richard was a big addition. His jazz background added a deeper harmonic sensibility to the music and his personality was very cool and a welcome addition amidst the tension. Ironically, Wolf was the worst druggie in the band as far as I knew. These were the '60s and '70s and despite their early family-friendly image they were reputedly known as a serious party band! He would drink, snort or swallow pretty much anything and we had issues with him. One time he fell off the stage in Maryland! I was unaware of Terry's issues at that time. Maybe I was naive. We were together a lot and I never saw anything..."

After seven years of continual touring across the vast nation, month in month out with barely time off in-between, all of the band members were now reaching various stages of burnout, and none more so than Terry Kirkman. Both alcohol and drugs were now playing an active part of his daily routine on the road, despite Mike Berkowitz remaining unaware of it all, and having seen the downfall of one of his bandmates he was all too aware as to the potential fate that awaited him, should the constant demands of the road continue.

"I was tired... I was burned out and I needed to go home. Essentially I just got up and walked out," he says. "I did it formally, and there was no malice, but I was done. I didn't discuss it with Pat Colecchio initially, I discussed it first with Lee Colton, our attorney, who was a very close friend, and I discussed the legalities, the timing and the integrity, so I wouldn't do any undue harm to the band, and I tried to do it well but Pat was furious with me because I didn't converse with him first.

"I remember having lunch at the Rainbow Bar & Grill on Sunset Boulevard with Clive Davis, or maybe he had just come over to my table while I was there, but he asked me about Pat. Why was he so hysterical and hard to get along with? He said that Pat had been screaming at him. I don't remember in what context it was but I would imagine that it would have been around Clive's view of us as being new to him and to his stable at Columbia, and the stability of us as an entity with him, and also of his choice of single from 'Waterbeds…' I personally had been very disappointed with the choice of 'Darling Be Home Soon', but we were locked into a deal with Columbia. But Pat had so offended Clive, that (the deal with Columbia Records) was over, and Pat was going to go over to Hal Landers and Bobby Roberts and they were going to create a label around us, and I just thought 'how sad is that?'

"I had caught wind that, without discussing it with us, Pat was taking us to Landers and Roberts, and his ability to handle us at that point was really shaky at best. We were sinking faster than your average rock, and that was when I decided that 'I'm out of here'.

"I was cooked, I was fried and I was so embarrassed to be doing the music we were doing, with everything else that was happening in the country and the world, and I just longed to sink myself into the anti-war movement…"

Ultimately, Terry parted company with the band in late 1972, returning home to his wife Judy and their young daughter Sasha… and stayed there. All of the internal business interactions, disagreements over musical developments and the general day-to-day lifestyle of being a rock star on the road, had ultimately become too much for the founding member and for the sake of his family, and for himself he needed to break away. Completely. Enough was enough.

"We were both political activists," he continued, when discussing his longtime marriage to Judy, "so royalties from music gave us income to pursue our activism. I didn't particularly like the music that we (the band) ended up doing. The music that I was writing, I didn't want to have arguments with anybody about that. I am a natural-born civil rights activist from Kansas, and I was on the road with three guys who were really conservative reactionary people. I stood back thinking, 'That's cool. That's completely fair.' You know, walk and talk, live your life but it's not the art that I want to make. I want the art to be about something besides jumping in the back seat, kiss me. Doo-wop, doo-wop." [7]

Terry's imminent departure also brought about the exodus of both Wolfgang Melz and Mike Berkowitz from the touring bandwagon. Both had brought in and added a considerable amount of quality and a dynamic rhythm and backbone to the recent live performances, but certain band members felt that they were too aligned to Terry's vision to be considered for permanent status within the band, and with the year now drawing to a close two new personnel, a drummer and a bass player, were soon brought in to take on the mantle of performing Associates.

"I was let go when Terry quit the band," says Mike today. "He and I were too aligned for Larry Ramos and Ted to keep me on and truthfully, without Terry, I wouldn't have stayed anyway. Pat Colecchio called me and said he wanted me to stay but the guys had voted me out…"

The departure of Terry Kirkman was, ultimately, the closing chapter for the original Association. It really was the end of an era. The band would continue to function for the foreseeable future and would also go on to achieve a certain level of success for their efforts, but without Terry up front, adding his voice and his guiding light into their stage presence, it was a totally different band who stepped up to the plate for the 1973 schedule. Jules, Jim, Larry and Ted were all still there, as was Richard Thompson, but from the original hit making band they were now three down, and with the recording deal at Columbia Records rapidly unraveling it was time for a new direction. A new beginning and a new lineup.

Maurice Miller, it has been said, was born to the blues. Born in 1931, he grew up in Alton, Illinois and, as many had done before him, took to music early, first as a singer and then as a drummer. Nicknamed 'Daddio' by age eleven, Maurice, or 'Mo', had a band and his own blues radio show by the time he turned sixteen and just one year later, in 1948, he was playing drums on the road with blues legends Memphis Slim, Chuck Willis and Big Joe Turner. Shortly afterwards, as a member of one of the earliest black rock 'n' roll bands during the 1950s, he found himself touring the deep south where he experienced the grim reality of Southern racism first hand, where driving from one club date to another was an experience in terror.

"We'd drive through towns in Mississippi and Alabama as late at night as possible," Miller later recalled. "We'd have our hearts in our throats until we reached the black section where we were headed. One night, we were on a road that went right past a burning cross at a Ku Klux Klan rally in a field in South Carolina."

Ten years later, and with a decade of touring behind him, he wound up in Hollywood, studying alongside Stan Levey, one of America's greatest bebop drummers, playing the clubs and recording sessions with Los Angeles' top jazz musicians, supporting headlining artists and acts such as Ike & Tina Turner, Nancy Wilson and Lena Horne, all of whom were to benefit from his immense percussive abilities. In addition, he had a special sensuous texture to his strong voice, and an inimitable and consummate stage presence that suggested his addition to ranks of The Association would be a valuable asset to the band's progression. Such was his vocal ability that, during 1970, he been asked to supply his voice to the title song for the *Halls of Anger* movie.

David Allen Vaught meanwhile, was a youthful, handsome 24-year old, sixteen years younger than Maurice but still with a wealth of experience behind him. Having started his career back in '62, playing bass guitar alongside his brother in the L.A. surf band Bob Vaught & The Renegaids, he continued playing in various smalltime lineups before joining up with Jerry Yester in Rosebud for their one album, released in 1971. Following the disbandment of the quintet, David then linked up with Jerry once again, aiding the folk-rock duo Aztec Two-Step with their debut album sessions, the result being the eponymous *Aztec Two-Step* LP for Elektra Records, produced by Jerry during 1972. That same year also saw the Vaught-Yester partnership work together on Robb Reiner's *Peter & The Wolf: A Contemporary Version*, released on the United Artists label, whilst yet further studio work for the now-in-demand player saw him undertake some demo sessions for the legendary Los Angeles-based producer Gary Usher as well as performing and recording as a member of the L.A.-based band The Flaming Pitts (releasing the *Bite The Baby* LP: VSR-101).

"I don't recall how either of them actually came on board with The Association," stated Jules, during early 2017 "but Maurice was absolutely fantastic! An incredible person. And David was a fine bass player, very technically adept. In those times it was when the music business was starting to change to… what it's become now. Of course, there was no computer stuff around but, technically, it was getting very interesting and David was very much involved in all of that, but I really don't remember who suggested them…"

With Miller and Vaught now added into the band (although Jules' former sparring partner from the Joshua Fox group, Joe LaManno, also recalls occasionally aiding the lineup on bass during this period whilst Vaught was establishing his availability), the next step was to introduce the new membership to a live audience, and to consolidate Pat Colecchio's deal with the new recording label.

Mums Records was a small company, operating out of the Creative Management Associates building on Beverly Boulevard, off La Cienega in Hollywood. Launched by a former executive of Dunhill Records, Bobby Roberts, in partnership with film producer Hal Landers, and with contributions from songwriter/producer Don Altfeld, the label had been created with the assistance of Clive Davis' financial backing during April of 1972, with full distribution by Columbia/CBS Records, as a means to release new product by none other than P.F. Sloan, by then (in Altfeld's own words) 'a drugged-out, burned-out hippie'. [38]

The first issues pressed by Mums during the spring of 1972 were credited to the artists LAX (a studio creation, fronted by session players Hal Blaine and Joe Osborn) and Charlie Starr respectively, but neither saw an actual release, and so the first official 45 to bear the neon-italic Mums logo was "Down By The River", written and released (Mums ZS7-6009) by the UK-born, Gibraltar-raised singer-songwriter Albert Hammond, during June of that year. Just scraping into the Hot 100 at number 91, this was followed up by P.F. Sloan's debut for the label, an unsuccessful version of his own composition "Let Me Be", along with a further release by Hammond, the delightful "It Never Rains In Southern California", a Top 5 *Billboard* smash, and a Top 10 hit in at least five other countries around the world. Needless to say, overshadowing Sloan's credentials, this rocketed Hammond's credibility and status as both a performer and a songwriter, and he became very much in demand (although, sadly, he would never reach such lofty heights in the U.S. chart lists again, despite further success in the U.K.).

Now, despite the potential fallout between Pat Colecchio, Clive Davis and Columbia Records, and the questionably underhand way that the deal was procured, The Association signed with Mums Records during late 1972 with the proposition of a single and an album deal. As related by producer Gary Usher during an early 1980s correspondence with Australian author and historian Stephen J. McParland (for his extensive Usher biography; *The*

California Sound), he had been the first notable suggestion for the producer's seat on the band's sessions for their new label, as he was experienced enough and potentially sympathetic enough to their needs, having been familiar with their work for a number of years.

"When Columbia hired me as a producer back in the '60s, they asked me to review all of their talent on the west coast, and Larry Ramos was on their roster as a singles artist. This was before he had joined The Association, and even then I thought he was extremely talented. It was around this time that I also first met Jules Alexander through Curt (Boettcher). Both Jules and Curt were very close at one time and worked together on writing, arranging and producing. I used one of their compositions, 'Would You Like To Go', on the Sagittarius album."

By late 1972, their association (no pun intended) had arisen once more, with Usher continuing: "I had been using David Vaught, who was The Association's bass player at the time, to cut some of my demos and it was through him that the connection was made. I had found out about this little studio he ran and he offered me free time there when he wasn't on the road with The Association. We were doing some amazing things together, such as speed variations, echo things, a lot of texturing and little production tricks."[16]

The studio in question was the small Van Nuys rehearsal set-up, located on the corner of Cedros Avenue and Aetna Street, in which the group had set up a sound stage and an 8-track recording facility, utilizing an expansive, and expensive mixing board, specially built for them by revolutionary audio engineer Daniel Flickinger, and initially carried around on tour for a number of years. With David overseeing much of the work being undertaken in the studio (often referred to as The Association Clubhouse), and impressed by these Usher-produced demos, he then suggested the possibility that his new partners and Gary work together for the new Mums deal.

"He talked to the guys in the group and they expressed a willingness to work with me. I then went over and met Bobby Roberts at Mums Records and had some discussions with him. At the time The Association were playing at the Santa Monica Civic Auditorium, and he asked me to go down there to see them. Well, the place was packed, and I was impressed with their live performance. I remember going backstage and we took it from there.

"Roberts set up a further meeting with an older guy (Hal Landers) who I actually had negotiations with. We talked about how the group should be handled and how they should be produced, and I was told to start rehearsing and to work up a budget. We had two or three rehearsals with the group in their studio, and I started working on songs for an album. One of them was a Jim Weatherly song (but) I can't remember the title. Everything was going fine."

According to his comments in McParland's biography, Usher himself was under the impression that the collaboration was paying dividends for both sides, and a strong productive partnership was forthcoming. He then reported back to Mums Records with a proposed budget figure for what he had planned for the group.

"I told them that to record an album the way the group wanted it done would cost somewhere in the vicinity of $40,000."

Landers reportedly exploded at such a figure, retorting, "That's outrageous! You should be able to do it for half that much! Let me talk to my partners and get back to you…" [16]

Shortly afterwards, and despite Usher's protestations that such a lowly figure would render the quality of such a product unworkable, Landers came back with a blunt refusal, noting that the label was not willing to spend that much on the band because, at that time, "they just weren't selling". With Usher committed to his proposed figure to deliver the quality the band wanted, and the label refusing to budge, the Association/Usher sessions collapsed, with the proposed album deal in tatters. Disappointed with the outcome, and no doubt concerned by the label's lack of support, The Association instead turned to focus on the songs of fellow Mums artist, Albert Hammond. For his part Hammond, now settled and living in Los Angeles, encouraged the band to record a complete album of his material and whilst that never came to fruition they did take one of his songs, the enjoyable "Names, Tags, Numbers & Labels" and cut a version under the production guidance of Hammond himself, along with Don Altfeld (an established west coast producer and songwriter with a number of Top 10 hits under his belt). Co-written by Hammond with his long-term musical partner and fellow Brit Mike Hazelwood, the song was a smooth, dreamy production, with vocal arrangements by the band members themselves, keyboards and drums by Mike Melvoin and Hal Blaine respectively, topped off with a sweet string backing, arranged by renowned conductor Jimmie Haskell.

Hammond's original demo of the song actually contained two additional lines within the lyrics that, in a similar move to their earlier recording of

"P.F. Sloan", The Association chose to omit when cutting their own rendition of song.

> Names, I know a man, who speaks the language of another class
> He sees nothing in the looking glass. Phony
> Tags, I know a kid. Somehow the ball game doesn't interest him.
> Isn't this where it all begins? Sissy
>
> "Names, Tags, Numbers & Labels"
> Words & Music by Albert Hammond-Mike Hazelwood

Maybe the slang term, 'sissy', referencing a boy or a man who doesn't display the characteristic behavior of stereotypical masculinity failed to hit home with a proposed American rock audience, especially coming from the pen of a sensitive English songwriter, but for whatever the reasons behind the omission the band's delightful recording of the song, released during February of 1973 (Mums ZS7-6016) and featuring Larry Ramos handling the lead with delicate precision, finally got the band back into Hot 100, peaking at number 91 in the *Billboard* listing, number 85 in *Cash Box*, and reaching the dizzy heights of number 27 on the U.S. Adult Contemporary charts (a secondary *Billboard* listing, comprising of the best-selling soft-rock/MOR 'pop' songs). Coupled with "Rainbows Bent", an Alexander-Carey composition from the *Waterbeds In Trinidad!* album (and already licensed to CBS for distribution), it may not have been Top 10, but it was back in the charts and that counted for a lot...

Of particular interest, amongst the other songs composed by the Hammond-Hazelwood team, but which the band had opted to reject, was a song that Hammond himself had already recorded for his debut album the previous year. Shortly afterwards, Phil Everly had also seen the potential this particular tune had to offer and cut a version for his own 1973 solo *Star Spangled Banner* LP. However, it wasn't until the hugely successful British band The Hollies heard it, and recorded their own version, that the song really took off. Released in the U.S. on the Epic label during 1974, and in their homeland on Polydor Records, "The Air That I Breathe" went Top 10 worldwide, racking up gold and silver awards for the band. And not that this was the first time The Hollies had capitalized on The Association's lack of foresight. "He Ain't Heavy, He's My Brother" had previously seen global success for the Manchester-founded harmony outfit and dismay for L.A.'s finest.

On March 2nd the band appeared on one of the first broadcasts of what would become the long running, and hugely successful *Midnight Special* TV show, pre-recorded and broadcast from the NBC network studios in Burbank. In addition to promoting the new 45 release, the band, now comprising of Jules, Jim, Larry, Ted, Richard, Maurice Miller and David Vaught, also ran through a shortened but stunning live version of "Along Comes Mary", with both Jules and Jim sharing the lead in unison, Ted striking a mean cowbell stage left and Richard, stage right but often out of shot, hitting some hard chords on the baby grand. A rockin' version of the unrecorded "Crazy Songs & Looney Tunes", originally a honky-tonk bar-band composition released by Oklahoman quintet Buckwheat the previous year (and written by three of that band's members), was also performed to complete the appearance. Then, shortly afterwards, they settled back into the well-acquainted surroundings of Doug Weston's Troubadour Club along Santa Monica Boulevard for a five-day residency on the familiar stage.

Interestingly, although the bookings in many of the larger concert venues around the nation were slowly fading away, despite Pat Colecchio squeezing every drop of the touring schedule out of the band he could seemingly find, they could always rely on selling out in a number of favored hot-spots across the country, and six weeks prior to the Troubadour residency they had achieved a similar series of sell out shows during a 5-day run, with two shows per day, held at the popular Paul's Mall venue in Boston, Massachusetts, sandwiched in-between residencies from the upcoming New Jersey artist 'Rick' Springsteen [sic] and the million-selling Dr. Hook & The Medicine Show, themselves hot off the successes of their "Sylvia's Mother" and "Cover Of Rolling Stone" 45 releases. The following day The Association flew the 1100-mile journey down south to Jacksonville, Alabama, just 80 miles from Jim's hometown, to honor a further concert booking.

From that point onwards 1973 was the beginning of an endless revolving cycle for the band. Later scheduling throughout the spring and early summer of that year would see the band perform at the third Greater Southwest Music Festival in Amarillo, followed by two dates at the Knott's Berry Farm theme park in Buena Park the following month. The Chemung County Fair in New York, the Brown County Fair in Green Bay and a show in Margate, New Jersey were also included in the touring diary. And over the course of the following six years at least fifteen musicians would come and go, claiming their right to be referred to as an 'official' Associate for their moment in the spotlight for however long it may have been. Before the decade was out there would even be one band on the road, a six-piece lineup playing popular smalltime venues and selling tickets, without one true official member on board, and yet claiming to be 'The Association'. This version of the 'band' even managed to convince the top-selling *Goldmine* magazine to devote an entire page interview to their cause, claiming that 'it hurts, that the former members didn't stay in touch' with them. C'mon guys, it's gotta be real…

THE
ASSOCIATION

AT THE
TROUBADOUR
MAY 8·13

CHAPTER TWENTY-TWO

LIFE IS A CARNIVAL

The first significant change to the new formation came with the departure of Jim Yester during the summer of 1973. He had begun to take on the responsibilities of the tour manager role himself, and was consequently finding himself having to liaise with the venues and the hotels, in addition to working with the band at rehearsals and sound checks on the road and, after eight years of constant touring, it simply became too much to handle.

Jim: "I left the group after burning out doing all the road managing. Hotel bookings, airplane flight reservations, as well as liaison with whatever management we had at the time."

Then, adding yet a further blow to the reduced lineup, it wasn't too long afterwards that Jules Alexander also decided that enough was enough.

"We'd just been on the road for so long" was Jules explanation as to why he also left the band, for the second time in his case. "I was just tired of it all, and I didn't want to do it anymore."

The endless days on the road, keeping the band alive, with few new recordings to promote, had simply worn both Jim and Jules down and, following on from Terry's departure the year before, both subsequently handed in their memberships, initially leaving Ted as the sole surviving original member, supported by the ever-reliable voice of Larry Ramos up front. However, in response to Jules' departure, and in a somewhat surprising move, Jerry Yester stepped in to fill the void on rhythm guitar, an outcome that almost immediately brought Jim back into the fold after just a short absence.

"When Jules left and Jerry joined, I decided to come back in order to work with Jerry again…" Jim continued, when discussing this ever-changing era. This revised lineup then continued together for the next nine months or so, playing at venues of variable capacity across the country such as Six Flags Over Texas, near Dallas during September, followed by the Jacob Brown Auditorium in Brownsville shortly afterwards, performing alongside Mac Davis. Later dates would then find them performing in low-key supporting slots, situated in small town university halls. Reviews were becoming mixed as well, with many in attendance now finding much of the reduced humor within the set tiresome and, occasionally, of an unsuitable adult nature. Jerry, too, despite only a relatively brief tenure in the band, began to find the touring regime increasingly unpleasant, particularly in relation to certain aspects of the set.

"When I was in the group," he later recalled during a 1992 interview, "both Richard and I began to hate 'Cherish' after playing it so many times! I just dreaded it because I was a tenor and it just killed me every time. It was painful. I would see it coming at me like a steamroller on the set list, like 'God! It's only a song away!' It was awful.

"I was in the band and Jim, Ted Bluechel and Larry Ramos were the original members there then, but it wasn't really considered like original members. It was still the first run of the group and so it was still kind of The Association. We just changed over the years. Maurice Miller was playing drums and I guess Larry sang 'Cherish', and Ted probably." [21]

Early 1974 saw them add some further television appearances to their résumé, although neither of the two shows were primetime broadcasts and history would now suggest that the watching audiences for *Yesterday: Soft Rock Music*, appearing alongside The Cowsills, Harpers Bizarre, The Four Tops and Wayne Newton, or *In Session* drew in little by way of high response ratings. The latter show, an obscure short-lived series for the ABC network, for which little more survives by way of detail (other than listing that the band appeared in two episodes alongside Steve Mandel and Eric Weissburg), reportedly had the group performing live versions of "Rainbows Bent" and "Along The Way", along with a bluesy rendition of a new Albert Hammond-Mike Hazelwood composition, "Praise The Lord (And Pass The Soup)", and a beefed up version of "Life Is A Carnival", written and popularized by The

Band on their 1971 *Cahoots* album, and featuring Larry in impressive form up front.

> Supergroups have to face reality; there'll come a time when audiences grow tired of you.
>
> The seven-member Association, at the top of the Silver Dollar Survey a decade ago, aren't ready to give up yet and are still more or less together and waiting impatiently for that next hit record. But fame is fleeting as the wind and glory fades away. Last year The Association started taking club dates. Their shows are now attended by the nightclub regulars and the nostalgia buffs. And tho' the 1974 repertoire includes better and more diversified stuff than what they've done in the past they still suffer because of what a large percentage of the audience is paying to hear.
>
> "We have to answer peoples requests," Jim Yester points out. "But the ideal situation would be to do pieces of the old songs, a sort of dribbling 'overture'".
>
> The price of traveling has hurt groups too. The Association has had to pass up gigs in small town like Buffalo, N.Y. because after the price of moving bodies and equipment they'll make "about $1.95." This is not to imply that The Association guys are sitting around passively getting bald. Most of their collective energy is aimed at working out a deal to make another hit.
>
> "We've now landed what we hope to be a very successful deal" says Ted. "We already have enough material for an album and we're looking for a 'A' side... something that they'll play on the radio."

Clearly, from a financial viewpoint, the band was struggling to meet the demands of the constant touring. But it was the constant touring that, in fact, kept the band very much alive. Catch 22...

> All the career management that bothered The Association's heyday has been cleared up, they think. "It's not a matter of learning from your mistakes. It's living with them," says Larry.
>
> "When we had a lot of money," Ted continues, "we were just too damn busy. We went through a bundle then, but we got a lot of business education."

When the stint at the London House is over this Sunday, The Association will return to the homes in Southern California that they bought when there was money everywhere. "We'll sit around and fool with new music," Ted says, "actively pursue a hit record and wait for someone to deliver us from poverty."

The Chicago Tribune
September 6 1974

Then, in an incident that few recall with relish, the uncertainties that ran throughout the ranks came to a head whilst on tour in one of the many small towns and cities across the country. Both Jerry Yester and Richard Thompson, high on alcohol and frustration at the endless cycle of events unfolding before them, the same set lists and daily routines, and both on the way to becoming victims of the many pressures that a life on the road brought along as accompaniment, jointly trashed the hotel rooms that they were staying in, in typical rock 'n' roll fashion. Big time. The band had to foot the bill, whilst both Jerry and Richard, the latter having been an official member of the band for approaching three years by that point, were subsequently fired.

"That was one of the hardest decisions we ever had to make," recalls Jim Yester, particularly in light that it was his brother who being removed of his post, before adding, "fortunately, it worked out for everyone and it got them some help they needed. The road can be a cruel mistress..."

Clearly Jim's comments highlighted that there were additional underlying factors that brought about the duo's dismissal from the band. Certainly, trashing a hotel room, to whatever degree, was *de rigueur* by certain rock 'n' roll bylaws and bands such The Who, Led Zeppelin, or even The Eagles may never have gained the reputation they achieved without the obligatory, raucous hotel after-show party, complete with television-to-swimming-pool rearrangement or rubble reducing chainsaw incident attached. The Association themselves, as acknowledged previously within this book, were known for being one of the hardest of the L.A. party bands during the late '60s era and so to actually dismiss two members for such outrageous, alcohol-induced extracurricular activity may seem, from the outside perspective, a touch harsh and even a touch foolish, but with alcohol proving to be such a destroying addiction sometimes it pays to take the high road, and certain actions are often undertaken with the best intentions, and not without due reason and consideration...

*

There was also one further record release during this period. As Ted had suggested, with the deal with the small Mums Records label having fallen through in light of the differing opinions over budgeting costs, the band had entered a one-off release deal with the huge RCA Records Corporation and, with Canadian producer Jack Richardson manning the desk of the Nimbus 9 studios in Toronto, they cut a hopeful series of non-original recordings for the label, still looking for that elusive big hit record.

Richardson had seen significant success whilst working with The Guess Who and Alice Cooper during the early part of the decade whilst, to a lesser degree of success, seeing some of his best work with country-rock pioneers Poco for a fine series of albums, and he was a strong choice to get the band back across the radio airwaves. Four tracks were recorded during early 1975, with the initial emphasis on a composition written by 'Scuffy' Shew [sic]. Little is known of this particular composer/performer, other than a one-off 45 released on the Metromedia label two years previous and an alleged former link to the Beatles' Apple label, but his composition "One Sunday Morning", as released by The Association during May of 1975, was a pompous piece of brass 'land of Liberty' patriotism, with Jim waving the flag and a fine production on the bridge, full of harmonies and a slice of fuzz guitar. Accompanied by a funky, brass-arranged studio version of "Life Is A Carnival" (from the mighty collaborative pen of Rick Danko, Robbie Robertson and Levon Helm), the 45 was issued with little promotion as RCA PB-10217, and duly slipped underneath the radar of most radio programmers and pluggers. A second release was also readied for issue on the RCA Victor label, with promotional copies pressed for distribution around the key stations, but with little attention paid to its predecessor it was to little avail and the proposed follow up to "One Sunday Morning" never reached beyond the promotional stage, failing to be heard by the general population. Later newspaper reports also suggested a further reason for the non-appearance of the 45:

> Love song writer can reap fortune if he can be found:
>   There is a young man, a songwriter believed to be living in Chicago, or maybe anywhere else, who is worth thousands or possibly hundreds of thousands of dollars if he contacts Canadian record producer Jack Richardson.

Richardson has produced a love song the young man wrote. The Association has recorded it on RCA. But it cannot be released until the writer is found. And nobody knows who he is.

Last November The Association was playing at the London House in Chicago when one of its members, Jim Yester, was approached by the young man.

"This guy had a tape recorder and ear phones with him and he insisted Yester listened to some songs he wrote," Richardson said. "Usually you tell people to mail the tapes, but this guy persisted."

Yester listened and liked the songs. He gave the tape to Richardson in Los Angeles. The producer liked the love song 'Sleepy Eyes' and produced it, and then everyone realized they didn't know the songwriters name or address, and they can't release it until they get his permission.

The News Journal
Wilmington, Delaware
February 18 1975

Comprising of two further songs recorded under the auspices of Richardson's watchful eye, with arranging credits on the lead side afforded to longtime collaborator Bob Alcivar, this second pressing (initially given the RCA Victor catalog reference of PB-10297) featured the above song, "Sleepy Eyes", as written by a young mid-western record producer named Steve Sperry – the young man who had initially approached Jim was finally reported to have been a friend of the songwriter – along with a Larry Ramos-led version of the Elton John-Bernie Taupin tune "Take Me To The Pilot", a composition that the band had taken to performing the previous year, with Richard Thompson still in the line-up.

The ballad "Sleepy Eyes" almost takes one back to the Alcivar-arrangements of the glorious 1968 *Birthday*-era productions, full of delicate harpsichord fills, a steel guitar embellishment and deep vocal harmonies, all topped off with Jim Yester's delicate tenor. Sadly, the actual composition itself falls someway short of the mark set by those earlier songs, a fact that perhaps also contributed to its non-appearance, although the accompanying flip-side, a piano-riff filled rendition that remained faithful to Elton John's original recording (as featured on his eponymous 1970 album), and featuring a horn arrangement by Tower of Power member/arranger Greg Adams, was,

305

essentially a far stronger recording, although with Elton having issued his own version as the U.S. partner to his 1971 breakthrough hit, "Your Song", the potential was somewhat muted.

By this stage, there had also been the additional arrival of one other newcomer to the level of Association membership, with blind keyboardist Dwayne Smith, a native of St. Louis 'who plays and sings with the fiery, raunchy passion of a gospel preacher gone astray'[41], coming in at the recommendation of Maurice Miller during December of 1974 to fill the void left by Richard Thompson's departure, adding his ivory-tinkling contributions to the RCA sessions. His ballsy-yet-soulful style of piano playing, developed whilst gigging alongside Ike & Tina Turner, Wilson Pickett and B.B. King, consolidated the jazz and r'n'b inclinations and direction that the line-up was now prone to taking during their concert appearances, especially once Maurice stepped out from behind the drums and up to the microphone. A soulful, black frontline singer was not what long-term followers of The Association were expecting to see or hear.

And yet, despite the addition of such a talented player as Dwayne, this was of little comfort to the group once Larry Ramos, central to the core of the band and more often than not the focus for the performing line-up, announced his departure from the ranks during the early months of 1975.

"We were butting heads many times." Larry reflected, citing musical differences as the reason for his decision. "It was basically on the taste of music that we were doing. It wasn't anything personal, but we were all writers. I didn't give a damn if they recorded my stuff or not, because I liked my stuff and I didn't have to prove it to anybody, (but) that was basically the biggest area of contention, when it came time to select music, and that was the only time that we would butt heads. After listening to eight bars of a song you'd know if it would grab you. [1]

"But everybody got tired. We worked our butts to the bone and I had to hang it up…"

With both Jerry Yester and Larry Ramos having relinquished the guitarist position the now vacant slot was filled by one Art Johnson, a formidable jazz player and a friend of Dwayne Smith (the two had played together with blues legend and Hot Tuna founding member Papa John Creech earlier on in their careers), who had previously learned his trade alongside Tim Buckley and Barney Kessel, worked on recordings by Tim Weisberg, Paul, Horn, Shelley Manne and John Klemmer, whilst also earning his stripes as a member of the jazz-rock-psyche band The Advancement, who cut their one and only album back in 1969, and Gas, Food & Lodging, an impressive five-piece fusion of jazz, rock and country Americana. Another recommendation by Mo Miller, Art was to remain with the touring group for the next few months, before the temptation of more studio work and gigs with Lena Horne, Barbra Streisand and Engelbert Humperdinck lured him away. Meanwhile, with a line-up now consisting of Jim Yester, Ted Bluechel, David Vaught, Maurice Miller, Dwayne Smith and Art, The Association continued on, playing shows wherever they could get a paying booking, venturing up across the U.S.-Canadian border on occasion, still striving to keep their name in the lights.

Recalling his initial audition for the band, Art Johnson was to recount in his own book, *Memoirs Of A Sideman* (published by Storymerchant Books in 2008): "Jim (Yester) was an unassuming blond-haired singer, songwriter and guitarist whose smile could move mountains. He was, for all his previous stardom, humble and a truly regular guy who sang like an angel. It was immediately apparent to me that Ted was just the opposite. He considered himself God's gift to the female gender and I knew I would have my work cut out for me in this environment. The rest of the group consisted of Mo on drums, David Vaught on electric bass, who played great and was also a fantastic recording engineer, and another old friend on keyboards, Dwayne Smith. Anyway, I arrived for my audition and my chops were hot that day, and the fact that I could solo great, read their music, and make up neat guitar parts behind their vocals, meant I also had another great advantage."

He continued the theme in discussion with the author: "They were also really thrilled that I had a high falsetto voice, as I could carry the high parts on 'Cherish', so we just played all afternoon and they just said 'you're in' and we started rehearsing the next day.

"I basically took the job because Maurice and Dwayne were there. Maurice was just the most personable human being ever. Forget the color of skin... every time he took the microphone and smiled everyone was in his corner. He was just an addition to every band he was in. Always smiling, positive attitude and a workhorse above and beyond. There was never any conflict with the audiences over his color. In the restaurants we were eating in, there were often threats, this was Alabama in 1975, but onstage there was never a problem. He was just so damn likeable that any racial thing just disappeared around him...

"Dwayne did a wonderful impersonation of Walter Cronkite, and I did an impression of Ed Sullivan and so, at each show, with the curtain closed, I would do Ed Sullivan introducing The Association, and he would do Cronkite! We also did a tune I wrote, a blisteringly fast bluegrass/country-western one called 'Corn 'n Taters' that Jim and Ted stuck in the middle of the set, and I sang lead on it. We had a lot of fun with that! They would also have Dwayne play the second movement from Ravel's 'Piano Sonatine', just to throw people a left-hand turn! It was a pretty wild time! A loose cannon era… but we were very well received everywhere we went. We had crowds everywhere."

"I either played Ravel or 'Arabesque in C Major' by Debussy," recalls Dwayne Smith, "and I remember the greatest response I got for playing that was during a show at a country fair in Iowa. I played the 'Arabesque…' and the place went silent. I could just feel everyone watching me, and then it just erupted into applause!

"And 'Corn 'n Taters'?" he adds with a laugh. "I got to introduce that one. It came straight after the classical piece in the set, so I would continue on and go 'and now, we're going to hear the lovely aria 'Corn and Potatoes' by Johnson. This performance will be sung by the composer…'"

> Corn 'n Taters, corn 'n taters, early in the morning
> Corn 'n Taters, corn 'n taters, start the new day
>
> "Corn 'n Taters"
> Word and Music by Art Johnson

"I did all my own guitar arrangements," continues Art, during the discussion. "I just did them the way I would do it if I had been there first. I just tried to add to the song what I heard should be there. We did 'Never My Love', 'Cherish' and 'Along Comes Mary' of course, and Maurice also performed a tune called 'Sister Sara' and Jim had a couple he had written. 'Along Comes Mary' has a very jazz flavor to it and we used to really jam on that with the band, we'd stretch out the solos, and that's the thing about Jim and Ted; they wanted to keep The Association credo, but they were not afraid to let Maurice and I sing our original songs, and for Dwayne and I to stretch out a little bit, because the audience liked it!

"I recall we played a new club in Toronto and I know they recorded the sets but I don't know what happened to the tapes…"

Larry's exodus wasn't the only significant departure during this mid-'70s period. Another longtime survivor of the endless Association bandwagon, one who had seen it all come and go, was Pat Colecchio, but he too had finally left his position as the band's manager in recent months, with a succession of nameless faces now operating behind the scenes on behalf of the surviving six-man band. Pat would return shortly afterwards, rehired to assist with the ailing touring band's fortunes, but his initial withdrawal had been a significant reason for Jim Yester adding so much more responsibility onto his own shoulders, arranging much of the touring itinerary as a result. A role he would continue to administer for a further year or so. And then, to make up the trio of departing key members, Larry's exit also brought about his brother, Del Ramos, quitting his post as sound technician.

"Dwayne Smith was an unbelievable talent," remembers Del, when reminiscing over that mid-'70s era, prior to his own departure. "He was such a great piano player, and he sang really well as well, and I was good friends with Maurice too. We used to hang out all the time and he used to tell me things that the group was saying about me that I didn't know about. It was important for me to learn because then I could know how to deal with it. I could fix it, but you can't fix it if you don't know anything about it. But that group of guys reached a point where the only strong point they had was a few really strong instrumentalists. The group was very weak vocally at that time and it was that way for around six months or so, and we started looking at each other because (as the sound technician) I didn't like the way the group sounded, vocally, because I knew how it was supposed to sound. And that's when I stuck my nose into it, and realized that maybe I shouldn't have done that! But somebody needed to say it because otherwise it wouldn't have started moving forward. I wondered if the group was even going to survive. As it was, there was so much time and effort being put into the band, the sweat, that you couldn't just throw it out of the window. We finally got the band sounding better, vocally again, but even with that line-up there were a lot of politics that we had to deal with, affecting the music. Sometimes going out on the road was a real chore..."

Larry meanwhile, having just left the band, had started working on his own material, influenced by his newly laid-back, west coast surfer's lifestyle, composing works such as the sun-kissed sounds of "Pacific Coast Lady" and "A Swell Is Coming", whilst performing a few small shows on his own. On one occasion, whilst playing a solo set in Seal Beach, Del was in attendance.

"He was doing OK and so I went to see him that night and he asked me to sit in with him. He had a bass in the corner that wasn't being used so I sat in with him, playing bass, and singing a few songs that we learned together when we were just kids. We even did 'Yesterday' by The Beatles, and some traditional Hawaiian music. We had a really nice vocal for the 'Hawaiian Wedding Song' in two parts, and when I started doing that with him he said 'what do you think about singing together, whenever you're in town?'

And I just replied 'Well, I've been with the group a while and I need to take a break. I don't particularly care for all of the politics, so why don't I just take off for a while?'

Opting to relinquish his touring role with The Association and follow his brother out the band, Del linked up with Larry and pulling together with a talented cousin, Miles Unite (*pronounced u-nee-tee*), they formed a family trio that they labeled Homegrown (but also appearing as The Brothers Ramos & Cousin Miles), performing a series of intimate shows up and down the California gold coast, from San Diego up to Santa Barbara.

"There's something about a family act that can't be duplicated by anybody else. We played everything from blues to bluegrass. That's probably the most fun I've ever had," said Larry.

Again and again people ask, "Where can we hear something mellow? No dancing. No heavy amplification. We like songs, sweet harmony and interesting instrumental arrangements. Darned if I didn't hear exactly that kind of musical approach the other evening at Los Castillos Mexican Restaurant, Westminster. Wednesdays through Saturdays starting at 8.00pm the plush but informal cocktail lounge offers the music of Brothers Ramos & Cousin Miles.

Tedd Thomey
Long Beach Independent

"There were a million and one clubs to work in," adds Del. "They were paying good money and we worked whenever we wanted to work. I had a lot to do with arranging all of that, but it was good work. We had a great following and we would do a couple of Association songs, and my brother and cousin would do a lot of guitar and five-string banjo stuff together so here were these guys from Hawaii, doing a lot of top quality bluegrass material!"

Playing a combination of bossa nova, island rhythms, California beach music, country, light pop and jazz, mixed in with some original compositions, the trio worked through such established tunes as "Yesterday", "Foggy Mountain Breakdown" and "Dueling Banjos", the latter two featuring both Larry and his younger cousin 'catchin' fire' on banjo, a selection of New Christy Minstrel and Association numbers including "Billy's Mule", "Wabash Cannonball" and "Gotta Be Real", and some of Larry's newer offerings; "California", "My Kauai" and "Pacific Coast Lady". This trio would continue to work together for the following three years, picking up gigs when they felt the need to share their music with their audience, sometimes six nights a week, sometimes three. And it wasn't just Larry and Del keeping the music of former Association members alive. Two other members had also reunited and had even released some new product to their loyal following.

Since leaving The Association back in 1971, Russ Giguere had also kept his musical options open. As well as forming, rehearsing and playing with his own elite band of musical brothers in either The Beachwood Rangers or Hollywood bands, he had also helped a number of friends with session work over the subsequent years, one of which had been for Craig Doerge's debut solo album, released on Columbia (KC-32179) during 1973, with both Russ and Bill Martin credited as a part of the 'Champagne Chorus'. Then during 1975 he once again linked up with former partner Jules Alexander, forming the studio creation Bijou, a five-piece vocal harmony group made up of Jules, Russ, and three former members of a female quartet named Honey Ltd.

Comprising of the Sliwil sisters, Alex and Joan, alongside Marsha Temmer and Laura Polkinghorne, Honey Ltd. had recorded one sunshine pop-folk album under the guidance of pop impresario Lee Hazelwood for the small LHI label back in 1968, albeit with limited distribution, before Alex had left the ranks, marrying songwriter J.D. Souther. The remaining trio then renamed themselves Eve and had cut one more album for the label before disbanding during 1970 to develop solo careers. Five years later, Alex, Joan and Marsha then regrouped, combining with Jules and Russ to create Bijou.

Jules recalls: "Russ and I put the group together. We got a contract with A&M and put out a single. It immediately went to Number 40 in St. Louis but A&M put out "Love Will Keep Us Together" on the same day and it got a bigger response. We just got left in the lurch. We cut several things including one called "Couldn't Put Out The Flame" and another, "Children Of The Highway", and one of the band, Alex Sliwin, her ex-husband was an executive at A&M Records and he had said 'look, we'll sign you guys and we'll give you a little time and see what happens.' They didn't know exactly what we were except they said we looked more like the Symbionese Liberation Army at that time! Anyway, they put $10,000 or something like that into it, and we started cutting a little bit. But after a couple of months, at the end of the time, they said 'thanks, but no thanks.' However, what we found out later was that, apparently, they had several bands like us that they were dealing with, that they would spend 'x' amount of money with and then drop them, and use it as a tax write-off. So that was the end of that..." [20/37]

Fortunately, this brief sojourn with A&M Records did result in one new product on the market, when the delightful composition "Carry On", co-written by Jules and Steven Carey, appeared on the label during March of '75, issued as A&M 45-1678, with production credits on the label shared between Jules and former Association engineer Henry Lewy. With additional instrumental support coming from Tony Greco on keyboards, Mike Williams on drums and, accompanying Jules on guitar, Kit Lane and solo-Beatles sideman David Spinozza, and coupled with a funky Jules Alexander composition entitled "Take Me Down To The Dawn", the Bijou 45 swiftly sank into obscurity, remaining a highly collectible release to this very day. The depth of the five-piece male/female vocal chorus remains a joy to hear but, certainly, being issued during the same A&M schedule as the aforementioned Captain & Tennille single, and on the same day as The Carpenters "Only Yesterday" 45, could not have helped the cause.

Disappointed and somewhat demotivated by the entire experience, and of the whole music industry in general at that point, the band fragmented and Russ chose to distance himself from the music, opting to devote his time and talents over the coming months onto the local comedy circuit instead, taking his partnership with Bill Martin into unchartered but, perhaps, comfortable surroundings. Russ had always maintained a comedic vein running throughout his body, and he had often been seen as the driving force behind many of the Association's comedy skits and routines during their formative touring years, and so this was simply a natural progression for him.

"Russ was a big fan of a number of the comedians back then," says his old friend Mason Williams. "Biff Rose was a performer that he liked and I have to say that he and the Ice House were a big source for material when I was writing for *The Smothers Brothers Comedy Hour*. I would call him up and say 'hey, we're looking for new talent, new this and that', and I've still got a rack of cassettes of people that he sent me. The Association were always looking for comedy material and Russ had seen so much of it going down at the Ice House that he knew who to get in touch with, to write patter and to find comedy songs."

Calling themselves simply Martin & Giguere, Bill and Russ took to the stages of the Pasadena venue (supporting on various occasions, The Modern Folk Quartet and singer-comedian Ron Coden), The Improv on Melrose Avenue (located on the site of the former Ash Grove Folk Club) and a number of the small comedy ventures around Los Angeles, paired in matching white suits and shirts.

"Our comedy was very conceptual." Russ recounted to both Marti Smiley Childs and Jeff March during 2011. "It was rock-um sock-um. We did everything. For instance, friends told us we couldn't do stuff about death, so the first bit we did was called 'Dream Death of a Lifetime'. It was like an ad. We'd say, 'Friends, are you dead or dying? If you die in the next 60 minutes you will receive...' and we built this thing up. 'Your yellow Samsonite coffin will be lowered into the world's largest active volcano, Mt. Kilauea!' But it worked, and every time we did it we'd edit it more and more." [1]

They also created a number of comedy albums for general release, all of which remain extremely difficult to locate from the completist and collector perspective

"Russ and Bill were great friends," summarizes Jules. "And Bill was a friend of mine. We'd sit, laugh and smoke! They did some real interesting things together. There was one album that was one side men's humor, and one side was women's humor! It was a really funny piece..."

Indeed, their 1977 release, *The Wolfman Speaks*, a collection of short horror story scenarios written by the duo, and featuring the archived voice of the late Lon Chaney Jr. (who had died four years prior to the release) remains a truly bizarre conceptual work, issued by Garrison Records and packaged in a sleeve that, somewhat erroneously, featured a still of British actor Oliver Reed dressed up as Chaney's alter-ego The Wolfman, from the 1961 movie *Curse of The Werewolf* (a film that Chaney had no connection to).

The 30-minute recording itself, cut and compiled at The Annex Studios on Santa Monica Boulevard, features six Martin-Giguere collaborative works (including "In The Graveyard", "The Laboratory" and "The Rumpus Room"), with the duo undertaking the various speaking roles themselves, contains no music whatsoever, other than a number of sound effects and instruments added for dramatic effect. Besides the reverse cover sleeve notes that make reference to Russ's perchance for collecting precious metals (six gold record awards and one platinum) during his five year, eleven-million record relationship with The Association, there is no connection whatsoever to his previous life as a wandering troubadour. Nevertheless, it makes a nice period piece for the horror genre...

By the mid-1970s it was clearly becoming a lean period for The Association. The rapidly reducing amount of original band members from their peak era, coupled with the changing attitudes and listening patterns of the American audiences, had seen a rapid decline in popularity for many of the '60s bands still touring, those who had seen their glory days of 5,000 seat arenas and stadiums gradually eaten away by the fickle tastes of the record buying public. Without a European audience to fall back on, something that a number of the American bands capitalized on during this era, The Association toured relentlessly, earning what they could to keep themselves alive, playing in the smaller halls and outdoor fairs, including the 1975 annual 'Rodeo Of The Stars' show in Tucson, Arizona during July of that year. Mixing in newer songs alongside the required classic hits, many now being sung by unfamiliar voices, the band members still managed to return to the good times each night, bringing smiles to those in attendance as "Cherish", "Windy" and "Never My Love" were churned out with harmonic familiarity. And yet, the band could still also rely on bookings in a number of the regular college venues and seasonal tourist resorts, particularly those that paid the band well, and 1975 saw short residencies at such popular destinations as Houston's AstroWorld theme park and the recently constructed Harrah's Casino and hotel complex in Lake Tahoe, Nevada as well as in the more lenient surroundings of Stetson University in DeLand, Florida.

Russ Giguere having departed back in 1971, followed by Brian Cole and Terry Kirkman two years later, for differing reasons, had taken away the backbone of the original band. And then with Jim, Jules and Larry now having left – albeit with Jim returning shortly afterwards – it was a largely unfamiliar line-up that, more often than not, appeared on stage to the many in attendance, those hoping to get an original album or 45 autographed, but not quite sure who was who anymore. And replacing such a charismatic front man as Larry Ramos was never going to be an easy option. However, continuing the misfortunes of the seemingly unstable band history, Art Johnson now also chose the same moment to depart from the line-up, taking up the option to add further studio credits to his increasingly impressive résumé. Nevertheless, by the early fall of 1975 a new guitarist and vocalist had stepped in to the role. Albeit one who, initially, wasn't as tuned in to the sound and the history of the band as one may have hoped for.

"I was pretty much neutral toward the band at that time," states Larry Brown today. "I had been born in Queens, New York and had come to California as a baby with my folks, but I was a blues player and most of the music I liked was generated by black musicians. I primarily joined the band for two main reasons: firstly, I needed a job and secondly, this was a chance to play for a band that worked all the time and they had great name recognition. As a writer myself I thought it would give me a big leg up, but I was a fan of blues, jazz and rock and they were really none of those things. The truth is I thought they were very 'Caucasian' and I had very little interest in their music, especially songs like 'Windy' which I thought was just painfully 'pop'. Yet, after I got the gig and began playing with them I gained a greater appreciation of the harmonies, which for me were far more fun to sing than to listen to. 'Never My Love' quickly came to be one of my favorite songs, and not just Association songs but overall.

"I had previously been working for three years with The Smothers Brothers. Tommy was married to my ex-wife's aunt and suffice to say this was during the days when there were a lot of drugs floating around and some uncomfortable situations had developed. We were playing at Harrah's in Lake Tahoe and (for whatever reason) I was angry with Tommy and I had confronted him and we got into one of these 'you're fired', 'fuck you, I quit' type things and I told him to go fuck himself. After the gig I flew back to town and the very first day back someone called me to sub for their regular guitar player on a club gig in North Hollywood. That night, while at the club, the phone rang and it was Jim Yester to see if I would do The Association gig. They had intended to use a very dear friend of mine by the name of Peter Klimes (as a replacement for Art Johnson). Peter was a wonderful guitarist and musician and I had worked previously with both Peter and David Vaught in the recording studio with Jerry Yester, Jim's brother, producing. Peter himself occasionally called on me to play things he knew I excelled at. Anyhow, Peter was having some health issues at that time and couldn't do the gig so he suggested me. I was terribly amused at the fact that I hadn't been out of work for even half a day!" [42]

For the record, Peter Klimes was the son of seasoned Capitol Records arranger and producer Bob Klimes, who had previously worked on the vocal arrangements for "Birthday Morning" with Jim Yester and Peter had also worked in the studio with the band previously, albeit uncredited. Nevertheless, fate fell in Larry Brown's lap that day and the good looking, curly haired guitarist with a penchant for Nudie shirts, was front line and center when the band posed for a new series of publicity shots shortly afterwards.

Settling in to a line-up that now featured Ted Bluechel on congas and percussion, with Jim Yester, Dwayne Smith, David Vaught, and Maurice Miller alongside him, Larry immediately found the band accommodating to his own input and each of the six members were, in his own words, "a co-equal corporation and we voted on everything together".

"We knew that our audience had come to hear the hits and we always enjoyed giving them what they wanted. Anyone who has been around the block in the music biz knows that people tend to most like what they are familiar with and they loved the hits. Audiences are easily bored by a set heavily weighted in favor of new originals that nobody knows. So much so that Rick Nelson wrote a song about it, that being 'Garden Party'. With that in mind we constructed our sets so that we were able to weave new original things in between hits so they we never lost the audience's interest and in that context they often really dug the new stuff which was much more rock and roll and bluesy." [42]

The band gelled together quickly, to the extent that they began to compile songs that, potentially, they saw developing into new recording possibilities. The line-up was certainly adding a number of strong enough new material into their live shows, but they were also keen to maintain the ethos of the old, original band as well. A line of humor here, or a comedy song there, and newcomer Larry Brown was swift to add in his own contributions, coming up with the song "I Hold Your Hand" to lighten the mood.

I hold your hand in mine dear
I press it to my lips
I take a healthy bite
Of your dainty fingertips…

Over the course of the next few months the band began to cut a series of new recordings in their own studio and rehearsal complex in Van Nuys, with the intention of releasing the first brand new Association album for three years or more. Amongst the new recordings chosen were a number of cover versions, old but familiar inclusions, mixed in with a series of original songs from the newer members, although, for whatever reasons, neither Jim Yester nor Ted Bluechel, whilst perhaps still seen as the leading members of the band by the loyal following that still followed them around the touring circuit, brought many of their own compositions into the mix.

"Ted was still so valuable to the band," comments Dwayne. "He was our connection with the original concept. He was historic!"

In fact, there was to be just one new Yester composition that graced the studio. Instead, it was Maurice, David and Larry Brown that were the dominant force for much of the time, perhaps to the unbridled relief of their more experienced counterparts, keen to see the old democratic principles falling into place once more. Certainly, the confidence and the ability that David Vaught had in the recording studio, both musically and technically, was a welcome addition to the collective, and he was often to be found at the forefront during the recording, production and mixing process, whilst the band members themselves, all six talented individuals, played all of the music. There was not a session musician in sight.

One of the newer tunes, and certainly one of the highlights that resulted from this fresh hive of activity, was a composition of Maurice's entitled "Faces", and this was also the closest that the band came to touching the quality and beauty of former glories. The harmonies simply ooze from the deliciously sounding composition, with a wailing Larry Brown guitar break rising out of the complex arrangement before a subtle synthesizer takes the song back into Dreamsville U.S.A. Not that this was the only highlight, and of the nine or ten songs that were initially cut during this period, the mood and patterns shift swiftly from ballad to soulful funk, from gentle acoustics to bluesy r'n'b, but always with a familiar harmony never too far away, drifting into the mix just as the listener starts to wonder exactly *who* they were listening to. But were there many people who actually did get to hear these recordings? With the eventual non-appearance of the proposed album, for the various explanations that have been offered up over the years, it remains one of the many tragic events that befell this band throughout their troubled history.

Although no specific track selection was ever forthcoming there is one particular pairing of songs that, to the select few who have heard the recordings, defines what would have been the opening salvo for what eventually became known as *The Association Bites Back!* album. Albeit still in unreleased form, this commenced with a contribution that Jim had brought into the band, based upon a melody by Johann Sebastian Bach ("Aus Meines Herzen Grunde"), with an updated lyric by poet and songwriter Larry Beckett. Featuring an *a cappella* vocal arrangement by his brother Jerry, the recently reformed Modern Folk Quartet, still comprising of Yester, Diltz, Douglas and Faryar, were also to be found performing the piece, entitled "The Sun Is Like A Big Brass Band", in concert during that period (a version of which can be found on their *Live At The Ice House* 1978 release). The Association rendition, a lovely blending of the six vocal harmonies, was cleverly linked with a new composition that Larry had recently written and had brought into the sessions. As the last distinctive harmony note fades away a neat blues Larry Brown guitar riff takes the song into the thumping "Good Ol' Rock 'n' Roll", as composed by Brown himself, whereupon both Larry and Dwayne offer up some nice additional harmonies throughout.

Little has been written or recorded about Dwayne Smith's contribution to the history of The Association. Blind since birth, his work was certainly not helped by the simple truth that the band was going through a noticeable lull in publicized activity during his tenure with the line-up, In fact, even before the sessions were deemed near completion, he became yet another member to fly the coop, and yet, with the ability of hindsight and the surviving session tapes it becomes apparent how essential he was to the band in creating the distinctive, contemporary sounds that emitted from these 'lost' studio recordings.

His piano contributions and vocal support to "Stuck In Chicago", a Maurice Miller cover of the Sylvester Johnson funk anthem from the composer's own 1974 *Diamond In The Rough* album, were a perfect example of Smith counterbalancing the work of his fellow band members.

"We just loved the stuff Mo did, because it was real blues and we had fun playing it," says Larry, when reminiscing over the *Bites Back!* sessions. "And Dwayne Smith played piano on this and was all over it, also harmonizing and ad libbing with Mo."

"Yes, I reluctantly sang!" admits Dwayne, recalling his vocal contributions. "I don't sing very well... but well enough!"

"Dwayne was just a monster keyboard player," chimes in Jim Yester, "in any bag. He was on all these 'Bites Back!' recordings…"

A studio version of Albert Hammond's gospel sounding "Praise The Lord (And Pass The Soup)" was also attempted with Maurice once more leading from behind the microphone, whilst the final contribution that he brought in was "That's What She Said", a real steady piece of hardcore soul and, in Larry's opinion "Maurice's funkiest tune and to this day, arguably the coolest guitar solo I have ever played. I was so fucking high when we recorded this I was just pushing the strings around with little regard as to where they would end up and it worked out real good. This might not be my most technically proficient guitar solo ever but it may be my favorite. Pushing strings without any thought as to where they might end up and remembering how high I was when I played it. My altitude was definitely part of the composition of it."

He also adds in that on "Praise The Lord (And Pass The Soup)", a particular sound effect was utilized to great effect on the recording:

"That song was about being hungry enough to do virtually anything while at a Salvation Army-type place, and one thing which is probably only noteworthy to me is that for a special effect, which would have only made sense in the condition we were in at that particular moment, we piled a ton of random junk on the roof of the recording booth, put a microphone on the ground and pushed the pile of junk off the roof causing a hellacious racket! You can hear all the crap crashing to the floor!"

With such an infusion of jazz and blues, and other random influences, into the song selection it was only natural that the remaining additions to the collection be closer to the origins of the band, and in what some may say as more comfortable surroundings for both Jim and Ted.

"Traveling Boy", a delightful smooth ballad composed by the formidable songwriting partnership of Paul Williams and Roger Nichols, and a modestly successful single release by Art Garfunkel two years before, was a near perfect choice for Jim Yester to handle, whilst the acoustic, country harmonies and the subtle pedal-steel arrangement on the wonderful Yester composition "One More Time" highlight the varying genres and styles the band were prepared to travel and, once more, shows that bringing the instrumental abilities of Larry Brown into the band was indeed a wise choice. With Jim playing the acoustic guitar on the track, Larry's contribution shines through.

"I love Larry's guitar work on it," says Jim.

"I played the pedal steel stuff with a Telecaster equipped with a b-bender and harmonized myself in an over-dub on the solo and ending," Larry comments, when discussing the technical details of the song. Certainly, the arrangement and feel of one this tune is akin to the material that The Byrds were cutting during the early 1970s Gene Parsons-Clarence White (creators of the stringbender accessory) era.

Rounding out the sessions was a cover version of the Paul Stookey 1971 love song, "Wedding Song (There Is Love)" – originally composed by Stookey as a wedding gift to his fellow Peter, Paul & Mary band mate – and an attempt to update The Association's own 1970 recording of "Just About The Same", perhaps a strange choice to revisit but a tune that had proven to be popular during the live performances over the subsequent years. David Vaught was behind the microphone for the former, with Jim supplying the accompanying lead during the bridge, but Larry remembers this one as being very much David's creation: "That is a signature David Vaught production. The layers and texture of the instruments herein is the very essence of what I know about Vaught. I suspect he may have been influenced quite a bit by Jerry Yester who I was fortunate enough to record with on many occasions as well, and whose taste in production reminds me very much of what Vaught did with this song. He played all the instruments and arranged the layered vocals. Vaught was a genius…"

"Just About The Same" on the other hand, a far weaker cut that the original from five years previous, has a totally different 'feel' to the production given to it and other than a nice guitar break sadly remains void of any directional clarity or group enthusiasm. Bland, is the only word that springs to mind, with but a hint of disco. It was also as if the band was going through the motions for the sake of it, although this may well have been cut at the very tail end of the *Bites Back!* sessions, once the group had become involved with producer Mike Curb, the perpetrator behind, what can only be viewed by many as, the criminal recording activities that were subsequently to follow.

"At that point we had no record deal and I believe that's the short answer as to why this stuff never came out. The timing was just wrong and the management was not good either. I also think part of the reason for that is that we had entered the disco era, disco dominated the pop charts and more importantly nobody recognized the band. The Association that people *knew* were a bunch of white choirboys, not a funky blues band with a black guy singing some of the lead vocals. It was impossible to get away from the original sound and look. Needless to say, the reason we called the album 'Bites Back!' is because of all the backbiting that was taking place! There was a lot of infighting – how much to tour when the money was not so good, who owned the name and a whole myriad other issues." [42]

Recently, Jim Yester also shed light on the fate of the *Bites Back!* tapes which, despite the commitment from all those involved, never appeared publicly: "About ten years or so ago I sounded out David Vaught, the producer of 'Bites Back!' about the tapes and he said that because of their age and condition that they were now unplayable, and any tape transport would shred them."

It remains undocumented as to how producer Mike Curb became involved in the project. None of those interviewed for this book can recall any specific details, or choose not to, and Curb himself is a notably reticent character, however by 1976 Curb was an up and coming force to be reckoned with within the industry, having risen to previous prominence fronting his own vocal chorus, The Mike Curb Congregation and aiding such artists as The Osmond Brothers on their rise to superstardom. It may well have been his love of original rhythm and blues, having grown up in the South Los Angeles/Compton district of the city, coupled with the band's new direction into a similar field that drew the two together but, whatever the connection, by 1976 Mike Curb was financially supporting the band for a series of upcoming recording sessions.

"I can't remember how the relationship with Curb came about," confirms Larry, "but I think he approached one of the guys with the suggestion of cutting the hits disco style. He didn't really 'work with us' at all. He really just put up the money for the disco recordings but he was never present at a session that I can recall. He wasn't involved in any way with the 'Bites Back!' album." [42]

For Dwayne Smith however, his period in the band was drawing to a close and he soon vacated the piano stool, opting to take his keyboard talents elsewhere, commencing with a series of soundtrack works, the first being for the 1976 movie *Welcome To L.A.* Later years would see his name grace the soundtracks for *UFOria* and *The Best Little Whorehouse In Texas*, along with a debut solo release, *Get Directly Down* (1978), and later reunions with Art Johnson on *Heartbound* (1985) and *Bar Talk* (2000). Coming in to replace him on keyboards, albeit for just a relatively short period, was Andy Chapin, previously a member of the reunited Steppenwolf for their 1975 *Hour Of The Wolf* album. However, by mid-1976 he too had gone, only to be superseded by the equally short appearance of Jay Gruska, who subsequently left to join up with Three Dog Night, replacing founder member Danny Hutton for their final tour during the summer of 1976, before quitting the road to concentrate on TV and soundtrack work closer to home. That brought about the arrival of David Morgan, although in the interim between the departure of Gruska, and the arrival of Morgan, Dwayne Smith briefly returned, helping the band out for one short tour in the northern states. Fortunately, upon David Morgan's entrance, the ever-changing piano position would remain stabilized for a further two years.

Larry explains further: "Andy Chapin was fairly demanding. Pat Colecchio, who had been rehired as manager by this time, was selling the band in what Andy felt was an increasingly wholesale manner and some of our accommodation on the road sucked. Andy didn't like staying in shitty motels and he had a terrible temper and could pop off over the slightest provocation. The official line of why he had quit Steppenwolf was over his reluctance to tour. The preparation of our road manager, Kent Neilson, was also a big sticking point and the touring schedule was a big issue for the entire band.

"In the case of Jay Gruska, I think his aspirations were more towards film and TV writing and initially he felt that being out of town was an impediment. He was also a solo artist and that too might have been amongst his motivations. David Morgan had been close friends and played in bands with Peter Klimes, who recommended him to us. It was Peter who had also recommended me for the band when he was hospitalized and unable to take the gig." [42]

"I wish I could remember more details of my time with them," laughs Jay today, when asked about his brief stint. "I recall I did a few small shows with them in and around L.A., including Knotts Berry Farm, and then we did a short tour, lasting several weeks. I played the keyboards and sang one of the three to five vocals parts, and I do remember everyone being kind and welcoming, albeit a tad road weary. Larry Brown was a fine guitarist. However, I wasn't involved in any recording, and my stint was really very short because I was on to some new projects as a singer-songwriter at that point..."

CHAPTER TWENTY-THREE

TIME TO GET HIGH

"We had entered the disco era. Disco dominated the pop charts." Two brief sentences from Larry Brown that seemed to perfectly sum up the latter part of the 1970s music industry. Rising out of the rhythm 'n' blues scene, but with more than a touch of soul and funk added into the equation, and then watered down to a meek assimilation with a certain white pop gloss on top, disco music now ruled the airwaves. Dressed in glitter and glam, dancing precariously on high-stacked heels amongst a wealth of shimmering glitterballs, the music charts scattered around much of the western world were now awash with the syncopated, synthetic rhythms of dance music. But it wasn't dance music with *soul* any longer. It was simple and, too often, plastic, neatly created with sharp creases by a vast industry that knew a moneymaking machine when it saw one. Credible artists such as KC & The Sunshine Band and, most notably, The Bee Gees, who had previously created a wealth of classy white-pop or soul compositions in the preceding years (*Cucumber Castle* anyone?) had their careers rejuvenated once they discovered that the churning, rhythmic funk beat that ran throughout "Jive Talkin'" was a journey worth following. And once the New York club scene, and those of its west coast and London counterparts saw the impact that the music brought to their patrons, then *boom!* – the Saturday night fever took over...

Needless to say, a number of other established artists and acts looked at the burgeoning scene with curiosity and whilst many derided the spectacle, joining in with the mass burning of disco record releases at various organized protests, others carefully dipped their satin socks into the waters, experimenting with the sounds and styles. Some managed it successfully, whilst others failed spectacularly in the process. The Beach Boys, Chicago, ABBA, Rod Stewart…

For their part The Association, working to whatever degree with Mike Curb, opted to test the aforesaid waters and cut a series of songs with the dreaded disco beat lurking alongside. Choosing to resurrect and revitalize two of their classic compositions from the golden age and introduce them to the new, all dancing audience, both "Cherish" and "No Fair At All", two of the tenderest ballads the original band had ever produced, were selected and pushed through the disco meat grinder, hoping that some good would come out the other side. Or, to use a phrase that Jim Yester had often turned out time and time again over the years, 'run them up the flagpole and see who salutes…' In this particular case, no one did and the songs never reached a wide market.

The recognizable harmonies were still intact, the melodies were still beautiful, but the incessant thud of the disco bass, the chucka-chucka rhythm guitar and the syncopated hi-hat shuffle, coupled with the omnipresent synthesized string arrangement (and even a sax break on "No Fair At All", played by session musician Mike Carnahan), was just too much. Both songs suffered accordingly. Even a third brand new offering, a Larry Brown composition titled "It's Time To Get High", arranged with similar feel, along with a hyped-up synthesizer and a wah-wah pedal close to hand, failed to hit the mark. As much as his partners were steeped in their glorious past, with a wondrous pop history, Larry was a bluesman at heart and his efforts to get down and boogie, despite the slick quality of the production, just didn't gel. And, with a lengthy instrumental break mid-way through, it ran for an astonishing six minutes as well, the longest recording in The Association's catalog.

"I played on all three songs," he confirms, "both disco re-makes and my song, 'It's Time To Get High', being the third. It was Mike Curb's idea to record the disco stuff and it was funny that he chose my song to be the only new original because he was a straight laced Boy Scout type and my song was basically about sex, drugs and rock and roll!

"This was all early enough so that the hits were still recent enough that we might have been able to resurrect the band if we had not been so *artsy fartsy* with our attitude. Mike Curb wanted to spend a whole bunch of money on us but he wanted session player Jim Gordon to play drums on the recordings and we told him to go away. I am not sure at that point it would have mattered who played drums but it definitely mattered that we refused to cooperate with the money guys!"

Seeing fit to wisely keep the new arrangements out of the concert set-lists (The Beach Boys were later widely criticized when, on one misguided evening during 1979, they debuted their disco intrusion upon a disgruntled audience, and were roundly booed for their efforts) the band still felt the need to keep abreast of the fashions and the times. After all, one couldn't live in paisley bell-bottoms or denim and Nudies forever, and so on many a stage occasion during this era, Jim Yester could be seen proudly sporting a widening permed hairstyle or Ted, with his horseshoe mustache drooping down towards his chin, would unsubtly allow his shirt to unbutton that little further towards the naval, exposing copious amounts of chest hair. Thankfully, there remains no record of gold medallions sprouting from within. Nevertheless, with the line-up having seemingly gotten over the revolving cycle of keyboard players upon David Morgan's arrival, the band continued with their never-ending touring regime and by late 1976, going into 1977 the line-up was once again receiving glowing praise for the variation of their set lists, despite the lack of any new product being foisted upon a record buying world and drawing in the concert audiences.

A return visit to Six Flags Over Texas, during early December 1976, saw the band praised in the *Irving Daily News* for the inclusion of "Time To Get High", as performed by Larry 'the Guru of Groove' Brown, whilst Maurice's "Faces" was also picked out as a crowd favorite. Indeed, during the show, Miller had jokingly told the audience that in the interest of 'ethnic purity' his contract specified that one in every eight songs performed that night 'had to be a blues number'. Such was the variation of their set list that one could almost believe it to be true.

"I get grumpy when people ask me if I'm an original member of The Association" reflected Ted, when interviewed for the newspaper. "We are The Association, all of us, and we are a new group. 'Lazarus Resurrects The Association' should be a headline for our new album" he added with a laugh, referring to engineer and record producer Bill Lazarus who had helped the band with the recent *Bites Back!* sessions. Clearly, at this stage, the band was still hopeful that the latest recordings would result in a new album release.

However, that period would also coincide with the departure of one further dominant member of the band, and although Larry Brown was viewed by many to still be a relative newcomer to the line-up, and maybe by some mark he was, his musical contributions during his two-year tenure were a vital ingredient in keeping the band sounding fresh and contemporary. His excellent guitar abilities, and his vocal and songwriting input into the unreleased *Bites Back!* sessions were, without question, one reason why the band had survived such a rocky period during their history. And whilst his own musical background was at odds with much of the band's repertoire, the endless night after night performances of "Cherish" and Windy", he had fitted into the mold with precision and he would be a hard act to replace. But then again, as had been proven when he himself, had stepped into the Art Johnson/Larry Ramos spotlight, the band was not, and never would be a vehicle for one man's talents. It was a united line-up, made up of many individual pieces. A puzzle that came together once all of the pieces fit into their correct slots.

Larry explains the reasoning for his departure as such: "Mo and some of the guys just wanted to keep working because they needed the money, whilst others, like me, worked when we were in town and had other sources of revenue. So I was not so hot to be on the road all of the time. This is what really caused the friction that brought my tenure to an end. I simply was not willing to go out for the kind of money Pat was booking the band for. It began to seem like some members were satisfied to rest on our laurels and just do lounge gigs for income and had less of a vision to resurrect the hit recording group, and I was simply not interested in playing lounges." [42]

"You can't keep your earning power and a career from your reputation. We've proved that," said Jim, when questioned during this period about the ongoing need to keep the touring band alive.

Early May 1977, and whilst The Eagles and their million-selling "Hotel California" were in the process of removing Glen Campbell's "Southern Nights" from the peak of the U.S. *Billboard* singles charts, and Fleetwood Mac's *Rumours* album was dominantly static at the very pinnacle of the album lists, The Association, the forerunners to the California sound that these musical heavyweights now represented, were playing to a sparse, yet enthusiastic crowd at The Cherry Tree in The General Washington Inn, Fredericksburg, Virginia.

Playing a lengthy three-hour set that included just a smattering of hits, under the guidance of David Vaught, who was now also acting as musical director for the tour, and with a second keyboard player filling in the sound where, once, either of the two Larry's had occupied, they continued to push the boundaries of their performances. Three hours, spread out over two sets, and a whole host of new material to try out before the small yet attentive audience.

One of the songs in the first set, 'Praise The Lord and Pass The Bread' [sic], is an upbeat, gospel sounding song, whilst 'Goodbye Columbus', a fast tune with a beat that keeps toes tapping, came midway through and brought people to their feet and a round of applause. "Shucks, y'all probably just liked the movie," said Yester.

The song following 'Goodbye Columbus', a bluesy southern-rock ballad called 'So Long San Antone', reminiscent of Pure Prairie League in the use of four and even five-part harmony, demonstrates one direction that the music of the group has taken.

"Our music has changed quite a bit since 1967 and 1968, but then so has pop music as a whole," said Yester. "Pop has gone through change and so have we. Each new member had added a different direction to the group, which I feel is a healthy change."

The Free Lance Star
May 7 1977

"I had brought in 'So Long San Antone' to the band," states Larry Brown today. "An old buddy of mine wrote it…"

The inclusion of this new song in the 1977 set, originally composed as an acoustic country tune by Stephen Geyer back in 1973, was an indication as to the influence that the former guitarist had brought into the show during his spell in the line-up. A lovely, gentle composition in its original demo format (as played to the author by Geyer himself), the band added their own originality to the song, as was their want, turning it into the southern-rock experience noted above, but maintaining the pure harmonic sound the band were famous for.

It's a race I'm bound to lose, it's an endless getaway
Like an outlaw on the run I've learned to pray
But the desert makes no deal, and I've got no time to spare

And it looks like no-one hears a cowboy's prayer
So long San Antone, hello Mexico
I been ridin' all night long and I got a long, long way to go

"So Long San Antone"
Words and Music by Stephen George Geyer

Ted Bluechel, the other original member, gives the group an 'island sound', much like Jimmy Buffet of late. His vocals and congas give 'Trying To Get To You', a song in the group's first set, a Jamaican-reggae flavor. 'In Search Of The Truth', a farcical song about a conversation with an island guru, has the same island feel.

Another strong influence on the group's style is provided by the pedal-pushing piano work of Dave 'Catfish' Morgan, He sings the blues and provides excellent keyboard work on 'The Sun Shines Bright On My Old Kentucky Home', a Randy Newman song. Morgan also shows his roots in Texas country music in 'Goin' To Jail', a song about spending a night in jail in Texas that he describes as 'country cookin'.

Maurice Miller, the drummer for the past five years, provides the band's mellow and 'soul' sound. His two showpieces were 'Faces' a slow love song that takes full advantage of newcomer Rick Ulski [sic] on the synthesizer and 'Seasons Suite', a four-part song that ranges in musical style to match the seasons of the year.

Giving the band a newer, disco flavor is David Vaught on bass. His strong vocals and pounding bass lines on 'Come On In' and the comical 'King Kong, the Leading Man' add another dimension to the group.

But the musical center for The Association are the old and new songs written and sung by Yester. The old hits, which Yester said are not as much fun to play but are still comfortable are still the musical soul of the group. Some newer efforts, 'Canadian Sunset', with a big-band '30s sound, and 'Traveling Boy', written by Paul Williams, are every bit as good as the older hits, thanks to Yester's clear piercing vocals. But his best song, and the best song on the night, was 'One More Time', a mellow, introspective look at the not so glamorous part of a musical career.

The Free Lance Star
May 7 1977

The review and article in the above newspaper also went onto make reference to the recent recording sessions, with Jim Yester even commenting to the reporter, Rob Hedelt, that "we're going to do (an album) all on our own this time. We've had some trouble with producers and recording in the past. This time, we'll do like we want in our own studio," before adding that the new release, tentatively titled *The Association Bites Back!* "should be out by June". Without a current recording contract in place one is led to assume that Jim's talking up of the recent sessions was more for publicity purposes than promotion, however, behind closed doors recent detailed discussions had been taking place with legendary recording engineer, Stan Ross, co-founder of Gold Star studios, who was proposing starting up his own record label. It was never to be.

"The day before the signing date Stan had a heart attack, and that was the end of that" sighs Jim ruefully.

As it was, there would be no completed album ready by the following month. In fact, with Larry Brown's recent departure one wonders if the proposed release had already been locked away in the studio vaults by that stage, destined to never surface publicly. Nevertheless, Hedelt was impressed enough by the band's show to summarize up in his review that 'if the album is as good as the three hours of music at The Cherry Tree, The Association should have another hit on their hands, 11 years after their first, and seven years after their last'.

This period also saw the start of a belated reappraisal for much of The Association's earlier years, now that enough time had passed in the media to be able reflect on their history with the benefit of rose-tinted glasses. It was always better that way. The 1970s had been a troublesome era for many in the United States. Watergate, Vietnam, Kent State, the Manson trial; they had all put the new decade off on a wrong footing and by the middle years much of the population was now happy to look back upon their earlier life, the 1960s, reminiscing about days long gone, the days of innocence, sunshine pop, peace and love. Was it really ever two girls for every boy?

The underground music magazine *Dark Star* was one of the first to touch upon the band's legacy with a positive overview, with editor Steve Burgess offering a full three-page critical praise to their recording career:

The Association were belligerently straight as a Midwest highway, wore suits, held graduate degrees, who fooled who, and how and why, is a question that comes up 'insufficient data'; certainly they had stumbled upon dope by 1970 but, then, who hadn't?

'Windy' hit the shops, sold four zillion in July '67 when there was a rampaging beastie called rock music to send pop straight to the liquor cabinet, and The Association stood as American and socially acceptable as Ed Sullivan and police brutality, what with these new-fangled hippies stinking out the pages of *Life* magazine and all. No right-on dude has given them a thought since.

Know what they're doing now? Playing Vegas, supper clubs, nightclubs. The only band in the world apart from The Beach Boys who can play soft pop/rock with finesse and mile-high harmony on stage. Just recorded a disco version of 'Cherish'. What's wrong? Wake up. Come back.

What a place to begin a love affair.

Steve Burgess
Dark Star Magazine (December 1976)

Perhaps aware as to the American public rediscovering the dawn of a new age, or simply rediscovering their youth, Jim Yester and Ted Bluechel seized upon the opportunity to make a few extra $$$ in-between the constant touring dates haphazardly pinned to the studio walls. With Warner Brothers holding on tightly to the original master tapes of their 'hits', and with the non-appearance of any new material forthcoming in the stores, the offer was put to them by K-Tel Records to cut a series of new recordings, simple re-workings of a selection of the 'big' ones, whilst remaining faithful to the original arrangements, thus negating any future need to license the original tracks and pay the heavy costs from the Warner vaults. Not that they were the first band, or artist, to attempt such a scenario. Far, far from it. And they certainly wouldn't be the last either, as a vast business of small, marketable record labels had popped up across the nation, and throughout all of Europe, whereupon, for the price of a newspaper advertisement, hundreds and thousands of potential customers could be reached, all of whom would have the opportunity to purchase their favorite songs from a bygone era, and by the original artists, all delivered via mail order straight to their doorstep. And at a special low, low price to boot!

Alternatively, record stores were suddenly being hit by a surge of budget-price LPs and labels, Pickwick Records, K-Tel Records, Era, Arcade... all packaged cheaply and at prices everyone could afford, and – surprise, surprise – they all featured your favorite songs from a bygone era, and by the original artists! Of course, if the buyer were to pay close enough attention to the sleeve they may well see the disclaimer 'these selections are re-recordings by the original artists, or by one or more members of the original group', which may have explained why the recordings didn't sound... quite... right.

Five songs were re-recorded by 'The Association'; Ted, Jim and David Vaught, for such purposes with Ted handling the lead vocals for "Windy", "Cherish" and "Never My Love", leaving Jim revisiting his own original vocal on "Along Comes Mary", and standing in Terry's shoes for "Everything That Touches You". The resulting recordings, in all truth, were weak in comparison, programmed to the extreme, synthesized and synthetic. The multi-layered harmonies were in evidence, albeit mixed a little too far back at times, but the production was considerably thinner than the original cuts and suffered accordingly. Not that it halted the release of the tracks, and over the years they have appeared on a multitude of records and cassettes, the most visibly seen was with the LP *Back To Back*, released first via Era Records during 1983, where The Association recordings were paired off with, ironically, a series of *original* 1960s songs by The Turtles (Era BU-5660).

"I do recall those recordings," says Jim today, "and I'm still getting the royalties for them! Thank you very much K-Tel!"

With the recent departure of guitarist Larry Brown, and the band having brought in a second keyboard player to fill out the sound onstage, it was all change on the endless Association merry-go-round as, shortly afterwards, the alternating line-up moved along one further notch.

For a brief period Jim Yester was the only guitarist up on the stage, a role he was able to fulfill but, as a predominantly rhythm player, with few notable leads to him name, the instrumental accompaniment of the band was becoming predominately keyboard-based during this era.

Jim recalls: "I always pretty much stayed with rhythm. I've always played a few licks, but no solos *per se* since the very late '60s. I used to play the solo on 'Changes' after Jules left, that was fun, but since then I'd just do a few lead licks, no solos..."

Then, in a move that saw the band reduced down to just one original member, Jim departed from the ranks once again, tired from the same revolving routine and the endless one-nighters. He returned to low-key performances, standing alone onstage with just a guitar for company, in-between working outside of the industry for a period. August 1977 saw him revisit his roots, performing a series of solo shows at the Ice House in Pasadena, 'forging a career in music and wit' ran the publicity byline, but it proved popular enough that he returned to the familiar venue a number of times over the subsequent months. In his place, albeit for a short period of time, and stepping into Larry Brown's lead guitarist boots, came Cliff Woolley, a young, fair-haired player from Torrence, CA, similar in appearance to Russ Giguere, scarred by his experiences as a volunteer support in Vietnam six years previously (alongside Bob Hope), yet blessed with a tenor vocal range that fitted like a glove into the band's harmony stack.

"It was a great honor for me to have been in the group" he says today, long distance from his home in Japan. "I was playing with Armando Compean, a great bass player who had worked with Little Feat, an extremely soulful singer and nurturer of talent. He took a liking to me and we practiced and had a duo together, and he introduced me to a vocal coach, and he somehow knew about the audition for The Association, so he set it up. I knew Larry Brown from Armando as he had played with him as well. I guess I was a cute little puppy or something, as I had never played that kind of music in my life! I was never really a rock or pop player, I was more funk and jazz, so we incorporated that into one or two songs, but I was the only guitarist in the band and I found myself center stage! I practiced my part so hard. I remember on the way to my first gig in Phoenix we were singing *a cappella*. Because the tunes and the arrangements were already there it was just a case of fine-tuning them, honing them up once I arrived. The only non-Association tune I recall working on was the jazz standard 'Canadian Sunset', which was very good for our vocal arrangements, and one old one we modified so I could play blues-harp on it.

"I was tenor and had a good falsetto, and David 'Catfish' Morgan might have chimed in on a couple of high parts as well. David was without doubt, hands down, the finest musician in the group. Singer, songwriter, pianist..."[45]

This line-up, which ran through until the closing months of fall 1978, comprised of Ted, David Vaught, Maurice Miller and David Morgan, along with newcomers Ric Ulsky on Hammond B3 organ and Cliff providing lead guitar, and without any recording schedules planned, and no record label or company supporting them, survived on the meager pickings of whatever concert dates they could pick up, including a September 1978 performance at Chicago's infamous Playboy Club on East Walton Street.

Ulsky had paid his dues working the bars and clubs of the industrious 1960s music scene in his home city of Seattle, WA. As keyboardist for a number of the local bands, such as The City Limits, and Rocky & The Riddlers (the latter of whom capitalized on the then-current fad for all things *Batman,* by releasing the 1966 45 "Batman"/"Flash & Crash" on the local Panorama label) he then furthered his career by joining up with the popular Washington-garage band The City Zu, contributing his distinctive B3 sounds to their live performances during the late '60s/early '70s. By the time he joined up with The Association, almost a decade later, he had branched out of the Pacific North-West scene and had diversified his music to tackle such variable deviations as Epicentre's 1978 disco/funk anthem "Get Off The Phone" and the all-encompassing Los Angeles music scene.

Then, when both David Morgan and the long-serving Maurice Miller chose to move on, Woolley also opted to step away from his short role in the band. Demoralized by the departure of David Morgan, his roommate for much of the recent touring schedule, coupled with the band's reluctance to develop his proposal of a long term career overseas, Cliff saw his future elsewhere, moving on to work with the progressive rock band Ambrosia before creating a life and a career for himself in Japan.

"I had some great plans for the group had they listened to me," he says with regret. "I had already toured Japan at the invitation of surf-guitar greats The Ventures before I joined The Association, and I had said to the guys 'let me spearhead this and I will get the band into Japan and we will have lifetime, loyal audiences. We will go over for two or three months a year and we'll never have to work elsewhere again'. But they were so fucked up, and so dysfunctional by that stage that the band simply couldn't get its act together. There were two factions in the group as I saw it. There was David Vaught and Ric Ulsky, who was just a very quiet guy, and then there were the rest of us.

"When David Morgan left it just broke my heart," he adds. "He was the guiding light, in my opinion. I thought, man, you just lost the best guy in the group. I don't recall how it happened but I know Dave left first, then Mo. It's just a real shame…" [45]

Morgan, an integral part of The Association's touring sound for the previous two years, subsequently signed up with Rick Nelson and his Stone Canyon Band soon afterwards, touring with Rick until mid-1985 when family commitments necessitated he leave the popular touring line-up. At his recommendation, fellow former-Association member Andy Chapin stepped into his role as keyboard player, remaining with Rick right up until the fateful day on December 31st 1985 when the airplane carrying Nelson and his entire touring party, Chapin included, came down, north-east of Dallas, killing all on board apart from the pilots. Maurice Miller meanwhile, reverted to his jazz roots, picking up gigs with like-minded souls across the years, earning a living in local bands such as Sweet Grease, a 1990s Valley-based outfit that also featured Dwayne Smith in the line-up. He also wrote jingles for several TV commercials. He passed away as a result of complications from diabetes on October 10th 2005. He was 73 years of age.

As the early months of winter 1978 loomed on the horizon, The Association was in poor shape. Ted Bluechel and David Vaught were still leading the line-up front stage, but soon enough it was yet another band of unfamiliar faces harmonizing alongside, playing the hits that, in some cases, were almost as old as the performers themselves.

John William Tuttle, a classically trained violinist, had been born in Santa Monica back in 1950 and was barely halfway through his teenage years when The Association first released their opening salvo of recordings on the Jubilee and Valiant labels. And here he was, in the golden months of a 1978 fall season, barely twenty-eight years of age, standing alongside founding member Ted Bluechel, offering up lead and harmony vocals on these classic hits, whilst adding guitar to the onstage mix. Russ Levine, on the other hand, had been a member of the Massachusetts-based psych-rock bands The Uniclops and, more successfully, The Ultimate Spinach, providing his drum patterns to the latters *Behold & See* and *Ultimate Spinach III* albums, both released during the late 1960s, and he came along with a wealth of experience attached.

"When I got the Association gig I had been playing in bands for a long, long time, since 1961 when I was 15," says Levine today. "I had spent a lot of my band time playing in bars, six-nights-a-week, five-shows-a-night doing covers. Pop hits and the drum licks to those hits were burned into my brain.

I had heard those Association songs so many times that playing them was second nature really. Coincidently, I had a pair of Timbales, like Ted, and used them for those two little licks in 'Windy'. In a sense it was surprising they chose me. I had a very hard-hitting and kicking style that was honed from drummers like Buddy Miles and Jim Capaldi. I always thought the Association hits were really beautiful but they were miles away from what influenced me as a drummer.

"Ted was just basically done schlepping around, setting up and breaking down a set of drums. He felt that standing up front with the rest of the band was a lot more fun. Also, because the band was so vocal heavy, it was a lot easier to have that vocal control without worrying about keeping perfect tempo or being hyper conscious of drum dynamics or locking in with the bass player. I just laid it down and David Vaught followed along. I guess it must have somehow worked because David was very particular but never had a complaint about how we gelled as a rhythm section. I was also one of the baritones; all six of us sang, and the blend was just magical. That was also thanks to David who was totally tuned in to everyone's part, making sure no one was the slightest bit off key.

"John Tuttle was one of the nicest people, just a really sweet guy. He had a voice like an angel but in a sense he was a stranger in a strange land. The rest of us were way harder edged than John because of our individual rock band experience. John would have been happy playing occasional Malibu coffee houses as a solo artist. He grew up in Pacific Palisades, the son of William Tuttle, filmdom's great make-up pioneer and he traveled for a time backing up Ramblin' Jack Elliot and that should tell you that a rock guy he wasn't!"

A third new addition, and a second guitar player, Jack Harris, joined shortly afterwards. And so it was that, with yet another new line-up in place, The Association – Bluechel, Vaught, Ulsky, Tuttle, Levine and Harris – took the show back on the road, and whilst no audio evidence survives publicly from this barren period, the ability of each band member, under the musical direction of David Vaught, would suggest that the integrity of the brand name remained intact... for now.

"Jack joined around the same time I did," continues Russ Levine. "He was a very decent lead guitar player, a rocker really with a beautiful tenor voice. He had played around in L.A. rock bands doing the typical five-set club dates. Unfortunately, the gigs were getting harder and harder to find for us. We were playing college dates around the country and it was basically just a lot of fun. There was a lot of camaraderie among all the band members and everyone had a self-designated roommate when on the road. The sloppy guys teamed up with the sloppy guys and the neat guys with the neat guys. Ric Ulsky and I always roomed together because we liked our room neat. When you walked into our room it looked like no one lived there, all our stuff so perfectly stowed. But some of the other guys... wow! It looked like a homeless encampment!

"The set list were all the hits, including some of the more obscure ones. There were also a number of original tunes from that incarnation, some of which were quite good and probably could have been hits. We even recorded a number of these..."

Unfortunately, the new recordings from that era, taped at the Cedros & Aetna studio and overseen by David Vaught, remained unreleased, locked away under Ted's watchful eye, without a record label or notable finance to issue them to their loyal, yet significantly smaller following. Nevertheless, despite the concerns and the lack of regular gigs the band persisted, playing as and when the offers came. Filling out the sound short term, whilst adding a sense of long-lost credibility to the fast fading act, the line-up was briefly reunited with another familiar face from the past.

"I did about four gigs with them during this period," says Jerry Yester, despite his previous dismissal from the line-up, three years before, "and there were these young guys, including John Tuttle on guitar, and he was singing lead. We had to do 'Cherish' of course, but I didn't have to do the bong bongs! I said 'I ain't doing no bong bongs, no way!!'" [21]

Sadly, Jerry's reassuring presence didn't remain within the line-up for long (although he did undertake some studio work for himself, utilizing both Vaught and Tuttle, during this period) and by early November, when the group stepped onto the stage at the Pasadena Ice House, a home from home for the only original member, it was a standard six-man band that appeared before the loyal audience. Excerpts from their appearance at the club were subsequently videotaped, dubbed with the original 1960s recordings for the *Echoes Of The 60s* TV Special, airing on July 25th the following year. This rather amateurish documentary, hosted by John Ritter, Suzanne Somers and the U.K. model Twiggy, was, essentially, a 60-minute journey through 1960s rock and roll music, highlighting the influences *en route* of Liverpool, the Carnaby Street fashion, Woodstock and Vietnam, whilst also blending 1960s archive footage with 1970s reunion performances and interviews. Featured interviews came from the likes of Brian Wilson, Gerry Marsden, Alan Price, Donovan, Micky Dolenz, Bobby Sherman and Sonny Bono amongst others, whilst the mid-'70s performances featured selections from Gerry & The Pacemakers, The Searchers, The Four Tops, Frankie Valli, Mary Travers and The Association. If it weren't for the fact that long-term followers of the band were all-too familiar with the original vocalists then these performances of "Cherish" and "Windy" would cause nary a raised eyebrow. However, seeing the likes of John Tuttle and Jack Harris, gamely lip-syncing along to the vocals of Kirkman, Giguere, Ramos and Yester, with a 1970s technology offering little by way of high quality footage, remains largely uncomfortable viewing.

And yet the end was inevitable and, as the winter winds of 1978 set in, the largely unfamiliar six-piece set-up finally confirmed what their dwindling audiences had been acutely aware of for an increasing period of time. The concert draw was no longer sufficient to keep the band on the road, the finances were in poor shape, and they were simply touring to earn the money to pay back the taxes. Ted Bluechel, effectively leading the band from the front of the stage, decided to gently lay the band to rest. The Association, twenty-four members strong over the thirteen-year life span, quietly disbanded.

"David Vaught was trying to self-manage the band which really sent us into further obscurity," summarizes Russ Levine. "And having no real management meant having no real direction. At that point we just couldn't make a living playing in the band and everyone just moved on, there was nothing else to do."

"The industry was getting stiff," recalled Ted "and we became known as a group without all of the original members. Our management had changed and was being poorly handled, and I was the only original one left. My name was signed to thousands of dollars of corporate debt, which were being called in. I found myself in deep financial trouble. The money ran out and, eventually, I had to lease the name to get out of debt. On November 20th 1978, I leased the name to Bill Larson, who packaged groups of musicians..."[20]

No record can be traced today of a Bill Larson, music promoter, but it soon became apparent that the lease had, in fact, fallen in to the hands of Rob Grill, lead singer, bass player and front man for The Grass Roots, one of The Association's principal competing bands during the late 1960s and a band that had seen twenty successful chart entries onto the *Billboard* Hot 100 between 1966 and 1975. This incredibly popular quartet, featuring *Joel* Larson on drums (initially during 1965 and then, once more, when he returned to the line-up in 1971) had finally floundered during the middle years of the 1970s and Grill, who by now owned the rights to the band's name, continued on performing through a succession of alternating band members, promoting themselves as The Grass Roots *featuring* Rob Grill. Larson had quit during 1979, whilst Grill, all-too aware as to the revitalized interest in bands of the 1960s, continued to promote the band on the 'oldies' nostalgia circuit. Utilizing a series of previously unknown but experienced musicians, performing under Grill's promotional guidance, a circuit of 'reunited' bands from the golden era of American '60s nostalgia subsequently began appearing across the country. One night it was The Grass Roots appearing on stage, then the following night, subject to demand, the same team of performers would appear onstage as The Buckinghams or, it would transpire, as The Association. It was a profitable business, but a misleading one.

JUST SING THE HITS AND THE CROWD IS HAPPY

Nostalgia is a bread and butter business for an awful lot of entrepreneurs. The Grass Roots, The Turtles, The Association, The Temptations, The Four Tops and dozens more 'revival' acts seem to be perpetually on the road, like contemporary flying Dutchmen, often performing together on oldies package tours. In some instances, there are several versions of a single group touring at the same time, each with few if any original members. This controversial practice has resulted in lawsuits initiated by controlling trademark holders, disappointed patrons and hoodwinked promoters who've been forced to issue refunds. Bogus tours have been launched by groups calling themselves Badfinger, The Byrds, Spirit, The Supremes and others with lineups completely unrelated to the best-known recording versions of those bands.

In the late seventies, groups from the Woodstock era became dependable draws on the nostalgia circuit. Jason Mershon, who was a show promoter in Colorado at the time, recalls: "I was in the entertainment promotion business, and The Box Tops were one of the bands I promoted. Alex Chilton wasn't with them anymore, and they were going through different singers. I was booking a lot of similar acts. Cory Wells from Three Dog Night, I was booking him. We didn't call it One Dog Night or anything, but we promoted him as their original singer. There was a version of Steppenwolf going around without John Kay, just with Nick St. Nicholas (bassist on one Steppenwolf LP) and Goldy McJohn (keyboardist on the first five albums). People would complain about Steppenwolf. They were upset that John Kay wasn't in the band. And I'd say 'John Kay isn't with the band. This is Steppenwolf now and he isn't with them anymore.' "

"You can rationalize it in some way," he goes on. "They want to hear the music of the groups. People want to hear The Temptations; they want to hear The Coasters and The Drifters. I mean, how many of those members do you think are originals? None. Zero. But the thing is, they still have the licensing. I don't know how many Drifters or Coasters or Shirelles are floating around the country, but they're all doing the same thing. People are happy. As long as you put on the show, sing the hits in the same style, the crowds are always happy." What about obtaining licensed permission to sing the songs of The Box Tops? "That was no problem, because that falls under ASCAP and BMI. Any band can perform those songs if the venue you're playing at is licensed by ASCAP and BMI, so those are all covered under that."

Still, not all concertgoers are happy when they find out that they've paid to see what is essentially a cover band with few if any founding members. "I know this one agent who promoted a lot of bogus bands. He had a group on the road called Bread without David Gates, which I thought was completely ridiculous. He had all these names like Steppenwolf. There are a million Temptations. Even the ones out there now, there are no originals. I mean, The Guess Who are making a lot of money right now without Burton Cummings, their lead singer. It's mainly a nostalgia thing. Look at The Grass Roots, Rob Grill owned that name, and he rented it out to different groups. There were a lot of Grass Roots going around!"

By Jay Allen Sanford. 2004.
Reproduced with permission

CHAPTER TWENTY-FOUR

THE BACKSEAT OF HEAVEN

N ow in his second marriage, and with a third child (Eden had been born in 1967, David in 1969 and now, Amy, born in 1971), Jules Alexander had been keeping himself busy with a number of projects since he had left the band five years previous, and not all were music related. Immediately after the disbandment of Bijou, his side project with Russ, he had contributed backing vocals, alongside the Sliwin sisters, to Hoyt Axton's *Southbound* album as well as performing at a charity fund-raising gig for his children's pre-school, performing on stage alongside Terry Kirkman (whose daughter attended the same school), Wolfgang Melz, the Lovin' Spoonful's Joe Butler and Richard Halligan, founding member of Blood, Sweat & Tears. He also aided his old Troubadour compadre, Robb Royer, with some demo sessions for an upcoming movie soundtrack that Robb was contributing to, singing on the unused early versions of "Pass You By" and "Among The Yesterdays", both featured in the film *California Dreaming*. However, with bills to pay, Jules also took to work outside of the industry, using much of the technical expertise he had perfected during his training in the U.S. Navy and finding employment in both the aerospace industry and, at one stage, for a company named Kinergetics Inc., where he built small cryogenic refrigerators for use in infrared detectors alongside none other than Jim Yester (himself taking a short hiatus from the music business). Indeed, Jules used his experience well, later creating state-of-the-art optical devices for the CIA whilst working for McBain Systems.

"I just thought I wanted to do something else," says Jules, before adding with laughter "and with the technical background I had it was real fun! Doing all these odd and interesting gigs around L.A."

Terry Kirkman meanwhile, ever the activist, the free speaker and the free thinker, had initially involved himself with the anti-Vietnam movement following his departure from The Association. Linking up with the Vietnam Information Project, a self-funded program designed to impress information about the ongoing military involvement in Vietnam to the general public, he took to delivering lectures, presenting evidence over the conflict, all right up until the U.S. withdrawal of troops in April 1973, followed by the final removal of U.S. citizens two years later.

According to research undertaken by both Jeff March and Marti Smiley Childs: 'during those same years, Terry studied acting with Peggy Feury at the Lee Strasberg Theater and Film Institute, performing in plays while also writing for television game shows *The Crosswits* and *Name That Tune*. In the late 1970s he graduated from game shows to HBO variety shows, writing two musical specials and helping to develop others'. In addition, a stint as creative director for the legendary Motown Records label, recently relocated to Los Angeles, further aided his résumé, although it was not a project he would look back upon fondly:

"That was a profoundly unpleasant experience that inspired me to re-unite with my former colleagues and get back into the performing business full time."[1]

It was during the festive season of 1978, with the then-current Association band having barely unplugged their stage monitors and retired from the performing circuit, that the idea of reuniting the original surviving band members was first mooted for an upcoming HBO *Standing Room Only* television special, to be subtitled *Then & Now*, instigated by Terry as part of his new role with the cable TV network.

They're the singing superstars of the '50s and '60s who racked up 40 gold records. They're still here! They're going strong!

HBO Promotional byline

Terry: "That HBO show started out with, like, five acts, and The Association wasn't involved in it at all. It was going to be an introspective of before and after. I never wanted to be in the same room as The Association again. Not that I had any ill feelings towards the guys, it's just that I didn't want to be a part of that… conflict, for me. But the producers kept pitching it and finally they came up with a number to offer the band, for us to get together for the show. And I knew that all of the guys in the band were hurting financially, as was I, and I knew I had to do it. I could not have HBO offering me this without calling…"

It certainly wasn't something that was going to happen overnight but following Terry's calls to his former bandmates the proposal came to fruition.

"It was amazing!" recalls Jules. "When we finally sat down together again and started playing. It was holy shit! It was really beautiful. But we were all doing different things so a period of months had to go by before we could really juggle whatever we had happening to make it happen. But we did it…"

"We rehearsed on weekends, and we got together five or six songs and produced them for the show," says Russ Giguere. Terry was listed as co-writer and associate producer for the 90-minute broadcast that also featured the Brazilian-born Sergio Mendes and his bossa nova-tinged dance rhythms, focusing on the talents of his three female vocalists, along with a stunning medley of non-stop hits by The Temptations, albeit a restructured version of the legendary soul band, featuring just two original members from their hit making heyday. The televised spectacle also featured appearances by The Kingston Trio, Patti Page, Jimmie Rodgers and Frankie Laine. Certainly, it was an impressive group of acts that took to the stage at the Ambassador Hotel's Cocoanut Grove venue the evening of the recording. Hosted by comedian and satirist Mort Sahl the show was taped during early April 1979 and then first broadcast across various days during the final weeks of the month.

Financed for the reunion by HBO, The Association, with a five-man frontline comprising of Terry Kirkman, Jules Alexander, Jim Yester, Larry Ramos and a heavily 'tached Russ Giguere, supported in the rear by Ted Bluechel, resuming his position behind the drum kit, and accompanied by a returning Richard Thompson on piano, with their old comrade and musical arranger Ray Pohlman reading the bass sheets, put in an impressive performance. Their sweet harmonies showing no signs of aging, despite the passing of the years, and regardless of their rather mismatched appearance, open-necked shirts and casual jackets, especially in comparison to the slick, glossy sophistication of the other performing artists, they held the audience in the palm of their hands for their short set.

"This is what the Association should sound like," Ted Bluechel was heard to say after the show, and few could disagree.

"We'd stayed in touch very loosely" Russ later commented to *Billboard* magazine, "but we didn't know where each guy was philosophically, musically or any way."

"After the first rehearsal, for about 45 minutes, we just laughed," Jim chimed in. "It was there. It had been eight years but it really felt good. We decided what the heck, might as well get paid for feeling good!"

The band immediately put plans in motion for a reunion on a larger scale, once personal commitments could be completed although, once again, there were reservations. A one-off televised reunion for nostalgia's sake was one thing, but going back out on tour was a completely different ball game.

"I really didn't want to do that again," continues Terry, looking back at the 1980s reunion. Despite the success of the HBO special Terry was still fighting his own personal demons. "I had just come out of being the creative director at Motown and I knew what a horrible state the music business was in. The Iranian oil crisis happened in the middle of that, the petroleum allotment for the vinyl was dropped down, and there couldn't have been a worse time to contemplate putting The Association back together again, from a marketing perspective. Acts were being dropped left and right, but in the middle of my alcoholism I simply said 'great idea'...

They immediately made it clear that this simply wasn't going to be a visit to the nostalgia circuit, deciding very early on that, to make it work for themselves as musicians and performers, they would structure the set around just a small selection of the 'golden oldies', and introduce new material to fill out the remainder of the performance.

"We're still a vocal band," summarized Russ, during the interview with *Billboard* in 1980, "but we're going into areas that we never got into before."

With financial support courtesy of a series of investors – "a couple of guys who believed in us and had the money to play with" – aiding due rehearsal time and equipment hire, and any legal issues surrounding re-use of the band name *apparently* sorted, the five founding members, Jules (now sitting in the bass guitar chair), Terry, Jim, Ted and Russ, with longtime partner Larry Ramos making up number six, and keyboard player Ric Ulsky also coming aboard once more in place of Richard Thompson, began to put in the long hours of rehearsal over a relatively short three week period, re-establishing their musical rapport once their individual obligations had been fulfilled. Drummer Russ Levine also returned to the drum stool, making it an eight-man band, and thus allowing Ted to remain front of stage, concentrating on his harmonies. Additionally, Pat Colecchio returned to the fold to oversee the reunion shows, as did Del Ramos behind the mixing desk.

Russ Levine: "One day I got a call from Ted telling me that the original, surviving members were going back on tour and was I interested in going out with them. Are you kidding?? Sounded like great fun and an opportunity to actually play with Jules, Terry, Jimmy, Larry, Russ and Ted. That was a great time!"

"It took thousands and thousands of dollars to do this," admitted Terry Kirkman to the press. "Most people sit there and say they got back together again and leave it at that. For me, and our manager at the time, it was a ten-month job. A ten-month job getting the money so we could quit the work we were doing as individuals.

"The most awesome thing in getting back together was that now we were adults – responsible adults with kids and mortgage and car payments and everything else that drives you crazy. When we first got together we were living on $15 a week. For that today, you can maybe make a phone call..."

Kicking off a series of shows in, of all places, Anchorage in Alaska, followed by a week run at the Sahara Casino in Tahoe, working alongside Debbie Reynolds, the band gelled back together with ease, unaffected by the potential MOR tag that such a slot may place upon them.

"We're not worried about being middle-of-the-road, side of the road or anything," laughed Russ. "It's a good shot and we are being seen by a lot of people."

The reunion tour took in venues all across the country and by chance, one evening in 1980, whilst they were in Dallas, Texas, scheduled to appear on a televised charity show called *Ed McMahon and Company*, hosted by McMahon for the Showtime cable network, the band happened to walk past a poster in the lobby of the Hyatt Regency hotel, advertising an Association concert in their Playboy nightclub that evening. A concert the band knew nothing about. Del Ramos picks up the story:

"We decided to go to this Hyatt nightclub at the top of this big building in Dallas and as we walked in there was this big poster and it had my brother's image on it, surrounded by these four other guys we didn't know. Well, the whole band, along with Pat Colecchio was there so we all walked in and sat down directly in front of the stage, about four rows back from center, and then this band walked on and they started their show with 'Windy'".

Jules continued on the story during the 1984 interview for *Goldmine*: "When we walked in there were these strange dudes doing '… and then we recorded dah, dah, dah, and then we did this…' We sat in the audience checking this out and Pat wrote a note and sent it to the stage. It said, 'If the names of Terry Kirkman, Jules Alexander, Jim Yester etc., mean anything to you, we're in the audience'. The guy opened the note and you could see the sweat! It was beautiful!" [20]

"He turned white on stage!" Larry was to later add. "After the show he was so apologetic. He said 'Hey, man, we didn't know you guys were still out there, still working, you know?' And I said, 'Yes, we're still working… and you don't use this name anymore! I don't care who said you could use it, it's just not right! It's illegal what you're doing because we're still a working group', so after that night they stopped performing as The Association…" [44]

This 'bogus' band, passing themselves off as The Association, was clearly the result of the arrangement that Ted had been forced to undertake the previous year, leasing the band name out to lessen the increasing debts that were building up on him. Rob Grill, having been the successful recipient of the lease, clearly saw the opportunity and consequently hired this faceless band to capitalize and tour on his good fortune, a decision that brought about the confrontation and, subsequently, conversations with the original line-up.

Larry's daughter, Tracy, during research on this book, also recalled the series of events leading up to this bogus edition of the band: "At one time dad saw a poster with his face on it, as the current group of The Association. Not someone who looked like him; a photo of my dad had been added! That's what prompted the conversation with Rob Grill, who then tried to hire him for something like $200 a show! When dad and I spoke about the offer he was pretty insulted at what Rob had wanted to pay him, and that he would use his photo to sell tickets. Of course he declined Rob's offer and told him to stop using his photo on their posters…"

Grill also reportedly approached Russ Giguere about fronting a new version of The Association, to be managed and promoted by himself, but Russ too had rejected such an offer. Nevertheless, even without any original band members willing to participate, Grill now owned the official rights to the band name and, instead, continued formulating his own version of the group.

Del continued: "For many years afterwards my brother and Russell were very upset with Grill and wouldn't work with him. Especially as Larry's image was used on the poster. Finally, my brother decided to bury the hatchet and just forget about it, Grill wasn't a bad guy. He was just trying to make money. We're all just trying to make money..."

Operating mainly in the southern states, touring and playing the small clubs between Texas and Georgia, but occasionally venturing up to more northerly climes, this particular line-up comprised of Wesley B. Wright on lead vocals and guitar, John Mascola on keyboards, Ray Gillman on bass and Mark Hamilton on drums, along with two supporting musicians, and were recruited by Grill, under the auspice of title ownership, reportedly touring under whatever band name Grill needed them to. What is even more bewildering, is the extent to which Grill and company authorized/misused, call it what you will, the act to deceive the concert audiences. Not only were they falsely claiming during their show of their full participation in the recording of the original band's hits, but they even appeared in print, claiming their rights to be known as The Association. Unbelievably, *Goldmine* magazine, one of the leading lights in rock journalism since its foundation in 1974, and still active to this very day, fell hook, line and sinker for the deception and in their June 1980 edition, with Carl Perkins proudly rockin' out on the front cover, the co-headline name of The Association sat alongside. By opening up to page 11 one was then confronted by a photograph of the 1967-era band, Terry, Jim, Russ, Larry, Ted and Brian, accompanied by a full-page interview with Wright and Mascola, uttering such shameless nonsense as;

"It's weird. You're on top and suddenly you have to start all over again. The early '70s took its toll on The Association. We're amazed we still have such an impact on people. All of these people are coming to see us relive the '60s, and until our new album comes out that is all they'll want. We want to do new things. We've spent all our lives developing our musical abilities and we're getting impatient to do new things.

"When we tried to get another hit record again in 1973 everyone said 'Oh, The Association', and that was the end. We're not afraid to take a chance. We've paid a lot of dues and never lost our enthusiasm."

Billboard
June 1980

Wright and Mascola then went on to claim that they had eased into the band after joining up with the original members back in 1970, initially signing on as road musicians, and that they rarely see any of their former bandmates.

"That hurt," Mascola noted. "We thought they'd stay in touch…"

Needless to say, following the events at the Playboy Club in Dallas, this particular line-up subsequently and wisely quit the proposed tour and no longer took to performing under the name of The Association for fear of a visit from Larry's attorneys, and any further misunderstanding over the use of the band name was swiftly put to rest. After all, who could rightfully dispute who *was* The Association? However, Wesley B. Wright, a talented musician in his own right, continued to perform in and around his home state of Florida over the coming years, and still does to this day. He went onto become one of the founding musicians of the million-selling Miami Sound Machine, before striking out on his own and touring with a succession of bands, re-popularizing the hits of a bygone decade. Even now, as this book is being researched and written, his online biography continues to read 'he toured with sixties legends The Association'.

Encouraged by the success of the HBO televised airing, and the potential triumph of the subsequent tour, the revitalized band went back into the recording studio during 1980, producing a series of brand new recordings, although unfortunately, none of the six band members, all notable songwriters themselves, brought in anything of substance to the sessions from their own pens.

"I put that deal together with a guy named Bob Williams," sighs Terry, "and we were going to give him a percentage of what the band did, but it never happened. The money we invested into the sessions dried up, and we lost all of our investment. Bob had bought SunWest Records, a wonderful studio east of Sunset Boulevard that you could just go in and develop your stuff. We had been cutting our demos in there for a long, long time. 'Everything That Touches You' had been demoed there, 'Pandora's Golden Heebie Jeebies'… Joni Mitchell and The Turtles sometimes recorded their masters there. It was just this laid-back, relaxed space to work in…

"But we weren't writing new songs. We all loved what we cut there, but we were just caricatures of ourselves. There was only one new song that was written by a member of the group during that time, a song by Larry that was just a gimmick song, and that was just a part of the live act."

Working out of SunWest the group cut a series of new tracks, the majority of which were forming the backbone of their current concert set lists, with the final intention of completing a full album in the near future. Produced by the band members themselves, these recordings resulted in an eclectic mix of '80s sounding productions. Dated by today's standards, full of synthesized backdrops, but delightfully arranged and performed, albeit with a hesitant sense of trepidation permeating the finished tapes. Ranging from the delicate harmonies of Peter Klimes' "Bird Outside The Window" (featuring vocal arrangements by Jerry Yester and some exquisite recorder overdubs by Terry), the funk-filled dance drive of "Darling Girl" and Randy Sharp's humorous 1930s pastiche, "Rita's Letter" (also cut by Ray Stevens), paired with an updated rendition of the 1975 Alexander-Carey Bijou 45, "Carry On", the sessions provided all the proof that was needed to justify the band's return into the spotlight, however reluctant or unsure some may been feeling inside. Over the years, too many great artists had returned from years away in the musical wilderness, just to retread the boards and wallow in past glories. The Association members on the other hand, were putting faith in their abilities to move away from their history, however grand it may have been, and make new, commercial music for a 1980s audience. Rounding out the sessions was the mid-tempo rhythms of "Stringing A Line", along with another new tune from Randy Sharp; "Could It Be Love".

"We shopped (the songs) around," Terry continues. "We played them for a few A&R friends in town but the timing could not have been worse for the recording industry. Not only was there the oil crisis, the market crisis… but, as an example, the combined Columbia Records entity, which was around eight or nine different labels, controlled about 80% of the Top 100 albums at that time. It was unprecedented, the control that they had over the marketplace. It was almost a monopoly, and yet with that achievement their business was still so bad that they had recently fired around 300 of their top marketing people. Controlling 80% of the market was still not good enough to sustain their business. So having a product where you were already identified as a band that didn't quite 'make it' would have required a lot of faith in the recordings from a marketing department on any label to invest the energy, the time and the money, when they couldn't even get their *top* artists arrested. It was a horrible time for us to be trying to do that…

"We had these songs that were really pretty remarkable, really exciting, but when the money that had been invested at SunWest dried up we could no longer afford it… we were stuck!"

However, despite the lack of label interest the new recordings were generating, in view of the current climate, the band was somewhat sidetracked when Elektra Records, the renowned company founded by Jac Holzman back in 1950 and home over the ensuing years to The Doors, Bread, Tim Buckley, Judy Collins and Harry Chapin (and followed, more recently, by The Cars and Queen under the auspices of an Elektra/ Asylum label mergence), stepped forth and offered them a new recording and distribution contract; although how supportive the label actually was towards the deal remains a moot point. With Pat Colecchio keen to see a revival in their recording career he negotiated the deal and requested that Bones Howe also be involved although, with hindsight, it was clearly not a particularly favorable arrangement for the band members themselves.

"That was the most embarrassing deal ever," admits Terry. "Bones Howe had some leverage, but it was 'go cut five songs. Give them a $50,000 budget, and maybe we'll get lucky. Then, we'll honor the author of the singles deal, release the least likely, and then we're done. But I don't want that act on my label…'" Essentially, the band was to suffer a similar tax write-off scenario to that which had befallen Russ and Jules with the A&M/Bijou project.

Since he had last worked with the band, producer Howe had utilized his studio expertise to great success, working with artists and bands from across the musical divide; The Turtles, The Monkees, Sergio Mendes, Tom Waits, Ornette Coleman, Bette Midler, Jerry Lee Lewis, and his abilities were undeniable successful, but without the full support of the recording label itself the sessions were duly undertaken with apparent skepticism.

The reunited partnership began cutting a series of new tracks for the label at the Wally Heider Studios in Hollywood, using the core of Howe's current session team – Tim May on guitar, Neil Stubenhaus on bass and Ed Greene on drums, with the talented arranger Mike Melvoin handling keyboards. Howe had also brought in the John 'Moon' Martin composition "Dreamer"; a pleasant enough ballad that he believed had all of the right ingredients for the sessions, perfect for the harmonies of The Association. The band themselves were far keener to explore some of the newer, self-produced songs they had been working on during their recent SunWest sessions, or go with another of the latest Howe-produced offerings, an impressive new composition by Andy Goldmark entitled "Backseat Of Heaven", but reluctantly they went along with the inclinations of Bones, cutting the vocals for "Dreamer" under the watchful guidance of John

Bahler, an established name in studio arrangements over the recent years. Both Bahler and Melvoin had previously been the guiding lights, and one of the main reasons behind the phenomenal breakout success of David Cassidy and The Partridge Family's musical achievements the previous decade.

Paired with the lively, harmonious sounds of Stephen Geyer's "You Turn The Light On" (co-written with Louis Anderson and previously recorded by Kenny Rogers for his triple-platinum *Kenny* album from 1979) the first single for Elektra, issued with "Dreamer" as the leading side, was released during January 1981 (Elektra E-47094) and, somewhat surprisingly, given the lack of any significant record company promotion, propelled the band back into the *Billboard* Hot 100, climbing to a respectable number 66 position, whilst also going Top 20 in the smaller Adult Contemporary chart lists. Promoting the reunion with a series of impressive television guest appearances, including *American Bandstand, Tomorrow With Tom Snyder, The Mike Douglas Show* and *The John Davidson Show*, all broadcast during the opening months of the year, the band were once again relishing their return to the spotlight.

"We're having more fun singing now than we ever did," commented Terry, when questioned in front of the cameras by Dick Clark during the *American Bandstand* broadcast. "The shows are wonderful and we've had a wonderful response..." But, despite the positive response, the question should be raised; did the band really believe in the project they were promoting?

"We went and recorded two of the songs," remembers Jim, summing up their attitude towards the 'Moon' Martin composition, "and we spent about ninety-five percent of the time on 'Backseat Of Heaven', and about five percent on 'Dreamer'... and what did the record company release?"

The first month of 1981 had seen the band return to the Ice House in Pasadena for a two-week series of successful homecoming gigs. Russ Levine had exited the touring party after the initial few months on the road and Ted was now located back behind the drum kit. As were the initial plans when launching the tour, the set list was still predominantly based around a selection of the newer songs, mixed in with the old humor and skits from previous years. Just five songs from their original era were included – the four 'biggies' ("Cherish", "Never My Love", "Along Comes Mary" and "Windy"), plus an encore of "One Too Many Mornings". The remainder of the eighteen-song set was polished, professional but largely unfamiliar to those in attendance. Nevertheless, each song was roundly and enthusiastically applauded, with cheers and laughter ringing out around the venue for the entire 75-minute set.

Opening up the show with a new, jazz-styled Michael Sembello composition entitled "Years Of Tryin'", the band immediately highlighted the musical prowess they had resurrected for the tour. Clearly, their musical chops were back on top form, with Jules' thundering bass lines underpinning the dynamic rhythm guitars, topped off by Terry's wailing saxophone break, mid-song. Following this with a succession of new material such as "Backseat Of Heaven" and "Stringing A Line", alongside other recent additions such as "When I Need Love", "She Likes The Lights", "Across The Persian Gulf", "Unsmiling Angel" and "Carry Me Over The Water", as well as two compositions by Daniel Moore (composer of the Three Dog Night's hit "Shambala"), "Learn How To Land" and "Put Out The Light", it was a varied choice of styles played out on the now-famous stage. With Larry's bluesy "Unsmiling Angel", featuring his own sizzling guitar licks, greeted with thunderous applause, and the stunned silence that met the intricate opening harmonies of "Across The Persian Gulf" leaving the audience sitting in disbelief, the show was a vocal *tour de force*. Not to deflect the new sounds of the band from the more traditional voices that many of the audience had become accustomed to over the years the band also launched into a series of amusing anecdotes and humorous songs, none more so than with the controversial Bill Martin tune "Nuke The Whales" or with the cleverly-worded Mason Williams' *a cappella* vocal number "The Italian Art Song", composed back in the '64 Troubadour era, and also known as "Michelangelo Boast":

Mason recalls: "I wrote quite a few songs in 1964, and 'The Italian Art Song' was one of many shots at odd-ball concepts I explored back then. In thinking about arty ideas for songs, I began to wonder if there were any Italian art songs that were actually about Italian art? I researched it and there didn't seem to be, so I therefore thought, why not rectify this oversight and write one? However, just to be 'arty', back in '64, I'd frequently delve into putting the wrong kind of music to a lyric, the idea being that it would be like a beautiful gem in a garish setting, with neither the lyric nor the music complementing or supporting one another. An exercise in failing on purpose. So, the original 1964 version wasn't truly in an Italian art song style. The melody was in 4/4 and up-tempo to accommodate the getting to the joke."

Michelangelo was not just so-so
He painted better than most
'Nobody paints those religious frescos
Like me', Michelangelo'd boast

"The Italian Art Song"
Words and Music by Mason Williams

Perhaps the overtly sexual overtones that dominated the Russ Giguere spoken word tale, "The Uncle Teddy Show", was a touch out of the ordinary for their usual set-list, but in the confines of intimate night club setting it went down a storm, exhorting shrieks of laughter from the highly amused, smiling crowds. However, back out on the road for the subsequent shows this little piece of adult humor, a tale of fuzzy bunny ecstasy slotted in for their home crowd, was often omitted in favor of "Rita's Letter", another of the SunWest songs, with Jim Yester once again vocalizing in fine form.

Recalling that particular era Del Ramos, working from behind the mixing board, offers up these thoughts: "When I was doing sound on that tour it was 'Backseat Of Heaven' and 'Persian Gulf' which were, in my opinion, the two songs that were ultimate Association 'sound'. If you picked two songs that represented the group, vocally, from that period I would pick those two songs, but some of those newer ones had so many vocals on them that we couldn't duplicate them on stage. We could do it but we'd have to cheat, and we never liked cheating. We never liked having pre-recorded voices. We never did that...

"On one occasion I had just done the sound on 'Persian Gulf', and I was also calling the light scenes that we had coming up, and I was just about to start moving the faders on the mixing board, making everything even tighter, when I heard this voice saying 'Hey, Del!' and I turned around and it was Bones Howe! He said to me 'That's the best I've ever heard the group sound... anywhere!' and he shook my hand and added 'now, I'll let you get back to work!'"

By the early summer months of 1981 the busy touring schedule was ramping up. The band were now using a dynamic, young agent named David Fishof to book and schedule their gigs and he was starting to get them some prestigious slots on the circuit. Disney World in Orlando, The Poplar Creek Theater in Hoffman Estates, Fort Meyers, Philadelphia, Costa Mesa, Escondido...

"He's really turned the tricks for us and gotten us some gigs that are hard to get," confirmed Terry to the press at the time.

In his own book, *Rock Your Business*, published by BenBella Books during 2012, Fishof was later to recall how he became involved with the band: "This (Hollywood) agent asked whether I'd be interested in representing The Association. I was so young and new that my response was, 'Which Association would you like me to book entertainment for?' I was so used to my career in the Catskills, booking acts like Sammy Davis Jr. and Bill Cosby for corporations and Jewish organizations. I thought he meant some association wanted a show. After the press agent explained who The Association was, I jumped at the opportunity and caught a plane the next day to Los Angeles. I got to the rehearsal studio and met the whole band – all the original members, except Brian Cole. The band started to play me their new music. I didn't quite get it, so I asked them to play me some of their hits. When they launched into 'Cherish', 'Never My Love', 'Along Comes Mary' and 'Windy' I got goose bumps all down my spine because they sounded so amazing."

Soon enough, with Pat Colecchio stepping down once again, Fishof was put in charge of managing the entire tour. However, initially he faced the same old issues that had been dogging the band for the previous decade. Many concert promoters simply weren't interested in the group, they were old news, offering returns of only $2,500 per night – plus the band would have to pay for the travel, accommodation and equipment themselves. To a keen businessman like Fishof that was unacceptable. Instead, he took to offering the booking agents a percentage of his own fee, fed to them individually over an expensive lunch, in return for them booking the band. In his words, "Lo and behold, the next day my phone started ringing off the hook with dates. 'Is The Association available for two days at Bogart's in Cincinnati for fifteen grand?' 'Can The Association do a gig at Summerfest in Chicago for $25,000?' Of course, I said yes and yes!"

As the bookings kept coming in, Fishof reported back to the band, ringing them up and questioning as to whom would make the final decision over which shows to take. The response?

"Our old manager, Pat Colecchio, did everything for us. It's your job to accept the dates". Then the line went dead... [46]

Their performance at the Hart Plaza Amphitheater in Detroit, Michigan, held on June 29th, was subsequently broadcast via an FM Radiocast, and remains one of the few surviving examples of the band's live performances during this period, although perhaps one of the more memorable was the July 4th Independence Day performance at the Philadelphia Mall in Pennsylvania. For that particular show, performing alongside the Philadelphia Orchestra for much of the concert, they once more called upon the musical expertise of Jerry Yester and Richard Thompson to assist with musical arrangements.

"It was the most terrifying thing I've ever done in my life, and not something I'd do again," recalled Jerry. "But for the privilege of standing in front of an orchestra, that close, and hearing them play something that I've written, is a wonderful thing. I did two arrangements and my friend, teacher and mentor from years and years ago, Bob Klimes, who taught me so much about orchestration and arranging, wrote a prelude.

"The band hired me and Richard, two people who they had fired, to do these arrangements, but we hired one other guy to do 'Cherish'. Neither of us wanted to do 'Cherish'! We both hated that song after playing it so many times…" [21]

TURN TO EXCITEMENT

DEBBIE REYNOLDS/
THE ASSOCIATION
OCTOBER 21 - OCTOBER 26

Bob Mirenda Orchestra

COMING:

Nov. 2-3	SKI MOVIE
Nov. 4-9	THE SPINNERS/DUSTY SPRINGFIELD
Nov. 11-16	HELEN REDDY
Nov. 18-23	JOHNNY MATHIS/JEANNINE BURNIER

DEL WEBB'S SAHARA TAHOE
HOTEL — CASINO

CHAPTER TWENTY-FIVE

NEW MEMORIES

May 1981 had seen the second 45 to be released on the Elektra Records label but, sadly, that had failed to capitalize on the impetus that "Dreamer" had laid out. "Small Town Lovers", the second Andy Goldmark composition that the band had cut, was a Jules Alexander-led piece of light funk-fluff and was never honestly going to trouble the chart lists. It was just too weak in comparison to what the band were truly capable of and, indeed, with virtually zero promotion from either the label nor the band themselves the 45 swiftly disappeared. However, if the record buying public had taken the time to discover the release, then hidden away on the flip-side they would have been audibly delighted by a two-minute studio rendition of the impressive *a cappella* "Across The Persian Gulf", a further Jerry Yester-Larry Beckett combination which, much the earlier "The Sun Is Like A Big Brass Band", was based upon the melodies of Johann Sebastian Bach (in this case; "Christ Lag In Todesbanden"). Sadly, with such an opportunity to develop their reinvigorated career missed, very few ever got to hear it.

That August they appeared in residence at the Garden State Arts Center in Holmdel, New Jersey, appearing alongside the million-selling country artist Crystal Gayle, and shortly afterwards they occupied the stage in Monroeville, Pennsylvania for a three-week run at the 900-seater Holiday House. Extended stays at Harrah's in Tahoe and Reno followed, in addition to a return journey to Disney World in Orlando (appearing on stage with

Chuck Berry, The Ventures and Gary U.S. Bonds) along with State and County Fair performances in both Syracuse and Kalamazoo. 1982 also saw a more luxurious trip to Bermuda, along with a number of cruise liner performances, before December wound the year down with a show held at the Beaumont Café in Texas, filmed for posterity by one of the fortunate attendees at the small venue. 1983 commenced, still with Fishof at the helm, with a further return to the Ice House in Pasadena and then a prestigious week-long booking at the Sahara Hotel & Casino in Las Vegas, sharing the bill with the reconstructed The Mamas & The Papas touring line-up.

"The offers were coming in fast," continued Fishof in his 2012 publication. "We were headlining Atlantic City, Las Vegas, Tahoe, Reno, and tons of festivals. The casinos were great because they would paper the house with free tickets to their gamblers. As more and more dates came in, I kept okaying them. I'll admit, the majority of the shows were pretty empty, but we got paid. I didn't care. I was so proud of the fact that I had booked a million dollars of dates for a band that used to average $2,500 a night opening for the Kingston Trio. By the end of the summer of 1983, The Association had grossed a million. I had made nearly £100,000, and the agents made their money too…"

However, there remains considerable debate as to how much the band members themselves profited from the tour, and the overall finances and income were certainly being brought into questions by certain factions within the line-up. Somehow, despite the continuous booking schedule, the band was still in debt, running at a loss…

Certainly not all of the performances were successful, and despite the positive reception that the band received in a number of the higher profile shows in either Vegas or Tahoe, or at the sell-out appearances for their homecoming Pasadena shows, some of the more localized events, the county fairs and the family amusement parks, weren't as welcoming to the seven-man band.

At the 1981 Iowa State Fair, held in Des Moines, and billed as a part of a 'Rock 'n' Roll Oldies Show' the band were resoundingly booed by a less than courteous crowd, unimpressed by the novelty inclusion of the Pythonesque march on "Nuke The Whales" and the Kenny Rogers country-inclinations of "You Turn The Light On".

"If you don't like it, go home," Jules reportedly responded, at which point hundreds of concertgoers stood up and did just that.

"That was a total send up!" laughs Jules today, when recollecting that particular Bill Martin tune. "People thought we were being serious, but it was hilarious. It was a total laugh at ourselves..."

Hopes of further resurrecting their recording career had been dashed during the tail end of 1981 when, by mutual agreement, Elektra Records had chosen not to pursue their option on the band following on from the relative failure of the second 45, and declined to aid further investment in an album release. Further sessions had resulted in the recording of a brand new silky ballad labeled "You Made A Dreamer Out Of Me", along with Curt Boettcher's polished "Disappearing", but the label had never been truly supportive in its involvement with the band, and any further partnership was swiftly dissolved. The much vaunted session tapes from SunWest were also returned to the shelves, unreleased, and the band were once again cast adrift of label support.

"We quit!" summarized Jules. "Elektra at that time was not interested in promoting our new stuff and weren't giving us enough attention."

"We want the album to be representative of us," Terry was to confirm in the media, following the spilt. "There's still a market for us. I don't think there's ever not been one. There's a market out there for anyone doing good work. The phenomenal success of Kenny Rogers and ABBA is an example. We've been playing to as many as 11,000 people and that's very gratifying..."

"But we had to face the reality of the music business," he continued in a separate interview. "The people who are paying money to see you are not necessarily interested in what you're doing now. Record companies just aren't geared for anybody's comeback thing. They are desperately trying to find out who they are in relation to new artists, and bands like us, attempting to come back after we've been gone from the music scene for a while, bewilders them. We actually asked to be released from the contract. It was the wrong company, the wrong place and the wrong time.

"Pop historians consistently remember us as a commercial, middle-of-the-road band. In truth, we worked out some very complicated arrangements on our albums. We were actually quite an innovative group. But that's the strange destiny of The Association..."

Undaunted, the band played on, and by the end of the following year they were looking at a short album deal with CBS Records, albeit for a minor division within the giant corporation, 51 West Records, a New York-based subsidiary label. The subsequent album release, *Vintage*, issued during the early months of 1983 (51 West Records Q-17223), marked the start in a new era of recordings for The Association. The new songs and compositions that the band had jointly pulled together in the SunWest recording studio, just two years previously, were left untouched and the line-up instead construed to revisit their illustrious past, a regressive move that, perhaps in hindsight, they never really recovered from.

Jules Alexander: "Someone approached us with the idea. I think the producer (Paul Whitehead) perhaps. I think that using the old recordings was too costly to license from whomever held the masters so the whole album was the producer's concept. Recording is almost always fun no matter what is being done. Well, for me anyway!"

Jim Yester adds, with a laugh, "I actually have no recollection of that album whatsoever! (Listening to it today) the version of 'Along Comes Mary' blows my mind! I think my vocal is even better than the original! It sounds like Ulsky on keyboards and Larry on guitar. And that's definitely Terry on recorder, nobody else plays recorder like that! As for not using the SunWest recordings – that would have been a decision made by the record company, or the producer, who wouldn't want to use something *we* had produced, and not them. For obvious reasons!"

Marketed by CBS Special Products, more aligned to distributing mail order or TV advertised catalog releases, it remains puzzling as to the full reasoning behind this collection but, as Jules suggests, at the pushing of executive producer Paul Whitehead, it may have simply been to utilize the band's current wave of reunion popularity, but that the original cuts owned by Warners were too costly to license. It was a similar scenario to the earlier 1978 Yester/Bluechel/Vaught re-recordings for K-Tel Records. Nevertheless, this new direction, clearly intent in re-evaluating the past with a smattering of re-recordings and cover versions, was all-too apparent as the opportunities to develop their new music looked less and less likely. Certainly, David Fishof was still looking at all options to optimize the groups maximum earning potential and these new recordings could subsequently be marketed at the concert venues he was still actively promoting.

Nine new recordings were attempted and pressed onto vinyl and audio cassette, five of which – "Windy", "Along Comes Mary", "Never My Love", "Goodbye, Columbus" and "Cherish" – were simply new versions of the old favorites, cut with a 1980s technology, but remaining pleasantly faithful to the original versions (something that the late '70s renditions had failed to do). A lot of the instrumentation was cut beforehand under the guidance of Whitehead, and some suggestions indicate that these may have taken place in Nashville prior to the band adding their vocals in Los Angeles, but Jim's suggestion that certain aspects of the band may also appear on the music tracks suggest a degree of group collaboration. Indeed, the group themselves were listed as co-producers and would certainly have had some say in the final product. Nevertheless, the voices, the arrangements and the harmonies all remained satisfyingly intact, overseen by the band's old friend Bob Alcivar, along with Kingston Trio member George Groves. The remaining four inclusions were cover versions of some of the hits of the day – sadly unnecessary but, once more, pleasantly executed.

"Do That To Me One More Time", as originally released by The Captain & Tennille, was reworked into an overtly heavy saxophone dominated arrangement, typical of a 1980s smoky-lounge-feel, with Russ well out to the fore on lead vocals, accompanied by some rich, deep harmony backing vocals, whilst the version of Stevie Wonder's "Isn't She Lovely", driven by some nice smooth bass and electronic keyboards, offered Larry the opportunity to equally shine in the vocal department. The tables were then turned towards Jules, who had his moment in the spotlight for a tender re-reading of Billy Joel's "Just The Way You Are", whilst Russ rounded out the collection, handling the highlight of the album with a cover of Rod Stewart's glorious "You're In My Heart", a song ideally suited to Giguere's uncanny ability of storytelling lyrics and musical phrasings. Without doubt, it was an expertly produced and accomplished affair and yet, as previously noted, totally unnecessary in the eyes and ears to many of the band's loyal following, issued as it was without the slightest hint of any potential chart success.

July 1983 saw the airing of a short, televised performance from the band, broadcast as a *Billboard* Presents *Friends In Concert* TV Special. A selection of favored songs was taped before a live audience, intercut with various behind-the-scenes interviews. "Along Comes Mary", "Never My Love", "Goodbye, Columbus", "Years Of Tryin'", "Requiem For The Masses", "Cherish", "Windy", and an astonishing version of "Across The Persian Gulf" were all played out enthusiastically before the small, attentive audience, clearly appreciative seeing and hearing the band in such an intimate live setting.

"I appreciate doing something like that for the people," Ted later commented during one of the brief interviews for the broadcast, referring to the band's vocal prowess on "Persian Gulf", "because it leaves people spellbound, gaping in awe at the vocal performance which I think is what they want to hear, just the raw voices."

The band could certainly still cut it onstage as this impressive performance would testify and yet, regardless of potential setbacks in their continuing recording career, for better or for worse, a future on the 'oldies' circuit was certainly beckoning. The revised interest in the group as a contemporary performing outfit, and for the new music they had been creating on the recent reunion tours, was but a fleeting moment, albeit an extremely successful and enjoyable one, but one could not simply walk away from such an illustrious catalog. Certainly, an American public who, for much of the 1980s Reagan-era, returned to their youth for the nostalgia and joyful recollections of innocence, would not let such momentous musical highlights as "Cherish" and "Windy" fade away. The wish of the six/seven/eight-man band to look forward, and to develop new music during the 1981-83 reunion tours, restricting their history to a mere five-song interlude, was highly commendable, and to a group of such talented individuals it was too good an opportunity to pass by, but without the opportunity to share the music with a record buying public, to have people listen to it time and time again in the comfort of their own homes, then the appeal was limited to much of the attentive audience. Those who only knew The Association from the succession of Top 20 releases from a bygone era and who could happily put the million-selling *The Association's Greatest Hits* on the family turntable and reminisce. The self-proclaimed 'America's Band', The Beach Boys, had certainly discovered for themselves that, despite the personal inclinations of certain band members, the record buying public and, more significantly, the concert goer were more than happy to pass out the dollar tenfold in order to spend a nostalgic two-hour trip when seeing the band perform live. When an audience of one and a half million people reportedly turned out to see the Mike Love-fronted band perform two shows in one day at the annual 4th of July concerts in Philadelphia and Washington, two years later in 1985, there was simply no turning back. For that particular group, already in a recording slump, there would be no more new and creative record releases, solo excursions aside, until a 50th Anniversary celebration in 2012 saw a re-energized line-up issue an outstandingly strong reunion release. For The Association it was the recording of the 1983 *Vintage* album and the accepting abandonment of the SunWest sessions that was to become the turning point and a subsequent recognition of their destiny. Those loyal followers attending their shows *did* want to hear the hits, and, more often than not, more of the same please.

This period also saw the band continue to cut new recordings within the studio environment, whilst further consolidating their position as a future nostalgia act. To their credit, the recordings they were to cut still maintained an air of polished sophistication about them – they were never simple throwaway recordings, and it is worth adding that this particular era of recording history wasn't something that would generate much acclaim within the musical history books, with Michael Jackson, Lionel Richie and the UK cod-reggae/new wave trio The Police dominating the charts worldwide, and few artists who had survived the 1960s, and had then seen through the punk and new wave backlash of the late '70s, would survive with anything more than basic credibility hovering over them. McCartney, Daltrey and Townshend, the Gibb brothers – all produced a series of average-at-best releases during this period and the advancement of studio technology was wiping away much of the artistic nature and personal feel of the musicianship these established artists had previously fed off. At the touch of a button a synthesizer could do much of what a musician had previously taken hours, or days to create, but it left a hollow void in the experience. The programming and 'feel' of the synthesized music left one empty without any sense of texture and warmth. It felt, and sounded passionless.

The Santa Barbara-based Hitbound Records was a small independent label, created by Beach Boys front man Mike Love alongside producer Rex Sparger and distributed solely throughout America via an arrangement with the U.S. retail outlet Radio Shack. Only a small succession of releases were to appear bearing the Hitbound logo, initially designed to promote cheaply-pressed compact cassette-only productions, all overseen by Love and his friends, the first of which was the limited cassette issue, *Rock 'n' Roll City* (Hitbound 51-3009). A twelve-song collection, featuring remakes of various 1960s hits by a succession of artists including Mike Love, with and without The Beach Boys, Dean Torrence (of Jan & Dean), Paul Revere & The Raiders, The Rip Chords and The Association.

We took a trip down memory lane to select songs for 'Rock 'n' Roll City'. First we listened to the original versions of hundreds of the hits of the '60s. Very few were as good as we remembered. We decided we shouldn't 'cover' these old hits, unless the new versions were better, a lot better than the originals. That's what 'Rock 'n' Roll City' is – better than the original.

Promotional sleeve notes
Rock 'n' Roll City. 1983

"The project came about as a piece of a larger puzzle," Love was to relate in a 1983 article for *Orange Coast* magazine. "That is, the recording of the history of rock 'n' roll. That would involve 300 songs, the Top 12 of the last 25 years. This project is somewhat of a demo in the right direction. From Radio Shack's side, they've had great success with a Beach Boys/Jan & Dean compilation album that they've sold close to 100,000 cassette units so they were real interested in having Dean (Torrence) and I collaborate on a project. It just so happened that the project we're interested in doing, the big project, fit in with this beautifully."

Love's collaborator, Dean Torrence, added: "Having a cassette priced at just $4.95 and readily available to lot of people certainly beats the record business. I know many artists who go into the studio and spend six months of their lives there doing some pretty damn good stuff that never sees the light of day. So this is an alternate way, a whole new way of getting the product to the customer."

"We'll get our stuff in a lot more retail stores than we would in record stores." Love concluded. "You can't even guarantee once you do a product for a record company that they will even distribute it to a store. In this case, we are, and there are over 8000 Radio Shack stores."

With executive production on the cassette afforded to Love, The Association's lone contribution to the offering was an update of "Walk Away Renée", a successful composition by Michael Brown, Bob Calilli and Tony Sansone, and previously a Top 5 hit for Brown's own New York-based band The Left Banke back in 1966. As to whether this version truly improves on the original, as per the accompanying promotional blurb, is open to debate, although Larry Ramos supplies an undeniably fine lead vocal. As to whether *any* of the inclusions improve on the original renditions is equally as contentious ("California Dreamin'", "96 Tears", "Da Doo Ron Ron"?), but The Association turned in a fine vocal performance, overlaying the synthesized backdrop of instrumental sounds, created and produced by none other than Curt Boettcher, himself very much an advocate of 1980s programmed studio creations. Boettcher, having last worked with the band almost thirteen years previous, had reconnected with the various members in recent months and had been the prime mover in the recording of the song.

"I hadn't seen Curt in years," Jules was to state. "This writer from England came over to interview me and he told me he was a close friend of Curt's. So we began to hang out together again. When the opportunity to record again came up from Mike Love, Curt suggested we do the song. Curt's really into high techno-pop. The only instrument on 'Walk Away Renée' is a piano; everything else is synthesized." [20]

Boettcher was also a close friend with Bruce Johnston of The Beach Boys, having worked with him throughout much of the previous decade, and Curt had also overseen the disastrous 1979 disco-fied Beach Boys abomination, a 10-minute programmed *faux pas* that alienated much of their hardcore following during this period. Nevertheless, his production on "Walk Away Renée", whilst dominated by the swirling synthesizer and programmed drumbeats, was very much slick, polished and yet somewhat superficial.

The band also took to performing the song onstage, promoting the cassette release, as were a number of the other featured artists during their own performances, but it often left the audiences confused as to why these songs were being featured. Or were these the original artists? To a 1980s audience, many of whom were unfamiliar with the original recordings, it was a strange scenario developing. The lines were becoming increasingly blurred...

And yet being back on the performing circuit, performing a mixture of both old and occasional new songs, this couldn't truly satisfy the soul of one particular band member, who had seen and done it all so many times before, and spring 1983 saw the departure once again of Jim Yester, unable to face the relentless touring that was keeping the band very much alive. Opting to break away from the music industry altogether and develop a family life, Jim moved to Canoga Park, Los Angeles, and took a job with Delta Tau Data Systems, making computers, ultimately creating a new career for himself and becoming a production manager within the company.

"At that time I wasn't really aware of the signing with Mike Love's label at all," he recalls. "I was unaware of a lot of that was going on as the group left me out of the business meetings after I decided I was going to leave. I was the black sheep!"

Clearly, the loss of Jim would be a major setback to the band once more, with his high tenor vocal range being an essential part of the vocal blend. In addition, his rhythm guitar skills left a notable void in the instrumental layout of the performing line-up and so to compensate for this, Jules Alexander, having inhabited the bass player position for the past three years, switched over to rhythm guitar, aiding Larry with the role of frontline guitarist, and the band briefly brought in Keith Moret to supply bass to the performances.

Jules recalls, "I think Keith was a friend of someone we knew. He was a good player though, but he was only with us for just a short time. Maybe a couple of gigs. I don't really remember why he left but I think it had to do with his singing chops as opposed to anything else."

The next recording project, also undertaken for the Hitbound label, was truly a result of the era; a desultory television special, produced for the increasing home video market by Hitbound in partnership with the Tandy Corporation, Radio Shack's parent company, and titled *Scrooge's Rock 'n' Roll Christmas*. Scheduled to run during the upcoming festive season of 1983, the show featured the weathered Hollywood actor Jack Elam in the role of miserly ol' Scrooge, alongside a host of performers (although all of Elam's scenes were filmed independently) – Mike Love, Three Dog Night, Paul Revere & The Raiders, Dean Torrence, Bobby Goldsboro, Mary McGregor and The Association – all lip-syncing along to a number of pre-recorded tunes, whilst making merriment in their snow covered and pine scented surroundings. It was truly a horrendous spectacle to watch, poorly scripted and filmed on a somewhat restricting budget, and to make matters worse (or better, depending on the listener's state of mind) an accompanying soundtrack album also appeared, issued via Hitbound Records (HB-1003). This official eight-song collection featured just one contribution by The Association, "Sleigh Ride", originally composed by Leroy Anderson back in 1948, with lyrics added by Mitchell Parish two years later although, somewhat strangely, Hitbound/Radio Shack also opted to put out an extended version of the soundtrack LP shortly afterwards, including a number of additional songs featured in the video, retitled and repackaged as *Christmas Party*, and yet issued under the same catalog number (HB-1003).

Both releases appeared as a vinyl pressing this time, featuring all of the aforesaid artists covering a number of standardized festive compositions. For their part, on the second edition, The Association added their vocal harmonies to two pre-selected songs, with a third contribution on an additional cut. The first one, as noted, was "Sleigh Ride", which was actually one of the more pleasing efforts on the entire release, genuinely offering up a seasonal feel of good times, sleigh bells and holiday harmonies, whilst their second song on the extended package was "Home For The Holidays", the 1954 composition by Robert Allen and Al Stillman, and popularized by Perry Como three decades previous. This too offered up a nice variation on the original theme, with Larry well to the fore, albeit one that was overly laden with sentimental strings. The third recording to feature a contribution from the band, although listed as being performed by the entire ensemble on the rear of the album sleeve, was the widely familiar carol "We Wish You A Merry Christmas". Production credits on both releases were split, depending on the individual artists, and The Association's first two vocal offerings were overseen in the studio by producer Dick Hierionymous, a relatively unknown name in studio production but who is recognized for his work with Brian Hyland and Dick & Dee Dee, along with various roles as composer and arranger to a number of sub-standard b-movie soundtracks. However, for the uncredited performance of "We Wish You A Merry Christmas" the production reins were handed over to Jeffrey Foskett, Mike Love's right hand man on a number of these recording sessions (and still a touring Beach Boy to this very day).

"That song was performed by Jim Hoke on keys, Steve Nelson on bass, Paul Nelson on guitar and Scott Matthews on drums," said Foskett, during an interview for a 2010 edition of The Beach Boys *Endless Summer Quarterly* magazine, "with Randall Kirsch, Larry Ramos and me singing all of the vocals. The TV show was shown locally in the L.A. area but I don't know if it was televised nationally."

And the actual onscreen performances? "Sleigh Ride" saw the band, now minus Jim Yester, decked out in their finest winter warmers, wooly scarves and bobble hats, save for Larry who insisted on wearing his now omnipresent wide brim, riding along in… you guessed it, a horse drawn sleigh in the beautiful, snow-capped mountain locale of Goldmine Ski Resort, situated in Big Bear Lake, one hundred miles east of central Los Angeles. "Home For The Holidays" meanwhile saw the band, comprising of Terry, Jules, Ted, Russ, Larry and Ric, once again enjoying the holiday hospitalities, amiably sitting around, laughing and lip-syncing on a snow-covered chalet deck. It was all very pleasant and traditional, with "We Wish You A Merry Christmas" playing out as the credits rolled. However, it goes without saying that this vinyl release, in either edition, along with its predecessor, saw limited availability through its Radio Shack distribution network, despite the initial suggestions of accessibility throughout all 8000 retail outlets, and despite the efforts and contributions by all concerned, some for the good, some not so, it remained an obscure niche purchase.

Ever the businessman Mike Love was soon talking about a further project for the Hitbound label, a full length movie about the 'rock 'n' roll years', with a proposed budget already accounted for by his company. "You can have The Association do 'Yesterday' and 'MacArthur Park'" he was subsequently quoted as saying. "The Beach Boys can do 'The Battle of New Orleans'. You can do some really exciting things. Marvin Gaye wants to do 'Jumping Jack Flash'!"

Such a project never materialized.

The Association, which put together a string of hits through the '60s, brought their comeback tour to a grateful crowd at the Grand Opera House in Wilmington last night. The less-than-full house audience, primarily 25 years of age and older, were treated to a pleasant evening of nearly 90 minutes of music. The band warmed up through the first two numbers, then got the crowd going with the old hit 'Never My Love'.

The first set alternated between funky and mellow and included such oldies as "No Fair At All" and the moving and melancholy "Requiem For The Masses". A highlight was a song in tribute to Michelangelo.

The second set opened up with the old hit 'Along Comes Mary', which was well received, as was a vaguely techno-pop updated version of the classic 'Walk Away Renée'. The set also included a song called 'Across The Persian Gulf', which is described as The Association's tribute to Johann Sebastian Bach, and a light version of Rod Stewart's 'You're In My Heart'.

After a bluesy tribute to the late Muddy Waters, the group cut loose with sterling, tight, moving versions of 'Cherish' and 'Windy', which left the Grand crowd on their feet calling for more.

The Morning News : May 1983

Wilmington, DE

With Keith Moret only lasting in the touring party for a brief period, and Jules flitting back and forth between rhythm and bass duties, the call went out to a friend of Jules to fill in the role of bass player, allowing him to vacate the position on a permanent basis. Former Joshua Fox bassist Joe LaManno, who had previously filled in the role on a couple of occasions during the mid-'70s, was that friend.

"I joined on July 4th 1983," says Joe today, in conversation with the author, "I didn't actually do a show on that day but I flew into Chicago, landing around 9:00 PM. It was a dazzling light show from the air with fireworks going off all over the city. I went straight to their hotel where I met up with the guys; they had already done their show that day, and traveled with them for a week or so with Jules continuing to play bass while I learned the show. I don't remember which show was my first actually playing.

"The call had come from Jules so I assume it was his idea I joined up, although I immediately felt welcomed by everyone. However, I was never a *proper* member of the band, but a salaried player: my preference. The boys had been back touring for a few years and they sounded as lush and full as ever. At this time, all of the originals were back on board except Jim, and Brian of course, plus we had Ric Ulsky on keys and vocals.

"I loved working with Ted in the rhythm section. While he was the first to admit he wasn't the consummate drummer, he was *the* drummer for that band. He played with so much heart and love for the music and his band mates. I'd previously played with him when I had briefly toured with the band during the mid-'70s. I also sang on most of the songs when I joined up again, but only as a harmony voice, second tenor or baritone, no leads. It was the same with Ric. I never kept a touring log of all of our shows but I'd guess we were out for maybe half the time. It was busy!"

Buoyed by the reception from the Tandy Corporation towards the publicity generated by the recent succession of releases, Hitbound Records continued to release products throughout 1983. The next issue to appear on the label was *Paul Revere Rides Again!* (HB-1004), a much maligned nine-track collection of cover tunes by Paul Revere & The Raiders that did little to enhance their reputation. This was followed shortly afterwards by the release of *New Memories* (HB-1005), a new gathering of recordings by The Association, lined up alongside songs by three other artists – Bobby Vee performing "Fever", Mike Love, turning in a version of the folk standard "Stagger Lee", and Mary McGregor with a techno rendition of "Sugar Sugar" that has to be heard to be believed… and then swiftly turned off.

"We've just signed a long and involved deal with Hitbound Productions," Jules was to state at the time. "We are just beginning to see all the possibilities for our music today." [20]

With production overseen by Jeffrey Foskett a list of possible songs for inclusion on the album was presented to the band beforehand, giving them the green light for the final selection and as to how the arrangements would come together and, despite the seemingly forced nature of how the album was compiled, the band appeared appreciative of the opportunity. Unlike the previous releases for Hitbound, whereupon the group simply supplied their own voices onto pre-recorded tracks, for this new album they were given total freedom to record, arrange and perform the songs as they saw fit.

Jules: "I've seen this in other bands and artists too, but you get to a certain point in your career when you go 'God, I love these old tunes! I'm gonna do them…' You've already got the hits yourself, and are established, so you want to go and record some of the old classics…"

With Ric Ulsky, now seen as a permanent resident within the current line-up, and new arrival Joe LaManno sitting alongside the core surviving membership, the band settled into Ulsky's one bedroomed cottage in Venice, CA, which also doubled as a recording facility, to create the new songs.

"Ric's 'studio' was, I think, a 24-track board located on his kitchen counter!" laughs Joe, "with some outboard gear on a nearby shelf and a few mics. Everything was recorded direct into that board except vocals. We played all our own instruments with the exception of the drums, which were recorded with a Linn drum machine programmed by a studio pro. However, the cottage was in the flight path of LAX so, during vocals, we had to stop now and then to let air traffic go by! Personally, I was given complete freedom in creating all the bass parts and I don't recall anyone really dominating the project. Jules, Ric and Jonathan Houston, Jock, our road sound mixer, mostly led the production end, but everyone had a voice and was heard…"

Settling on a seven-song selection of "Memories Are Made Of This", "Love Me Tender", "Breaking Up Is Hard To Do", "Pretty Woman", "World Without Love", "Dock Of The Bay" and "It's All In The Game" the final mixes reveal very pared down productions, with the synthetic drums dominating much of the proceedings, although the highlight of the album, noticeably when the Linn is unplugged, is the gorgeous soothing rendition of Neil Sedaka's "Breaking Up Is Hard To Do", with Larry Ramos leading the line over a smooth acoustic instrumentation and faithful Association harmonies and arrangements at work. Sadly, elsewhere, the results sound at times like a confused variation of '80s synth-pop idols Duran Duran lost in a 1960s timewarp, although the pure quality of the vocals, with the leads shared between Terry, Russ, Jules and Larry, can never be brought into question.

Packaged with a distinctly unflattering line drawing of the band members, minus Joe, dominating the front sleeve the album appeared in the Radio Shack stores and mail order catalogs during the latter end of the year, coinciding with the promotion for the upcoming airing of *Scrooge's Rock 'n' Roll Christmas*, followed up by a swift placement (in Joe LaManno's words) "straight into the bargain bin."

With production credit afforded to the band themselves on their seven inclusions, it was by no means a glorious addition into the band's catalog but this was the 1980s, a time of rediscovery, reassessment, peacock punk and leg warmers, and much of the music industry was still coming to terms with the advent of electronica, despite the obvious scenario that the legendary Moog synthesizer had initially made its appearance during the heady, hazy days of 1967 when The Monkees had first plugged in its vast array of patch cables and Micky Dolenz twiddled randomly on the impressive assortment of buttons and dials. However, at least Dolenz or Eddie Hoh, both of whom supplied percussion on the glorious *Pisces, Aquarius, Capricorn & Jones Ltd.* LP that year had a full drum kit in front of them as they played along on the tracks. Roger Linn had a lot to answer for during that heavily shoulder padded 1980s era.

"That album was horrible!" laughs Terry today. "Radio Shack! I thought 'Oh! Here's where my illustrious career has gone!'"

The 'long and involved deal' with Hitbound that Jules had so eloquently made reference to within the pages of *Goldmine* magazine never came to fruition and, with the release of *New Memories*, their association with the label came to an end. Hitbound Records ground to a halt shortly afterwards and, coincidentally, and barring one later issue the following decade, featuring a stripped down version of the original band, so did the recording career of The Association as a collective.

Sunrise, sunset…

CHAPTER TWENTY-SIX

HAPPY TOGETHER

Throughout the summer months of 1983 The Association had been performing as part of an 'oldies' package tour, with Gary Puckett & The Union Gap and, on occasion, legendary rock 'n' roller Chuck Berry also on the bill, and by October the schedule had wound its way around to the Meadowlands Arena in New York. David Fishof, still successfully acting as the band's manager whilst also overseeing the managerial careers of various headlining football and baseball pros, approached Puckett about signing him up to his stable of artists and, shortly afterwards, he also added The Turtles, now comprising of original front men Howard Kaylan and Mark Volman (also known as The Phlorescent Leech and Eddie) along with a selection of supporting musicians, to his roster.

Commenting about this growing organization at the time, Fishof was to say: "I was very excited. I thought I was making great strides in the music business. But my agent friends told me I was nuts. 'You're representing the biggest athletes in the world! Fishof, you own New York City, and you're spending your time managing these oldies acts!' But I didn't care. I liked these people. They were fun to listen to, and most of them were very nice." [46]

Realizing the continuing popularity and the potential draw that these bands still had, Fishof approached the William Morris Agency and together they came up with the concept of the Happy Together tours, a combined package of artists, four or more bands and a night whereupon the audiences

372

would hear a succession of smash hits, one after another – and *only* the hit songs. No room for filler, no room for egos.

Adding Spanky & Our Gang to the bill, million-selling hitmakers of "Sunday Will Never Be The Same" and "Lazy Day", the proposed tour, scheduled for a spring 1984 commencement, immediately began selling out. Promoters in Ohio, Michigan, Illinois began booking bulk performances. New York City came on board. Tucson, Pittsburg, Ontario…

Before they headed out on the long road however, the band undertook one further, exclusive concert appearance, making an all-too rare journey across the seas for a private corporate show, held in Athens, Greece. Joe LaManno recalls; "This was a gig for a major American corporation. It was a bonus for the top employees of the year. We were there for a week staying at The Intercontinental Hotel, which is also where the performance was. If memory serves, we did two shows the second night we were there and the rest of the time was ours to spend as we wished. And spend it we did! We became consummate tourists, seeing and doing all we could in the time we had. On the way back we had a layover in London, so three of us extended it for a day and did the town."

Also during this period, The Association taped an appearance on the popular syndicated *Solid Gold* TV show (broadcast on July 15th 1984), hosted by Marilyn McCoo; founding member of the 5th Dimension, whereupon the band appeared on a 'Salutes The Songs Of Summer' slot, performing both "Cherish" and "Windy". That time period also saw Jules, Larry, Terry and Ric contribute backing vocals in the studio to a new 45 by The United States Of Existence, a Maryland-based '80s psych band acclaimed for using vintage instruments and antiquated recording techniques to fully embrace the authenticity of their sound. The release on U.S. Fidelity Sounds, "Anything Goes!" (USFS-1003) failed to achieve any real mainstream success but is a pleasing example of the rejuvenated interest in the original era, and the foursome add some nice *ba-ba-ba* harmonies throughout the recording.

Running through until the early winter of 1984 the inaugural Happy Together tour, a 125-date run of performances, was a resounding success for David Fishof and all of the promoters who backed the initial concept, drawing more than 750,000 attendants, with eighty-five of the shows being complete sell-outs. "No other show offers as much for the dollar," Fishof was to report to the press, whilst basking in the aftermath of the success. "Where else can you get 40 gold hits for the price of one ticket?"

The Association went through near-perfect renditions of 'Windy', 'Enter The Young', 'Goodbye, Columbus', 'Cherish' and the rest of its hits. 'Never My Love', perhaps the groups finest moment on disc, was performed with appropriate soft intimacy. The outstanding pop chorale group of the '60s still sings flawless harmony, still has its dense vocal sound and still shares its lead vocals amongst members. Chattanooga native Jules Alexander was particularly effective on 'Along Comes Mary', the song that launched The Association in 1966. Terry Kirkman, Larry Ramos, Russ Giguere and Ted Bluechel each had equally good moments on the mic, and they all shined on the excellent new arrangement of the 1966 Left Banke classic 'Walk Away Renée'.

The Tennessean
August 3rd 1984

"It's a very fast, very entertaining show," Terry Kirkman was to say to *The Tennessean* in the lead-up to the concert. "We get standing ovations for some songs. Each act has its impact. Each one is onstage for 25 minutes, and we each have our own audience. Some people come to see Gary Puckett; some are fans of Spanky & Our Gang, and lots of people are really into The Turtles' zany and unpredictable Flo and Eddie."

However, within The Association camp all was not well. Larry Ramos later recalled the incidents surrounding the tour in a 2011 interview with writer Sam Tweedle:

"During the Happy Together tour the guys got tired because we had been out for four weeks. They said, 'Oh, I can't go out anymore. My wife wants me to go home!' I swear to God. Wives have been the ruin of many groups! Anyways, four of the six guys decided to go home. I said, 'Go home. That's cool. I can't go. I still owe money.' We had borrowed money to get the group working together again because you need finances to buy instruments and equipment. It's not a freebie. So we still had outstanding debts, and some of them were held by friends of mine, some of them who decided that they wanted to help the group get back together again, and I couldn't turn my back on my friends. So I decided that I'm going to finish up the tour. I'll get guys to sit in with us." [23]

Ted Bluechel, Terry Kirkman and Ric Ulsky were the three band members who initially raised doubts about continuing on with the tour, although Jules also had his reservations but along with Russ Giguere, who was keen to remain on the tour, he ultimately decided to stick around and see through the outstanding dates. For Ted Bluechel however, the simple calling of a wife back home was not the main reason for making the decision to walk away from the band. He had a far greater need.

That year Ted's wife, Carol, had given birth to their son Michael but he was born three months prematurely and he experienced health problems early on in life, resulting in autism. Although he didn't walk away from the band immediately, these mid-1984 Happy Together shows saw Ted opt to vacate the drum stool once more, moving back to the front of the stage and adding his harmony to the mix from there, occasionally supplying rhythm guitar. A quick fix was found to fulfill the drumming position but, even then, Ted couldn't make it work, coming and going as and when family commitments would permit, and he departed soon after.

"I wanted to stay on, doing what I could do as time would allow, but we have a motto in the group; 'you're either in the group or you're out of the group', so I really had no choice but to cut the cord and step back," Ted was to say during 2011. [1]

Leaving behind the band that he spent the majority of his adult life being a part of, was not an easy decision, but Ted clearly had his priorities in order, putting the welfare and upbringing of his son first, and taking a less stressful view of life.

"Stress is a big factor that has had its way with me, but as I'm getting older, I really look to enjoy what's left of the span here on earth. I just go on looking after my own household." [1]

His friend and former 1970s bandmate Cliff Woolley looks back on Ted with affection: "Ted gets along with everyone, he's unchanged from all these years. He retired to raise his son, and that's incredibly fatherly of him. He's an incredibly wonderful guy..."

With Terry and Ric leaving the tour during that same period it was with a hastily revised line-up of Larry, Russ and Jules, with Joe LaManno still holding down the bass guitar role, and a selection of temporary sit-ins filling out the musicianship that finished up the remaining commitments on the heavy schedule.

Larry: "Russ had decided that he wanted to stay too, and I figured that if we could just convince one more person we would have half the group and still be original. We got Jules Alexander to come with us, and we got the drummer and, I think, a keyboard player from Gary Puckett's band. The drummer was Gary's brother (Brian). They played with both bands. They just changed clothes..." [23]

"There were so many stellar venues," recalls Joe LaManno, "both classic and modern. And the Caribbean cruise was beautiful. Jules was such an intuitive musician and Brian Puckett is such a solid player and a gentle soul."

Replacing Ric Ulsky, and briefly coming in on keyboards and filling out the vocal sound was Michael Leroy Peed, who was himself replaced shortly afterwards by Donnie Gougeon, a former member of a Christian metal band named Joshua. He had big boots to fill, with Ulsky having been an essential part of the touring band, on and off, since 1977, but he fitted in quickly and comfortably within the line-up.

Ric meanwhile moved on to play in Chuck Berry's touring band, ultimately becoming his bandleader and keyboardist for the next decade. He also performed alongside one of the many incarnations of the '50s doo-wop legends The Coasters. Fellow Seattle-born musician Bill Majkut summarized up Ric for an online article during 2001: "He's worked with Stevie Wonder, The Association and countless other national acts. He works with everyone! Ric is a musician's musician. He's the kind of keyboardist that other players come out to just listen to. He has deep and funky jazz/blues roots, extraordinary technique and a hypnotic sense of rhythm. As far as B-3 players go, he is by far and without a doubt the best in the Pacific North-West, and one of the top three on the West Coast. Ric takes crap from no one." [47]

Terry Kirkman not only left to pursue a quieter life, away from the road, but also to finally conquer his demons. Having been in the band, constantly on the road for the past three years, former addictions had once again gotten the better of the founding member. His participation in the reunion had never been a wholly comfortable situation for him, a reluctantly necessary scenario more than a creative desire, and his dissatisfaction over how the band's affairs were being handled also frustrated him immensely, with reportedly thousand and thousands of dollars falling into the wrong hands.

"I walked into our manager David Fishof's office right before I left the group," he states. "I just stopped in New York and surprised him because I was supposed to be in Philadelphia with the Happy Together tour. It scared the shit out of him because we didn't really like each other, and I said 'I have a question to ask you.' 'You have a question to ask me?' he replied, and he was nervous. I was intimidating him. He said 'what's the question?' and I replied 'short of us four-walling our whole career, is there any way we can keep you from stealing from us?' He looked at me, and sat back and smiled, 'that's the question?' he said, 'No!'

"We were being paid about a third of what we were actually earning…"

Opting out of band life on the road, he now took the opportunity to turn his life around. "I am a recovering alcoholic," he candidly admitted to both Childs and March for their 2011 publication. "I was a screaming cocaine addict and I got sober October 21st, 1984, six weeks after leaving The Association, and I've remained so ever since."

"I was in spin-dry for about three years, trying to figure out who I was, what had become of me. I was mortified, disappointed, really embarrassed that I'd participated in that mess again. It was so not what I'd set out to do…"

Returning to his previous occupation, prior to the reunion, he began writing for television once more, whilst always offering to help others who had and still were suffering from the same addictions he'd been through. He was later invited to work in a recovery program for the Hollywood Community Hospital, a worthy experience for him and one that led to him attending UCLA where he passed his certification board exams in order that he could undertake a career in chemical dependency counseling. He continues to talk and fight the cause to this very day…

"There's no comparison to anything else I've done in my life. It was one of the best jobs I could ever imagine having in the recovery profession. Someone would call up all helpless and hopeless and broke, and if they met our minimal requirements, I could have them in a treatment facility within minutes. I'd go home with a great feeling of gratitude every night." [1]

Between 1984 and the turn of the following decade the performing band known as The Association, with three official members still on board, toured relentlessly, picking up slots on various 'golden oldies' tours, or appearing at individual performances whenever they were booked. With Larry Ramos now being seen in the media as the prominent driving force, a succession of supporting band members came and went in the intervening years, with Joe LaManno being the next to depart from the ranks, linking up with The Turtles during early 1985 where he remained, an essential part of their touring band for the next five years. In his place came Paul Beach on bass and tenor vocals, a seasoned yet youthful pro on the revival circuit and a touring member with both Gary Puckett and Spanky & Our Gang.

"My connection to the Association goes back way before I joined the band," recalls Paul, when questioned for this book. "I knew Larry Ramos from surfing at Trestles years before I joined the band. I first met him there around 1976 and I remember seeing him out in the lineup at Lower Trestles, my favorite surfing spot. He and I made that connection one night, backstage in New York, when I was still working with Gary Puckett. I worked many of the same shows The Association was on when I was working with Gary, and also with Spanky & Our Gang. Gary and Spanky had hired me to lead the band for Spanky's show; write the charts, rehearse the band, etc. and then I first joined up with The Association as vocalist in the middle of the Happy Together tour, when Terry, Ted and Ric Ulsky left the band. I added first baritone, second tenor and, occasionally, some first tenor. The band tended to listen to blend more than assigning specific voices to this or that vocal range, and most of the guys had pretty wide ranges, so they had the luxury of changing vocal parts, pretty much at will. At this point I was in three of the four bands on that tour!

"Afterwards The Turtles hired Joe LaManno (on a permanent basis), which left a vacancy in The Association and I think it was Jules that called me, to see if I was interested in joining them as bass player, which I was, of course. It was an easy transition for everyone, in my opinion. I already knew the vocal parts, and had a working knowledge on bass for most of their show. All of the bass players in the Happy Together tour had learned each other's shows, in the event of illness or a family emergency. As it turned out, thankfully, we never had to do that."

In addition, another Puckett alumni, Bruce Pictor, also signed up on drums, baritone and tenor, filling in the role now vacated by Brian Puckett.

"Brian wanted to settle down," says Bruce, looking back over his many years with the band that continues to this day. "I joined the group in February 1985, and at the time they were playing around two hundred and fifty shows per year. I was recommended by Jim Dotson, who was Gary Puckett's manager, and I received the phone call from Paul Beach who had joined Gary's group during my time there.

"I recall I auditioned against two drummers who were also highly recommended from the Los Angeles area, but I got the job. From what I was told, it was no contest. I'm a self-taught drummer and singer, beginning at age twelve when, for Christmas in seventh grade, I received a drum set after years of begging, and I've been a huge music fan all of my life, always listening to the radio and recordings. Any '50s groups, all '60s groups… Hendrix, Cream, Chicago, Beatles, Stones, Herb Alpert, Beach Boys, Four Seasons, Motown…

"Before I joined I had played any and every musical situation I could; just hundreds of local groups, show bands, commercial jingles, studio musician, club bands, jugglers, strippers, jazz groups…"

Clearly Bruce's pedigree was of a high standard and his ability to take on the role that had seen five predecessors come and go was unquestionable.

"Although I was influenced by the group's recordings, I use that as a map, or referral and I recreated the parts with my own style. Hal Blaine, 'the Clown Prince of Drumming', was a major influence on me but my style is more jazzy and complex than Hal's. I play my own patterns and style. The original recorded parts, *per se*, were easy for me and the original arrangements, with a few exceptions, such as 'Kicking The Gong Around', are rather important but not especially challenging. The rhythm section is the bedrock of all of the songs using instruments. It influences definition, song structure, and dynamics, as well as keeping the group in time."

With Paul and Bruce now signed on, Donnie Gougeon also remained with the band until 1987 when Chris Urmston briefly replaced him on keyboards, followed shortly afterwards by Paul Holland. Gougeon then returned to the line-up in 1989. By this stage, another voice was also being added to the harmony mix, albeit from someone who didn't actually appear on the stage with the band…

Del Ramos: "Talk about multi-tasking! I was now singing with the band, on a live vocal mic from the mixing board, calling lights on another headphone mic and running sound simultaneously as well! There were certain parts I had to sing as no-one else was singing that on stage and I would put that part in, and make sure it wasn't overshadowing anything. I never let my ego get in the way of the mixing the sound, but the band would give me a special introduction of me singing from the mixing board, and I used to have a lot of people sitting around me that would actually ask for seats to watch me do what I was doing!"

The Association is one of the most popular and successful bands to have come out of the sixties and (they are) to be featured during Decatur Celebrations with performances at 4.00 and 7.30pm Sunday on the Anheuser Busch/AE Staley Show Stage. Their album, 'The Association Greatest Hits' continues to be one of the longest best-selling albums in the history of Warner Brothers and during the last five years, The Association has sung and played every state, most of the Canadian provinces, Bermuda, Athens, the Philippines, the major showrooms in Atlantic City, Las Vegas, Reno, Tahoe, musical festivals, colleges, fairs, every large theme park on the continent, supper clubs, hotels and conventions.

From a February 15 1985 review:

"Remarkably, not only did the six-man band sound as fresh as it did in the old days, it looked even fresher... dancing and laughing throughout the show, the finely-tuned outfit swept through the room like a summer breeze complete with blue skies and sunshine, smoothly and confidently exchanging leads, then blending in precision vocal harmony."

Herald & Review
Decatur, Illinois. July 31 1986

The Association's music remains cherished because it reminds fans with their first close encounters with the opposite sex, says founding member Russ Giguere. After all, how can people not respond to a song that accompanied their introduction to romance?

In addition to Giguere, the current six-man Association also includes original members Jules Alexander and Larry Ramos. It keeps busy singing 'Cherish', 'Never My Love', 'Windy', 'Along Comes Mary' and other oldies at colleges, casinos, county fairs, amusement parks, conventions and cruise ships. Between dates, The Association is rehearsing material for a new album 'that's a little more electric, a little more sophisticated,' said Giguere. 'We're not recording yet, but we have a lot of great stuff. Some of it we try out on stage. That's how we picked 'Cherish'.

Chicago Tribune
June 25 1987

With an expanded seven-piece vocal ensemble now providing the sound, the band also began adding to their on stage repertoire, accepting their position as a representation of the swinging '60s for the audiences who paid good money to come and see the band, and rekindle lost memories. Taking guidance from a popular U.S. movie that first appeared during 1983, "The Big Chill Medley" was a selection of songs from the original era, popularized once again by their inclusion in the Tom Berenger/Glenn Close/Kevin Kline movie of the same name. The Oscar nominated film, *The Big Chill*, featured a host of classic recordings from a bygone era, and for their mid-1980s tours The Association began including a medley of "I Heard It Through The Grapevine", "Wouldn't It Be Nice", "My Girl", "Bad Moon Rising", "The Weight", "It's The Same Old Song" and "Joy To The World", although such an addition to the set was not always universally accepted by the media, and their varied performances were often greeted with mixed emotions:

Hero worship to the Nth degree was displayed Saturday night at the Westport Playhouse, when a few tenaciously loyal fans stuck it out to see The Association, a soft-rock and ballad band. They were greeted by rousing applause that barely filled half the theater-in-the-round. Still, the audience unconditionally accepted every song. Nostalgia was the theme for the evening; so the group also performed a lengthy medley of other songs from the 1960s. Fans who came to relive old memories certainly got their money's worth.

St. Louis Post Dispatch
Missouri. April 21 1986

The Association sold more than 15 million records in the 1960s with hits like 'Along Comes Mary', 'Cherish', 'Windy' and 'Never My Love'. Unfortunately, the group scheduled them in the first half of their hour show – before anyone worked the kinks out of the sound system. Instead of perfectly balanced harmony, bits of random voices stuck out like warts would on Marilyn Monroe. After the 20 years you'd think the group would know how to make its own sound. The Association had better luck with music that wasn't theirs.

They closed with a medley of music from the Big Chill that showcased the three '60s singers. Ramos put out a little soul with the lead in 'I Heard It Through The Grapevine' and 'My Girl'. Jules Alexander provided a smooth, rich tenor when he took the lead on The Beach Boys 'Wouldn't It Be Nice'. Giguere did a nasal interpretation of 'Bad Moon Rising'. He had a lot of energy, not a lot of voice.

Given Tuesday's mostly empty Arena, maybe it's time to conclude that nostalgia shows have worn out their welcome in Sioux Falls.

Argus Leader
Sioux Falls, South Dakota. September 30 1987

"When the band were having a good night, no-one did it better," says Paul Beach. "I have a lot of favorite moments from my time in the band but those that stand out include the 1984 Happy Together tour which, in my mind, was one of the best. Then there was also The Grand Ole Opry, where our shows always sold out months in advance, Madison Square Garden and the NASCAR Winston 500 in North Carolina. We sang the National Anthem and played to over 200,000 people at that one!"

"We had a concert scheduled many years ago in downtown Kansas City," adds Bruce Pictor, "which had been delayed due to weather. We circled the airport for three hours waiting for the weather to clear before we could land, making us late for the start time of the concert. We changed clothes in the car on the way to the stage, which was in the heart of downtown, surrounded by skyscrapers, hotels and office buildings. 30,000 people waited in the pouring rain for us to arrive! I was the first one up the stairs to the stage and as my foot hit the stage and the lights went on, everyone that was watching from the buildings and the crowd below broke into a thunderous ovation..."

Not that their popularity was solely restricted to the concert circuit either as, once again, the esteem to which the band were still held in ensured occasional bookings on the various television networks across the country. 1988 saw a return appearance on the popular *Solid Gold* series, followed by a performance on *Live! Dick Clark Presents*, a relatively short-lived collaboration between Dick Clark Productions and the CBS Network that briefly ran during the fall season of 1988. Early the following year they also guested on *Classic Rock*, a popular show out of Nashville, hosted by Wolfman Jack, performing a 15-minute collection of the hits; "Windy", "Never My Love", "Cherish" and "Along Comes Mary"

The former show saw the reconstructed line-up, consisting of Jules, Russ and Larry, ably abetted by the youthful presence of Bruce Pictor, Paul Beach and Donnie Gougeon, perform an astonishingly polished live performance of "Along Comes Mary", void of any novelty and showbiz, with a lead vocal from Jules that, with respect to Jim Yester's original leads, simply kicked. However, for the second 1988 televised slot, appearing on the same show as Tony Orlando & Dawn, the band (now with Paul Holland replacing Gougeon) performed a three-song medley made up of "Along Comes Mary", "Cherish" and "Windy". This airing was perhaps most notable not only for the zeal that the six-man band now had for undertaking their craft, but also for a suggested weakening into a softened cabaret approach, one they hovered perilously near to. Dressed impeccably in the now-regular Association uniform of all white, the frontline trio performed live vocals with aplomb, smiling and dancing for the audience and camera, although during the segue from the slick performance of "Cherish" into the closing homerun of "Windy" Russ Giguere, with a dazzling diamond earing in his left lobe, hair combed back into a 1980s mullet, broke out into a near-frenzied middle-aged dance sequence. It was highly enthusiastic; it was pure 1980s *Footloose*, but it wasn't The Association of old. With Larry placing his guitar to one side, encouraging the audience to clap along, the threesome then launched into a high-kicking routine that made the old-time enthusiasts wince at both the routine and the breathless gusto these all-round entertainers were prepared to go. A step, or a high kick, too far?

On January 1st 1989 the same sextet appeared during the half-time show at the Mazda-sponsored Gator Bowl, the annual college football showcase, again performing their three-song medley. Accompanied by the Heritage Festival Band, three thousand high school band members, dancers and cheerleaders, the group performed admirably within the tough conditions, with poor open-air acoustics hindering a rushed performance before the 72,000 capacity crowd, although the accompanying brass band arrangement offered a nice variation for the short set but it was one that ultimately culminated, once again, with the staged high-kick routine.

Nevertheless, continuing with the band's seemingly relentless tendency for ever-rotating personnel, bassist Paul Beach was the next departure, handing in his notice after the Gator Bowl appearance, for personal reasons.

"The 1980s were good to us and I loved my time with the guys," he reflects today. "There was a resurgence of popularity for '60s music and just about every band that had any kind of hit from the '60s was working, and most were working a lot. The 1984 Happy Together tour had the second highest gross in ticket sales for any tours in the U.S. I think the Stones were the highest. The tour had 28 gold records between the four bands: The Turtles, The Association, Gary Puckett, and Spanky & Our Gang. It was a well-balanced show stylistically, and is one of the few shows I've seen that was comprised of all hit songs, but I felt it was time to go. Jules left fairly shortly afterwards. I don't remember the exact date ..."

Jules Alexander subsequently opted to retire his services from the band during that same spring period of '89, quietly placing himself in self-imposed semi-retirement, and reverting to a peaceful family lifestyle in his adopted hometown of Wimberley, Texas.

"I screwed around for a long time after I left the band. I did a couple of other jobs. A friend of mine had a tree-trimming company in Texas and I managed that for a while, which was great. It was really a cool job." [1]

The band name now fell into the direct co-ownership of Larry Ramos and Russ Giguere under the corporate name of Laruju, a name initially put together from the first letters of Larry, Russ and Jules. With Jules' departure the remaining duo simply retained the name, employing their touring partners as hired hands.

Beach's departure resulted in former supporting keyboard player, the multi-talented Paul Holland, rejoining the touring band on bass guitar and Bob Werner, one of the band's former road crew from earlier years, stepping onto the stage and filling in the instrumentation on rhythm guitar. This six-piece gathering of Giguere, Ramos, Gougeon, Pictor, Holland and Werner, accompanied by the vocal contributions of Del Ramos from behind the board, consequently and, some may note, somewhat surprisingly became the most stable line-up in the band's entire history, lasting a full decade of revival and golden-oldie performances. They may no longer have been a headlining act, often sharing the circuit billing with similar nostalgia performers, but it was good work and The Association duly accepted the offers and the tours put to them, the first of which was as a part of Dick Clark's *American Bandstand Tour* of 1989, performing alongside The Spinners, The Guess Who and The Drifters.

"That was interesting," says Bruce Pictor. "I drove 27,000 miles in ninety days! We had three days off that tour, and each night we played one or two shows. The other groups had bus drivers, but we didn't. We rented two new Cadillac Sevilles and a brand new Chrysler LeBaron convertible, each car carrying two members, and I drove Russ and myself that whole tour. Some drives were short, three hours, but others were eight to ten hours. And then sound check... every day! And then the shows..."

After having brought the Headbanger's Ball and Club MTV tours to South Florida, MTV Networks is now rolling out the promotional carpet for the 120-city 'Dick Clark American Bandstand Tour'. Appearing with the headlining act The Spinners will be The Guess Who, The Drifters and The Association.

Russ Giguere, who would not give his age, said last week that The Association will perform the group's hits, such as the million-selling No.1 smashes 'Cherish' and 'Windy', as well as 'a surprise or two.'

'We're a classic rock 'n' roll band,' Giguere commented. "A lot of people who have never seen us have always thought of us as a singing group in front of a band. That's not the way we are; we play and sing all of our music. This group is like family. I'm not just a member of The Association: I am The Association. I'm like the gold seal on the Campbell soup can.

'Every time it's changed, it's gotten better. When a guy doesn't want to be on the road I think it shows in his performance. There's nothing as personal as your voice. The singing is directly tied to your spirit, your psyche and your mind. All of the guys, who are on the road now, love being on the road. We love doing the shows, and it shows.'

The Palm Beach Post
July 7 1989

CHAPTER TWENTY-SEVEN

A LITTLE BIT MORE

Since leaving the band in 1983, Jim Yester had never fully left the music behind. Two years after his departure, having climbed the ladder of success of his new profession, the lure of performing and recording was calling him back with the occasional solo performance in some of the small clubs around Los Angeles. Then, in 1985, his brother Jerry got back together for a series of concerts with Chip Douglas, Henry Diltz and Cyrus Faryar, reforming the Modern Folk Quartet and even reuniting in the studio to record the delightful *Moonlight Serenade* album. However, shortly afterwards, Diltz was called away on business and had to fly back to the east coast for a prior commitment. With concert bookings still scheduled, and not wishing to cancel, Jerry asked Jim to stand in Henry's place for the shows, singing Henry's parts and playing guitar and keyboards. Happy to oblige Jim stepped back into the spotlight once more and became an honorary MFQ member for those shows. However, when Henry subsequently returned to the line-up, instead of thanking Jim and pushing him aside he was asked to remain in the band, becoming one of a five-part vocal unit in the process.

"Henry did his part and then I went either unison with Jerry or, occasionally, we put in a fifth part,' recalled Jim. "We had fun. But then a couple of guys moved back to Hawaii and it scattered again. Then Jerry moved to the islands and I also wound up moving there as well, so there were four of the five in Hawaii, so we started doing local gigs over there.

For about eight or nine months we worked around Hawaii as the MFQ." [21]

Setting up home for his family in Hilo, Hawaii near to where Jerry had recently built a new recording facility (prior to which Jerry had just cut his first 'solo' album: *Just Like The Big Time... Only Smaller*, featuring a number of supporting contributions from his elder brother), the brothers also formed a new act, combining with a local singer-songwriter named Rainbow Rastasan/Page, and naming themselves Rainbow Connection. Using computer technology to create synthesized dance instrumentation this newly formed trio developed a strong following around the islands over the following months, many of who were unaware as the musical legacy performing on the stage before them.

"We were mostly a performing group," states Jim, "although we also did a lot of TV shows in Hilo. Those were pretty good..."

However, such was the popularity and continuing demand for the MFQ, particularly in the Far East where they had always maintained a loyal following, that further tours for the quintet were put together, with the first one being undertaken in Japan during December of 1988.

With Jim remaining as vocalist and keyboard player, the band's sell-out appearance Tokyo's Club Quattro, held before an adoring audience during that December, was subsequently captured onto tape and featured on the Japanese issue *Live in Japan*, released on the small Pony Canyon label during 1989 (Pony Canyon-D22Y0319). A fascinating audio experience, starting off with a stunning rendition of "The Sun Is Like A Big Brass Band", segueing nicely into the joyous Michael Stewart composition "Sing Out", a song originally featured on the band's 1964 *Changes* LP, the new 21-track collection highlighted the dexterous versatility of the talented line-up with Jim even stepping into the solo spotlight for a rendition of "Never My Love". Featured within a four-track medley of hit '60s songs that the individual band members had participated in, the tune blends nicely into the following renderings of "Happy Together", "Daydream" and "Daydream Believer". His high tenor also features prominently on a number of the *a cappella* highlights, scattered throughout the 2-disc set.

The following year, 1990, saw the five-man MFQ release a brand new studio album, an impressive 12-track affair titled *Bamboo Saloon*. Again only issued in the Far East (Pony Canyon PCCY-00061) Jim was once more a significant contributor to the album, overseeing the mixing for a number of the tracks as well as supplying keyboards, harmonica and the distinctive tenor voice for much of the recording. With familiar sounding songs such as "Walk Away Renée" and "Across The Persian Gulf" featured within the selection, along with the joyous performance on Jerry's "Whatever Happened To The Lovin' Spoonful", the collection also featured two significant songwriting credits, firstly with the Yester brothers joint collaboration on "She's A Dancer", an enchanting ballad featuring Jerry's lead vocals backed by the sumptuous harmonies of the band and an exquisite musical arrangement. This was, in fact, as Jim would point out during a 1992 interview, the first song the brothers had written together for over thirty years. Secondly, and of particular interest, was the mesmerizing title track, the impressive six-minute "Bamboo Saloon", featuring the co-songwriting credits of Jules Alexander and Steven Carey amongst a series of harmonies that equals anything the more illustrious career of Messrs. Crosby, Stills and Nash could offer at the time.

"I brought that song to them," says Jules today. "That was written by Steven and myself and we were all still fairly close at that time."

The year would close out with, firstly, a one-off CD single for the Japanese market, "Together To Tomorrow", released to aid a Japanese school for the blind, followed by the third album to feature both brothers in the same line-up: *MFQ Christmas*, a collection of traditional seasonal numbers, arranged in pure MFQ fashion with a dense layering of vocals, banjos and *a cappella* harmonies. It would indeed bring joy to the world… or at least to the Japanese audience that it was once more exclusively released for (PCCY-00165).

There would be one more release on the Pony Canyon label featuring the five-man MFQ line-up. *Wolfgang*, the 1991 issue (PCCY-00284), was an interesting concept from the get-go. With the original idea coming from their Japanese record label, the thought was that, with the two-hundredth anniversary of his passing coming up, the band would get together at Jerry's studio in Keaau, Hawaii and create a series of new works based on the music of Wolfgang Amadeus Mozart, with the band's own lyrics and arrangements, plus additional contributions from Jerry's close friend Larry Beckett, accompanying Mozart's melodies.

"The 'Wolfgang' album wasn't our idea," confirmed Jim, "but the material was selected by Jerry and Chip."

It was a fascinating concept and one that, perhaps on paper, bordered on the surreal and ridiculous, but it worked in so many ways as the band's complicated harmony lines wove throughout the interchanging layers of the original Mozart melodies. And with Jim's vocal range shining through on songs such as "Across The Universe" and "Love In Return" it remains a sad story that this succession of Japanese-only releases never reached the wider market they deserved. It must have been a truly rewarding experience for all concerned to be involved in such a creative collection of releases, without a hint of nostalgia in sight…

"They treated me like one of their own," reflects Jim today, when reminiscing over his time in the band. "They couldn't have been better. They had their own group dynamics that they dealt with, they had been together since '63 and there is a lot of history there, but that was a special time in Hawaii. We then did two tours of Japan, in 1988 and 1990, and a lot of recording. I was always a big fan of theirs, so it was a delight to be with them. Enormous talents in a lot of different directions…"

Then, in 1991 another opportunity came knocking at the Yester door when factions of The Lovin' Spoonful saw an opportunity to reunite in the aftermath of a heavy and lengthy financial battle that they had been fighting for many years.

"I didn't leave the MFQ as such," he continues, "but they kind of stopped working, soon after the '90 tour of Japan (and the *Wolfgang* sessions). Henry went home to L.A., and Jerry wound up moving back to the mainland, to Portland in Oregon. I stayed in Hawaii and was working a bit at the studio that the group built, doing small projects for local people. Then, in 1991 I got a call from Jerry saying that the Spoonful's case against Kama Sutra Records had been settled and Joe and Steve wanted to put the band back together. Zally (Yanovsky) hated the music business by that time, and had a successful restaurant in Toronto, and John had pretty well lost his voice and was playing househusband in the Catskills, and passed. So, would I be interested in joining?"

Finally free from royalty restraints, drummer Joe Butler and bass player Steve Boone, having failed to lure back the band's principal singer-songwriter John Sebastian, or former guitarist Zal Yanovsky, turned to Zal's original replacement in the band, Jerry Yester, to join up with them once again. This, in turn, led to an offer going out to Jim to make up the quartet, standing in Sebastian's boots for the proposed reunion tour.

They're back and they're hot!

Pollstar Trade Magazine: 1991

With tentative rehearsals for the revived Spoonful taking place during early October of that year the initial hope was that they could once again rekindle the magic of their mid-'60s successes.

Jim: "You always hope for that. At the time there was a great deal of work to be done just getting the show together. Bringing Joe up front and off of the drums made a huge difference, but it also brought about more work to be done, what with a new drummer, what to exactly *do* with Joe upfront, with no drum sticks in his hands! He had to have an Octa-Pad at first so he could do some percussion things but he eventually let go of it, and just occasionally used the autoharp. It was great. I got to do 'Darling Be Home Soon' and 'Nashville Cats' and I had a guitar controller that my brother programmed, that went to a voice apparatus, so I had all the car horns and French horns and stuff. Good, good time. And those guys are family. We've always remained close. It was lots of fun, and great music!"

With Jim taking on rhythm guitar and supporting vocals, and holding the center stage spotlight on such timeless classics as the aforementioned "Nashville Cats" and "Darling Be Home Soon", The Association's "Along Comes Mary", and the light-hearted interlude of "The Circus Song" (written by the New York-born singer-poet John Henry Raskin, accompanied by Annie O'Brien), the show was given a positive reception upon its debut in Ontario, Canada, followed shortly afterwards by a brief European visit for a New Years Eve TV Special, held in Athens, Greece (sadly hindered by an embarrassing mid-set technical hitch). Mixing in hits such as "You Didn't Have To Be So Nice", "Daydream" and "Summer In The City" alongside new band compositions, including contributions from Jerry's youngest daughter Lena, the band made its U.S. debut on March 1992 in Boca Raton, Florida at the city's annual spring festival but, unfortunately, it was never going to be more than a nostalgia trip for many, despite the promise of some potential new recordings. Sadly, such hope never came to pass and before long it was all-too clear that the new Spoonful were struggling to hold an audience's interest. Joe Butler, the new front man, was simply not used to the role and his onstage patter often went above the heads of their new audience.

A brief 16-date 1992 U.S. summer tour showed the media starting to build against the band, with some criticizing their 'bogus, sans Sebastian' stature although, as a counter balance, some were eager to praise their polished approach, something that the original band were often accused of lacking.

"Towards the end of 1992 they asked me to relocate to the mainland, as they were having to fly me in and out of Hawaii, so I wound up, during a break between gigs, going down to Arkansas to visit a dear friend from Hawaii who had moved there. I was there three days and bought a house with a handshake for $25,000. I wound up having to get an advance from the group to move my then girlfriend and her two teenage boys from Hawaii to Arkansas. This at the time didn't seem like a problem as there were a series of concerts coming up but then Steve called one day and said all those were cancelled, and there was no work for several months. So here I was in a financially depressed area, with no work and a family of four to provide for! I registered with a temp agency and was working for $5.00 an hour, loading and unloading semi trucks, digging ditches for restaurant construction, working at a Christian CD distribution center, repackaging CDs, running a wood lathe for a furniture factory making table legs… Needless to say, things were a bit tight!"

Fortunately, yet another opportunity soon came his way:

"About that time David Somerville, the founder and lead singer of the Diamonds, called and asked what I was doing. I told him I was with The Spoonful, but was in bad financial shape. He said 'come sing with us', and I asked 'who is us'?"

'Us' transpired to be the legendary Four Preps harmony group, hitmakers and recording artists since the late '50s, and best remembered for such popular million-selling songs as "Big Man", "26 Miles" and "Down By The Station". The quartet had recently reformed under the guiding light of original group members Bruce Belland and Ed Cobb, along with longtime member Somerville (who had known the members of The Association since sharing the billing with them at the Ice House in Glendale), and with Jim Pike, formerly of The Letterman, making up the foursome. However, the band now wanted to replace Jim Pike with Jim Yester.

"They sent me a ticket to Texas to watch one of their shows, unbeknownst to Jim Pike who I would be replacing. It was a killer show, but I went through about two weeks of terrible angst, trying to make a decision. I finally talked to my brother Jerry and he advised me that it should be an easy decision. 'It's work!'

"They sent me tapes so I could learn the material, and I went out to L.A. to help re-record their selection, replacing Jim Pike's voice with mine, and arranging and putting the Association's songs in instead of The Lettermen's, and away we went!

"That was just a new thing for me, singing without my guitar! It took me a while to get used to it, but it was cool..."

Decked out nightly in smart tuxedo and polished brogues, Jim contributed to the impressive harmony stack as the group took to the easy-listening road as the 'New Four Preps', a sell-out journey that would continue on for a further fourteen years under various guises. Accompanied by five musicians at each venue, and the occasional taped orchestral element as accompaniment, the repertoire was made up of various medleys from the members numerous chart hits, alongside popular songs of the day made famous by the likes of Elton John, Mariah Carey and Chicago.

"The oldies stations, bless their hearts, keep this stuff alive," David Somerville was to comment. "Although a lot of children now hear this music."

Jim: "We were doing almost exclusively corporate dates, with the occasional exception, like a month at The Outrigger in Waikiki filling in for The Society of Seven. That was a great gig. We did that one twice!"

The re-recordings that Jim referred to subsequently appeared on the 1993 CD release *Better Than Ever: Three Golden Groups in One* (FPD-2626), an adaption of an earlier 1991 issue, recorded with Jim Pike in the line-up. Credited simply to The Four Preps the eleven-track selection, comprising mostly of the extended stage medleys, containing both old and new songs, was a mixed, if polished affair. The old songs were still a joy to hear, with the classic 1950s and '60s sounds of "Big Man", "Why Do Fools Fall In Love", "Little Darlin'", "Silhouettes" and a gathering of five Association tunes ("Cherish", "Never My Love", "Windy", "Along Comes Mary" and "Everything That Touches You") combining well together, whilst the newer compositions such as "In The Air Tonight", "Glory Of Love" and "Hard Habit To Break" all sounded uncomfortable amidst such a nostalgic mixture of easy-on-the-ear harmonies. Sold via a limited distribution the release swiftly disappeared. Meanwhile, a second gathering of songs was also collected onto disc that same year, compiled exclusively for the month long residency at The Outrigger venue in Waikiki.

"We called that one WEBE50!" Jim laughs. "It's a play on UB40! Ed Cobb wanted us to be incognito on that second release. No names, no pictures. It was made expressly for Hawaii where we were going to play for a month and he thought we might do better sales if people didn't know who it was. A strange experiment!"

That second set was, perhaps, a stronger representation of the quartet, containing a selection of straightforward recordings with just one extended medley included ("Rhapsody In Blue Jeans"), although it was still the classic compositions from days gone by that benefited most from the four-piece harmonic treatment with a lively doo-wop rendition of the 1962 Bert Berns composition, "Tell Him" (a hit for The Exciters), coming out best.

Meanwhile, Jim's former partners Larry Ramos and Russ Giguere were still to be found driving The Association bandwagon around the country, appearing at venues still crowded by an over 50s audience with copies of *Insight Out* and *The Association's Greatest Hits* safely stored on their hi-fi shelving. The hits were never going to go away and yet, to their credit, the group continued to look towards the future and by the mid-1990s the five/six-man band, still consisting of Larry and Russ, ably accompanied by Bruce Pictor, Paul Holland and Donnie Gougeon, with Bob Werner still aiding the onstage sound and Del Ramos harmonizing from behind the mixing board were pulling together material for a series of new recordings, albeit one that they had been promising for the previous six or seven years.

During 1994, they participated in the unsuccessful launch of a new theme theater, SierraLand, located in Oakhurst, CA. where a reunion of many of the original New Christy Minstrels took place, and Larry brought along the current Association touring band, including Russ, along with his brother Del and their banjo-playing cousin Miles, to participate in the venture. The enterprise, created and financed by the reunited Minstrels themselves, proved to be a popular draw amongst the local community for a period, but it failed to reap success in financial terms, with many investors losing heavily, and the vision was short lived. A somewhat belated, limited edition CD issue of the reunion, *A Gathering of Minstrels* (Bearmark Music), appeared during 2006, featuring Larry and the band, most notably on the popular "Rocky Top", a lively Felice and Boudleaux Bryant bluegrass composition that saw the reunited Homegrown trio in full flow.

Nevertheless, the following year was to see a full Association recording project finally come to fruition with the release of *The Association: A*

Little Bit More, issued on compact disc via Track Records (OTD-1001-2). Unfortunately, and despite the unified longevity of the current touring band, the eventual release wasn't a group effort as such, with the instrumentation performed by a trio of New York-based session players; George Small on keyboards and the dominating synths, Allan Schwartzberg, the former drummer for Mountain, providing all of the percussion, and Steely Dan, Billy Joel, Paul Simon, Hall & Oates (and countless others) sideman Hugh McCracken supplying the guitars. With all decisions and production duties overseen by Stan Vincent and John Allen Orofino, the former having worked alongside McCracken and Small during the 1980 sessions for John Lennon's ill-fated *Double Fantasy* comeback album, the recordings were initially cut in New York's On Track Studios before the tapes were shipped out west, whereupon the band cut their vocals at the Rusk Sound Studios on North La Brea Avenue in Los Angeles.

"Everyone was involved," comments Bruce Pictor, "Larry, Russ, Del, Paul Holland and myself. I sang baritone, tenor and some bass on every song and, in fact, I sang multiple harmonies in both registers, overdubbing several parts. Donnie Gougeon even lent a part on one song…

"All the instrumental tracks were cut in New York, but I did however, think of a great idea, or so I thought, for putting a 'round', a cyclical, or repeating pattern of music or vocals, at the end of 'How Much Love'. When I approached Stan and sang it to him, he said it was a great idea! When I asked him if he was going to use it, he simply said 'No!' That was a valuable, interesting and informative experience. If it doesn't come directly from the producer, it's likely not going to be used. Intellectual property I believe…"

This new eleven-song collection, comprising of many new additions to the band's catalog, kicked off with yet another version of "Walk Away Renée", albeit one that maintains a similar arrangement to their earlier 1983 rendition. Another licensing issue one assumes. This was then sweetly followed by the title track to the album, "A Little Bit More", a Bobby Gosh composition widely recognized courtesy of the 1976 Top 10 hit by Dr. Hook. With the lead vocals dominated by Larry Ramos, leaving Russ with barely a recognizable moment in the spotlight, the overall sound of the mix is unbearably synthesized and unnecessarily bland to a degree, offering only a hint of the vocal spark that ignited so many a heartstring throughout the previous three decades. It's all very pleasant, but…

The Randy Sharp contribution "Could It Be Love", featuring Rick DePofi on saxophone, was a re-recorded hangover from the 1980s SunWest sessions and it stands as one of the few highlights on the resulting album, alongside the band's melancholy interpretation of Eden Ahbez's "Nature Boy" (a 1948 hit for Nat 'King' Cole). Likewise, "Learn How To Land", the one noticeable moment for Russ to share the lead, had also been a factor during the 1980s reunion, appearing during the resulting tour set-list, whilst "I Wanna Be Your Radio" came about as a result of Russ's friendship with songwriter Bill Martin. Sadly however, there are no songwriting contributions from the leading duo themselves, new or old, with the remainder of the collection being made up of various agreeable, but non-descript tunes such as Stephen Geyer's "How Much Love", Daniel Moore's "Dreamland", Christopher Max's "If It Take Me Forever" (co-written with London McDaniels and Phil Roy) and an emphatic piano-driven power ballad entitled "The One". Rounding out the set, perhaps limiting its all-year round appeal, was the (acceptably delightful) seasonal Christmas tune, brought into the sessions by studio session player George Small. This one inclusion even had the potential to appeal to a wider Christmas market... were it not misplaced mid-way through such a benign collection of recordings. Even the actual packaging of the CD release, undertaken by New York-based designer Christine Heun, was somewhat lacking in inspirational content and, bar the acknowledgment of the current members as the 'official' Association line-up (notably including Del but omitting Bob Werner), accompanied by a cartoon line drawing of the sextet, the release had very little substance to offer, and the limited distribution of such a small record label only added to the lack of any subsequent success.

Drawing off the album as a promotional tool, the label issued the updated-update of "Walk Away Renée" as a CD-single release but, without significant publicity or promotion, it was to little avail and, with their recording career seemingly sliding silently to a close, the group gradually began to slip away from the limelight. There was talk briefly of a successor to the album, with the band reportedly in discussion with Dick Clark's newly formed Click Records label, with a view to a further series of recordings and releases, but the label then lost its distribution deal with Sony/Columbia and negotiations broke down over the choice of material.

In 1997 the focus was briefly placed upon the younger of the Ramos' brothers when Del was featured in a U.K.-made television documentary, *Daydream Believers*, made by Principle Films for the Channel 4 TV station.

Appearing alongside L.A. disc jockey Rodney Bingenheimer and former Love guitarist Bryan MacLean, Del was filmed and interviewed about his involvement and his subsequent life since unsuccessfully auditioning for *The Monkees* TV series back in 1965. Highlighting his love of playing pool, a characteristic he inherited from his father, and working part-time in a local billiards store, Del was also shown operating the soundboard and adding background vocals for The Association as they performed a relatively low-key gig, out on a pontoon at the Lido Isle Yacht Club in Newport Beach. It was nice to see him getting recognition for his contribution to the band after so many years out front of house. Then, two years later, having spent almost three decades working for the band in one capacity or another, Del officially stepped onto the stage as a verified member, taking up the bass role when Paul Holland, himself a member for almost twelve years, stepped away to concentrate on his own business plans. It would be a further few years before Del became a stage regular as, shortly afterwards, a further change of personnel saw Bob Werner consolidate his position in the line-up as bass and rhythm guitarist, with Del only appearing alongside his brother as and when needed, but by the middle of the following decade his appearance onstage was assured in the band.

Donnie Gougeon had also departed the group towards the latter part of the 1990s, although he would periodically assist during future performances, and in his place had stepped a young man with a particular pedigree and loyalty towards the band name.

Born on June 17th 1961 Jordan Cole was the eldest son born to Brian and Vicki Cole and by the middle of the swinging sixties he was living in the center of the Hollywood community in a small fourplex along Western Avenue with his parents and his younger brother. However, as his teenage years were approaching Jordan was finding schooling particularly difficult and, just prior to his father's tragic passing, he found himself back in Oregon, placed into a residential care home, having to deal with his personal issues. As he was to relate to Marti Smiley Childs and Jeff March during 2011: "No-one could reach me. I was cutting myself off from the world. I wouldn't do the work. What I remember is that everyone was out to get me. There were real problem children there. Basically, what they taught me was that no matter whose fault it is; when it's on your lap it's now your problem. Deal with it and just move on."[1]

Having returned to school he dropped out in his senior year, attended an engineering college in Phoenix, Arizona and began to discover a deep passion for music, following in his famed fathers footsteps. Teaching himself various instruments, all of which he soon became extremely competent on – keyboards, guitar, drums and saxophone – he finally quit study completely and found his way back home, to his birth city of Portland, and by 1982 was playing in his first rock band; Kordrah ('*hard rock*' *backwards*). The subsequent years would see him earning a living with various assorted groups and line-ups, including a stint playing the Top 40 hits with a traveling show band, touring Japan and numerous U.S. forces bases.

"I would do the Top 40 thing and tour until I had enough money to start an original band and try to get some airplay. I've always had ideas for songs. I can't shut my head off at night when I need to sleep" he says. [1]

However, ever keen to learn more about his father of whom, sadly, he got to know very little about during his early life, in 1998 he contacted his father's former band mates to see what further detail he could uncover.

"I had always longed to know my dad. He's a big hole in my life; somebody I thought was so cool and never got a chance to know. I would listen to the live record and look at the silent film footage we have of him, and it was not anything other than getting a hold of some of the original members and I really, really wanted them to just tell me more about my dad. [11]

"I had gotten ahold of Jules first and he told me that Larry now lived in Idaho, so I called him next. After a few chats Larry asked if I played at all and I said 'yes'. He asked me for a tape and so I sent him one with ten or twelve songs that I had written and sung on. After hearing it, Larry asked what part I was playing and I told him I was actually playing all of the instruments, so about a month later he called again and asked if I'd be willing to play bass on an upcoming show for them. No one ever gave me music or showed me specific parts; I just knew the material that well. I knew all the parts by heart having grown up on them all. I borrowed a Dean bass and flew out to Miami and met the band in the lobby on the way to the airport before we flew on to Jamaica to board a cruise ship. It was actually the first time since I was a child I had seen any of them.

"The show was on board the ship and on gig day I showed up to rehearsal and we were a five piece: me, Larry, Russ, Bruce and Donnie the pianist. Paul Holland was the bass player at that time and I was sitting in for him on this occasion. There was also an eight-piece orchestra. They handed us sheet music, as we were to play the cruise ships opening theme ourselves, and I could read music at the time but very slowly, however it didn't take me long to figure out it was actually the David Letterman theme! I knew that one pretty well! So here I am teaching Donnie the chords as if I'm an expert reader."

Subsequently, during the closing month of 1998, Jordan Cole officially stepped in to his father's role for a temporary slot as an Association member during the winter Caribbean Cruise. Then, when Donnie Gougeon announced his departure for family reasons shortly afterwards, Jordan was invited back on a permanent basis, this time filling in on keyboards and vocals.

Larry Ramos, upon greeting his former partner's son into the band on a full-time basis, was genuinely enthusiastic about his appointment, but reportedly spent time warning him off following in his father's footsteps, and not wasting the inordinate potential he had at his beckoning.

"I don't recall his exact quote," confirms Jordan. "But early in my tenure in the band he certainly said words to that effect."

Vicki Cole, Jordan's mother, also commented when it was announced that he was stepping into her former husband's shoes: "Brian had a fantastic sense of humor but not everyone got his jokes. He was a little cerebral for many people. Jordan is quite like him in many ways. When Jordan first joined the Association, other musicians who knew Brian remarked about the similarities in their personalities."

Having maintained a friendship since the mid-1980s sessions for the Hitbound Records label Larry Ramos and Jeffrey Foskett reunited in the studio during the year 2000, with Larry contributing backing vocals to "I Can't Let Go", a cover of the Evie Sands 45 from 1965, also given the Top 10 treatment by The Hollies the following year. The song appeared on Foskett's own album; *Jeffrey Foskett IV: Twelve and Twelve*, issued on the New Surf Limited label. The duo then set about working on a series of other recordings, the result of which was the 3-track 2002 CD EP *Never My Love/'A' Ole La Ku'ulei*, featuring a remake of The Association's 1967 hit, sung in Larry's native Hawaiian language (with translation credited to acclaimed Hawaiian performer and producer Tony Conjugacion) and initially released exclusively for the Hawaiian market.

The tune, on a three-song CD released by Tom Moffatt's Paradise Productions label, features Ramos on lead vocals as well as guitars and ukulele. Conjugacion provided the Hawaiian lyrics expressly for Ramos and the island spin should become a quick favorite on radio's play lists and, presumably, at record shops.

Moffatt said the release would initially be marketed in Hawaii, with eventual expansion to cities on the Mainland.

The Honolulu Advertiser
July 14 2002

With additional steel guitar embellishment from Gary Brandin this updated version of the Addrisi brothers composition maintained the musical and vocal arrangements from the original recording but, despite the addition of Foskett's multi-tracked sweet harmonies, lacked much of the original spark. Nevertheless, paired with "God Loves Laughter", a song Larry had composed alongside Damon Leigh two decades previously, and a Foskett rendition of the popular Hawaiian flavored "Honolulu City Lights", composed by Keola Beamer, the CD single received a favorable response amongst the local Hawaiian media.

Then, in 2003, Larry, along with Russ, Jordan, Del, Bruce and Bob, reunited with another familiar group of friends, some of whom they hadn't appeared onstage with for almost twenty years.

Founded in 1998 the Vocal Group Hall of Fame was organized by Tony Butalla, an original member of the popular close-harmony trio The Lettermen, to honor outstanding vocal groups throughout the preceding years. Located in Butalla's hometown of Sharon, Pennsylvania, a somewhat backwoods location for such an awarding body, as opposed to the more visible and higher profile position for The Rock & Roll Hall of Fame, situated in Cleveland, the Vocal Group museum was still seen by many as a prestigious honor and with such acclaimed names as The Beach Boys, Crosby Stills & Nash, The Platters, The Four Seasons, The 5th Dimension, The Ink Spots and Peter, Paul & Mary having been inducted in recent years (amongst many others) it was only a matter of time before the dense, intricate harmony lines of The Association were duly acknowledged within the theater walls. On September 17th 2003 all of the surviving members of the original band came back together to accept their induction, place their hand and footprints into the awaiting tablets of wet cement for posterity, and perform before an appreciative audience at the annual ceremony, held at the Cafaro Field in Niles, Ohio.

Jordan later recalled: "Before the show started, and during rehearsal, I'm looking at the guys onstage, saying 'wow!' this should be really cool! And when the guys started performing, I went right into performance mode and I totally forgot that I'm up there with Terry Kirkman, who wrote 'Cherish', (but) I was watching the thrill on his face and I knew exactly where he was coming from…"

With a ten-voice chorus of all the members onstage – Jules, Terry, Jim, Russ, Larry, Ted, Del, Jordan, Bruce and Bob – the band, dressed in their white matching jackets, launched into an enthusiastic live rendition of "Along Comes Mary", followed by a brief chorus of "Windy" before they took their bows, waving to a cheering crowd as they left the spotlight, returning later to participate in the closing chorale of "America The Beautiful" (with Jules actively snapping away on his camera during the opening bars). Rejuvenated by the warm response and overdue acceptance within the industry the briefly reunited band appeared once more together, the following year, when they appeared onstage for the televised PBS *My Music* series; *The '60s Rock Experience*, taped on December 9th 2004 at the Dover Downs Showroom in Delaware. Appearing alongside Roger McGuinn (representing The Byrds), Chuck Negron (Three Dog Night), Eric Burdon (The Animals), John Kay (Steppenwolf), Robb Grill (The Grass Roots) and Scott McKenzie, The Association once again turned in a fine performance of "Along Comes Mary", paired this time with a smooth "Never My Love" and despite the graceful aging process that was clearly catching up with a number of the band members, all of whom were now in their sixties, their love of the music, and for each other, was all too apparent. With greying, thinning slicked back hair and expanding waistlines all too evident, and individual voices perhaps betraying the strength and depth of former years, the harmonious blending of all the members as one could still stir the heart and soul. Sadly, this 2004 appearance this would prove to be the final reunion to date of all surviving members.

CHAPTER TWENTY-EIGHT

JUST THE RIGHT SOUND

For Ted Bluechel, now bringing up and supporting his family in the temperate climate of Ventura County, California, music had gradually drifted back into his life in the ensuing years, following his departure from The Association back in 1984. Recent years had seen him venture back onstage, performing as a part of a local trio, Sweet & Dandy, and even returning to the arena with his former band, playing a one-off concert with The Association (as was Jules Alexander) during late 2001 when he sat in for an absent Bruce Pictor behind the drums. He had also taken to striking out alone, playing solo sets in small clubs and coffeehouses around Santa Barbara, Ventura and Thousand Oaks, and singing old Association material alongside a mixture of Caribbean-flavored songs, with a few self-compositions thrown in. It was far less stressful than a seemingly endless life on the road, and it allowed him that precious time to be at home every night with his wife and their son and, despite the overwhelming reception given to The Association at the two recent reunion shows, he had no desire to return to the business full-time. His privacy clearly meant too much to him, eschewing all requests for nostalgic interviews and barely tolerable of modern technology and the increasing demand for social media.

Meanwhile, The Association's music catalog continued to be reassessed, reappraised and, ultimately, repackaged for a newer generation; the clean, crisp, remastered audio reproduction of a digitized compact disc bringing out the splendor of the harmonies once again to an audience, all-too

401

familiar with the snap, crackle and pop of a twenty-five year old slab of black vinyl.

Following the positive reception to a 51-track deluxe 2-CD overview of the band's collective career, *Just The Right Sound*, compiled in 2002 by the reissue specialists Rhino Entertainment in liaison with Warner Bros., and featuring a host of deep album cuts and rarities alongside the familiar hits (note: a 52-track European edition featured a slightly alternate track listing), the bulk of the band's original 1960s and 1970s albums began reappearing onto compact disc courtesy of the Collectors' Choice label, and all to a healthy reception. No longer viewed by the music buying market as a throwaway sunshine-pop band, a fate that they had wavering towards for the past decade of revival tours, the reappearance of such overlooked products as the 1966 *Renaissance* album, *The Association* and *Stop Your Motor* made it abundantly clear to the inquisitive as to how deep the talent pool went within the ranks of the band. For every "Along Comes Mary" or "Cherish", there was a "Come To Me" or "Memories Of You". For every "Windy" there was a "Sometime". For every "Everything That Touches You" there was a "Toymaker" or maybe a "Silver Morning". Unfortunately, the group's final release drew short shrift in the reissue stakes, with *Waterbeds In Trinidad!* receiving a somewhat belated 2006 reappraisal, courtesy of Sony/Japan and the U.K.'s Rev-Ola album.

2005 saw the first official DVD release of the band, issued as a part of the *Pop Legends Live!* series by SRO Entertainment; a sixty-minute recording of the current touring band with Paul Holland back in the line-up for the show, smoothing out the vocal depth and adding additional rhythm guitar alongside Larry, Russ, Jordan, Bruce and Bob. Del was, by now, also performing as an official stage member.

"Paul came back to help with the vocals on that gig," recalls Jordan Cole. "I had to sing top tenor parts for the first ten years I was in the band, and I'm not a tenor!"

Interspersed with short interviews with the two principal members, recalling events of the past 40 years, the twelve song selection encompassed the obvious hits from the early days, including their debut offering for Valiant, "One Too Many Mornings", and more recent contributions such as "Years Of Trying" and "Walk Away Renée". With tight harmonies right from the opening number, "Just About The Same", the current touring band remained one-hundred percent faithful to the original arrangements, bar the substitution of Jordan's keyboards for Terry's recorder solos, and they all turned in a polished performance for the cameras, even if there were only two performers onstage who could justly regard themselves as hit-making members. Maybe the lead vocals didn't always hit the high benchmark set in previous years, but the silky smooth ballads, with Russ highlighted on "No Fair At All" and a seven-voice chorale on "Cherish", remained particularly notable for their overall production and sound. Closing with the co-leads on "Along Comes Mary" from Bob Werner, Jordan Cole and Paul Holland the audience were clearly having a blast, up on their feet and dancing as the song brought the show to a close, with frenzied applause and cheers ringing out, prompting Russ and Larry to once again venture into the closing high-kick routine to the sounds of "Windy". To some it may only have seemed a mere representation of original The Association sound, and the absence of Terry Kirkman, Jules Alexander, Ted Bluechel and Jim Yester may have made the release negligible to many of the faithful, whilst to others it was that journey back once again to the former era of innocence. It was always in the music…

Between 2005 and 2010 there was a certain amount of fluidity to the touring party as band members came and went, and a 2006 collaboration in the recording studio with the maestro of easy-listening, Barry Manilow, would hardly ease the troubled minds of the loyal follower. At Barry's personal request, having called Russ to ask if the band would care to participate, the partnership produced a polished medley of "Cherish" and "Windy", a combination that jumped uneasily between the re-arranged tempos, and which subsequently appeared on Manilow's 2006 best-selling offering *The Greatest Songs Of The Sixties*, a surprise Top 3 hit on the U.S. *Billboard* charts during the festive season that year.

However, the latter part of the decade wasn't always the smoothest of rides for some of the group, and during 2007 Del was struck down with colon cancer, leaving him unable to tour for a seven-month period whilst he successfully recuperated. With a visit to the Philippines on the schedule a friend of the band from the 1960s, former Hearts & Flowers and Dillard & Clark sideman David Jackson filled in on bass guitar for the duration. Two years later and Del was cruelly hit hard again when he tragically lost his wife, Garlena, shortly before her 50th birthday. Then, when Bob Werner became unavailable for a period, the familiar image of Jim Yester appeared up on the stage, adding an instantly recognizable voice to the mix. It wouldn't be long before this, once again, became a permanent arrangement.

"It's all part of the game," Jim was to comment during an interview with Russ Karr from the online *Swerve* magazine, during 2013. "It was difficult, with the comings and goings because you lose different parts or arrangements when someone leaves the group.

"A few years ago, our drummer Bruce had to depart for a back operation, and a drummer I worked with in the past (whilst with The New Four Preps), Blair Anderson, joined the group. He is fantastic on arrangements and he knew the music and was a huge fan. He helped us straighten the parts back out again. We did that sitting on a back porch of a motel in Northern Michigan. Just us and an acoustic guitar. He had all of the notes written down."

However, despite Bruce Pictor coming back to line-up after his 2008 surgery, no one could take for granted their position in the band, as Jordan himself became all-too aware, despite his history with the group:

"At one point I was given a months notice, and I was only told at my supposed very last gig that I'm not being fired after all! It was much later that I found out it was for having too much energy and upstaging certain members of the band!"

Since Jim had joined up with The New Four Preps during early 1993 he had been kept fairly busy with his schedule. The quartet was proving to be a popular attraction on the corporate circuit and performances in the popular tourist and business resorts kept the act in high demand. In addition to his role within the quartet Jim had also formed a relationship, both professionally and personally, with another performer, a phenomenally talented concert pianist who was affectionately known as the 'Piano Princess'.

"The New Four Preps came to Atlantic City to play at the Taj Mahal casino for a month," he says. "And the third night there, I met a gal who was performing in one of the lounges. She was a piano entertainer, not just musical but she had a show as well. She had been a protégée of Liberace when she was a teenager, and really went to school on him. I started going to her shows, she came to ours and we wound up getting involved. When the gig was over, everybody else went home, and I stayed! We wound up living together…"

Linda Gentille, a native of California, had built up a reputation not only for her outstanding virtuosity on the keyboard but also for the all round entertainment she provided during her spectacular tours and shows around the world. At the time of their meeting Gentille was effectively handling her own business affairs but, after rejecting Jim's suggestion that a former agent for The Association represent her, she indicated that Jim himself should represent and manage her, an offer that he duly accepted. At first, he was content in remaining in the background, dividing his time between commitments with The New Four Preps and managing Linda's business affairs but, eventually, and at Linda's prompting, he began to step on stage behind her, somewhat reluctantly at first.

"I got brave enough!" Jim laughs. "She said, 'you're here every night anyway, so would you mind coming up and singing?'"

As the occasional appearance began developing into a regular nightly performance Jim's confidence grew, often providing both guitar and bass to the act. The duo even began working a musicals theme into their set, including a tribute to *Phantom Of The Opera*, whereupon Jim would don the musical character's signature mask whilst singing alongside Linda's piano.

"It has expanded my repertoire and improved my voice," he went on to say. "I think I sing better now than I ever did."

A beloved entertainer in China, now recognized as having performed more shows in the vastly populated country than any other western entertainer, 1997 saw Linda perform one of many Piano Concert Tours of the Far Eastern state, with Jim traveling alongside and performing on stage with her. He also joined up as a part of her 'Get High On Music, Not Drugs' school assembly program, performing numerous concerts across the country to the younger generation, promoting the message of music, health and well-being. The following year saw the duo commence work on *Touches Of Love*, a collection released on the RKO Records label during 1999, credited to Jim Yester, with Linda Genteel [sic], The 'Piano Princess', initially comprising of nine delicate yet sparse piano/vocal interpretations of some of the duo's favored cover versions.

> I did not choose the particular love songs for this recording. These are the songs most requested of us, over a period of time, by the clientele of the Taj Princess Lounge. It is for them, their support, their touches of love and affection that we have done this project.
>
> Jim Yester. 1999
> *Touches Of Love* sleeve notes

The requested song selection included renditions "Lady In Red", "Hello", "Memory", "Love Is A Many Splendored Thing" and "Music Of The Night", along with two additional, fully arranged band productions of "Never My Love" and "Cherish", heavy with backing vocals.

"Those two tracks were not on the original selection", says Jim. "I recall I did a video shoot for RKO, whereupon Ron Dante did the tracks and the backing vocals for 'Cherish' and 'Never My Love', and I just sang the leads. There were a whole slew of retro artists included; Lenny Welch did a shoot the same day. I got a couple of grand and a promise of royalties, but I guess RKO added those two tracks to the CD. Linda and I sold the original collection at concerts but it is possible that we gave it RKO to market and they added those tracks so they would get more money..."

Interestingly, Dante, an acclaimed session singer (and the original lead vocalist on the 1969 million-selling hit for The Archies; "Sugar Sugar") used the same backing tracks, but added his own lead vocal when issuing the two songs on his own album, *Favorites*, released on the RKO label during 1999, whilst Jim's versions also ended up on the multi-disc RKO *Rock 'n' Roll Legends Live* CD series that same year. There is no record of how the video was utilized...

Combining his partnership with Linda, Jim also maintained his calendar as an occasional solo performer and a member of The New Four Preps, although September 1999 saw the sad passing of founding member Ed Cobb, following a short battle with leukemia. Nevertheless, despite the loss of such a key member of the quartet the remaining trio continued on with their performances, renaming their act Yester, Belland & Somerfield (later YB&S, Triple Gold and finally The Three Tenors of Pop) – and reissuing their two albums, repackaged and rebranded. *Better Than Ever: Three Golden Groups in One* was repackaged simply as *YB&S* (YB&S26-2), whilst *WEBE50* became known as *Triple Gold* (YB&S52-2), later reissued on the Snailworx label as *Triple Gold: The Original Lead Singers of The Association, The Four Preps & The Diamonds* (SN-02040).

1999 also saw Jim reunite with Terry Kirkman at a country music songwriting seminar, held in Paramus, New Jersey, with the duo formally invited by music publisher Dan Maxcy to participate as judges on the panel. In addition, they also performed a brief set for the attendees that day. Then, the following evening they moved on up to the Sugar Loaf Performing Arts Center in Chester, New York, where, supported by a country rock band by the name of Circles End, they made a second appearance together, performing a full show for a rapturous audience.

"There were two concerts put together," recalls Jim. "It was started by Dan Maxcy, now sadly deceased, who put together a back-up band for us that learned the charts and most of the background vocals. The first was, indeed, for a songwriters showcase in Paramus, at which Terry and I were to act as judges for the songwriters, as well as perform for the general audience. The following day we went to Sugar Loaf, which was a performance theater, and this was just a concert appearance which actually went quite well and was well received. We did all the major hits as well as a few things like 'Come The Fall' for Terry, although I don't recall what song of mine we did. It's been too long! The band members were really great players and I stayed in touch with most of them, rehearsing for some other things in Jersey, which never materialized. I even taught them 'Requiem For The Masses', which sounded really good…"

Unfortunately, for the first seminar appearance the duo were billed as 'The Association Revisited', a fact that didn't go unnoticed by Larry Ramos and Russ Giguere once the event was publicized. As owners of the band's name, neither Larry nor Russ had given authorization for use of the name, and Jim humbly apologized for the confusion.

"They were a bit upset but the promoter, who was told he couldn't do that, did it anyway! I patched it up as best I could and I think the second show had a different billing. I also remember I did another show with those same guys at an outdoor amphitheater up in Strausstown, Pennsylvania, owned by a country artist named Pat Garrett. Terry may have been on that show as well, but I don't recall exactly!"

"It was the millennium, Y2K time," adds Terry, "and I so wanted to call our duet YK2 for those two little shows, but those were the only times that 'Come The Fall' was ever performed live. I had never previously considered it for our concerts so it was a precious opportunity for me to see how it would work live. Ironically, 'Come The Fall' was also the last (of my songs) that I ever recorded with The Association. It was an absolute psychic precursor to what my 12-step recovery path would consist of fifteen years later…"

Take a look inside your soul; sort out all the things you stole
Return them to their owners if you can
Things like trust love and time, the other person's place in line
If you tell the truth I think they'll understand…

"Come The Fall"
Words and Music by Terry Kirkman

Fours years later and Jim found himself sharing the limelight once again with his former Association band members as they were all inducted into the Vocal Group Hall of Fame, and the following year they had regrouped for the PBS *60s Rock Experience* TV Special. He then returned to his own musical career and, in between his commitments with Bruce Belland and David Somerville, he began assisting his brother Jerry in the recording studio who, along with his own talented daughters, Lena and Hannah, was stockpiling songs for an upcoming family collection, ultimately (and belatedly) released on CD as the delightful *Yester* album, via the self-distributed Zerva label during 2009.

Jim recalls: "That's mostly the work of Jerry and Lena. We all sang on it but they did most of the writing. It was a fantastic recording and Jerry shopped it to several major labels but nobody bit. Then the project was pulled back because Lena wanted it to go a more unplugged format. She writes great songs, and there are some killers on that CD. We followed it up with an unplugged performance at a local coffee house, Uncommon Grounds in Harrison, Arkansas; just Jerry playing acoustic and the four of us singing, and people were blown away! It was real sad that it didn't go further..."

"Working with my dad was always great," commented Jerry's daughter Hannah, during a conversation with the author in 2016. "He was very encouraging and insightful, and it was also fun to learn the various vocal arrangements he created. My uncle Jim is very similar. Very laid back. It was fun seeing him and dad work together again. There were lots of laughs. All of the male leads were done by my dad, although he shared them with Jim on 'One Of Us'..."

With six of the thirteen songs listed on the album as L. Beckett-Jerry Yester compositions, with six further Lena Boone credits, the selection initially looks evenly shared between father and daughter but it is only once it becomes apparent that the initial half were composed during Lena's brief tenure as a touring member of the Lovin' Spoonful, performing alongside her father, and that she used the pseudonym of Beckett (in recognition of Jerry's friend, Larry) to differentiate between the 'Yester's' on the tour, that her dominance to the songwriting process becomes apparent. And the fact that she had since married the Spoonful's bass player Steve Boone… thus making Jerry's younger bandmate (by just eight months) his son-in-law.

From the opening bars of the commercially sounding pop of "L.A. Riverbed" (originally demoed as a Spoonful song by Lena and Jerry back in 1994), through to the gentle four-part vocals of the delightful "One Of Us (El Amor Que Sentio)", an adaption of the 1996 *Grammy* award winning hit for Joan Osborne, the album was a pure delight to those who were fortunate enough to hear it. With the gentle smooth pop-jazz of "Tijuana Moon" paired with the MFQ folk-origins of "Showboat" and the Gaelic nuances of "Far Away", accompanied by Lena's own delicately fragile vocal on "All I Ever Wanted", the album was a crossover of the varying genres that highlighted the sheen of the family harmonies as they interacted and supported each other to perfection.

A number of further songs were also cut, including a rendition of the Peter Klimes composition, "Bird Outside The Window", a familiar choice for Jim, courtesy of the earlier 1980 SunWest sessions with The Association, but, following the failure to achieve any significant label support for *Yester*, the resulting outtakes remained unreleased.

Shortly afterwards, and having briefly filled in for Bob Werner with the band, Jim went to see his former colleagues once more: "I went to see them perform in Wildwood, New Jersey. At the time, I was still performing with Triple Gold but David Somerville was entertaining the idea of possibly leaving. I told Russ and Larry that if that happened, I would think about coming back. They had asked me before about it and said they really needed help in the tenor range, and then about two or three weeks later, Russ called me and asked when I was coming back, as if it had already been decided! So I told him I would come back if I could juggle being in both groups at the same time. I would be replacing Bob Werner in the band, so Larry said he would keep Bob on call for times when I had a conflict of schedules and couldn't make the gig. I don't remember how long it stayed like that, possibly most of the year but, eventually, Somerville accepted a year long booking in Branson, Missouri as a single act, so that was effectively the end of Triple Gold. I was back full time with The Association…"

With Bob happy to step aside, exhausted after a seemingly continuous existence on the road, Jim returned during 2009: "I came back as an independent contractor. We are all like that. Russ and Larry owned the band name and if we were employees they would have to pay extra taxes. They initially offered me less money, which I refused, so they then agreed to pay me the same as they were making per show. Of course, they were making more money from the business itself, but c'est la vie!"

Jim would link up once again with David Somerville during the turn of the decade when, having accepted an invite to appear on Italian TV under the guise of his former 1950s band, The Diamonds, David found himself short of performing members.

"David later called me and asked if I wanted to go to Rome and do a TV show with him, to perform just one song; 'Little Darlin''. However, he was still short of one singer. I had just worked with Dennis Tufano from The Buckinghams on a show in Jackson, Tennessee and I suggested him, and I gave David his number. David Jackson, our close friend from the '60s, who had recently filled in for Del in The Association, was also there. It all worked out and we went to Rome for four days, David Somerville, David Jackson, Dennis Tufano and myself as The Diamonds. The show took one day and the rest of the time we were tourists! And we got paid! I love those kind of gigs..." he laughs.

By 2010, The Association were making a steady living on the 'oldies' circuit, bolstered by the continuing sales of their past catalog, a factor increased by the reissue program, once again, of the original albums onto compact disc. Remastered from the original tapes in the Warner Bros. vaults by the revivalist Now Sounds specialist label, the first five long-players were reissued with extensive liner notes, featuring interviews with all of the surviving original band members, along with the added bonus of unreleased tracks and/or alternate mixes where available. An impressive 2-CD gathering entitled *The Complete Warner Bros. & Valiant Singles Collection* also appeared two years later (CRNOW-35D), but the continuing absence of the *Stop Your Motor* album, or Columbia's *Waterbeds In Trinidad!* (as of the time of this writing), stoked the flames of fury for many of band's loyal hardcore following.

In 2011 the key touring ensemble of Larry, Jim and Russ joined up with the revived Happy Together 25th Anniversary Tour, linking up with The Buckinghams, The Grass Roots, Mark Lindsey (from The Raiders) and The Turtles for an extended run of performances across the country during the summer months. It was purely from a financial and logistics perspective that the remaining touring members of the band, Bruce, Del and Jordan, were not involved on this tour. It certainly made the set-up of each performance a lot simpler and a smoother transition onstage between bands, as the tour backing band simply remained on stage for the entire length of each show, supplying additional vocals and instrumentation for every act on the tour, but it certainly was a touch harsh for the loyal band members left behind.

"We're looking forward to The Happy Together tour and working with old friends," Larry was quoted as saying, as the detailed preparations for the tour ensued. "When you get the opportunity to tour with your buddies, there's no downside to going to work every day. And if I had a quarter for everyone who 'got lucky' to an Association song, I'd be driving a Lamborghini!"

Performing a six-song set, comprising of "Windy", "Everything That Touches You", "Never My Love", a cover of The Mamas & The Papas' "California Dreamin'", "Cherish" and "Along Came Mary" the tour was another financial and commercial success, proving the longevity that the classic songs and the 'oldies' acts from the '60s still had to offer. However, demand on the human body, certainly as the body weakens with age, can affect the ability to continue with such extended tours, away from the relaxing comforts of home, the rigorous daily schedules of moving from town to town, city to city, set-up, sound check, performance…

For the past few years Larry Ramos, working alongside multi-instrumentalist Jordan Cole, had been working on a collection of his own songs, with the intention of releasing a long overdue solo collection of his work. It was a labor of love, and one that he returned to frequently. However, it was also one that he felt comfortable with stepping back from as well, particularly when the recording wasn't coming out quite to his satisfaction. It was often better to walk away from the project, and return later, with fresh ears and a new approach, although his inability to play much of the instrumentation for himself, both arthritis and neuropathy were now becoming issues for him, was becoming a frustrating business.

Jordan recalls: "Larry was against digital recording until he worked with Jeff Foskett on some solo material. After seeing how easy it was to fix an error instead of doing the whole track again, he was sold. Since my studio is my own hodgepodge of equipment that I had modified myself, along with various obscure software, I charged much less per hour, and after discovering how well I could recreate any song and arrange original music, and noting Jeff's much higher studio price, he was satisfied. By then I had

The Association 'Cherish'

also undertaken several of the symphony orchestrations for the band. Jeff's work is very good, but I underbid him.

"We started recording with the song 'Dear Joanna'. He gave me a homemade, bad quality tape of him singing with an electric guitar, and then told me to do whatever I wanted. He couldn't play much, if anything by then, as his hands were numb and harder to control. I know that frustrated him but he shrugged it off. I played all instruments and he complimented my electric guitar work by saying it was exactly what he would have played. Then he became more serious and we then tackled 'Hawaiian Condominium Fund' with much more of his management."

> This recording is a collection of songs that were written in four decades, the '50s, '60s, '70s and '80s. I never felt that these songs lent themselves to the styles of either of the groups I was in, The New Christy Minstrels or The Association, so I thought I'd record them someday and did – taking only 8 years to complete.
>
> Larry Ramos

On August 31st 2011, just twelve hours after arriving home from the recent Happy Together tour, Larry Ramos had suffered a heart attack. Fortunately, it was non-fatal, but it naturally sidelined him for a short period of time although his drive to return to the stage, despite the recuperation, was unshakable. Less than two weeks later he was back on tour, although the schedule wasn't too frenetic during the latter part of that year, and he was able to sit out the occasional back to back show without causing undue stress. Nevertheless, with the age-old story of 'the band played on' ringing true, The Association continued with their pre-booked commitments, bringing in New York-based guitarist Godfrey Townsend at short notice to fill in the vacant lead guitarist position whenever Larry was feeling overly fatigued.

"I was first introduced to members of The Association when they were brought into the Happy Together tour, back in 2011," remembers Townsend. "I'm the musical director for those tours and my band backs up all of the acts. After touring with Jim, Russ and Larry that whole summer I was then asked to learn their entire show so I could fill in for Larry who was having some health issues at the time and couldn't perform. I played six shows with them, including BB Kings in New York, The Infinity Hall in Norfolk,

Connecticut and the Dover Downs Casino in Delaware. Then the following January we were in Alabama and Florida…"

Then, by the turn of the year, 2012, with Larry still unable to commit to a heavy touring schedule, another familiar face reappeared on the stage alongside them.

Jules Alexander: "The Association is a pretty high mark to go up against. If I'm going to perform, it's got to be at least as professional, and (up until now) I just really haven't found that much around. I haven't been looking for it too much either!

"After I left in '89 I took up photography, and I had a little band for a while. I did a Christmas album with some people and a few things. Oh, and I wrote the music for a musical! It was produced in this little town that I live in, a tiny little town, and I was involved in that, and my wife was involved in it. I wrote all the music for it and recorded it. It was in ten parts, a classical farce on Wimberley's early history. It put me a whole different thought space. Basically a fellow named Russ Marlett and I wrote the show; it was called *The Blanco Was Blameless or It Was Balcone's Fault*, and Russ and his wife Shirley decided to start their own theater company and chose this musical as their first production, drafting me to be the musical director as well. It was produced a few years ago to very good reviews."

Despite his relatively low-key existence in the rural settings of Wimberley, mid-way between the Texan cities of Austin and San Antonio, Jules had stayed in occasional touch with his former partners and in 2012 returned to the band, in a similar capacity to Jim, as an independent contractor, supplying his distinctive harmony and guitar and filling out the onstage mix in Larry's absence

"Up to that point I had decided not to ever be in the music business again. I was out of the band and then I had damaged my thumb with a table saw, and I had decided that I really couldn't play guitar any more. So for about sixteen years I didn't really touch a guitar but when Russ called me up and said 'we want you back in the band,' I thought 'Oh gee! I'd better go get a guitar! And when I picked it up there was no problem (with the thumb) so I started learning again!"

Larry would still appear with the band over the coming months, whenever the tiring regime permitted, bringing the band membership up to seven, with four of the core members from the 1960s back on stage together, but excessive traveling continued to take its toll on him, further accentuated by issues with his kidneys, and during 2013 he received yet another devastating setback when he was diagnosed with metastatic melanoma, a form of skin cancer. Nevertheless, he remained at peace with his condition, stood strong, but chose to keep the news private.

During 2012 he had finally finished the solo collection that he and Jordan had been working on for the past few years, between the various commitments and periods of recuperation. The resulting CD, a 13-track collection entitled *Poipourri*, was made available via the internet and gathered together a number of compositions that Larry himself had composed over the years, and in some cases had performed live, but which had never been previously committed to tape. From the 1950s rock 'n' roll of "Sippin' Lemonade", through to the gentle Hawaiian tempos of "My Kauai" and "Hawaiian Condominium Fund", and the laid back, west coast lullaby of "Pacific Coast Lady", it stands as a delightful and fitting climax to Larry's recording career.

"There were a lot of songs that were turned down because it didn't sound like The Association. Good tunes, but it didn't sound like us. I put a lot of those songs on my first, and last CD. Songs that I thought wouldn't apply to The Association or The New Christy Minstrels that I had written. The songs come from about four decades of writing from the '50s on to the '80s. These are songs that just rattled inside of me. I thought I'd just keep these songs and eventually I'll record them, but a lot of these songs have gone past their prime! I should have recorded them a long time ago, but I finally did and I'm glad I did it. The CD is called 'Poipourri'... It's potpourri, except it's 'Poi'. It's Hawaiian!" [23]

By early 2014, despite his condition, the determination, loyalty and love of life was unquestionable, and he always maintained a familiar air of grace and positivity. Unfortunately, a recent checkup at the hospital had assessed his cancer as worsening, and he knew he could no longer continue on the road but he had it in mind to say his farewells, and so it was announced shortly afterwards that he would perform one last show, a benefit concert for the disease, his final goodbye with the band on February 24th at the Blue Fox Theater, in Grangeville, Idaho, Larry's adopted hometown. His manager had suggested Las Vegas may be a suitable location to bow out but Larry wanted to pay due acknowledgment to the Idaho city, near to where he had set up home on a 300-acre ranch with his wife of nearly 50 years, Helene, and where he was happy. It would be a thank-you to family and friends. And yet, surprisingly, this wasn't to be the only departure from the band as, during January, it was also announced that Russ Giguere was leaving the touring line-up.

> As of January 2014, Russ will no longer be touring with The Association. He will ALWAYS be a part of The Association family and we wish him well in his retirement!
>
> The Association Official Band Statement

As noted, with the word 'retirement' formally bandied around, one is led to believe that it was a mutual parting of the ways, with both Russ and his bandmates and business partners acknowledging the fact that time had simply caught up with him and that fifty years on the road had simply taken its strenuous toll. Indeed, some of the more recent concert reviews had publicly suggested that, just maybe, his lead vocals were no longer as strong as they should be, and he was struggling with both the range and the pitch, forcing him to graciously accept that his voice was no longer as resilient as it needed to be for such a strenuous harmony-focused performance, night after night, and that the ability to maintain the potency it took to reach the standards of "One Too Many Mornings" and "Windy" was, at times, no longer within his control. In addition, he too was suffering with health issues, along with close personal loss, but whatever the reasoning, from an outside perspective, taking his cue with grace, Russ appeared to accept that retiring from the band was potentially the best option, moving his control of the organization, his band, to a behind the scenes role.

At this stage, with Larry now unable to fulfill regular duties, and with Russ also absent from the line-up, Del Ramos stepped forward to take control of the touring operation, upon the request of his stricken brother, with Jim now taking the central focus onstage A hastily organized band meeting, held backstage in Alexandria, Virginia saw the group restructure their show, deciding on who would handle the vocals on which song and, to a rapturous reception, the band played on…

"I had needed to be asked to be put into that bass players spot," says Del today, recounting over his increasing role in the band, "as I had always wanted to earn my way on to that stage. My brother then asked me to do that. I was earning my way, and so I guess, in the long run, it came true as I'm now playing bass and singing in the band. But to start from where I started, singing from the mixing board, covering vocals for Jules who had appendicitis at the time, and being asked to be sound man, to pretty much trying to lead the band, which is again what my brother asked me to do… I don't really do that. We kinda share that, Jules, Jimmy and myself. They deserve that respect. It mattered to me what my brother said, but I didn't agree with that, so I just decided to have the three of us make the major decisions together…"

Bringing Paul Holland back into the band was one early move, with Larry central to the decision of bringing him back as, from a vocal and instrumental viewpoint, he was one former member who knew all of the parts inside out, back to front. On February 21st the band, now consisting of Jules, Jim, Del, Jordan, Bruce and Paul performed at the popular Yoshi's venue in Oakland, CA. performing a full set comprising of "Windy", "Just About The Same", "Everything That Touches You", "Enter The Young", "Walk Away Renée", "Never My Love", "California Dreamin'", "Six Man Band", "Learn How To Land", "No Fair At All", "Dubuque Blues", "Cherish", "Along Comes Mary" and, as an encore, "Goodbye, Columbus". They also took to performing a Bill Martin spoof version of The Eagles' 1971 Henley-Frey classic "Desperado", humorously retitled with typical Martin-wit as "Avocado", and later popularized by 'Weird Al' Yankovic.

Jim (onstage): "When we go into a recording project we listen to, possibly two or three hundred demo projects a day. It start to get a little tedious and if you don't hear something in the first ten or fifteen seconds you wind up going 'next!' and turning down songs that end up being pretty big. We turned down a lot. We turned down "Joy To The World, "The Air That I Breathe" and "MacArthur Park". Anyway, one day we heard a demo when we were listening, and I loved it… but nobody else did. I lobbied heavy for it, but they turned me down. A couple of years later The Eagles had a big hit with it. They changed it around… but I'd like to do the original…"

Avocado, what makes you think you're so holy?
You're just guacamole to me
You're a green one,
You know that you're out of season.
These hands that are squeezing you are gonna eat you some day

"Avocado"
Words by Bill Martin
Music by Don Henley-Glenn Frey

Three days later and the above line-up stood on the stage at the Blue Fox Theater in Grangeville alongside Larry Ramos for the final time, performing the second of two, seventy-five minute sets.

"I had expected him to just do one or two songs with us," says Del "because it was now very difficult for him to perform. But he came up and did both full sets…"

"Actually, I'm a little nervous," Larry had said during an interview with the local radio station, just days beforehand. "I haven't sung with the group in nearly a month and a half. It's been doing well without me and I don't want to mess them up."

Needless to say he didn't, and it was an emotional appearance all round as the band went through their repertoire for the second time that day, although, with limited abilities in his fingers, a frail looking Larry appeared for some of the time without his familiar guitar, gently harmonizing alongside his musical partners, all of whom were wearing a white rose in their lapel as a sign of support. Yet, he was not down and out by any stretch of the imagination and, at one stage, he brought out an old ukulele to play, smiling happily before his attentive audience as the band performed "'A' Ole La Ku'ulei (Never My Love)", but the event drained him, both emotionally and physically, and for the latter part of the performance he sat on a stool, still giving what he could, albeit struggling to hit the pitch perfect notes.

"It was a big deal for him." Del was to comment. "After the concert I went over to my mom's house where my brother was staying, so my mom could watch over him, and I remember sitting in the kitchen area and seeing how much it had taken out of him. He was a real pro, and he did the very best he could do, which was phenomenal…"

He had wanted to participate in a further show, as a part of the band's upcoming performance in Florida, sharing the billing with Paul Revere & The Raiders, but ultimately he remained at home.

In March he traveled down to Arizona, the home of his daughter, to celebrate his and Helene's 50th wedding anniversary along with family and close friends and then, just one month later, he journeyed the 3,000 miles to fulfill a desire to see his birth island of Kauai once more, ignoring his increasing inability to travel such long distances. Celebrating his 72nd birthday whilst there, he saw more friends, ate his favorite foods, and took in the beautiful Hawaiian landscapes one last time.

Del rang him whilst he was there, and wished him a happy birthday, but it would be the last time the two would talk. Having celebrated his birthdate on the 19th, tired but presumably elated, he duly returned home to Idaho the following week. Just two days later he attended the hospital in Clarkston, Washington, for his routine kidney dialysis but, upon noticing a fever, he was checked in to stay. He never left. On the 30th April 2014, surrounded by his close family, he peacefully passed away. His daughter Tracy, on behalf of the family – his wife Helene, mother Pat, his siblings Carmen and Del, his five children; Stacy, Tracy, Larry, Keli and Terry, along with five grandchildren and one great-grandchild – posted the following heartfelt announcement:

It is with immense sadness I write this. My Dad, Larry Ramos passed away this evening. As you all know he had been ill for the past three years following his heart attack in 2011. What you don't know is he was diagnosed with metastatic melanoma last year (he wanted that diagnosis to be kept private while he was alive.) While his illnesses were trying at times, his passing was peaceful and he was surrounded by family.

We are devastated beyond words at our loss and will miss him tremendously! I personally will miss his endearing salutations but find comfort in a conversation I had with him upon learning his condition was terminal.

I said, "Well Daddy, it looks like we're going to have to finish your bucket list, what it is you still want to do?"

He simply said, "Nothing honey, I've done it all."

Not many people can honestly say that but Daddy did and meant it. He had a wonderful life (got to go home and eat the biggest and best LauLau on the islands) and will forever be remembered and immortalized in his music.

At his retirement concert in February he asked my sister how he did and was happy when her response was, "You did great Daddy!"

He said, "Good honey, cause that's how I always want you to remember me."

We will and hope you do too!

Thank you for all your love and support, it has meant so much to us. Daddy loved performing and genuinely loved connecting with fans.

Aloha

The Ramos Family

CHAPTER TWENTY-NINE

ONE MORE TIME...

The music of The Association was never about one member. In truth, it was never about two or more members. Or even the collective, from whichever era from across the decades. Time has proven that. People were still coming to see The Association, and listen to their timeless music, after co-founding member Brian Cole tragically passed on. They continued to come and watch following the departure of the band's musical backbone, Terry Kirkman, and even when Ted Bluechel was left as the sole performing member during the 1978/79 period, people still came to listen to "Cherish", "Along Comes Mary", "Windy" and "Never My Love".

Yes, one could argue that The Association was only ever *really* The Association once there was collective gathering of either Alexander, Kirkman, Yester, Giguere, Cole, Bluechel or Ramos on the stage, but such is the demand for the music of that original era these days that concert attendees today are, at times, no more familiar with the line-up in front of them than they were, or their parents were, fifty years beforehand when they first handed their hard-earned $$$ across the record store counter and walked out with a pristine copy of *And Then Along Comes... The Association* under their arm. To many, they needed no more than the sound of the harmonies, *those* harmonies, wafting across the hi-fi speakers, the family radio or the concert hall monitors to be taken back in time. It's as if the 1960s were this magical nirvana, surrounded by an omnipresent vision of color, bubbles, beads and flowers, where everybody was happy, everything was perfect, and there really *was* love, love, love. And was "Cherish" *really* playing across the airwaves every time the young romantics held each close in the backseat of the car? Was it really like that? The saying goes that 'if you remember the '60s you weren't really there'… but people like to imagine how it was, and the music helps takes them back.

With the sad passing of Larry Ramos, and the retirement of Russ Giguere, the involvement of the performing Association membership was reduced further, with only Jules Alexander and Jim Yester justifying their status as the original band, but such was the devotion of all current performers on the stage that so many hundreds, nay thousands of concertgoers still came away from a performance with smiles on their faces and warmth in their hearts. With Del Ramos taking over the role of touring mentor from his brother, accompanied by Jules and Jim, and with loyal support from Bruce Pictor, himself a touring band member for over 30 years, Jordan Cole and Paul Holland, the next phase of the band kicked in. The show must go on.

On May 9th 2014, with just over one week having passed since Larry's death, The Association was booked in to play a show in North Carolina. Del Ramos was now handling many of his brother's lead vocals, and none were more central to the act than those for "Never My Love". As Del was to relate to the author: "I always consider that song my brother's song and, when I sing it now I always turn to my right, where my brother used to stand, as a tribute to him, But during that show, as I was singing it, I couldn't hear any of the other guys vocals anywhere, so I turned around and I got kinda upset as I saw everyone was so emotional. They were crying and couldn't sing, so I had to say 'c'mon you guys, get it happening!'… and all of a sudden I could hear all their vocals coming in! Everybody gave their heart out for that show…

"Jim told the audience that we'd like to dedicate the show to my brother, who had just recently passed away, but he just couldn't say any more."

In 2015, Russ Giguere, now acting from behind the scenes as band manager and decision maker, got the band booked onto the annual Happy Together tour once again, another prestigious round of performances across the county.

Del: "Russ still has a lot to do with making decisions for the group, along with my brother's wife, who my brother gave his share of the group to. She doesn't have a lot to do with it but she is often advised by Russell, with signing contacts, but Russell does a lot, even though he doesn't perform anymore…"

A lengthy summer schedule ensued, sharing the stage and the fun with a number of their old friends – The Turtles, The Grass Roots, The Buckinghams, The Cowsills and Mark Lindsay of The Raiders – although, once again, for the majority of the shows it was only Jules, Jim and Del in attendance, with Godfrey Townsend and his own backing once more providing the musical accompaniment for every act on the tour. However, for the Costa Mesa performance, held at the Pacific Amphitheater in Orange County on July 26th, they were joined on stage, and in harmony by Bruce Pictor and Paul Holland.

2015 also saw the release of two further additions into the band's solo catalog, when both Jim and Jules had individual products issued onto the market. For Jules the release came in the shape of a limited 6-track CD EP, sold at various concert venues *en route*, and titled *EP Number 001*, credited to The Jules Gary Alexander Band. And what a release it was. Performed by a nucleus comprising of Jules himself on guitar, synthesizers and bass, local Texan players Val Roessling, also on guitar, and Jeff Hogan sitting in on drums and percussion, with the Florida-born fiddler Erik Hokkanen on violin and guitar, all ably accompanied by Jules' daughter, Eden, on backing vocals. Whilst Jules' own lead vocal abilities may, at times, have seemed softer in comparison to many of his former partners, no one can find fault with the astonishing collection of self-composed compositions and arrangements on this fine set. From the opening instrumental arrangements of "El Camino Terlingua", the beautiful lyrical visions and new age wash of "The Bed In The Bay", "Cactus and Cowboys" and "Boston Days" (the latter featuring lyrics by the late Steven Carey), through to a delightful reworking of his own "Caney Creek" composition (the AM version), the love was so clearly still in the music and the proverbial icing on the cake was an additional, extended 15-minute (FM version) of the latter song which dissipated into a joyous elongated jam of Gaelic-influence and vastly inspired proportion that it left the listener spellbound. The interplay between the fiddle and the electric guitar tracks (both played by Hokkanen, each in one take), underpinned by the percussion and a hypnotic rhythm, was simply wondrous.

"I love Clannad and their early Gaelic stuff..." enthuses Jules today. "It just knocks me out! That sound appealed to me very much and my wife and I listen to a lot of Gaelic and Celtic music. We like to listen to several of those kinds of bands.

"Tennessee, where I grew up, was settled by the Scots, that was where they ended up, in the mountains, and so being into folk music I really hooked into that..."

Jim's release, meanwhile, was also of particular interest, as it was the belated debut issue for a recording taken from the legendary *The Association Bites Back!* sessions of 1974.

"That was for a collection put together by Ron Foos," says Jim. "Ron is currently the bass player for Paul Revere's Raiders and we did a lot of shows with them. He was compiling this *Voices For The Voiceless* charity CD and he asked me if I had any tunes he could use that weren't hung up by record labels and contract. So I sent him the song 'One More Time', but it was such a bad copy that he almost couldn't use it. Fortunately, he managed to salvage it in the studio."

Released to raise awareness and funds for Pet Place International, a non-profit organization located in the Yucca Valley, this 18-song compilation appeared on the Audio & Visual Labs Inc. label during July of 2015, with Jim's contribution being a particular highlight, although the quality of the recording, coming from his own personal copy, as opposed to the long-discarded original master tapes, was certainly sub-standard, with aspects of hiss, crackles and pops sadly proliferating throughout. Nevertheless, it was such a strong composition, accompanied by Larry Brown's original Telecaster steel guitar overdubs, that it deserved the praise and a long overdue public release.

Not that Larry Brown had been idle himself since departing The Association four decades previous. The ensuing years had seen him continue to play his music and his guitars, contributing to numerous sessions and live performances whilst building a family and a comfortable life in his home state of California. However, he had never gotten around to releasing any music of his own until, during the middle of 2014, he began to compile what would formulate into his first solo CD, featuring contributions from his fellow former-Associate David Morgan. Released online during 2016, the 7-track *Better Late* was a fine example of his guitar abilities and his finer love of the blues and it stood out as a tremendous delight to those who were blessed enough to discover it.

And what about his fellow former-Association alumni? For there have been many of those throughout the years. Some went on to maintain a notable presence in the industry, achieving further acclaim amongst their musical peers along the way, whilst others chose to step away from the limelight, disappearing into the darker recesses of the infamous lost and forgotten files, out of sight and sound of the public's awareness.

David Vaught, having been an integral part of the band during the mid-late 1970s, continued working, contributing to a number of underground cult-releases (including two albums credited to Jon Wayne: *Texas Funeral* and *Two Graduated Jiggers*), whilst raising his own profile as a much in-demand producer and engineer. His undeniable abilities, and that of his own recording facilities in Van Nuys; Suite 16, utilizing his former band's expansive Flickinger-built console, aided the early successes of Maria McKee & Lone Justice, Counting Crows, Vic Chesnutt and Toad The Wet Sprockett. Sadly, he died in 2013, aged 64, the result of pancreatic cancer.

Richard Thompson also lost out in his own battle with cancer, having been diagnosed with the disease during 1998 and finally passing away after a defiant fight the following January. His story was posthumously retold in the tender readings of his wife's emails and recollections, published as *Minus One: A Correspondence* (Dog Ear Publishing: 2006).

Former manager Pat Colecchio was the third Associate to fall foul of this cancerous demon, having spent a number of his final years of retirement in the close confidence of Jules Alexander and the Wimberley, Texas community.

"He fell in love with Texas," laughs Jules, recollecting his time with his former manager. "Pat had a cowboy in his heart trying to get out. It was hilarious. When Pat got here in 2006, he practically took over the town. By the time he left, everyone knew him. He was the godfather of this club we liked to go to…" [1]

Upon being diagnosed with colon cancer Pat moved back to New Jersey to be with his son, Rick, before succumbing to the disease during the early summer of 2008.

Rick Colecchio adds; "I stayed with the band until mid-1974, and after '75 I moved back east and really lost touch with everyone, including dad. I was gone by the time he left the band for the first time, but I know dad loved the guys, and they him, and they were all good friends until his passing. Dad still worked for them to some degree, taking care of royalties and the usage of all Association music and memorabilia, that which I am in charge of now. Then, in 2003, when the guys were inducted into the Vocal Group Hall of Fame they asked if their lifetime manager could also attend, so dad and I went along. There we all were, thirty-eight years later, together again, naturally. The family was back together."

Others no longer available to play the music on this wayward journey, or recount the stories and exploits, include John Tuttle (1991), Maurice Miller (2005) and Andy Chapin (1985). Former manager Dean Fredericks also passed away during 1999.

Mike Berkowitz, Art Johnson, Jay Gruska, David Morgan, Cliff Woolley, Russ Levine, Ric Ulsky, Joe LaManno, Donnie Gougeon and Paul Beach all still keep active profiles in their chosen field, some musical, others elsewhere, whilst some former members, such as Dwayne Smith, Wolfgang Melz and co-founding member Bob Page, maintain a quieter outlook on life. Others still, have simply disappeared.

2016 saw the ongoing recognition for The Association's contributions to the industry continue with their induction into yet another of America's continuing fascinations with Hall of Fame establishments. America's Pop Music Hall of Fame, based in Canonsburg, PA. sits quietly alongside its more celebrated and, at times, controversial partners, and it gains little notoriety for its induction process, but it still stands as further acceptance to those fortunate enough to be chosen by their musical peer groups. The 2016 inductees included not only The Association but also such celebrated artists as Barry Manilow, Barbra Streisand, Dion DiMucci, Neil Sedaka and The Temptations.

Meanwhile, there was seemingly no let up as the touring band themselves entered into a heavy phase of performances, celebrating their 50th Anniversary during 2016 followed by the early months of 2017 seeing a long list of venues with the band's name highlighted on the outside marquees. May 2016 had seen the line-up change once again, albeit briefly when, for one appearance at the Monroe Arts Center in Wisconsin, Texan guitarist Paul Wilson (who had been an earlier consideration for a place in the band when Larry had first stopped touring) stepped in to deputize for an unavailable Paul Holland but, other than that, the touring line-up stayed consistent, and with over forty shows booked for the 2017 Happy Together tour – although, once again, only Jim, Jules and Del participated – the future, and the past, looked healthy for The Association as a touring band and/or business, and for the many, many audiences who feed on their one night of nostalgic interaction.

"I feel an ownership and I'm deeply vested in the group's sound and energy, using my own style and parts," summarizes the band's longtime drummer, Bruce Pictor. "This is now my 33rd year with the band, and we've done cruises for each major cruise line, we've played the Grand Ole Opry three times, we've sung the National Anthem *a cappella* in front of 100,000 people, and we've played at all the major venues in the country. We played The Rainbow Room in Rockefeller Plaza the week of July 4th, 2012. During that time, ground zero was still smoking and steaming and I later met the men from Fire Station 54, directly around the corner from our hotel, who had been part of the fire fighting team on 9/11 and the following weeks. They were very hospitable and humble, gave me pins and Station patches and in return I gave them an Association tape which they promptly played through the sound system of the station. It was a great honor…

"Many times Vietnam Vets have also shared with us their kind and compassionate words on how much our music meant to them while stationed overseas…"

Nevertheless, despite the amazing talent that has fed down through the many members across the years, the authenticity of the group will always be there whilst a representation from the original line-up still steps onto the stage each night. The late Larry Ramos was an avid supporter of Truth In Music, a legislation adopted by a number of states in the country since 2005 that protects the trademark of recording artists, by assuring that any act must include at least one original member.

"I think we will always need some of the original guys there, on the stage," says Del, reflecting on the future of the band. "That's where all the sound comes from. But if we get to the point where some of the guys can't do it anymore, that just might be the time for me to retire as well, but its just so much fun now, so until then…"

And as for a perspective from the original membership? Jim Yester has his own philosophy as to why these songs, and this era have stood the test of time.

"Music from that era wasn't only melodic," he says. "The lyrics were also meaningful and people related to those songs in particular times in their lives. I never tire of playing them as, not only are they great songs, but some of them, 'Cherish' for example, are quite difficult to play. When you do it right, you can feel the response from the audience. You can feel it so much that there are times when I get choked up that it's hard for me to sing.

"We're also very concerned about how well we do everything now.

There's a great deal of care taken in the band… and that wasn't always the case. We actually had a reputation to overcome because of some years when it wasn't up to snuff. Some people had a drinking problem, some people were losing their voice… but we're getting the most amazing response now, we're just having so much fun. [52]

"It's very visceral and it's that kind of thing that keeps it going. And the oldies stations help a lot, too. You would not believe how many times someone has come up to say that 'Never My Love' was 'our song' or that 'Cherish' was played at their wedding. Even 'Windy' has broad appeal from little kids to grandma and grandpa. So, I feel so blessed to, at this point of my life, do this. It's just absolutely wonderful…" [48]

Of all the band members who came together to form The Association the music still continues to live on in a number of them today and, perhaps, none more so than with Jules Alexander. Today, both Ted Bluechel and Terry Kirkman maintain a lower profile, shunning much of the media spotlight, although Terry, away from the music industry for over three decades now, and content to divert all of his efforts into aiding those in need on the often difficult road to addiction recovery, remains happy to step out every now and again, upon request, to fondly recall and recount tales of days gone by, but he has no desire to retread the floorboards of the stages around the world:

"When I'd left the group in '72 I really didn't want to become a caricature of who'd we'd been, and as happy, *truly* happy as I am for Jim and Jules, and before that Larry, that they have this niche, I could not fathom myself singing those songs more than six or seven times a year as a nostalgia thing. I have never, *ever*, in the eight years of not being in The Association the first time, and then thirty-two years since, sung 'Cherish' alone on a stage, excepting once at a musicians Christmas party! I'll never be that guy, walking around, milking what I can out of something I did in my twenties. I've done so much more than means more to me than being a pop star…

"Yes, I would love to sing 'Requiem For The Masses', but then who'd I get to do it with me? I was present when a high school choir did it, along with 'Cherish' in Jackson, Michigan, around 2005, and I also wrote a song just for them called 'Singing Our Way Through Jackson', so I still have music in my life. I also had an AA choir that I put together, I sung and arranged for, and we did that for fifteen years, and I still make music in my closet. Can anyone else hear it? No! But my last job, actually working on somebody else's payroll, was as a clinical director for M.A.P., the Musicians Assistance Program, in Hollywood, which is now a part of the *Grammy* Foundation.

"My biggest claim to fame these days is that I get to work with Artists in Recovery, in forty-six states and in eleven countries... and that's really my passion."

By contrast, Russ Giguere still operates the business side of The Association touring entourage and has recently been compiling his own thoughts and recollections of the band onto paper for a potential autobiography. He remains private, saddened by personal events of recent years but affable to all who approach him, and anyone asking for an autograph or wishing to share a treasured memory of earlier days with him, goes away happy.

Jim Yester, recently remarried, still lives on the Eastern seaboard of New Jersey, just fifteen or so miles from the heart of Atlantic City. He also prefers the quieter life when not on the road with the band, and is still fascinated with his love of falconry, although the lure and the thrill of a live performance remains strong. In 2013 he reunited with Linda Gentille on the stage, performing as a guest at her eight-concert season appearance with the Jersey Shore Pops in Cape May, accompanied by a New Jersey-based show band appropriately labeled The Yesterdaze, and he often appeared at the Caravan of Stars bi-annual concerts, held in Jackson, Tennessee, sometimes in partnership with his brother Jerry, but such appearances are now few and far between.

"When not on tour I'm mostly retired these days," Jim says. "I'm not involved in the local music scene any more although I have toyed with the idea of open mic nights locally, but so far haven't done it. And as far as future plans outside of The Association? There are none yet, at present, but I'm working on improving that!"

But it is with Jules Alexander that the music still flows most freely. When not on the rigorous touring schedule that shuttles him to all four corners of the vast country he still spends his down time at home, in deepest Texas, in between family time, thinking about his music. Whilst he doesn't perform locally anymore, preferring to spend his time watching the resident acts rather than playing, his friendship and musical partnership with Eric Hokkanen and also that of Ike Eichenberg, a fellow well-traveled musician, shows no boundaries as they often explore the musical landscape together, working alongside a selection of local talent.

"A lot of the performers down here are solo acts," he says, "so I don't perform locally. After all, I'm in a band myself so I don't need to! But I like to go and watch them, with a glass of wine in my hand..."

"The music scene in this part of Texas is both vast and localized," says Paul Wilson, another of Jules' Texan friends who had recently subbed for Paul Holland during an Association show.

"By that I mean that you can make a living just playing in the state, and yet there are also several great local music scenes. Erik Hokkanen is from another planet in terms of musical ability and is quite renowned as both a fiddler and guitarist, so he mostly does country, swing and gypsy jazz, and Ike Eichenberg mainly plays jazz. Jules recently recorded an album's worth of Ike's material that we all worked on, but the local scene around Austin and San Antonio is quite diverse. It's just one great musician after another."

Indeed, having spent the best part of fifty years, writing, producing, arranging and performing, working by himself or alongside a host of equally-minded folk, some may say that the music has never left Jules, ever since that fateful day when he descended the hillside on that warm, rainy evening, heading away from the ongoing party, high above Pearl Harbor...

The music of The Association, and the interplay between the members, both past and present, may have changed over the years, relationships were formed, friendships were tested, troubled waters were crossed, and the road ahead may still be rocky in places, but there can be no denying the talent that each and every individual has brought to the table.

Longtime friend of the band, Randy Sterling, who was there alongside the original sextet during the Ice House and Troubadour days, and who traveled an equally rocky road himself over the ensuing years, looks back, commenting; "My whole take on the thing is, from beginning to end, was the fact that they started off as a bunch of troubadour kids, full of it, ready to go out there, change the world and make their music. And they did! I got to watch them from the embryonic stages, the absolute beginnings, and they got together, woodshedded and got themselves better, and each one made the other better. Each one made the other rise to a better level. It was a beautiful thing to watch..."

What does lie ahead? Well, whatever that may be, the road behind it is a well-traveled one. It's been tested to the limit but, as with many great American institutions, it's been roadworthy throughout the journey. And long may she run. Cue the song that started it all off on that road...

Every time I think that I'm the only one who's lonely
Someone calls on me
And every now and then I spend my time in rhyme and verse
And curse those faults in me
And then along comes Mary

"Along Comes Mary"
Words and Music by Tandyn Almer

AN OUTRAGEOUS CONCERT

HAPPY T☮GETHER

TOUR 2018

THE TURTLES

CHUCK NEGRON
FORMERLY OF THREE DOG NIGHT

GARY PUCKETT ⟫⟫⟫ & THE UNION GAP

THE ASSOCIATION

MARK LINDSAY
FORMER LEAD SINGER OF PAUL REVERE & THE RAIDERS

THE COWSILLS

SELECTED DISCOGRAPHY

U.S. ALBUMS

AND THEN... ALONG COMES THE ASSOCIATION
Valiant VLM-5002/VLS-25002 (1966)

Enter The Young (Kirkman) / Your Own Love (Alexander-Yester) /Don't Blame It On Me (Addrisi-Addrisi) / Blistered (Wheeler) / I'll Be Your Man (Giguere) / Along Comes Mary (Almer) / Cherish (Kirkman) / Standing Still (Bluechel) / Message Of Our Love (Almer-Boettcher) / Round Again (Alexander) / Remember (Alexander) / Changes (Alexander)

RENAISSANCE
Valiant VLM-5004/VLS-25004 (1966)

I'm The One (Giguere) / Memories Of You (Yester) / All Is Mine (Kirkman) / Pandora's Golden Heebie Jeebies (Alexander) / Angeline (Alexander-Kirkman) / Songs In The Wind (Bluechel) / You May Think (Alexander-Kirkman) / Looking Glass (Alexander) / Come To Me (Alexander-Yester) / No Fair At All (Yester) / You Hear Me Call Your Name (Alexander-Kirkman) / Another Time, Another Place (Alexander)

INSIGHT OUT
Warner Bros. W-1696/WS-1696 (1967)

Wasn't It A Bit Like Now? (Parallel 23) (Kirkman) / On A Quiet Night (Sloan) / We Love Us (Bluechel) / When Love Comes To Me (Yester) / Windy

(Friedman) / Reputation (Hardin) / Never My Love (Addrisi-Addrisi) / Happiness Is (Addrisi-Addrisi) / Sometime (Giguere)/ Wantin' Ain't Gettin' (Deasy) / Requiem For The Masses (Kirkman)

BIRTHDAY
Warner Bros. W-1733/WS-1733 (1968)

Come On In (Mapes) / Rose Petals, Incense And A Kitten (McClelland-Yester) / Like Always (Alcivar-Ortega-Ramos) / Everything That Touches You (Kirkman) / Toymaker (Comanor) / Barefoot Gentleman (Carmel-Yester) / Time For Livin' (Addrisi-Addrisi) / Hear in Here (Bluechel) / The Time It Is Today (Giguere) / The Bus Song (Kirkman) / Birthday Morning (Carmel-Yester)

GREATEST HITS
Warner Bros. WS-1767 (1968)

The Time It Is Today (Giguere) / Everything That Touches You (Kirkman) / Like Always (Alcivar-Ortega-Ramos) / Never My Love (Addrisi-Addrisi) / Requiem For The Masses (Kirkman) / Along Comes Mary (Almer) / Enter The Young (Kirkman) / No Fair At All (Yester) / Time For Livin' (Addrisi-Addrisi) / We Love (Bluechel) / Cherish (Kirkman) / Windy (Friedman) / Six Man Band (Kirkman)

GOODBYE, COLUMBUS (SOUNDTRACK)
Warner Bros. WS-1786 (1969)

Goodbye, Columbus (Yester) / Goodbye, Columbus (*instrumental*) (Yester) / It's Gotta Be Real (Ramos) / So Kind To Me (Brenda's Theme) (Kirkman)

THE ASSOCIATION
Warner Bros. WS-1800 (1969)

Look At Me, Look At You (Kirkman) / Yes I Will (Boylan) / Love Affair (Alexander) / The Nest (Carmel-Bluechel) / What Were The Words? (Yester) / Are You Ready? (Ortega-Ramos) / Dubuque Blues (Alexander) / Under Branches (Alexander-Carmel) / I Am Up For Europe (Cole-Alexander) / Broccoli (Giguere) / Goodbye Forever (Alexander-Kirkman-Martinson) / Boy On The Mountain (Kirkman-Thompson)

THE ASSOCIATION LIVE

Warner Bros. 2WS-1868 (1970)

Dream Girl (Bluechel) / One Too Many Mornings (Dylan) / Along Comes Mary (Almer) / I'll Be Your Man (Giguere) / Goodbye, Columbus (Yester) / The Last Flower (Thurber) / Get Together (Powers) / Wasn't It A Bit Like Now (Parallel 23) (Kirkman) / Never My Love (Addrisi-Addrisi) / Goodbye Forever (Alexander-Kirkman-Martinson) / Just About The Same (Rhodes-Stec-Fennelly-Mallory-Edgar) / Babe I'm Gonna Leave You (Bredon) / Seven Man Band (Kirkman) / The Time It Is Today (Giguere) / Dubuque Blues (Alexander) / Blistered (Wheeler) / What Were The Words (Yester) / Remember (Alexander) / Are You Ready (Ortega-Ramos) / Cherish (Kirkman) / Requiem For The Masses (Kirkman) / Windy (Friedman) / Enter The Young (Kirkman)

ONCE UPON A WHEEL (SOUNDTRACK) (Various Artists)

Warner Bros. PRO-444 (1971)

First Sound (Kirkman-Thompson) / I'm Going To Be A Racin' Star (Kirkman) / Once Upon A Wheel (Kirkman-Thompson) / Time For Livin' (Addrisi-Addrisi)

STOP YOUR MOTOR

Warner Bros. WS-1927 (1971)

Bring Yourself Home (Bluechel) / Funny Kind Of Song (Alexander) / That's Racin' (Kirkman) / P.F. Sloan (Webb) / Silver Morning (Kirkman) / It's Gotta Be Real (Ramos) / The First Sound (Kirkman-Thompson) / Along The Way (Yester) Traveler's Guide (Spanish Flyer) (Cole) / Seven Virgins (Spheeris)

WATERBEDS IN TRINIDAD!

Columbia KC-31348 (1972)

Silent Song Through The Land (Davies) / Darling Be Home Soon (Sebastian) / Midnight Wind (Alexander-Carey) / Come The Fall (Kirkman) / Kicking The Gong Around (Alexander-Carey) / Rainbows Bent (Alexander-Carey) / Snow Queen (Goffin-King) / Indian Wells Woman (Ramos-Hickman-Ramos) / Please Don't Go ('Round the Bend) (Alexander) / Little Road And A Stone To Roll (Stewart)

BACK TO BACK (Various Artists)
Era Records BU-5660 (1983)
Windy* (Friedman) / Cherish* (Kirkman) / Never My Love* (Addrisi-Addrisi) / Along Comes Mary* (Almer) / Everything That Touches You* (Kirkman)
*Re-recorded version

ROCK 'N' ROLL CITY (Various Artists)
Hitbound Records 51-3009 (1983)
Walk Away Renée* (Brown-Calilli-Sansone)
*Single contribution to this compilation release

NEW MEMORIES (Various Artists)
Hitbound Records 51-3022 (1983)
Walk Away Renée (Brown-Calilli-Sansone) / Memories Are Made Of This (Gilkyson-Dehr-Miller) / Love Me Tender (Matson-Presley) / Breaking Up Is Hard To Do (Sedaka-Greenfield) / Oh, Pretty Woman (Orbison-Dees) / World Without Love (Lennon-McCartney) / The Dock Of The Bay (Redding-Cropper) / It's All In The Game (Sigman-Dawes)

SCROOGE'S ROCK 'N' ROLL CHRISTMAS (Various Artists)
Hitbound Records HB-1003 (1983)
Sleigh Ride* (Anderson-Parish) / Home For The Holidays* (Allen-Stillman)
*Single contributions to this compilation release

VINTAGE
51 West Records/CBS Special Products BT-17223 (1983)
Windy* (Friedman) / Do That To Me One More Time (Tennille) / Along Comes Mary* (Almer) / Isn't She Lovely (Wonder) / Never My Love* (Addrisi-Addrisi) / Goodbye, Columbus* (Yester) / Just The Way You Are (Joel) / You're In My Heart (Stewart) / Cherish* (Kirkman)
*Re-recorded version

A LITTLE BIT MORE
Track Records OTD-1001-2 (1995)
Walk Away Renée* (Brown-Calilli-Sansone) / A Little Bit More (Gosh) / Could It Be Love (Sharp) / How Much Love (Geyer-McCann) / Learn How To Land (Moore-Clark) / Nature Boy (Ahbez) / I Wanna Be Your

Radio (Martin) / Perfect Gift (Small-McDonald) / Dreamland (Moore) / Forever (Roy-McDaniels-Max) / The One (Rowley-Dukes)
Re-recorded version

JUST THE RIGHT SOUND : ANTHOLOGY
Rhino Entertainment R2-78303 (2002)
51-track compilation includes: Better Times (Boettcher-Mallory) / It'll Take A Little Time (Lynch-Godding) / Pegasus (Alexander) / Names, Tags, Numbers, Labels (Hammond-Hazelwood) / Carry On (Alexander-Carey) / One Sunday Morning (Shew) / Dreamer (Martin) / Small Town Lovers (Goldmark) / Across The Persian Gulf (Yester-Beckett)

THE COMPLETE WARNER BROS. & VALIANT SINGLES COLLECTION
Now Sounds CRNOW 35D (2012)
37-track compilation includes: One Too Many Mornings (Dylan) / Forty Times (Alexander)

U.S. SINGLES

1965

Babe I'm Gonna Leave You/Baby, Can't You Hear Me Call Your Name (Jubilee 5505)
One Too Many Mornings/Forty Times (Valiant 730)

1966

Along Comes Mary/Your Own Love (Valiant 741)
Cherish/Don't Blame The Rain (Valiant 747)
Pandora's Golden Heebie Jeebies/Standing Still (Valiant 755)

1967

No Fair At All/Looking Glass (Valiant 758)
Windy/Sometime (Warner Bros. 7041)
Never My Love/Requiem For The Masses (Warner Bros. 7074)

1968

Everything That Touches You/We Love Us (Warner Bros. 7163)
Time For Livin'/Birthday Morning (Warner Bros. 7195)
Six Man Band/Like Always (Warner Bros. 7229)

1969

Enter The Young/The Time It Is Today (Warner Bros. 7239)*
Goodbye, Columbus/The Time It Is Today (Warner Bros. 7267)
Under Branches/Hear In Here (Warner Bros. 7277)
Withdrawn release

1970

Yes, I Will/I Am Up For Europe (Warner Bros. 7305)
Dubuque Blues/Are You Ready (Warner Bros. 7349)
Just About The Same/Look At Me, Look At You (Warner Bros. 7372)
Along The Way/Traveler's Guide (Warner Bros. 7429)

1971

P.F. Sloan/Traveler's Guide (Warner Bros. 7471)
Bring Yourself Home/It's Gotta Be Real (Warner Bros. 7515)
That's Racin'/Makes Me Cry (Funny Kind Of Song) (Warner Bros. 7524)

1972

Darlin' Be Home Soon/Indian Wells Woman (Columbia 45602)
Come The Fall/Kicking The Gong Around (Columbia 45654)

1973

Names, Tags, Numbers And Labels/Rainbows Bent (Mums 6061)

1975

One Sunday Morning/Life Is A Carnival (RCA 10217)
Sleepy Eyes/Take Me To The Pilot (RCA 10297)*
Withdrawn release

1981

Dreamer/You Turn The Light On (Elektra 47094)
Small Town Lovers/Across The Persian Gulf (Elektra 47146)

OTHER RELEASES OF NOTE (non-definitive)

Alexander, Jules 2015 CD: The Jules Alexander Band: EP Number One (No Cat.No.)

Bijou 1975 45: Carry On/Take Me Down To The Dawn (A&M Records 1678-S)

Cherry Hill Singers, The 1964 LP: An Exciting New Folk Group (Hi-Fi Records L-1020)

Giguere, Russ 1971 LP: Hexagram 16 (Warner Bros. WS-1910)

MFQ 1989 CD: Live In Japan (Pony Canyon-D22Y0319)

MFQ 1990 CD: Bamboo Saloon (Pony Canyon PCCY-00061)

MFQ 1990 CD: MFQ Christmas (Pony CanyonPCCY-00165)

MFQ 1991 CD: Wolfgang (Pony Canyon PCCY-00284),

New Christy Minstrels, The 1963 LP: In Person (Columbia CS-8741)

New Christy Minstrels, The 1963 LP: Tell Tall Tales! (Legends and Nonsense) (Columbia CL-2017)

New Christy Minstrels, The 1963 LP: Ramblin' (Columbia CS-8855)

New Christy Minstrels, The 1963 LP: Merry Christmas! (Columbia CL-2096)

New Christy Minstrels, The 1964 LP: Today And Other Songs (Columbia CL-2159)

New Christy Minstrels, The 1964 LP: Land Of Giants (Columbia CS-8987)

New Christy Minstrels, The 1965 LP: Quiet Sides (Columbia CL-2280)

New Christy Minstrels, The 1965 LP: Sing And Play Cowboys And Indians (Columbia CL-2303)

New Christy Minstrels, The 1965 LP: Chim Chim Cher-ee (Columbia CL-2369)

New Christy Minstrels, The 1965 LP: The Wandering Minstrels (Columbia CS-9184)

New Christy Minstrels, The 2006 CD: Gathering Of Minstrels (Bearmark 837101204637)

New Four Preps, The 1993: Better Than Ever (FPD-2626)
Later reissued as YB&S "Yester, Belland & Somerville" (YB&S 26-2)

New Four Preps, The 1993: WEBE50 (No Cat.No.)
Later reissued as YB&S "Triple Gold" (YB&S 52-2)

Ramos, Larry 1966 45: It'll Take A Little Time/Gotta Travel On (Columbia

4-43805)

Ramos, Larry 2002 CD Single: A Ole La E Ku'ulei/God Loves Laughter/ Honolulu City Lights (Paradise Productions: No Cat.No.)

Ramos, Larry 2012 CD: Poipourri (BigMouseWorks Productions: No Cat. No.)

Yester, Jim & Linda Gentille 1999 CD: Touches Of Love (No Cat.No.)
Later reissued as Touches Of Love (RKO-1021 with 2 extra tracks)

Yester 2009 CD (featuring Jim, Jerry, Hannah & Lena) (Zerva: No Cat.No.)

Yester, Jim 2015 CD: One More Time*: Voices For The Voiceless (Audio & Video Labs 10014361)
*Single contribution to this compilation CD

CREDITS

THE ASSOCIATION - thank you to:

Jules Alexander, Ted Bluechel Jr., Brian Cole, Russell Giguere, Terry Kirkman, Larry Ramos and Jim Yester

with Bob Page, Richard Thompson, Wolfgang Melz, Mike Berkowitz, Del Ramos, Maurice Miller, Art Johnson, David Vaught, Jerry Yester, Dwayne Smith, Andy Chapin, Larry Brown, Jay Gruska, David Morgan, Cliff Woolley, Ric Ulsky, Russ Levine, John William Tuttle, Jack Harris, Keith Moret, Joe LaManno, Paul Beach, Brian Puckett, Bruce Pictor, Michael Leroy Peed, Donnie Gougeon, Chris Urmston, Paul Holland, Jordan Cole, Bob Werner, David Jackson, Blair Anderson, Godfrey Townsend and Paul Wilson.

REFERENCES:

1   Where Have All The Pop Stars Gone? (by Marti Smiley Childs and Jeff March: Published by EditPros LLC 2011)
2   Sleevenotes for the Association Now Sounds CD Reissue Series (by Steve Stanley: Now Sounds)
3   Frank Zappa: Information Is Not Knowledge (website)
4   The New Christy Minstrels (liner notes by Bruce Eder 2009)
5   The Story of The Men (online article by Jules Alexander 2002)
6   How I Found Myself In The First Folk-Rock Group (by Terry Kirkman:

The Huffington Post 2012)

7   The Soul Of The Association remembers... (by Robert White: Review Magazine, Michigan 2015)

8   Goldmine Magazine (1995)

9   HeartBeat Magazine (2007)

10 Everyone Knows It's the Association (by Jim Newsom: Portfolio Weekly 2008)

11 Reaching Out To Capture A Moment (by Chuck Miller: Goldmine Magazine 2004)

12 Along Came... The Association (by Paul Freeman: Pop Culture Classics Online 2014)

13 KRLA Beat (1960s Los Angeles Music Newspaper: Various Editions & Writers)

14 Mr. Tambourine Man: The Life and Legacy of The Byrds' Gene Clark (by John Einarson: Backbeat Books 2005)

15 Along Come Tandyn (Sundazed CD sleeve notes by Parke Puterbaugh 2013)

16 The California Sound: An Insiders Story (by Stephen J McParland: CMusic Books 2005)

17 Curt Boettcher Interview (by Ray McCarty: Zig-Zag Magazine 1974)

18 Sleevenotes for The Association Collectors Choice/Real Gone Music CD Reissue Series (written by Richie Unterberger: various years)

19 Interview with Russ Giguere (by Mark Voger: NJ.com 2011)

20 The Association. Collectively Collectible (by Marty Natchez: Goldmine Magazine 1984)

21 Interviews with Jim and Jerry Yester (by Simon Wordsworth: 1992)

22 Terry Kirkman: Helpful Hints To Young Hopefuls (by Marilyn Doerfler: Teen Set Magazine September 1967)

23 Larry Ramos: Along Comes Larry (by Sam Tweedle: Confessions Of A Pop Culture Addict 2011)

24 Just The Right Sound: The Association Anthology (by Dawn Eden: Rhino Warner Bros. Records 2002)

25 Eight Miles Higher – The Blogspot for People Who Don't Like Blogspots (by Andrew Darlington 2011)

26 Interview with Bones Howe (by David Adams: Elvis Australia 2008)

27 Sound Explosion: Inside L.A.'s Studio Factory with The Wrecking Crew (Ken Sharp: Velocity Books 2015)

28 Interview with Dick Addrisi (by Larry Katz: Thekatztapes.com 2002)

29 The College Crowd Digs Me: Interview with Terry Kirkman (by Casey Chambers 2015)

30 The Billboard Book of Number One Hits (by Fred Bronson: Billboard 1988)

31 Just The Right Sound: The Association Anthology Outtakes (by Dawn Eden: Fufkin.com 2002)

32 Articles and emails written and supplied by David Pearson

33 Email conversations between the Author and Jim Yester (2016/2017)

34 McLane & Wong: Entertainment Law (by Ben McLane : 1998)

35 Hit Parader Magazine (1969)

36 California Dreaming: Memories & Visions of L.A. – The Photographs of Henry Diltz (Genesis Publications)

37 Interviews with Jules Alexander by the Author (2016/2017)

38 P.F. Sloan: Traveling Barefoot On A Rocky Road (by Stephen J McParland: CMusic Books 2000)

39 Steve Carey: Smith Going Backward (by Pat Nolan: Parole Blog 2014)

40 Rock, Roll & Remember (Dick Clark Radio Broadcast: March 1988)

41 Born To The Blues: Sweet Grease at Re$iduals (by David S. Barry: The Los Angeles Times 1993)

42 Email conversations between the Author and Larry Brown (2016/2017)

43 'Pleasant Valley Sunday' Online Radio Broadcast (Kevin Nolley: Ball State University, IN)

44 Interview with Larry Ramos by John Broughton (Radio Casey, Australian Public Radio 2012)

45 Interview with Cliff Woolley by the Author (2017)

46 Rock Your Business : What You And Your Company Can Learn From The Business Of Rock And Roll (by David Fishof: BenBella Books 2012)

47 The Smokin' Gun Has Been Found: Interview with Bill Majkut (by Michael Buffalo Smith 2001)

48 Park Record.com online article. (Park City, Utah 2016)

49 A Perfect Haze: The Illustrated History of The Monterey Pop Festival (by Harvey & Kenneth Kubernik: Santa Monica Press 2012)

50 Into The Next Stage (by Guy Aoki: Rafu Shimpo Media 2013)

51 Interview with Terry Kirkman by the Author (2017)

52 Interview with Jim Yester (by John Montagna: Radio418.com 2017)

53 The Cake and the Rain: A Memoir (by Jimmy Webb: St Martins Press 2017)

ACKNOWLEDGMENTS for contributions, emails, conversations and/or general support and encouragement – or just for being 'Associated'

Dean James Adshead, Jules Alexander, John Ansley, Guy Aoki, Karl Baker, Sherry Rayn Barnett, Paul Beach, David Beard, Donald Beck, Mike Berkowitz, Ted Bluechel Jr., Wim Boekhooven, Michael Brewer, Larry Brown, Steven Casto, Paul Chester, Randy Cierley-Sterling, Steve Cohen, Jordan Cole, Rick Colecchio, Dave Daugherty, Bill DeBlonk, Sharon Degonia, Andrew Darlington, Mike Dennis, Dave Fractman, Brian Gari, Stephen Geyer, Mike Gibb, Mike Grant, Jay Gruska, Lois Hatlelid, Paul Holland, Art Johnson, Graham Joiner, Candy Kayne, Terry and Heidi Kirkman, Joe LaManno, Russ Levine, Jeff March, Joseph W. Marek, Stephen J. McParland, Mark Meinhart, Jim Metropole, Rita Michalski, David Nakamura, Marty Natchez, Gray Newell, Michael Ney, Kevin Nolley, Craig Norton, Charlie Oyama, Bob Page, Tim Page, Darryl Palagi, Scott Paton, David Pearson, Jason Penick, Lloyd N. Phillips, Bruce and Linda Pictor, Art Podell, Ruth Pordon, Del Ramos, Tracy Ramos, Robb Royer, Ian Rusten, Darian Sahanaja, Jay Allen Sanford, Scott Shelly, Dwayne Smith, Pat Smith, Ray Staar, Bob Stane, Steve Stanley, Mike Stax, Diane Tartaglia, Stan Trachtenberg, Richie Unterberger, Chris White, Mason Williams, Paul Wilson, Sharon Miller Wilson, Cliff Woolley, Simon Wordsworth, Hannah Yester, Jim Yester.

I am also indebted to the writings of various folk who, over the ensuing years, have provided me with much detail, information and reading delight. A goodly selection of their works are hereby listed:

PUBLISHED READING RESOURCES

The California Sound: An Insiders Story (by Stephen J McParland: CMusic Books 2005)

Crosby, Stills & Nash (by Dave Zimmer: DaCapo Press 2008)

Desperados: The Roots of Country Rock by John Einarson (Cooper Square Press 2001)

Do You Believe In Magic: The Story of The Lovin' Spoonful (by Simon Wordsworth: CreateSpace Independent Publishing 2014)

Endless Summer Quarterly (compiled & edited by David Beard)

Goldmine Magazine (various articles: F+W Media)

Memoirs Of A Sideman (by Art Johnson: Storymerchant Books 2008)

P.F. Sloan: Traveling Barefoot On A Rocky Road (by Stephen J McParland: CMusic Books 2000)

Record Collector Magazine (various articles: Diamond Publishing)

Riot on Sunset Strip (by Domenic Priore: Jawbone Press 2007)

Shindig! Magazine (various articles: Silverback Publishing)

Sound Explosion! Inside L.A.'s Studio Factory (by Ken Sharp: Velocity Books 2015)

So You Want To Be A Rock'n'Roll Star: The Byrds Day-by-Day (by Christopher Hjort: Jawbone Press 2008)

The Steve Hoffman Music Forums (various contributors to online threads)

Swim Through The Darkness (by Mike Stax: Process Media 2016)

Waiting For The Sun (by Barney Hoskyns: St. Martin's Press 1996)

Where Have All The Pop Stars Gone? (by Marti Smiley Childs & Jeff March: EditPros LLC 2011)

… and, yes, Facebook also assisted in its own inimitable way.

EXTRA PERSONAL APPRECIATION goes out to:

Jules Alexander – for being there, patiently responding and offering assistance, time and time again!

Terry Kirkman – for generously giving his time and thoughts for a truly fascinating, and somewhat lengthy conversation…

Jim Yester – for regularly offering further insight into it all. A gent…

Larry Brown – for assisting without question.

Del Ramos – for those thoroughly enjoyable transatlantic calls.

Tracy Ramos – for her kind nature and courteous manner.

Jordan Cole – for being honest and open.

Art Johnson & Dwayne Smith – a formidable pairing…

Jim Metropole – for his unwavering patience.

Marty Natchez – not only for allowing me to access his work, but for writing the lengthy article in the first place. A good place to start…

Ian Rusten – for the detailed research without issue.
Graham Joiner at Audio Restored – for restoring the audio!
and to Steven Casto – for keeping the enthusiasm alive!

A big thank you to Jane Bozian for reading it all through and picking up on those minute details that simply escaped me...

And to Randy Cierley-Sterling (March 10 1942 – March 29 2018).
Rest easy...

ABOUT THE AUTHOR

Malcolm C. Searles has lived and breathed in the English Essex air for all of his fifty-seven years on planet earth. Married to Louise, with two boys – now men (Sam and Matt), and located in the county's capital city of Chelmsford, a mere forty miles to the north-east of London, this is his second publication; the first one being the biography of BREAD: A Sweet Surrender – The Musical Journey of David Gates, James Griffin & Co. (Helter Skelter Publishing 2014). However, a love of all things musical, and in particular of the harmonious pop variety, has seen various written works appear online over the preceding years, including extensive writings on The Beach Boys and The Monkees.

What next? Watch this space...